Bring Me A Minstrel

Shared Songs Of The Salish Sea

Robert B. Greene

ISBN-13: 978-1478373971
ISBN-10: 1478373970

Dedication

To Sheryl Lea, my light, my love and my guiding star,
thank you for everything.

FOREWORD

In ancient times two powerful kings agreed to assist a third in punishing a rebellious tributary. Recklessly, the three men sent their united armies on a roundabout route through the desert to attack the malefactor. Instead of a quick victory over a weak opponent, their great force bogged down in the desert and nearly came to ruin for lack of water. With disaster looming the potentates all agreed that the only way to save their soldiers was through divine counsel. Unfortunately, the primary sovereign had neglected his god and had mistreated his god's earthly representative. Nonetheless, desperate to escape their own folly, the rulers sent for the shunned prophet. When the old seer appeared before the chieftains, they informed him of their need. His consent notwithstanding, the oracle rightly perceived the difficult position he was being forced to occupy. Thus, needing to calm his mind and find an answer in prayer, the wise man ordered: "Bring me a minstrel." The soothing performance of the musician gave him the serenity he needed to hear and deliver the saving message. In like manner, the good little ship "Minstrel's Song" provides respite and insight to those who seek answers.

CONTENTS

INTRODUCTION

The dictionary defines boat as "...*a small vessel propelled by oars, sails, or an engine.*" To that I say: BILGEWATER! The proper definition of boat is more like this: "...a *mental construct capable of lifting people of every age, size, color, sex, creed and inclination directly up out of their hum-drum lives and transporting them unswervingly forward into their wildest dreams!*"

Since the beginning of time man has yearned to find ways to float on water. From whenever that first event actually occurred, the minds and imaginations of people everywhere have transformed that rather mundane act into great visions of new worlds, unrivalled wealth, sheer pleasure, commerce, peace and tranquility, to say the least.

Inextricably intertwined with the obvious benefits of getting from here to there by sea – whether actual or only fancied – is the fact that unlike most other things that people dabble in, the water provides us concomitantly with a medium that is both a means and an end. Pragmatically we use our oceans, lakes and rivers to put food on our tables and to move our goods and services over long distances; psychologically, however, it lifts our souls, forms our dreams, provides escapes and creates special lifestyles.

Beauty is said to be in the eyes of the beholder. But when it comes to things oceanic, one might argue that it lives somewhere else. What if, for instance, the extreme delight evoked by an old master's oil painting of some lonely seascape issues neither from the mind of the observer nor from the artist himself? What if, instead, these human imitations are nothing more than the pale reflections of the exquisite subjects crafted solely for our pleasure by a greater hand? Perhaps, just perhaps, that's why we go down to the sea in boats.

Have you ever packed the whole family into the SUV and driven to the nearest interstate to watch dreamily the 18-wheelers roll past? Have you ever awakened on a Saturday morning longing to sit in the parking lot of the local mall just to watch the cars come and go? Have you ever dreamed of being able, someday, to while away the hours bouncing cross-country in a Greyhound bus? For that matter, have you ever longed to journey halfway around the world just to spend a week lazing on someone else's lawn? Yet who hasn't reveled in the sound of the ocean breaking on a warm beach? Who hasn't sought out a window table at a restaurant overlooking a marina? Who hasn't been entirely willing to fight maddening crowds and to endure countless inconveniences just to while away a few days on a floating palace? Who hasn't been stopped dead in their tracks by an orange orb sinking quietly into the sea? Who hasn't dreamed of decorating their homes with nautical curios the proper names of which are not even known? Who hasn't seen a Winslow Homer painting of ships and the sea and not been transported to a world of wind, and waves and the glory inherent in such a special place? The point is that the sea is an extraordinary thing, a unique destination that beckons almost all of us, incessantly. And, Walter Mitty-style, even when we are cast up high and dry up on the shore, the very thought of those conveyances we call boats lifts us out of our ordinary lives to experience, even if just for a moment, some of the wonder and the awe that permeates the watery parts of our globe.

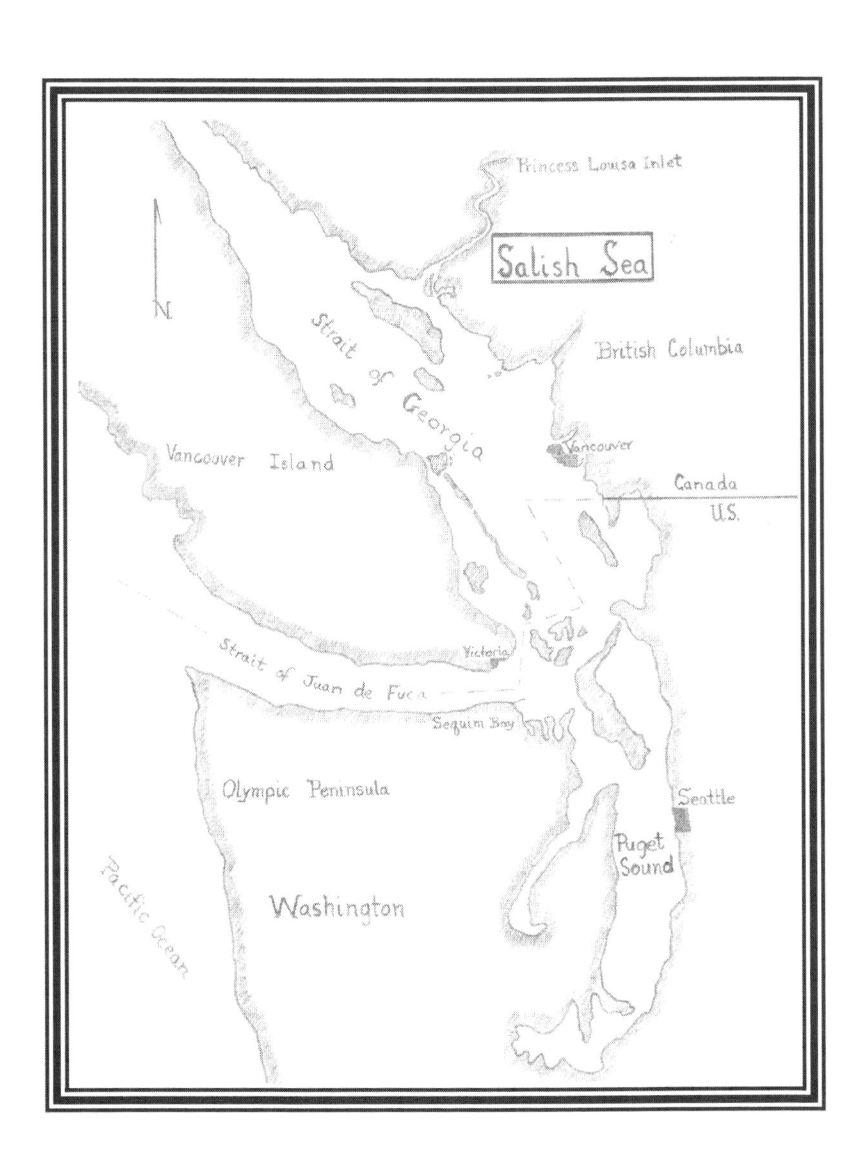
Princess Lousa Inlet
Salish Sea
N
Strait of Georgia
British Columbia
Vancouver Island
Vancouver
Canada
U.S.
Victoria
Strait of Juan de Fuca
Sequim Bay
Olympic Peninsula
Seattle
Puget Sound
Washington
Pacific Ocean

The Siren-song of the sea is loud and alluring. Its attractions myriad. Mostly, each of us hear in it a different tune and each of us finds in it different shapes in the distance. Ships and boats are the creations that let us follow these illusions to their ultimate source. Whether we rise and fall on the backs of the great, rolling greybeards that challenge even huge supertankers out on the Seven Seas, or we choose to sit in our snug living rooms, safe and dry, reading the words that others have used to describe that magical world, the pull is strong. Follow it and we find exciting new domains. More importantly, if we look and listen carefully, through this medium sometimes we can find ourselves too. It's a journey well worth making! Welcome aboard, matey, it's good to have you along!

THE SALISH SEA?

The great comedian Bill Cosby used to quip that Seattle enjoyed at least 365 rainy days each year and, he would add, the people of the area thought it both normal and fashionable to look as moisture wrinkled as prunes. To a greater or lesser extent, this traditional view of the Pacific Northwest lives on today. Ironically, this area's image of a land of perpetual rain, clouds and dreariness is being undermined by the presence therein of by a body of water: the Salish Sea. The Salish Sea, you say?

Yes. The Salish Sea!

Believe it or not, this geographic construct didn't exist prior to late 2009 and early 2010! In those two years the national and local governments that control the lands surrounding this entity agreed that the jumble of waterways and the names appended to each should give way, a little, to a more manageable, single designation. Consisting entirely of the inland waters that divide the northwest United States from western Canada, as well as those separating mainland British Columbia from Vancouver Island, this newly appointed expanse includes what used to be known separately as the Puget Sound, the Strait of Juan de Fuca, the Strait of Georgia and all the sub-waters that were a part of them. While these objects continue to exist individually, the grateful mariner may now properly refer to the entirety by the simple appellation Salish Sea.

But it was not this consolidation of names that has worked to transform the public image of the region. What began to change it was the ever-increasing number of tourists who wished to enjoy the awe inspiring trip to Alaska aboard ocean liners transiting via the Inside Passage,. As both the southern terminus of that famed waterway as well as the primary embarkation/debarkation region for the behemoths that cater to the trade, millions of vacationers flock annually to and cruise through the Salish Sea each summer. These passengers usually begin and end their travels in one of the area's leading cities, either Seattle, Washington or Vancouver, British Columbia. Because the sailing season stretches only from May to September, these sojourners are treated to the best weather this part of the world has to offer as they come and go. It is not unusual, then, for them to return to their homes having experienced a time in the Pacific Northwest considerably at odds with the humorous picture painted by Mr. Cosby.

The tale that follows is true, mainly. It is about a voyage into the heart of the Salish Sea, an area of unparalleled beauty that lies, nonetheless, just a stone's throw from the aforementioned population centers. Despite its proximity to the hustle and bustle of the modern world, much of this domain continues more or less untouched by the blessings of civilization. Most of the nearly 5,000 miles of shoreline that border this sea still remain inaccessible except by boat or float plane. More surprisingly, perhaps, is the fact that this is a microcosm where fjords cut deeply into the land, where hundreds of remote, forested islands dot the surface of the ocean and where glaciers, perched jauntily atop their mountain homes look down on it all. Few other locales combine alpine heights, protected seaways, island beauty, absolute solitude, and proximity to great population centers as does the Salish Sea. For those desirous of something different, something special, there aren't many places easier to reach or more worth the trip.

DISCLAIMER

As do so many things in life, this book began with good intentions. Having enjoyed an 11-day cruise through paradise I sought only to share the experience, briefly, with family and a few friends. The friends, being fellow travelers, would be entertained and even enlightened, I imagined, by what I had seen and done; the family, generally thinking me to be wholly beyond the pale anyway, might be convinced to reconsider that view.

What at first seemed to be a harmless endeavor soon got out of hand. I found early on that one thing could not be properly described to everyone before four other things had been explained. Worse, all of the 'whys' and 'wherefores' of my musings got in the way of my, "We're just going from here to there!" expectations. The entire thing became so overwhelming that I finally threw up my hands and declared the project "a book"! What follows is the result of that pusillanimous decision.

As the reader quickly will discern, all of the work that follows is my own. So too are any and all of its errors, commissions and omissions. It is my hope that the reader can forgive and forget, or at least, in the case of my older followers, forget.

On the positive side, I am especially indebted to my wife for all of her help. Without her continual encouragement, her willingness to put up with my artistic idiosyncrasies and, especially her income, the whole thing might have become shredded packing material long before it saw the light of day. Additionally, her computer skills were invaluable in converting my simple copy into the product required by the publisher. Most importantly, her expertise in this realm was instrumental in saving, on multiple occasions, the mechanical life of an otherwise perfectly functional P.C.

Over time a number of people have glimpsed bits and pieces of my work. Their input and support has helped to move this project toward completion. It is my strident hope that they will enjoy the fruits of our collective labors. I am grateful to all of them. I would especially like to thank Doug Schwarz, Past Commander of the U.S. Power Squadron in Sequim, Washington for his constant friendship, for the hours we spent sailing together and swapping lies and for his kindness in allowing the use of his photograph of the author on the back cover.

Finally, as pertains to the content of this book I am forced to endorse and echo the sentiments of Mark Twain: "Persons attempting to find a motive in this narrative will be prosecuted; persons attempting to find a moral in it will be banished; persons attempting to find a plot in it will be shot." Amen.

Robert B. Greene
Ronan, Montana
December 2013

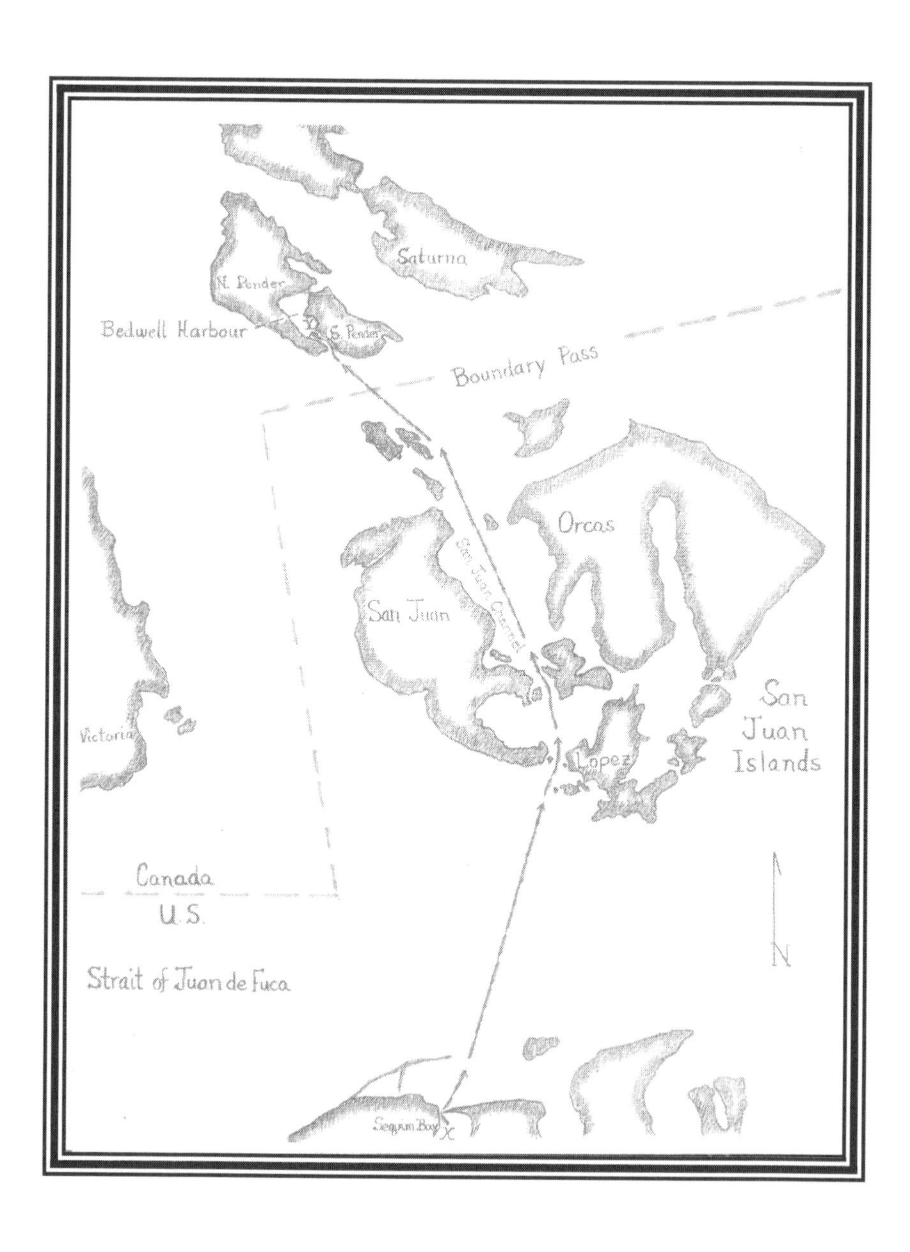
Saturna
N. Pender
Bedwell Harbour
S. Pender
Boundary Pass
Orcas
San Juan Channel
San Juan
San
Juan
Islands
Victoria
Lopez
Canada
U.S.
Strait of Juan de Fuca
N
Sequim Bay

DAY ONE

Sequim Bay to Bedwell Harbour
Or
Chinese Fire Drills and Other Foreign Stuff

Looking more like a nervous version of "Little Toot" than a tough, cruising tugboat, *Minstrel's Song* creeps out of her snug berth at John Wayne Marina in Sequim Bay, Washington and points her bluff bow north. Outward bound on an 11-day passage, her destination is Princess Louisa Inlet, a remote glacial fjord cut deep into the west coast of British Columba. Her mission is to convey The Captain and The Crew safely through the southern waters of Canada's famed Inside Passage. The ultimate objective is to search out the new vistas that will become the colored threads used to weave the tapestry that we know as life itself.

At about 35' in length – dripping wet and counting the rubber inflatable boat (RIB) mounted on her stern – *Minstrel's Song* is not a large vessel. In fact, she reaches no higher than large-ish, on the small end of the size scale! This day she carries on board her preferred compliment of two people. Laden with just enough food, fuel, freshwater, games, books, charts and assorted equipment to circle the world five or six times, she plows a straight furrow toward Canada. Her single diesel engine drives her along at a comfortable cruising speed of eight and a half knots (almost 10 mph).

Working her way slowly out of the bay's protective channel, she soon leaves (passes) to port (the left side) the Dungeness Light

House and begins the trek across the dreaded 'Strait.' The sea ahead of her is unusually calm and flat. The tiny ripples that play on the surface of the dark, blue-green water gaily scatter the crystal rays of the bright yellow sun that still sits low on the horizon. Even at this early hour that giant, yellow orb dominates the cloudless blue dome that arches overhead. The vibrant colors, both above and below the miniature ship, accented by the dancing sparkles that trip gaily along the surface of the ocean create a holiday atmosphere. And indeed, it is!

Seventy miles off to the northeast, volcanic Mt. Baker fills the skyline like a giant, vanilla ice cream cone, carelessly dropped, upside down. To the south, behind the little boat, the snow-capped peaks of the Olympic Mountains stretch their mighty arms east and west across the Olympic Peninsula until they disappear into the hazy greyness that is neither land nor sea. Ahead, dark humps of something rise up out of the watery world, sprawling helter-skelter on top of the water as if to block the progress of any vessel not absolutely determined to get through them. *Minstrel's Song* inches her way forward, toward them.

The Chinese thinker, Laozi, once said, "...a journey of a thousand miles begins with the first step." Both The Captain and The Crew of this diminutive craft agree, however, that even when propitious, the best beginnings should not have to start with a crossing of 'The Strait.'

At risk of dealing in tautology, the southern extreme of the Pacific Northwest's Inside Passage would be neither inside nor a defined passage were it not for the placement of Canada's Vancouver Island directly off, and parallel to, the west coast of mainland British Columbia. Serving as a slender, oceanic barrier, this 275- mile long island holds the worst of the North Pacific's weather at bay while giving form to the protected inner waterway known so well to the Alaskan cruising trade.

The sounds, channels, bays, passes, inlets, coves and canals that find shelter behind Vancouver Island – upward to 25,000 miles of them -- are filled, drained and re-filled daily by the tidal rush of seawater that sweeps from the open ocean around the north and south ends of this mountainous impediment and then penetrate deeply into the lowlands of the coast behind it. Vancouver Island's southern extreme dips down from its heights and gives way to a narrow-ish stretch of ocean know as the Strait of Juan de Fuca. Washington's Olympic Peninsula rises up again to 7,000' feet and more on its south shore. Separating the two entities this way, the "Strait" cuts a 100-mile long, 20-mile wide, east-west swath from the Pacific Ocean directly to Seattle and the Puget Sound. In doing so it also serves to physically divide the U.S. from Canada.

With the mountains of the region pulling back momentarily to accommodate the interloping water, not only does the sea crash inland through the narrows of the Strait, but the prevailing west wind romps down the resulting corridor too! In the latter instance, the funnel effect created by the adjoining high terrain speeds the air on its way so that what begins as a fair breeze coming in off the open Pacific ends as a full blown gale by the time it reaches the eastern extreme of this slot. In consequence, high winds, heavy seas, and the Pacific "Northwet's" famous rains and fogs – sometimes all together – caress this special part of paradise with some frequency. When it is in one of its shrieking moods, the non-professional sailor is well advised to trifle with something other than this body of water for fun.

As if nature's creation alone proved insufficient to entertain, humankind has found ways to bolster the Strait's potential for more and better thrills. To that end, we have planted several great shipping ports (e.g. Tacoma, Seattle, Vancouver, B.C.) and a number of naval bases (e.g. Bremerton, Bangor, Esquimalt, B.C.) in the general vicinity. This has the effect of spawning a never-ending parade of ships in and out of the constricted Strait. Freighters, tankers, container ships, aircraft carriers, submarines, tenders, cruise ships, ferries, tug boats, barges, trawlers, Coast Guard cutters, pilot boats, log booms and pleasure craft regularly steam through it. Thus, man's attempt to coax chaos out of reason exceeds all expectations. Daily the nautical daredevil is rewarded with plentiful maritime traffic to dodge in addition to the common high winds, rough seas, rain and fog that he can enjoy there almost any time of year!

It should be no wonder, then, that we find our little ship poking her bow out of her safe haven, cautiously sniffing the wind, casting eyes all around, nerves all atwitter like a Serengeti gazelle with the scent of a lion in her nostrils. Both The Captain and The Crew know that what the sea probably will not do to *Minstrel's Song* this beautiful, calm day might still be accomplished by any number of great, fast moving, seaborne behemoths that care not for tiny boats at play.

With her miniature radar whirling frantically and her Automatic Identification System working overtime to pick up even the faintest hint of danger, our intrepid mariners stand an anxious vigil in the pilothouse, ready for anything. And, as often happens in situations like these, the anticipatory worries are far worse than the experience itself. *Sans* a screaming gale, great breaking waves the size of skyscrapers, visibility limited to the length of an arm held straight out or even the telltale wisp of smoke on the horizon to warn of an on-rushing ship, the Captain and The Crew pour grateful coffee libations – into their insulated cups – in hopes of keeping Poseidon firmly on their side!

In retrospect, one would be tempted to say that the crossing of the Strait made by *Minstrel's Song* this morning was picture perfect. And it would have been had it not been the opening day of halibut season! For scattered over the face of the mirror-smooth water lay a fleet of pleasure craft so densely packed that a sardine tin would have looked roomy by comparison! Big ones, little ones and sizes in between, there were vessels of every shape and description, each filled to overflowing with determined sportsmen. Back and forth randomly the members of this fleet ranged, up and down and even round and round they went, dragging invisible threads attached carefully to the bristling array of rods that poked out from their hulls in every imaginable direction. And, like a great school of herring, they all swung and swerved in marvelous unison, driven by the same idea: catch the biggest fish!

Skillfully The Captain dodged this way and that to keep from cutting their lines or from cleaving their hulls! And although neither chore could be ignored safely, being relieved of his greater worries about the weather, the sea and the potential nightmare of being pulverized by a super-sized ship, The Captain and The Crew allowed their minds to relax some and turn to the mundane. It was that mental wandering, in fact, that led them to discover a new law of physics. Based on the empirical data immediately at hand they concluded that at least when it comes to non-commercial boats fishing for halibut, 'The size of the vessel employed is inversely proportionate to the distance it is from the shore.' Thus, they observed that the enclosed 60-foot cruisers skirted close to the shorelines, just a mile or two from the beach, while the open, 12-foot aluminum skiffs -- you know, the ones with decrepit six horsepower, two-stroke outboard engines that are hanging precariously from dented transoms and barely can remain afloat under the weight of the six, 250 pound (plus) beer-buddies standing on the gunwales peering down as if to pierce visually the 400' depths – were 12 miles offshore, smack-dab in the middle of the Strait! They could find no exceptions!

Weaving through the gauntlet offered by these boats this day, The Captain steered his craft somewhat east of north toward Cattle Pass. His intention was to use this opening to slip into the sheltered waters of the San Juan Channel – a pleasant byway that separates Washington State's San Juan, Lopez and Shaw Islands from each other. The plan was to follow that Channel north and later northwest to Boundary Passage and thereby cross the Canadian border.

Undoubtedly those readers not geographically challenged and/or those plugged into Google Earth, already are shouting wildly at The Skipper: "Look at the chart, fool! Your day's destination, Bedwell Harbour, is north and slightly west of Sequim Bay. By what perverse manner of steerage are you dragging this whole parade eastward into the San Juan Islands to get there?" The answer is relatively simple: The Navigator is a big chicken!

"How sharper than a serpent's tooth it is to have a thankless child!" Worse, perhaps, is to peer into one's own soul and see the foibles thriving within. To his credit, The Navigator did not try to hide from The Crew his reasons for taking the longer way around. Whereas he might have alibied his choice by claiming that this route was the more scenic, or that it kept them well away from the shipping lanes or even, in a fit of inventiveness, he might have suggested that he wanted to avoid disturbing the pod of Orca whales that often hunt off the west side of San Juan Island – all sound enough reasons on the surface – but he did not. Instead, he matter-of-factly confessed his general aversion to lee shores. With neither complaint nor derision coming from The Crew, The Captain spun the wheel slightly to starboard (the right) and *Minstrel's Song* churned her way toward Cattle Pass.

An *ex post facto* defense might serve, however, to keep the reader from judging too harshly. Note, for instance, that since boyhood The Navigator had immersed himself in reading, dreaming and writing about things pertaining to the sea. Beyond that, he rarely missed the chance to go out on the water or to learn something new about it. He was, however, particularly taken by the romantic age of sail – a period that began about 10 minutes after mankind first stood upright on dry land and continues through the present, if one allows for the inclusion of modern sailboats. And, he took seriously the vicarious lessons he learned from those long-departed seafarers.

At least from the days of Odysseus onward, seamen have been especially wary of "lee shores." A lee shore is nothing more than an extent of land, any land – and rocks and even reefs can qualify at times for this appellation -- that is located downwind of a vessel. These things were most troublesome when ships depended entirely on the wind for their motive power, but they are not without peril even to machine driven craft.

Through the ages man harnessed the wind, letting it push his ships and cargoes all over the place. As one might recall from 8th grade history, world exploration depended almost exclusively on this mode of transportation. Its flaw, however, was that things worked great when the wind was going in the same direction as the boat, but they did not work at all when it was not. Over the millennia, sail shapes, mast placement and even hull designs gave wooden vessels a bit of a break, increasingly allowing them to zigzag back and forth across the oncoming wind – a maneuver known as "tacking" that is practiced in the main by politicians today – and thus slowly and painfully to reach a desired point, even when the direction of the wind was not ideal. Unfortunately, the stronger the wind, the more difficult this was to do this safely (or even at all) and the harder it was to resist having to go with the flow. Thus, with impunity a ship might sail all day long within a stone's throw of a coast even if a gentle breeze was pushing in toward the land (lee shore). However, put her on that same shoreline with a gale roaring in from the sea and there is little that a captain or a crew can do to make her claw her way off the lee shore and get to safety. With terrifying speed such a hapless victim will be driven aground, up on the beach, a reef or into the rocks where whatever happens thereafter is never very pretty.

In sailing off a lee shore, the real danger derives not from being incapable of resisting the press of the wind, but rather from what happens when earth and ship inevitably meet. (It is a bit like the old saw that says, 'It's not the fall that hurts, but the sudden stop at the bottom that's painful!') Sadly for the mariner, the blowing wind almost always conspires with the sea to push up huge waves. These fling themselves with tremendous force onto anything, including land, silly enough to get in the way. Understanding this effect, and counterintuitive though it may seem, the first thing any prudent mariner does when suspecting that a hard blow is in the offing is to put as much water between himself and the land as he can get. In the case of great storms, like typhoons and hurricanes, hundreds of miles offshore might not be too much. To do otherwise is to court disaster.

'But surely those rules do not apply to motorized vessels nowadays, do they?' To which the reply is that they do not as long as the engine is running and as long that "cast iron mains'l" is strong enough to overcome the wind and the waves. It is important to recall, however, that hurricanes, typhoons, tsunamis and the like routinely lay waste to everything manmade that comes between them and wherever it is that they are pleased to go! One ought to consider as well that if the motor stops making those precious, growly-noises we all know and love – and it always does at the most inopportune instants – then the rules pertaining to sailing ships (multiplied by about a factor of 10) immediately become operative again.

So, despite the change in nautical propulsion systems from boats using large pieces of flapping cloth hung willy-nilly on poles in order to catch the air, to mechanical monsters that make great roaring sounds and belch black smoke, being driven 'onto the rocks' was, is and probably always will be, the single greatest threat to life and property a seamen faces. Even today, even in the relatively protected waters of the Salish Sea, the most common boating calamity outside of drowning is that of going aground. And contrary to the owners' expectations, pleasure boats probably are more susceptible to the dangers of lee shores than any other type of craft precisely because they aren't owned, operated or maintained by professionals.

"Impossible you say!" Not so, I reply! Here's the scenario: The Strait of Juan de Fuca's prevailing westerly winds unexpectedly kick up as you cruise the western shore of San Juan Island in search of killer whales. You've been happily motoring along, just a few hundred yards off the steep, rocky coast, having a high old time of it with your friends, your food and probably with a full portion or two of grog (or the modern equivalent). As the sea begins to turn rough, however, and the wind and the waves start to shove the boat in toward the shore, you decide to head for safety. You push your engine's throttle forward to pick up speed and to counteract the forces that are beginning to pound your craft, but instead of the normal, throaty roar you usually hear after doing so, you get instead two coughs, a splutter, a pop and then pure silence. Crank and grind the starter as you will, the engine refuses to cooperate. Now where is the boat heading? Bingo! Suddenly The Navigator's paranoia is not quite so paranoid!

After an uneventful crossing, *Minstrel's Song* passed out of 'The Strait,' slipping easily between Goose and Dead Man Islands – do you ever wonder who names these places -- to enter the southeast end of the San Juan Channel on a weak ebb tide. Although she was losing a knot (approximately 1.16 mph) or more to the current that flowed southward, if the various charts and tabulations available were to be believed, she still was making better time than she would have had she slogged directly north up Haro Strait (on the west side of San Juan Island).

Even when the weather's good, cruising in protected water is always better! Wrapped as they soon were in a diorama of evergreen covered barrier islands that served to keep wind, large waves and big ships at bay, The Captain and The Crew breathed silent sighs of relief. In fact, they were happily snapping photos of the picturesque Cattle Point Lighthouse, framed as it was against the distant Olympic Mountains, when their blissful reverie was shattered.

"What the hell was that?" I growled to no one in particular. Beyond surprise, I was chagrined by the unexpected appearance of a streak of orange and white rubber that came out of nowhere, shot past our starboard beam (right side) at something just under 1,000 mph (estimated) and then disappeared ahead in a roster tail of spray. As The Skipper of *Minstrel's Song* I pride myself on running a tight ship. The sloppy watch-keeping this event underscored cut me deeply. Adding insult to injury, The Crew rightly observed – as if I had not – that the comet that had just passed us belonged to the U.S. Coast Guard. As with police cars on our highways, the last thing you want to miss seeing when out on the ocean is a Coast Guard vessel screaming toward you!

Somewhere in that hazy mental construct we call the past, it seemed to me that both The Crew and I had been employed for a considerable period of time by a three-letter government organization that specialized in espionage. An integral part of that shadowy world included the 24/7 need to be able to determine if and when one was under surveillance. Doing that effectively -- even in trying circumstances – required, at the least, always being aware of one's surroundings. With lots of training, years of experience and much success, both The Skipper and The Executive Officer had been good at their work. Thus, letting a bright orange and white, government-owned meteor "sneak up" on us while we floated on the wide, flat sea, in broad daylight, was about as much abuse as any ego needed to withstand. At least half of us onboard pouted.

Perhaps it is because of the War on Terror. Perhaps it is because of the influx of illegal aliens. And perhaps it is because of us, John Q. and Jane R. Public, who take to our oceans, bays, inlets, arms, straits, reaches, rivers, streams, lakes, canals and sometimes, even, our swamps in ever-greater, ever-nutsier numbers. Whatever the root cause of the changes we have observed over the last decade or two, it seems that the challenges of 21st Century life have forced the Coast Guard's brave few to transform themselves from a body of waterborne good Samaritans into a phalanx of rough and ready warriors. Thus, when a gaggle of infantry-booted, gun-totting, stern-looking young officials blasts past at warp speed and then they carve a beautiful doughnut in the water and rocket back the same way they came, eyeballing you intently the whole time, it takes a fairly sturdy constitution to forego the temptation to throw up one's hands and beg for mercy for whatever transgressions these keepers of the public order suspect you may have committed![1] Fortunately, before we were able to run up a white flag, our prosecutors executed a nifty 90-degree turn and took off again. This time they seemed to be in hot pursuit of a likely looking boatload of criminals and assassins who were holding very malicious looking fishing poles!

With our pre-assault serenity totally shattered by these events, we take some solace in the fact that our shipshape boat -- properly documented, marked, tagged and festooned with every safety sticker, organizational identification, burgee and flag known to mankind – evidently passed muster and has saved us from the indignities of a Coast Guard brig or worse! Even better, we are now free to spend a very pleasant, self-satisfying 45 minutes or so of watching this buzzing government craft flit across the water scaring the bejesus out of a score of other unsuspecting miscreants. So engaged do we become in this

---

[1] *It is important to stipulate that the U.S. Coast Guard is an amazing organization. Populated by dedicated men and women who truly do protect and serve, it is hard to imagine what our waterways would look like without them. Their work is of inestimable value to all seamen; they contribute much to the health and welfare of our nation.*

sport that in Walter Mitty-fashion we begin to mentally vector the intrepid defenders of freedom toward vessels that do not come up to our high standards of legitimacy. Gleefully we imagine the panic that the various culprits feel when they learn that they've been found out!

It is likely that this amusement could have gone on all day, but the demands of boating safety intervened. We had reached the point where San Juan Channel makes its dogleg change of direction from north to northwest, curving around the appropriately designated Turn Island. The required maneuver is not especially tricky so long as one understands that a great pile of barely submerged rock, inventively dubbed 'Turn Rock,' lurks about a quarter of a mile north of the last speck of visible land. Those seamen who failed Chart Reading 101 or worse, those who dispense with charts completely, sometimes try to cut this corner a little short. At almost any season of the year one can find some otherwise happy group of boaters sitting high and dry up on these shallows, well on their way to learning a lot more than they ever wanted to know about what lurks in the fine print of their marine insurance policies. So, with the intention of floating around this rocky menace vice trying to motor over it or being driven up on it by the currents, The Navigator awoke from his reveries to give the upcoming change of course his full attention.

From its change of direction at Turn Rock, San Juan Channel runs off to the northwest without deviation and dumps the traveler out in the vicinity of Spieden Island. This stretch of ocean is a favorite of ours. With Shaw Island setting the northern limits of the waterway and San Juan Island doing the same to the south, the land presses in more closely here –about a mile and a quarter of sea separates them. This has the effect of transforming the heavily treed hills that resembled distant green smudges in the wider, lower channel into brilliant, 3-D pop-outs at this end. Houses perched on cliffs or intentionally hidden behind the heavy foliage, suddenly spring into view. The dark grey-brown rocks jumbled helter-skelter at water's edge, separating the sea from the steeply rising heights, seem to mock the deep blue-green water for its inability to drive them back up on land. On this particular day, the cloudless, azure sky hovers overhead as if to ensure civility amongst the various elements under it. Cruising rarely is more enjoyable than this!

Taking on larger proportions too, at this specific moment, is the whale watching boat that had been coming up abaft our port beam. (That is sailors' talk for 'from the back left side of the boat.' It seems a nice, even necessary touch sometimes when dealing with things nautical, but admittedly The Crew still responds much better to "over there!") Because we are good citizens and because there is a need for some regularity in our comings and goings on the ocean blue, we try to play by the rules. And the rules say that a commercial vessel of some significant size, engaged in its legitimate business pursuits generally has the right of way over tiny pleasure ships like ours. So we extend this particular craft all due courtesies by slowing to allow it to pass unimpeded along its merry way.

All would have been fine had the Captain of this aforementioned sightseeing platform not decided that his 'merry way' should include decreasing his boat's speed to that of a racing barnacle just milliseconds after he gained the lead. Adding insult to injury, he then zigged and zagged back and forth in front of us to the throbbing beat of the 1970s disco music that blared from his onboard sound system! The combination of these things caused us to change course repeatedly, to slow up, to speed up – to throw up? -- and ultimately to do the Hokey-Pokey while he wandered all over the place. Surely he did so in hope of scaring up a whale for his passengers to ogle; with equal surety the mental calculations of the financial loss his 100% money back guarantee was going to cost him if he did not rustle up some Cetaceans undoubtedly kept him from performing his piloting duties at a professional level.

The reader will be relieved to know that the invectives our Skipper used to fill the pilothouse of *Minstrel's Song* at this particular instant were not directed at the inconsiderate master of the other vessel, his mother, or any of his immediate relatives, past or present, canine or otherwise; rather, The Skipper rolled out a range of traditional marine vocabulary for the express purpose of keeping it immediately at hand and well exercised. Having these tools worked up and in shape in the event of a real emergency was little more than prudent seamanship. The Crew wisely said nothing, understanding that if practice makes perfect, her Captain was just about there!

When the excursion boat finally veered off to starboard (the right), into Spring Passage and all points north, we waved a fond farewell to our momentary nemesis and wished them a *bon voyage*...or words to that effect. Back on our original course, we chugged past desolate Spieden Island and left both Cactus and Ripple Islands off our port beam too. As the latter was cleared, we turned our bow a point or so to port (roughly 6 degrees for those still keeping score!) and beheld a brave, new world: Canada!

It is in this general vicinity that an outward bound vessel emerges from the confines of the San Juan Islands and first enjoys the vista created by the broad expanse of Boundary Passage, a substantial body of water that stretches far off to the north and northwest. In the hazy distance, dots and lumps and bumps clutter the briny horizon. These are Canada's Gulf Islands! Most exciting, however, is the fact that for the first time we identify the mountainous mass looming dead ahead as that of our immediate destination, South Pender Island. Bali Hai is calling...! Sighting it means that the day's cruise is nearing its end and a protected harbor awaits us just an hour or so away. Also, it means that it is time to call Canadian Customs to announce our ship's intentions.

We raised a Customs official on the cell phone and let her know who we were, gave her of our travel plans and certified that our first landfall in her country would be Bedwell Harbour. The polite young lady returned the favor by giving us an entry number and directed us to arrive at the government dock in the aforementioned port at 3:00 p.m. sharp. She said that if a Customs' Agent was waiting for us we should stop for inspection, but if not, we were good to go. Cool!

NEXUS COMPLEXUS

Some months before this moment, in an abject fit of

rationality, we decided that since we planned to voyage frequently to Canada, we should streamline the border crossing ordeal to the extent possible. The buzz on the street was that the best way to do that was via something called "The NEXUS Card."

When one goes on-line to order something from L.L. Bean, Amazon.com, Coldwater Creek, West Marine, or almost any other commercial entity, the drill is always the same. First, you register, and then you shop. After making your selections, you proceed to check out. There you review your purchases, select a form of payment, choose a delivery address and a shipping mode and you're done. Including the time it takes to sign up -- by filling in a number of mandatory blank boxes, always denoted by the accursed red asterisk! -- the whole thing usually takes no more than 10-15 minutes, max. The profit motive apparently pushes efficiency unmercifully; remove it and, well…you get government service.

Our quest for "The NEXUS Card" – a pursuit that ultimately resembled the medieval search for the Holy Grail -- began innocently enough. A quick Internet search led to a U.S. Government site that kind of…sort of…well…almost put us in the general vicinity of our goal. The word "general" is emphasized here because once we were 'there,' we discovered that we were not anywhere at all! Indeed, it required several additional internal site searches before we found anything even vaguely related to what we wanted.

Crawling through a maze of nearly nonsensical prose -- penned for certain by a school of irate Martians driven to madness by the need to use their claw-like appendages *sans* articulating thumbs to record their thoughts – we pursued dead end after dead end until finally we stumbled over something called "GOES." And, with no more that a few hours of careful study we discerned that that acronym represented something known as the "Global Online Enrollment System." Reassuringly we read that that we had arrived at the absolute, without a doubt, official, "U.S. Government Web Site to apply for Global Entry, FLUX, NEXUS, SENTRI, FAST" (and perhaps Martian citizenship as well!). While clarity may not have been the long suit of this site page, at the least it proved to us that what we sought actually did exist.

Although it was not explicit, we inferred from our review of the available materials that to get "The NEXUS Card" we had to slip through the GOES portal. We were encouraged, however, by the unrepentant assertion that were we to do just that, getting "The NEXUS Card" would be an easy, four-step process, to wit:

1. Apply On-line;
2. Schedule an Interview;
3. Interview Determines Your Eligibility;
4. Provide Identification

The fine print appended to this outline did stipulate that an up-front application fee of $100. (U.S.D.) was required for each card and that everyone who crossed the border together in a single conveyance had to possess his or her own card or the old, usual rules for clearing Customs would apply.

Having once been trusted members of that band of spooks who worked for a particular U.S. Government agency that is best known by its three-letter acronym -- the first of which stands for "Central" – we were no strangers to the land of background investigations and formal interviews. Thus, we might be forgiven for thinking naively that since there was little that Uncle Sam did not already know about us, getting cleared for "The Nexus Card" would be a snap. That, sadly, was proof that over the intervening years we had forgotten the first tenet of governmental survival: never assume anything.

Per our expectations we found that to make application on-line for "The NEXUS Card," one first had to register. Anxious to strike this chore off of the 'to do' list, I dove into that process enthusiastically ...and did a belly flop!

My first attempt to enter the inner sanctum netted nothing more than an indifferent screen with an error message. Again and again I filled in the boxes –denoted by red asterisks -- and again and again my offerings to the electronic gods were rejected. Accepting responsibility for the mistake(s) that I must have made – because computers are ALWAYS fault-free – I vainly checked and re-checked my work. Three days later I was still at the same registration screen, getting the same idiotic rejection notice.

Shamed beyond belief, again, I was driven to admit to The Executive Officer that maybe, just maybe, my computer skills had hit the proverbial brick wall. Would she please help? Cleverly masking the joy I know she takes in watching The Skipper suffer the indignities brought about by nearly-complete computer illiteracy, she commences to show off her prowess. Type, type, type, she goes. Scroll, scroll, scroll. Enter, enter, enter, and then, *voila!...* she gets the same stinking message I'd been getting! (Sweet vindication!)

You can do a lot of things to my Messmate, but do not muck with her when it comes to computers. (She rules electronic gizmos and it is a well-established fact around our house that recalcitrant machines have but two choices: submit to her will or die!) Glaring at the offending monitor, she re-checks her work, starts pushing keys and buttons like an accountant on tax day and emerges from her cone of silence with important intelligence! She advises that, "It's a long holiday weekend and the GOES people gave their computers these days off!"

"To let them visit their families?" I ask sarcastically.

"According to this, they won't be back on-line until sometime after opening of business on Tuesday," she responds, wholly ignoring my question.

"You're kidding," I blurt.

"Nope," she cheerily tells me, "It's the government way, you know."

"Yes, I know...all too well," I think to myself.

Come Tuesday I am back at my desk working on "GOES." (By now this moniker has taken on a comedic air in light of the fact that the government computer driving this show refuses to move off the dime.) Still, slogging forward as best I can I get to the place where I'm required to pick a password. I cleverly choose "It'sme,Fool" – a nice combination of capital and lower case letters with a symbol thrown in just for style, all reflective of my mood at that particular moment – and time and time again the government's soulless processor rejects my wit. After thirteen vain attempts to surmount this hurdle, I am reduced to consulting The X.O. again. She takes a couple of minutes to read the instructions, an act I deliberately disdained, and then advises that only a very peculiar combination of letters, numbers, marks and symbols could be employed. As described I complain that these are of sufficient complexity to make the Rosetta Stone look like the work of unschooled chimpanzee. Nonetheless, without any other recourse I acquiesce; my contrition is rewarded immediately, however, with an I.D. number.

The late T.V. huckster, Billy Mays, used to shout, "But wait! There's more!" as he added item upon item to the incredible list of wonders you could have for a mere $19.95 (plus shipping and handling!). Billy's shtick always was entertaining -- in a perverse sort of way. The government's approach is a great deal less so. For after jumping through an apparently endless line of registration hoops, I find that there is still more. In order to get permission to commence the beginning of the start of the application process one must wait! In fact, I read that a delay of a week or two intentionally is built into the system. "They'll be in touch," an unemotional grey screen advises me. "GOES, indeed, I mutter to no one in particular!

The next contact I have with the leviathan counsels that as soon as I pay the non-refundable $100 application fee they will allow me to look at, and perhaps even fill out, the requisite forms. I resist the temptation to ask the machine the existential question of why I have to pay 'extra,' beyond all of the tax dollars we feed into the maw of the governmental beast each year, just to get it to do precisely what it exists to do to begin with? Instead, psychologically reduced as I have been, I am ready to pony up the hundred bucks no questions asked if only they will let me continue!

They will, I infer from the fine print at the bottom of the notification I received, let me move to the next level but only on condition that should I make any mistakes at all – any! -- in supplying whatever it is that they might demand, and my Ben Franklin will disappear into the depths of the government's coffers never to be seen again. Oh, and by the way, the entire process may result in me having to go to jail, directly to jail, and certainly without benefit of passing go along the way!

The requisite form is hardly up on the screen when I see that they are throwing curveballs! Box 1 asks, "What is your name?" Undoubtedly a test question designed to ferret out the ill intentioned or the unwary prevaricator, its genius lies in its apparent simplicity! Don't we all know our own names? Well…maybe not.

Consider, for a moment, this situation: Several decades ago my ex and I had to choose a catchy title for our third child. Having expended more than a lifetime's allotment of psychic energy on giving precisely the right name to our previous progeny, we took the path of least resistance on this one. If we had a girl, we agreed, we would name her after a favorite grandmother; if a boy – a first for us – he would be a "Junior." As fate would have it, this final addition to the familial line was a boy. Thus, on paper he became me writ small! I continued, however, just to be me.

Since the beginning of my time here on earth, I have used my baptismal name for all things official. And life was good until I learned how to fly! On the happy day when I filled out U.S. Government form number something-something-something or-the-other in order to get my long sought after pilot's license, I was warned, sternly, that only absolute honesty on it would be tolerated. Screw it up and my permit might never be issued, and the bureaucratic ball of yarn that I would personally be creating might take years or even decades to untangle. "All the while," I was told, "you'll forfeit all of the fees you've paid already and you'll not be able to fly anything!" (Hmmmmm…was this *déjà vu* all over again?)

Forewarned that way, I dutifully recorded my full name, letter by letter, as I always had and I confirmed it three times against the appellations on my driver's license, my passport and my Social Security card. When done, my flight examiner asked if I affixed either Junior or Senior to it. "No," I said "I'm just regular old me." Undaunted, however, this government agent asked if I had any offspring that shared my name. Sure, I said, I have a son who is a "Junior." Having inadvertently sprung his trap, the keeper of my flying future gleefully screeched, "Ahaa! That makes you a "Senior!" Agreeing to that assertion and gathering at the same time that this representative of state power could have me taken out and publically horsewhipped for trifling with him this way, I acquiesced quickly to his demand that we append "Senior" to the end of the name then on the form. So, to this very moment all of my official, property of the U.S. Government, FAA-issued licenses add "Senior" to what had always been my full name.

Returning to the question of what I should list for the "The NEXUS Card," I had to think long and hard about who I was. I was not "Senior" on my drivers' license, my passport, my Social Security documents, not even on the Barnes and Noble membership card I tote to get good discounts on books, but I was a "Senior" according to the FAA of the USG in the US of A. "To be or not to be..." that truly was the question. Reasoning that getting the offending appendage stricken from one federal document, if need be, would be easier than adding it to a gaggle of others, I decided to go with the FAA version.

The questions I had to answer after that got easier. Mostly they reflected the usual bureaucratic myopia! After interminable hours, I thrashed my way to the end of the form and thankfully put the whole affair behind me by hitting the send button.

Given all of the other requirements and prohibitions, I was surprised to learn that I was allowed to keep a copy for my records. This specific condescension convinced me that "they" had some perverse reason for letting me see my own responses again, but despite my suspicions I took advantage of it anyway.

As mentioned earlier, one restrictive feature of "The NEXUS

Card" is that it only gives you a leg up if everyone traveling with you has one too. Thus we knew that The First Mate would soon be going through this same ordeal -- and paying another $100 for the privilege! Comprehending full well that skilled interrogators delight in differing stories about the same things, we definitely compared notes; truth be known, I gave her all of my answers! (Nowhere in the instructions did they forbid that, but I am sure it is not allowed all the same.)

In WWII, after the British turned Rommel back at the Battle of El Alamein, Winston Churchill made a speech in which he said, "Now is not the end. It is not even the beginning of the end. But it is, perhaps, the end of the beginning." So it was with us. With our applications submitted, we searched the Internet anxiously each day for proof that progress was being made toward "The NEXUS Card." As the outcome of the war hung in the balance for Churchill, so too did the fate of our $200 teeter on the whims of our government. About a week after dispatching our solicitations – which was a bit shy of a month after we first set out on this quest – news arrived: we were to be interviewed…in about 30 days!

The Breadwinner of our household – the one who goes out each day and actually gets paid for her work – took leave from her employer so we could make the three-hour road and ferry trip to reach the black rendition site. We carried with us all manner of documentation and proofs – without which "they" would not even consider our cases – and we spent the whole time we were together in the car plotting and planning how best to share the contents of our files while separately enduring the agony of the anticipated thumbscrews!

Dressed as much like Mr. and Mrs. 'We'reNotADangerToAnyone' as we could be, it was with great trepidation that we entered the halls of the august U.S. Customs House. (Actually, we arrived in front of a couple of doors marked "U.S. Customs" in a side corridor of an old air terminal. Surely, however, the imperial image of a magnificent edifice fits the image better.) We stood there understanding that life as we knew it, the future of western civilization and especially our 200 bucks, all rode on the success or failure of these "interviews." I was called first.

The Senior Inquisitor On Duty did not look like Torquemada. Instead, except for the uniform and the bored look on his face, he could have passed for an ordinary citizen. But I knew that in situations like these appearances were intended to be deceiving.

He had but 15 minutes to get the job done and waterboarding now was strictly prohibited. I knew that with time constraints like that he would have to work with great alacrity. I knew, too, that if I were to prevail, I was going to have move even faster to stay ahead. He motioned to a seat across the grey, government-issued desktop and as I took it we sized each other up. Then it began. Within milliseconds I determined that he was good, really good at his. Thus, his first question hit me right between the eyes, "What is your name?"

Perceiving immediately where he planned to take this thing, I calmly stated, "Senior, Your-All-Powerfulness."

"Do you have three proofs of that with you," he knowingly inquired.

"Of course, your Incredible Majesty-ness." I handed him my passport, drivers' license and Social Security card.

After momentarily studying those documents, he gave me 'the look.' While hundreds of psychology textbooks surely have dissected this phenomenon, none of us have to be schooled in it to know it when we see it! It is the ever-so-slight, but just-barely-perceptible sneer; the almost unnoticeable raising of a single eyebrow; the overly polite, honey-toned voice – all signs of the petty functionary callously marking out his next victim. Closing in for the kill, he delivered what I am sure he thought was to be his best stroke, "But sir, these don't say anything about 'Senior'."

Unbeknownst to our would-be defender of bureaucratic privilege, his target had been professionally trained by an official, three-letter, U.S. Government agency to counter with ease these sorts of minor annoyances. Thus, I parried his rather clumsy attack by calmly laying three plastic cards on his desk. Each of these displayed the telltale holograms and the embedded security strips of an official identification card. Each one of them had emblazoned across its top,

United States of America

Department of Transportation * Federal Aviation Administration

Casually, I laid a finger on the name line of one of them, visually underscoring the fact that they all included the word, "Senior." *Touché*!

Whether it was just a slow day and they had nothing else to do or whether a wave of psychic energy suddenly wafted through the interrogation chamber, I cannot say. But I did observe, with that kind of skilled detachment that comes only after years of practice in the field, that a worried hush had fallen over the agents who shared the space with the man I now had in my crosshairs. The over-frantic shuffling of papers, the pouring of cold coffee into colder, Styrofoam cups, the sudden interest in the latest inter-office memo all told me that despite the feigned looks of indifference on all of their faces, everyone within those four walls knew that the battle had been joined.

To my delight I noticed that sweat beaded on The Interrogator's brow. He knew that he had just lost Round One of the championship bout. Digging deeply within, I could tell by the way that he shifted in his chair that he did not intend to lose any more. Collecting his wits he half snarled at me, "Have you ever used any OTHER names?" (It was patently obvious that he wanted my hundred bucks and he was not going to give that bill up without a fight; whether those greenbacks would go directly into his personal account or only serve to pad his official reporting numbers remained a matter of pure speculation.)

Just as no toreador can pass up the opportunity for a brilliant *estocada* (final thrust) to conclude his performance, so, sadly, was I unable to relinquish center stage or step out of the limelight. Ego pushes us in all kinds of unattractive directions and before it even happened, I knew that what I was about to do was not truly professional and certainly it did not reach minimal performance thresholds for seasoned field officers. (Ultimately I had to rationalize this lapse as deriving from a lack of practice. In looking back on it now, I can see that it was a disgraceful waste of talent, but I just could not help myself.) Provoked as I had been, I automatically commenced doing my best Gomer Pyle imitation. Taking just a bit too long to answer his question – a moment used, I admit, only to savor the sweetness of the victory that I knew now was in hand -- I teased him with a very tentative, “Ahhh…gee….you see…ummmm, well I guess I’d have to say yes…and no to that question, Your Overwhelming Almighty-ness!”

“Really?” he said as he leaned every so slightly forward in his chair, with a look of total confusion on his face. Concomitantly, the office grew deathly quiet and all eyes were locked on me. None of them had anticipated an answer like that.

“Well, yes, your Very Ultimate Lordliness. But of course you need to understand…”

Drawing in a deep breath and then slowly expelling it – just for effect -- I underwent another metamorphosis. Looking directly at this poor little man, while shifting to a ramrod-straight sitting position, I addressed him most authoritatively this time. “As I’m sure you know from your computer base there,” I nod to the monitor on his desk, “For many years I was with that three letter Agency that starts with the word ‘Central’ and includes the word ‘Intelligence’ in its name. We weren’t always Boy Scouts there and we didn’t always play by the Marquis of Queensbury’s rules.”

An uppercut delivered by a heavyweight champion would not have stopped my tormentor any faster. Instantly he had been put between a rock and a hard place. I knew from experience and from the way he now was squirming in his chair that his computer told him nothing about my former employer, but I also knew that his sole defense against my attack was to pretend that his magical screen revealed everything. Adrift on a sea of uncertainty, he had been lured into uncharted waters. Even his colleagues began to look around at each other, raising their eyebrows and slightly shrugging their shoulders to indicate that they that did not know what to do in a case like this either.

As he stammered to buy time, I cut The Inquisitor short. "Since you're working in the national security field too," a stretch of the truth requiring all the self control I could muster, "I can share with you something that I couldn't with most other people. You must understand that I can't go into specifics, but here's the deal in a nutshell: Was 007 really James Bond's name? Was James Bond really 007's name? When did James get into the game? When did he get out of it? See where I'm going with this?"

To bring the entertainment to a tidy end I allowed as how he could rest easy about this whole matter since I had only used 'other names' – perhaps even many other names – with the approval of and at the specific direction of the U.S. Government. I assured him, too, that under normal circumstances I would not have revealed this to anyone, but since HE was a part of the U.S. Government as well and since I was required to tell the truth, the whole truth, and nothing but the truth, I felt a moral obligation to hold nothing back. (Appearing to go above and beyond the call of duty in situations such as these adds a ring of veracity that is hard to dispel. Not only is the listener bolstered and reassured – for no good reason – but, taking this tack generally obviates the need to produce additional *bona fides*!)

I waited for a few seconds to let all of this sink in and then, just to nail down any loose ends that may have remained, I added, "You can appreciate the pointlessness of asking anything more about the identities I might have assumed. That," I threw in gratuitously, "is highly 'Classified' and of course no further explanations could or would be provided!"

With this turn of events the seas suddenly parted, a rainbow broke through the clouds and all of the "unpleasantness" regarding that "Senior" thing was now a part of the distant past. We were, after all, comrades in arms -- albeit with vastly different statuses -- and short of going out for drinks together, my boy and his wide-eyed colleagues did everything possible to make up for the inconveniences the system had caused. Human compassion obliged me to stop him just short of the declaration he was warming up to making, that he was only following orders. I did not have the heart to let him go there.

Although little would have pleased my new found friends more than chatting for the rest of the week about the good old days and the work "we" had done to make the world a safer place for democracy, I feigned another, pressing commitment and implored the herd to take up immediately the issue of The Executive Officer's application. From the wings where she had been left to chill, The X.O. quickly was ushered into the interview room with all the pomp, circumstance and courtesy customarily reserved for foreign dignitaries.

Oh, it was simply wonderful the way we suddenly found such collegial commonality! As the afternoon wound down, we said our fond farewells with the absolute assurance that "The NEXUS Cards" would be in the next day's post. Best of all, we were pleased by the fact that our $200 finally appeared to be safe...and that once again, like the good "agents" we were, we had not been forced to kill anybody!

* * * * * * * * * * * *

The odd thing about crossing the border into Canada by sea is what happens when you do it. Actually it is a kind of an "anti-thing" since what occurs is nothing. Absolutely nothing! There are no signs, no fences, no security check points, no Customs officials, not even your ordinary swath of painted water to differentiate one side from the other. But change occurs at that boundary nonetheless. It is subtle, it is well hidden, but it is undeniable.

Take, for instance, the name of our first day's destination: Bedwell Harbour. Run those words past your spellchecker and it will spit them out like sour grapes! Why? For starters it is because Bedwell is some sort of a proper noun, British no doubt, and thus not listed in most dictionaries. But Harbour is far more interesting. The reader recognizes it for what it is, but the spellchecker rings the gong every time and says wrong, wrong, wrong! Why? Because of the "u."

Back in the day when most of Canada's residents were either French or Indians (the latter now known there as First People), and when the British colonies in America hardly extended inland off the East Coast beyond the reach of the saltwater, a bunch of malcontents began causing trouble, insisting that the English king was not doing his job very well. One thing led to another, there was a bit of pushing and shoving and soon folks were choosing up teams and threatening to settle the matter in the traditional manner. One jolly band of ne'er-do-wells, known as the "American Revolutionaries," thought they could and should go head-to-head with the (almost) undisputed heavyweight champions of the world (i.e., Great Britain, a.k.a. "The Redcoats"). An equally vocal gang, however, dubbed the "The Loyalists," said 'No Way!' These good people opined that if there was going to be a game they should support the team with the best record. Being prudent citizens, however, they generally determined that that meant staying in the stands and cheering for the monarch's team. As always, too, there was a collection of individuals who really could not decide what to do. Because their ultimate refuge amounted to pulling their heads into their shells and hoping that the whole thing would go away quickly, they could have been referred to as "The Trembling Turtles."

The action of the contest that ensued swayed back and forth, up and down and around and around for years. Occasionally a stand out competitor, such as Benedict Arnold, changed sides, and periodically both benches signed new players (e.g. German Hessians and French sailors) to bolster their ranks. After going seven or eight grueling rounds, "The Redcoats" finally threw in the towel, saying that winning the match was more trouble than it was worth. This caused the "Revolutionaries" to celebrate, "The Turtles" to breathe a sigh of relief, but "The Loyalists" were at a loss as to where to go from there. Having been transformed into the fans of the losing side, the away team, they could not stay in the stands any longer, but they had no home to return to.. So, they traipsed north to Canada and laid claim to front row seats for the War of 1812.

Neither the French nor the Indians, who already lived in that vast land, were too happy about this new arrangement, especially given "The Loyalists" belief they should be in charge of organizing all future events. Since the King was indebted to these stalwarts for their, well, loyalty, and since he owned this particular parcel of real estate anyway, when he insisted that they be housed there and that they be given a lion's share of responsibility for transforming the colony into a going concern, the earlier inhabitants had to accept the reality of their brave new world. Slowly these diverse groups learned to play together, sort of!

The interesting but perhaps not surprising upshot of this slice of history is that while "The Revolutionaries" immediately set out to rid themselves of all vestiges of His Royal Majesty, "The Loyalists" clung tightly to them. And therein, dear reader, lies the difference between the two entities to this day!

The British spell harbor with a "u." They also use that same letter for labour, colour and a lot of other words properly spelled with "or" in the land of "The Revolutionaries." In fact, having a lingering predilection for things English, the Canadians tend to retain many rather other apparently arcane forms of spelling. Weights and measures, too, follow this Continental pattern. Even architecture reflects a different point of view. So, when one crosses into Canada one begins to see little distinctions. Drive on Canadian roads and you will note that the speed limits are posted in kilometres (not even kilomet<u>er</u>s!) per hour. Look at their charts and observe that the elevations, distances and depths are calibrated in metres. Weights there are described in grams and kilograms. So highly do they value these touches of home that even to this day their world-famous national constabulary is officially called the <u>Royal</u> Canadian Mounted Police, despite the fact that there is no longer a binding, legal connection between the two nations!

It was into this familiar, but unique, society that *Minstrel's Song* now sailed.

As the old thought-meister Yogi Berra might have said, "You never know what a place is going to look like until after you've seen it!" Although fully burdened with charts, chartplotters, GPSs, tide and current tables, sailing instructions, cruising guides, satellite photos, etc., etc., we consistently discovered that our destinations bore little actual resemblance to the mental images of them we managed to construct beforehand. Our first inkling of this phenomenon came as we approached Bedwell Harbour.

The waters of Bedwell Harbour wash the shores of both North and South Pender Islands. A long, northwest-southeast oriented peninsula extending from North Pender proper protects the harbor (harbour for our Canadian friends) from the prevailing winds and the disturbed seas that mainly come out of the west. Off to the east, the whole of South Pender Island shelters this safe haven from the storm-driven weather that sometimes sweeps in from that quarter. Both islands wrap around its northern extreme. The protected area thus formed is about 2.5 miles long and a half a mile wide (4.02 X 0.80 kilometres for our northern neighbors).

On the proper tide and with favorable currents running, one can access Bedwell Harbour from the north via a slim tongue of water that connects it to Port Browning. The usual way of entering it, however, is through the open water that extends to the southeast onto Boundary Passage. Since we were arriving from that direction anyway, this approach suited us perfectly.

Even from a distance of seven miles (11.3 kilometres), South Pender's Curtis Peak was easy to identify. From that vantage point, however, the opening to the harbor was not. With the arm of North Pender extending southeast to Wallace Point and with Mount Norman looming in the background, we could not see anything except solid land dead ahead of us. Occurrences like this always make The Navigator nervous, so when an ever-deepening indentation into the rocky coastline slowly materialized, the little black cloud that hung over the bridge of *Minstrel's Song* lifted.

A quick glance at the charts suggests that the full extent of the harbor can be seen when coming in from the southeast. In fact, unless one holds a course a little further east than south, the tip of Wallace Point blocks the view of most of the bay. This, in turn, creates the illusion that the harbor stretches northwest and then cuts sharply back to the northeast. Even though such is not the case, that impression has the effect of forcing the edgy Navigator to glance, for the 10,000th time, at his precious charts!

Motoring slowly into Bedwell Harbour, we turn our attention to finding the government dock that we had been directed to be off at exactly 3:00 o'clock, p.m. Pacific Daylight Time. Certainly if a Canadian official was going to go to all of the trouble of welcoming us personally into his country, the least we could do was to arrive promptly for the event. Thus, all available hands were posted as lookouts and their eyes strained to catch a glimpse of anything that might be either a government dock or an official personage; this despite the fact that no one onboard could rightly say what a government dock or a Canadian Customs Officer actually might look like.

Steaming on a northwesterly course, we know that the area we seek will be off the starboard bow, just behind an unnamed point of land. Slowly a crescent-shaped indentation in the shoreline of South Pender Island opens in that direction. At about that same time The Crew spies a dock area and says, "That's where we want to go." The Captain hems and haws and then opines that maybe it is not. Motoring cautiously closer to the object of her insistence, The Skipper finally accepts the inevitable truth that once again The X.O. is right. Thus he turns the bow of the ship directly toward an empty wharf. Checking the charts and the depths, again, and mentally aligning what he sees around him with what is on the paper spread before him, The Captain orders 'Full Ahead Slow' and with a gentle pull on the throttle handle reduces engine's speed to an idle.

Within a few moments *Minstrel's Song* sits just off what is presumed to be 'the government dock,' exactly at the appointed hour. Because it is devoid of all life, including Customs Officers, all hands study the nearby outbuildings and the ramp leading down to the wharf like they would a newfound treasure map. Nothing moved.

In academic settings there are well-established rules of thumb concerning how long students must remain in the classroom while awaiting a tardy professor. Equally, in the espionage world certain recognized timing standards for critical events control almost every action. But who knows how long one is supposed to wait at a 'government dock' for a Customs Officer? Ultimately we decide that the minutes consumed by turning three slow circles in the water off the pier should suffice. Then, with no uniforms in sight and our doughnuts done, we head for the barn while making self-congratulatory noises about the wisdom of getting "The NEXUS Card!"

Weeks before our planned adventure, we determined that Bedwell Harbour offered three possibilities for overnight (boat) accommodations: marina slip, mooring buoy or anchor. And, the most desirable places to accomplish any of these activities were those parts of this safe haven known separately as Poet's Cove and Skull Islet. (How a place named Skull Islet came to exist within a stone's throw of the romantic sounding Poet's Cove, is a question we have yet to answer.)

The epicenter of Poet's Cove is located precisely where we had just been making circles in the sea, off the government dock. Co-located with the official quay is a private marina. In turn, the marina is a floating extension of the Poet's Cove Resort and Spa. And that entity consists of a tidy cluster of New England-style buildings populating the hillside that rises up immediately to the south of the wharf area. Because it is a rather modestly sized inlet, much of Poet's Cove proper is given over to these human contrivances.

Less than a half a mile to the northwest of this hub of excitement is that speck of land known as Skull Islet. It is the only part of a semicircular ledge of rocks that extends into the bay from South Pender Island that remains above water at high tide. So small, low and boulder-strewn is it that were it not for the short, white, navigational tower that sits squarely atop it, one could easily pass it without notice.

The happy combination of the northerly arcing shoreline that sweeps from the Resort around toward the Islet and the reversing, but complimentary curve of the craggy archipelago that ultimately rises up to form that tiny piece of real estate with the unsavory name, creates an especially cozy safe haven for boats. Neither snow, nor rain, nor heat, nor dark of night, nor even fierce winds blowing can threaten this snug little anchorage. Adding to its allure is the fact that some benevolent souls have affixed a number of mooring buoys within its inviting confines. These are part of the Beaumont Marine Provincial Park, a unit that takes in most of the anchorage, the beach and the heavily treed hills that overlook them. The areas in and around the buoys, as well as those between the Islet and the Spa are perfect way stations for small vessels in need of a night's respite.

SLIP-SLIDING AWAY

Boats and water are kind of weird things. Drop a brick on the ground and it stays put. Leave your house in the morning and it will not have moved an inch before you return at night. Park your car in a lot and it will be there when you come back – assuming local malefactor does not meander by, smash the window, punch out the ignition and deliver it to the nearest chop shop where it will disappear quickly into a cloud of parts, but that is another story! The point being that as land-bound creatures, we expect inanimate things to remain where we leave them. So, adapting to the watery world requires a bit of mental paradigm shifting.

Except when they have run hard up on some fragment of land carelessly overlooked on the chart, or when someone in full control of a boat intentionally directs the vessel toward some particular objective, the thing that boats like to do best is to wander from place to place. What we mean here is that floating things are not inclined to remain in a fixed place. Give them a lee shore and it is almost eerie the way they will throw themselves up on it. Enter a narrow passage with a running current and they will head in every direction except the one you want them to follow. Try to ease into a tight slip with the wind blowing and your vessel will delight everyone within a five-mile radius as it bounces around like a pinball, careening from pillar to post and then back again, all the while ringing up a most wondrous insurance claim. Vessels of every size just like to move; it is in their nature.

Over millennia the only remedy man has found for this wanderlust is to bind the floating things he treasures to other, really solid objects. (Note: This is an effective, temporary treatment for the malady, but it does not represent a permanent cure!) Having benefit of hard, cold, empirical data – derived from millions of practical experiments conducted through the ages by untold numbers of irate owners under all imaginable circumstances, spanning eons of time, and including legions of lost craft and empty bank accounts – reliable methods for achieving the desired aquatic stasis now are known to us. Unfortunately, despite technological breakthroughs in other spheres, in this important realm the solutions available remain extremely limited in number.

It is likely that the earliest attempts to keep boats from parading around on their own involved little more than pulling, pushing or carrying them to some pre-selected spot up on the shore where they could be dropped unceremoniously or otherwise left for safe keeping on the dry ground. The wondrous combination of gravity and friction having a naturally calming effect on the spirits of our waterborne conveyances, those mariners fortunate enough to be able to employ this common technique usually reaped the benefits of finding their vessels where they left them when they were ready to return to the sea. This seems to be because the "staying put" principle operative on land tends to overcome the wandering nature of things on the water.

But, because nothing is ever as easy as it seems, even the straightforward arrangement of beaching one's craft suffers some serious drawbacks. First, because about 70% of the earth's surface is water, the task of finding a convenient bit of *terra firma* at day's end is not without its challenges. Second, even when land is available, the sad truth is that not all shores slope gently up over white sandy beaches that then lead to lines of coconut-laden palm trees which sway alluringly in warm, soft breezes. Next, the chore of getting a floating something up on the land works really well if the object of one's attentions is small and light, like a surfboard, a kayak or even a canoe. But if it is a supertanker…well, you see the problem! Finally, while a properly beached vessel cannot go cavorting off on its own, it is not uncommon to find that the owners of the real estate on which such things are brought to rest object, violently, to the uninvited presence of said craft on their turf. Depending on the era, the resolution of this type of infringement frequently involved the use of spears, swords, guns, armies and today, phalanxes of litigating attorneys!

Despite these shortcomings, in many locales the restive natures of ships continue to be tamed as they were in the past, by way of putting them up on dry land. Although we tend not to recognize the primitive roots of these practices, our modern scientific inclinations leading us to view everything from the postmodern perspective, they remain nonetheless. The careful observer might see, for example, that there is a striking similarity between the modern boatyard, the dry dock and even the ubiquitous "Boat and RV Storage Here!!!" facility – all of which command substantial amounts of money to hire – and those earlier freebies designated with no more elegant names than "hard ground," "mud flats" or "exposed tidal rocks." In truth, one might speculate that the march of time reveals more about man's ability to sell innovation than it does about the improvements themselves!

In the earliest days of human existence conquering the briny deep and the things that floated upon it must have involved a lot of trial and error and an extra measure of courage. Progress, no doubt, came only in tiny increments. It is probable, then, that when sailors tired of dragging their boats up rocky cliffs or fighting to the death unhappy locals just to acquire an overnight parking space, they began to look for easier, less trying ways to keep their boats from wandering the world unattended. Thus, speculation suggests that the next step along the road to modernity was to leave the stinking thing in the water and try to find a way of tethering it to the shore. Such a scheme would have had the advantage of recreating that sense of predictability we expect on dry land (i.e., that the vessel will still be where we left it when we return to it). But what they hoped to gain in ease and constancy proved elusive.

Properly restrain anything that lives on land by affixing it stoutly to an utterly immobile object and it will remain in that place for thousands of years on end. But introduce water into the equation and suddenly you are dealing with something that is neither fish nor fowl! In this particular instance, it does not take a rocket scientist to understand that simply tying a floating object to something stationary near a shoreline is a little like chaining a pit bull to the front porch: He cannot run away, but he still can bite the heck out of the mailman! For example, finding your boat exactly where you left it, smashed to splinters by the pounding surf, really is not much better than not finding it at all!

Sans a satisfactory system to make the boat both available and useable while it continued in the floating mode, early mariners were left high and dry. But they did not forsake the search for a solution to the ongoing 'How can I keep-my-freaking-boat-safely-in-one-place-without-dragging-it-ashore' dilemma. At some point the ancient seafarer apparently stumbled onto the idea of affixing it sufficiently far from the shoreline to keep it from committing suicide on the rocks, while still having the craft close enough to dry land to allow him a modicum of access. With this "Aha!" moment behind him, he probably pursued two parallel courses of action: 1.) Extend the earth out into the sea; and/or 2.) Plant trees in the ocean!

Milliseconds after having these thoughts, our guy must have known that the first option was a bust. Not only would replacing the sea with dry land be one heck of a lot of work – and not very portable -- but even if accomplished it would do nothing more than put him back into the boat-wrestling business, albeit on terrain of his own design!

As to the tree-planting alternative, he must have discerned that this answer was not without its weaknesses as well. First and foremost among the drawbacks attendant upon it was the biological one. Surely it would not have taken our intrepid forebear too long to discover that just like people, most trees drown when they are held underwater for any period of time! So even if he managed to get the seedlings in place without killing himself, they would have gone 'paws up' and been driftwood by nightfall of the first day! And then too, it must have dawned on him that even if the trees did grow, his own modest lifespan would not allow for a wait of 20, 30, 40 years while the saplings matured to a useful size.

It is possible that the simple act of contemplating the

aforementioned problems might have sparked a thought worthy of consideration: Why not take a short leap forward and begin the whole process with a dead tree? Looking beyond all of the hard work involved in getting a large tree trunk to any given point in the sea, the great challenge would have been in finding a way to hold it down once there. After all, as soon as a log hits the water it assumes a lot of the same undesirable properties possessed by ordinary boats! So, just like any other vessel that is perfectly content to stay put when dumped on the beach, even giant pieces of wood develop an overpowering wanderlust the moment they start to float!

To surmount this hurdle our ancestors seem to have devised two ways to keep their tree restraints in place. They either could stand them upright and then ring them in with so many great boulders that they could not escape, or using a very heavy object to function as a large hammer they could drive the trunks themselves into the seabed. (Either way you take it, I am thinking that I do not want to be a part of that work crew, but that is probably what they did nonetheless.)

With their 'trees' planted, the seaman of yore now had something he could hitch his boat to without fear of loss. But like most silver linings, this arrangement came with its own dark cloud! Beyond just transportation, one of the great attributes of ships is their ability to haul a lot of stuff. Getting mountains of "stuff" – technically referred to as cargo – off and on a boat when it is tied some distance from anything that is not scientifically classified as a liquid, is not easy. Doing so would have involved a lot of wading or even swimming back and forth and not only would that have slowed the process to a crawl, but it would have required the participant to get very wet and cold to boot! The fix for that necessitated little more than setting a lot more trees upright in the water and then connecting them to land with a series of small logs. From there it was only a tiny jump to the development of wharfs, docks and marinas, all of which soon were for hire at exorbitant prices.

Despite these advancements, it must have become painfully clear to the roving sailor that his purely land-based schemes did not serve all of his needs. For while he might now be able to go out on the water and then return to the same spot, he still could not travel freely from place to place without having to stop each time to build a whole new support structure or to fight another land war. Comprehending the gargantuan amounts of work and the dangers involved in doing things that way, it is likely that he wondered how, if he devoted all of his time, money and energy to the peripherals, he ever was going to be able to sail again? (Sadly, that is a dilemma that continues to plague most mariners to this very day.)

In an attempt to resolve this quandary, our seafarer may have looked again to his landlocked cousins for ideas. And in doing so he most certainly noticed the similarities between boating and animal husbandry.

Most of our post-modern world is far removed from, and modestly ignorant of the agrarian scene. For example, I have personally conversed with educated souls who thought – really -- that pickles were plucked directly from "pickle bushes," that veal was a specific breed of animal that, in appearance, looked like a cross between a donkey and a cow and that the meat we find packaged in Styrofoam and clear plastic at the store was just another product manufactured on a factory assembly line. Fortunately our predecessors knew better, being closer to and more constantly threatened by the vagaries of trying to put food on the table when living in a world of scarcity, and that undoubtedly served them well when it came to mastering boats.

To retain the utility and the relative luxury that goes with owning living, breathing beasts such as horses, cows, goats, sheep, pigs, camels, even llamas, one had to devise ways of keeping them from gallivanting willy-nilly all over creation. Those who went before us fast discovered that if they could somehow detain these natural wanderers, they then would be available when needed. Despite their relative backwardness, these folks of the land somehow perceived that the very act of keeping their animals "up" conferred on them what all of our best economists now refer to as 'value added.' Additionally, constraining their creatures also meant that they could not become someone else's bounty the moment they went over the nearest hill.

Most importantly, however, was the fact that when their semi-domesticated servants were confined to a single location our distant relatives could devote most of their days to doing productive things that did not involve running flat out in hot pursuit of creatures who were both faster than they were and wholly disinclined to be captured. To obviate these drawbacks, domesticated brutes of any value were tied to things that would not move, like immense rocks and huge trees. Is the reader starting to get the picture now?

As the lessons of the agricultural realm began to seep into the marine world, they had to be amended somewhat to be useful. The first problem that had to be addressed sprang from the difficulty one could have in locating the underwater trees and rocks necessary to hold a boat fast. And once found, there was the somewhat unnerving question regarding who was going to brave the depths – populated as they were by monsters and other offensive being -- to tie ropes around them once they had been found? (The dimensions of both of these conundrums can be imagined if we keep in mind that the first and most important principle in marine architecture is and always has been: The water must remain on the outside of the hull. This obviously derives from man's primordial aversion to swimming long distances through seas filled with terrors while carrying heavy loads!)

There is no doubt that the general inconveniences associated with finding and then actually employing submerged objects for the purpose of holding a craft in one spot motivated the early voyager to explore the alternate possibility of hauling his own heavy item with him wherever he went. This arrangement turned on the idea that a big, heavy thing – tied to a vessel -- could be deposited on the ocean floor whenever and wherever the whoever in charge of the craft wished to stop.

Alas, this approach, too, had serious failings. First and foremost amongst them was that if the chosen item was too heavy -- and this applied especially when rougher sea conditions were encountered – it tended to plant itself on the seabed without getting prior permission from the captain. Worse, in many cases these errant weights did not just abandon ship, but they managed to take the hull and the entire crew down for an unanticipated visit with Davey Jones! That such side trips tended to be unappreciated by the boat's occupants seems patently true, especially since they violated the first principal of boat design (see above).

Have you ever noticed how even our very best inventions, while incredible, tend to generate an array of unexpected, new tribulations that are not, well, so incredible? Take cell phones for instance. Before the advent of these wonders, we did not have to worry about where our telephones were, whether or not they were charged or even how we were going to be able to use them to communicate surreptitiously with a friend while we attended another boring business meeting. In like fashion, our sailing forebears may have discovered that the virtues of carrying along a great chunk of something to pitch overboard when and where needed came with some serious drawbacks.

To start, if the mass of the body they brought on board was reduced sufficiently in size to keep it from sending the ship to the bottom, it might not be large enough to hold the boat in one place. Conversely, if its mass were increased to just under that which a gang of mighty men barely could leverage over the side, then they ran the risk of never being able to get the silly thing back up from the seabed! When that happened, all that would be left to do would be to cut the line and run free. Obviously that would leave them with no way to stop, except to ground the vessel, and they had already been there and done that, historically speaking.

A final hitch associated with limiting the movement of a boat by way of tying it to something heavy that then was tossed overboard had to do with the vertical distance between the surface of the water and the seabed. If that distance exceeded the total length of the tether even by mere inches – nay, even by a few millimetres -- then the entire lash-up effectively became a pendulum and nothing more. In that mode the movement of the vessel might be slowed somewhat, but it probably would not stop its incessant roaming. More likely, the good ship would head off on its own and continue its unfettered wanderings until such time as the crew tired of the game and hauled the stupid thing back onboard or the appendage came to rest on a higher part of the floor of the ocean. Recalling the basic nature of boats, we can be certain that the latter event would occur always at a place far removed from the stopping point originally selected by the craft's master.

Boundless as is man's ingenuity and determination, salty innovators ultimately devised a portable system of restraint for ships that suited their special environment. Starting with a heavy, semi-malleable substance, like iron, he fashioned an implement that had sufficient weight to drop to the bottom, but which was not so massive as to scuttle the boat or to be irretrievable when it was time to lift it back onboard. Essential to the performance of this contraption were some funny looking little pointy things, called flukes. Arms tipped with these were designed to dig into the seabed like a plow ripping into a stretch of virgin prairie sod and, at least in theory, to remain firmly affixed there once set. Since the device was not wholly dependent on its mass to get the job done, it did not need to be terribly heavy. And with the proper upward pressure on its tether, this thingamabob could be pulled back onto the boat with relative ease. We now refer to this item as an anchor!

So, despite having put a man on the moon and rovers on Mars, we find that there still are only three ordinary ways to make a boat stop, sit and stay. We can put it up on dry land. We can fasten it to a structure built out in the water. Or, we can anchor it to the sea floor. Two subsets of the latter category exist which are germane to our conversation as well: stern tying and mooring buoys.

When one is anchored close to land, it may be desirable to restrict the boat's ability to attack independently some other object, some group of other objects or even some number of other boats that may lie within the circle inevitably inscribed by the vessel as it searches through 360 degrees for a way to escape its restraints. (All of which can result, these days, in hefty insurance claims and lengthy lawsuits!) This is accomplished by running one or more lines from the stern of the craft to an immobile object located on the shore, like a large bolder or a mature tree. With an anchor holding its snout and a stout line rigged to its tail, stern-tied vessels can do little more than stay where they are put.

Mooring buoys are like anchors only better. Effectively looking like bobbing beach balls, these handy helpers each consist of a hard plastic sphere chained to a monstrous-great weight set directly on the ocean floor. Pre-positioned with a marine crane, these luxurious aids are not designed to be portable; even an average-sized hoard of alcohol-crazed modern yachtsmen rarely can budge them from the bottom! Employing this wonder requires nothing more than passing a hefty line through a ring on the buoy and then tying it securely to the selected craft. And, unlike the anchor, which is inclined to stop holding at exactly 2:00 a.m. in the morning when a fresh breeze unexpectedly wafts in, the mooring buoy almost never fails. Harkening back to our history lesson, the defect of the mooring buoy is its fixed placement. Ironically, that is its strength as well!

Here the thoughtful reader might object that we have left a couple of possibilities off the list. It cannot be denied that excluded from consideration have been such options as running the boat hard aground, being pulverized on a lee shore by 20 foot rollers or colliding with semi-immoveable objects like huge ships in order to get stopped. Supported by the expert opinions of the good folks who populate the actuarial departments of insurance companies around the world, we do not view these alternatives as everyday prospects – especially since they are almost always one-shot affairs! And, while the author admits to having seen any or all of them tried in a variety of situations across a range of conditions over a span of decades, he still cannot, in good conscience, recommend any of them to others.

* * * * * * * * * * *

Long before the little tug chugged into Bedwell Harbour; in fact, long before the voyage even began, we knew where we were going to park on our first night in port. Having had the many long, dark evenings of the preceding winter to make our plans, it was unlikely that a single word had been written or even a lone photograph of the area snapped that had not received our close examination. So carefully had we scrutinized these environs that both the First Mate and I independently qualified for the Masters' of South Pender Island Studies Degree offered on-line by the famed Geographic Rectification

Department at the East-West Northumberford campus of the renowned Nonesuch University. (We have but to send the check to them in order to get our sheepskins!) From our detailed investigations we knew that the harbor possessed many fine anchorages. Also, we were aware that Poet's Cove Resort and Spa hired out marina slips a nightly rate that, as usual with such establishments, came in at something just shy of outrageous. But the prize we had selected was neither! Our bow was pointed toward the few, the oh so few, mooring buoys set just inside Skull Islet!

Intending to pick up a mooring buoy at any given location is both a blessing and a curse for us. We love using them because they keep the boat exactly where it belongs. That is the good news. Unfortunately, the dark side of the equation derives from the relative scarcity of said objects.

It was the classic economist Adam Smith, I believe, who first described systematically the power of mere supply and demand. Without plumbing those arcane depths, a reasonable summary of the principles he espoused might look something like this: 'The more there is of any commodity, the less valuable it tends to be and visa-versa. Concomitantly, the greater the demand for something of limited availability, the higher its value.' The combination of an apparent worldwide shortage of mooring buoys and a growing number of consumers (i.e., boaters) creates the perfect storm for Smith's market forces. We can see this whirlwind 'up close and personal' on any busy boating weekend in the Pacific Northwet. The scramble to lay claim to one of these prized berths, by comparison, makes the 19th Century Oklahoma land rush look like a well-organized sewing bee.

Mooring buoys are almost always at a premium and they are usually available only on a first come, first served basis. In the struggle to get one, the advantages any particular boater has over any other comes directly from careful planning, exquisite timing and great local knowledge. In other words, if you know when and where the vacancies are likely to occur and you are on the spot at exactly the right instant, then you will probably be a winner. The flaw in this strategy is that you can never be sure beforehand that your quest will be successful. Thus, your emotional tranquility may be unsettled for hours before your arrival at any given harbor -- even for days if you are inclined toward the obsessive like The Skipper -- especially if your plan turns wholly on plucking one of these jewels.

In our favor on this outing were three things: a.) We would be getting to the Skull Islet mooring grounds on a weekday and not a weekend; b.) We were traveling in early May, still weeks before what is considered the boating season in this region; and c.) The weather forecast for the coming days was "iffy" at best. Going against us, however, were several equally daunting negatives. First, Bedwell Harbour is a primary Customs clearance point for those seeking shelter in Canadian waters. Second, the number of mooring buoys there is limited to six, seven or eight (depending on which source you reference). And finally, we are coming in late, several hours after the prime buoy-grabbing period has passed. (This latter moment being defined as that instant when the sleepy-eyed, departing flotsam has bobbed away, but the incoming cruising tsunami has yet to darken the horizon. It occurs precisely between 9:30 and 9:31 a.m., depending on weather and day of the week.)

Having made our obligatory three circles off the government dock in Poet's Cove, we were anxious to get to the mooring area. Even allowing as how there was not another moving boat in sight and there appeared to be no more than two vessels anywhere near Skull Islet, we worried still that a mosquito fleet would descend suddenly on the buoy field and snap up all the vacancies. (Such is the sad condition of the psyche of the modern mariner.)

Motoring out of Poet's Cove, it was all The Captain could do to keep from jamming the throttle forward and screaming, "Damn the torpedoes, full speed ahead!" Fortunately, a dark, knowing look cast at him by The Executive Officer, and a finger directed toward the "no wake" sign posted prominently off the starboard beam forced what passes for rationality in him to take control once more. Thus, the engine kept turning at "all ahead slow" and the little ship idled the last few hundred yards toward its goal. The Skipper's impassive mask of command belied the total internal turmoil still raging within.

With a steady hand, The Pilot nosed *Minstrel's Song* up to one of the five unattended buoys off Skull Islet. The Crew deftly slipped a line through the ring on the float, doubled it, tied it off and signaled that the job was done. The deep throb of the engine gave way to dead silence as The Chief Engineer shut down all systems. Smiles were passed all around. Everyone on board knew there would be extra grog and liberty for the job well done!

Call me an old worrywart, but there always seems to be something that keeps me from attaining that Nirvana-like state that we all seek. After taking a few moments to slip out of our life preservers, to happily sit and survey our snug little harbor, to drink in the lush green hills and the lofty heights of the islands and to contemplate the joys of life, harsh reality intrudes again. Alas, some bureaucrat, somewhere, expects us to pay for the use of 'his' buoy!

We pony-up cold cash for similar services on-shore all of the time. When we roam by car, for instance, we are not surprised to find a coin-hungry meter lurking on the curb, a ticket-spewing machine guarding the gate of a parking lot, or a bored attendant strategically positioned near the front of a subterranean car cave, all wanting the same thing: our money. No, these encounters are all part of modern life. So why is it different when you 'park' your boat in somebody else's watery lot?

We human beings like our routines. We get up. We get ready to face the day. We spend our hours laboring at something we deem important. We return to our nests. And then we finish our evenings doing as we see fit. Whatever the pattern, whatever the choice, we pretty much follow the same regimen day in and day out. To a greater or lesser extent we know today what tomorrow is going to look like. And whine and complain as we will – we are human aren't we? – the truth remains that repetition within acceptable confines makes us happy. We want to come home each night and find the house exactly where we left it.

For most of us the blessing and the curse of going to sea is that it breaks up all of our routines. Nothing is exactly the same as on land.

And while this makes our hearts sing it can also cause consternation.

Take picking up a buoy in a new port. In and of itself it is not a big deal. The trauma arrives, however, when we are face to face with the ambiguity of the new and the uncertain. Two quarters is what the parking meter says it needs for 40 minutes; $3.00 for the first half hour reads the sign at the lot gate; "Don't forget to get your ticket validated," intones the sleepy-eyed man in the booth. Everything about these situations is known ahead of time and thus is completely cut and dried.

But pass your line through the ring on a buoy and the world turns upside down. How much does it cost? How soon after you tie up do you have to pay? Where do you deliver your lucre? Should you look for a box at the bottom of the sea? Should you search for the official-in-charge up on dry land? Or, can you just mail "them" a check next Tuesday for the berth that you want to occupy today? Questions. Questions. Questions.

Breaking out of this mental paralysis, The Skipper orders The Bosun's Mate to prepare The Captain's gig. He has decided to go ashore.

The contraption he deems necessary for this event is a 10' rubber inflatable boat (RIB) that usually travels vertically (standing up on its side) on the stern of *Minstrel's Song*. When not propelled by a tiny set of oars, an equally diminutive 2.5 horsepower outboard motor is pressed into service. That water-thrasher rides up on the ship's rail when not in use on The Captain's barge.

To deploy the RIB, a stout soul must detach the stainless steel rods that hold it upright and then pivot the hulk via davit hinges affixed to the lower pontoon, by hand, down toward the water. No one on the ship is muscular enough to ease it gently to the water; thus, it always flops unceremoniously and without constraint the last few feet. If it is desired, the engine then is wrestled off its perch, carefully transferred over to the bobbing RIB and quickly clamped to the little boat's transom. (Each time this juggling act is performed – whether coming or going – all involved envision watching the fairly expense chunk of aluminum that drives the dinghy sink quickly and irretrievably out of sight beneath the waves mid-way through the process.) Once floating and outfitted, this undersized, always dirty, grey life raft will take us anywhere we wish at a blazing 4 mph – so long as neither wind, wave, nor current object!

With no more and no less acrimony than always accompanies the transfer of personnel from the big boat to the little boat (e.g., 'Keep your center of gravity low!' 'Try not to capsize the silly thing!' And, 'For Heaven's sake, don't let go before I get the motor running!'), The Captain and The Crew prepare to go exploring. They agree that a good place to look for the answers they seek is back at the marina in Poet's Cove. As always, the RIB conveys them in royal splendor; as usual, its occupants are impressed by the similarities between its ride and the thrashings of the mechanical bull at the State Fair!

Because most of the marina slips are empty and there is scant little activity anywhere to be seen, we head toward the fuel dock. The possibility of viable commerce in the form of selling some gas or diesel usually is strong enough to incline the owners to keep a lookout posted for prospective buyers. As we slip alongside the pumps, two young men of college age amble out of the shack that appears to serve them both as business office and clubhouse. Clearly these kids are studying rocket science, for upon receipt of our inquiries regarding the workings of the buoy system, they reward us with two utterly blank stares followed by two simultaneously mumbled, 'I don't know.' When pressed with, "Do you know how much a night on one of them costs?" or even "Where's the collection box located?" their blankness continued.

Resisting the temptation to grill the youngsters further – and thus losing a first rate opportunity to conduct a scholarly investigation into exactly what it was that they did with all of the vacant hours they spent in their hovel – we politely thank them for their assistance. With no viable intelligence in hand, we head back toward the mooring area while surveying the scene and plotting our next move.

Although we had enjoyed a full day of sunshine, the climate gods chose this particular moment to remind us that they were in charge and could do whatever they darn well pleased. (That we were in an open boat, without raingear, surely had no influence on that decision whatsoever!) As raindrops the size of jawbreakers began to pelt us, The Crew and I agreed that we needed to revise our plans immediately. With little debate and no formal vote on the matter we decided that our first priority now was to get back to the mother ship before the RIB filled with water and sank! As we clambered up the side of *Minstrel's Song,* Cookie declared that the preparation of our evening victuals superseded any further need The Captain might have for The Crew in the unprotected RIB. So abandoned, there was nothing for the latter to do but to retrieve his rain slicker, grab a bailing pump and renew the search alone.

Although all of the guidebooks insisted that the mooring buoys were a part of the Beaumont Marine Provincial Park, The Expedition Leader remained skeptical! As with many other annoying little things that happen out on the briny deep, it is pretty difficult to establish the legal limits of any given chunk of water, much less to render judgment concerning who owns what and where that property starts and stops. In this instance, without corner stakes, fences or painted lines, it was just about impossible to tell where ordinary seawater came to an end and "park water" commenced. To complicate matters further, the buoys were made of a bright, unblemished white plastic that was devoid, apparently, of any useful information.

Surveying the little bay and the treed hills that dropped down steeply to it, I sought to identify with certainty anything that was "park." The only sign of human presence I could detect on the beach, an expanse that arced from Skull Islet all the way around to Poet's Cove, was a 10'X10' wooden float that was sitting high and dry on the rocks and appeared to be desperate need of repair. This derelict did not look like the gateway to a going concern much the welcome mat leading to a full bred Marine Provincial Park. Barely visible through the wall of trees growing some paces behind the wreck, however, I spied a structure that resembled the kind of wide, wooden platform one might find at the bottom of a set of stairs. With no better prospect at hand, I decide to land in that vicinity and scout around.

The closer to the "beach" I came in the RIB, the more I realized that there was not a grain of sand on it, just a continuous series of rocks ranging in size from pebbles to regular boulders. Worse, through the clear water I could see that the bottom did not come up quickly, but slopped very gently. That meant that to save the outboard's dangling prop from a catastrophic collision with a large, immovable object (i.e., a solidified chunk of pre-historic magma), I had have to gain some speed, drive strait for the shore and then, at the last moment, tilt the shaft of the outboard up out of the water and let the vessel drift on in. Imbued with all of the natural tracking qualities of a volleyball, the RIB lost all steerage the second the engine quit pushing it. Swinging wildly this way and that, my directional commands notwithstanding, the little boat gleefully picked out a most unappealing landing spot and ran itself hard aground betwixt a herd of rounded, slippery, moss-covered, basketball-sized stones all of which were under about a foot of water. With rain pelting my upper body, I stepped calf deep into the cold, North Pacific Ocean, trying desperately to set my feet down on solid ground so as not to break anything important. "Sure! Why not?" I figured. "This way I get to get everything wet!"

After dragging the "dingy" – my pet name for this small, air-filled, canvas tormenter that rebuffs all of my efforts to keep it clean – safely up on shore, I slog toward the platform and the steps I now see rising beyond it. Up into the forest I go, up the stairs I climb. Eventually I come to a landing that dumps me out on an established path and therein I find immediately a large information board and a metal lockbox. "Now I'm getting somewhere," I thought. Examining the surroundings carefully, I discover a wad of drenched envelopes floating in a plastic holder affixed to the side of a nearby post. These appear to be of the type typically used by a boater to "register" for a mooring buoy. I peel off a glob of them, study what is left of the printing on the soggy pulp and conclude that they constitute, indeed, both register and payment packet for the tie-up. All that remains, then, is to fill one out – providing the pertinent data about the boat, the mooring number, the date, how long we plan to stay, ya-da, ya-da, ya-da -- slip $12 (Canadian) inside of it, stuff the whole thing into the metal box and we are done. Not!

Although I knew our boat's name and the date, May 7th, I had no clue as to the buoy number. In fact, I had no memory of seeing one on that big white ball. So, how could I record what probably did not exist? Concerned, I weighed the alternatives, including going back to our little ship to check again for a numeral. The primary problem with pursuing that course, I determined, was that I was up there in the park – getting colder and wetter by the moment – and *Minstrel's Song* was not! "Regulations be dammed," I grumbled to myself. "A mean looking troop of Canadian Mounties isn't going to get me to make that trip again just for a stinking digit! I'll fake it!"

In preparation for doing just that, a quick glance around convinces me that there are no pens, pencils, magic markers, or even flint chips available to scrawl a message on the wet, now-disintegrating pouch. A frantic search of my pockets rendered nothing useful either. I am now in a quarrelsome mood – being wet to the skin and chilled tends to do that to me. So, I start to think: "If I can phoney-up the buoy number why not do the whole thing that way?" Yeah, I can almost hear the conversation. "Absolutely, officer! I filled out every part of that form, in triplicate, then carefully placed the money inside that special little envelope you folks provided and *strained the whole gooey mess* through that stupid, narrow slot in the metal box. It wasn't easy, I'm telling you, but I didn't quit until every gram of that slime was in there!" (From previous experience with officialdom, I knew that having a well-rehearsed cover story was more than half the battle.)

Resigned, but not happy, I turned back to the boat. It was just then that it caught my eye! There, affixed to the base of the information board, printed in the tiniest little grey letters imaginable was a message just for me. It said, "Thou shalt not...ya-da, ya-da, ya-da. Fees apply only after May 15th!" Ssssssss......ugar!

"Why couldn't <u>they</u> put that note on the buoys? How about a sign up on the beach? Or a word on their web-site?" Then I got this uneasy, paranoid feeling that sometimes comes over me. What if a bunch of them were hiding out there in a warm, dry, camouflaged bunker on that forested hillside, watching me slosh back toward my dinghy? What if at that instant someone was saying, "Look, Chuck, we got another one! Ain't it great? This guy's drenched from head to toe, too!"

It quit raining just slightly before the RIB bumped into the side of *Minstrel's Song*. The western horizon was clearing too and it looked like it might be a nice evening after all. As I climbed back on board, my shoes squishing with every step, I reveled in the realization that the warm, dry second pair of shoes I threw in my bag at the last instant would momentarily be cradling my sopping wet feet! More than that, I took pleasure in the certain knowledge that just beyond the cabin door was a heated saloon, a hot dinner and one of The Cook's warm smiles. All of these things, and more, soon would be the exclusive property of the 'Hero of the Great Beaumont Marine Provincial Park Expedition.'

Over the years The Executive Officer and I have developed a division of labor that works for us, mostly. The broad outline of our respective duties took form without any particular malice or forethought; there just were things that had to be done. The process works the same on land and at sea. For instance, when The First Mate collapsed in paroxysms of hysteria after I intimated that she might enjoy learning to pilot the boat, I inferred that her preference was to forego standing tricks at the wheel. We really did not discuss the issue or lay out any hard and firm rules about it, an accommodation just happened. Thereafter, excepting when we are in smooth, open water and an emergency in *Minstrel's Songs'* head demands The Engineering Officer's immediate presence there, it has been standard operating procedure for The Pilot to run the craft while The Crew tackles other critical duties, like keeping our coffee mugs full and preparing our meals.

Most mature men can fix a few things in the kitchen. Their base survival instincts drive them to master the intricacies of cold cereal, peanut butter and jelly sandwiches, hot dogs, canned chili, ramen and the odd package of lunchmeat. So adept at preparing such delights do the majority of us become that in male parlance these food groups serve as synonyms for breakfast, lunch and dinner. Perhaps because I perceived at a very early age the direct connection between staying alive and being able to cook -- and despite various forms of employment that had no connection whatsoever to *haute cuisine* – I became an excellent chef! But while my interests in the culinary arts sprang entirely from existential considerations, The Cook's participation in the field is one founded on complete, unadulterated love. Find me poring over a cookbook and it is likely that the library in the bathroom has been woefully neglected. She, on the other hand, thinks that a special gift amounts to a volume crammed full of advice on how best to prepare salmon Tlinglit-style or that a day in heaven is one spent whipping up a delightful lamb saag, a savory chicken masala and a mouth-watering pan of nan!

My skill notwithstanding, while The Commander-in-Chief occasionally deigns to allow me to enter the kitchen – that would be galley for the sailors amongst us – to fix some particular specialty, it is done with the greatest of reservations and only under close supervision. Although never voiced, I have always imagined that she is not pleased when I come into close proximity with the combination of perishable foodstuffs, hot pots and pans and sharp objects. The upshot of all of this is that she cooks and I drive (and eat).

Following our repasts together I usually busy myself by hauling the dirty dishes to the sink and by stowing the leftovers in their proper places. I am prohibited, however, from putting soap and water to anything associated with food. The origin of this arrangement comes not from slovenliness on my part, but rather from the unhurried pace at which I work. She is a speed freak and I am anything but. Another factor in this equation is my inability to keep the panoply of wet, slippery, and valuable things that easily break up off the floor and/or otherwise whole. Thus, I have perceived that Cookie would rather watch a sloppy four year old spend the entire afternoon finger painting on a priceless Persian carpet than to turn me loose with soap, water and a stack of good plates. And, no, I do not think either that ptomaine or food poisoning has anything to do with her feelings. But that is just a guess!

THE LATE SHOW

It was after we had turned to our respective duties following our dinner off Skull Islet, while The Scullery Crew labored over the sink and The Duty Officer stood at the chart table flexing his dividers, that we learned that the good folks of Bedwell Harbour planned some live entertainment for us this evening.

What we were privileged to witness that night was not your garden variety of laughs and giggles such as those frequently associated with the pleasing spectacle of a neighboring boater vainly trying to set his anchor in a seaman-like manner or even a bunch of newbies attempting to take up a buoy. Instead what riveted our attention was a legitimate Chinese fire drill!

We commented on the fact that over the course of the afternoon and for reasons never really known, our snug anchorage slowly filled with a disproportionate number of boats manned by Asians. By dusk the quantity of vessels fitting that description had swelled to include an oceangoing sailboat (flying a Japanese flag) and three or four other watercraft manned wholly by those whose ancestors clearly derived from the Far East. The denizens of these conveyances – who seemed to enjoy a degree of familiarity with each other – amused themselves in various ways, frequently heading off in their RIBs with fishing rods at the ready or transporting children to the beach for some casual combing. The actions of an immediate neighbor, however, demanded our particular attention.

A rather plain looking sailing sloop[2] of about 36' in length (8.23 metres, Canadian-style), and of an otherwise indifferent design dropped anchor roughly 150' away from us. We did not pay much attention to it when it came in, although in retrospect it did seem to

---

[2] *A type of craft having a single mast forward of the midpoint of the boat.*

take it forever to get its "hook" set in the bottom. And, we probably would not have given it any further thought had it not commenced to deploy two RIBs. Since our experience informed us that the standard number of RIBs carried aboard a boat of that description was one, seeing a second hit the waves roused our curiosity. So attracted, we began to enjoy the spectacle of four, twenty-something Asian women and one like male as they tried, desperately, to clamber into both of these small, unsteady boats. It was a bit like watching an old Keystone Cops movie!

It was clear that none of the female cargo had much seagoing experience. Getting them into the tiny craft that were tied loosely alongside the sloop and then distributing them according to some inscrutable order entailed inordinate amounts of finger-pointing, timid rail-grabbing, extended toe-pointing and group-assisted false starts. As this transpired, the waterborne RIBs did what vessels love to do best when left on long leashes: They began to drift away from the main ship. This, in turn, caused panic among those who had already taken the leap and had gotten themselves ensconced in one boat or the other. Instructions and demands shot back and forth between the sailboat and the inflatables – most of which went unheeded in the din. Even as lines tightened and reason set in, the overall effort to get both RIBs back alongside the home ship largely was negated by the counter-exertions of the girls in the rafts as against those who were not. Every time the RIBs got close to the sailboat, the ladies in them commenced to abandon ship. Concomitantly -- and with equal zeal – the women who were still on the larger vessel tried to climb into the RIBs! The upshot of this tug of war was that with one foot planted firmly on the larger vessel and the other positioned on the puffy pontoons of the inflatables, all four females, traveling in opposite directions, simultaneously pushed the boats apart. This action repeatedly caused the principals to retreat nervously back to their original platforms while the RIBs tried to head off to sea again. These machinations continued for a pleasant period and only came to an end when the leader of the horde – the singleton male – dropped, literally, the two girls still on the mother ship into one of the boats and then climbed in himself. This chap must have been pleased by the seating arrangements, for within seconds he loosed the lines and allowed the boats to swing free.

Having achieved his immediate goal of getting everyone off the sloop, our hero turned his attention to starting the outboard motor that was appended to the stern of one of the inflatables. Pull, pull, pull…wheeze, wheeze, wheeze… giggle, giggle, giggle… went the champion, the engine and the passengers respectively, but no running motor sounds were to be heard. Neither the continued pulling, wheezing nor giggling did anything to cause the outboard to run. It did wear the young man down something awful though. And it also gave the freed RIBs another chance to break for the open water!

The chattering and pointing and twittering that was endemic on the drifting boats as the lone master tried to coax his stubborn outboard into life took on a new intensity as it seemed to dawn on all of our erstwhile mariners at about the same time that neglecting either to keep the boats attached to the mother ship or at the least to tie them together constituted two major, strategic errors. Driven by the frantic encouragement of the lone woman seated in his vessel, our wilted captain was forced to abandon his work on the engine in favor of finding an alternate means of propulsion. This became increasingly important as the distance between the two boats lengthened and the wail arising collectively from the three fair damsels in the second craft rose into the three-digit decibel range. Seizing a lone, short-handled paddle, our Skipper began to give the water a wild, but undoubtedly well-deserved thrashing. This had the effect of causing his RIB to make much more progress around and around in circles than it did in moving it straight toward the other boat as was required. Bravely persevering, however, he eventually achieved his end and pulled alongside the second little dinghy.

That was the good news! The bad news was that once the RIBs were reunited – and tied together this time -- the outboard still would not respond to the ministrations of its now exhausted commander. Even from where we sat we could see a visible pall descend over both boats as it became clear that despite the gargantuan exertions of our protagonist, the only course of action left open to him was to somehow get both rafts back to the primary vessel.

The physical effort the star of the show had just expended in getting the drifting RIBs together again was as nothing compared to the work he did to regain the side of the sloop. Gamely he used his tiny paddle to stroke furiously on this side of the inflatable and then on the other. Gaining a bit of way, he would dip his oar here now, there then, back and forth and around and around, all in an effort to force both of the accursed rafts to go in the general direction of home. It was a sadder but undoubtedly wiser young man who finally flung himself up, like a played out marlin, onto the deck of his sailboat.

The accompanying disembarkation of the passengers assumed a more seaman-like quality this time around. Surely their bout with the perils of the great ocean wide served to sharpen their focus considerably.

For our part, we found the performance so enchanting that had we kept our wits about us we might have taken to the open cockpit of *Minstrel's Song* with large cards bearing scores in the high 'nines' for our fellow mariners to savor. As it was, I made a mental note to contact the local Chamber of Commerce as soon as practical to let them know how much we appreciated the work that must have gone into putting on this kind of performance for us. At the very least I would assure them that we would be telling all of our friends about the virtues of spending the night in Bedwell Harbour.

Oh, yes! After much more starter-rope pulling and thing-a-ma-bob tinkering the recalcitrant outboard motor finally sprang to life. With the roar of the engine singing in their ears our jubilant travelers took to their boats again, speeding off toward the Spa and Resort for an evening of fun and frolicking. A deep and satisfying stillness settled over the anchorage as they disappeared into the night. It was broken thereafter only by the inexplicable solo sorties that our male neighbor periodically made back to the main vessel. His comings and goings served as but afterglow reminders of the pleasure and good pace of the previous recital. Good times were had by all. Bravo! Encore, Maestro!

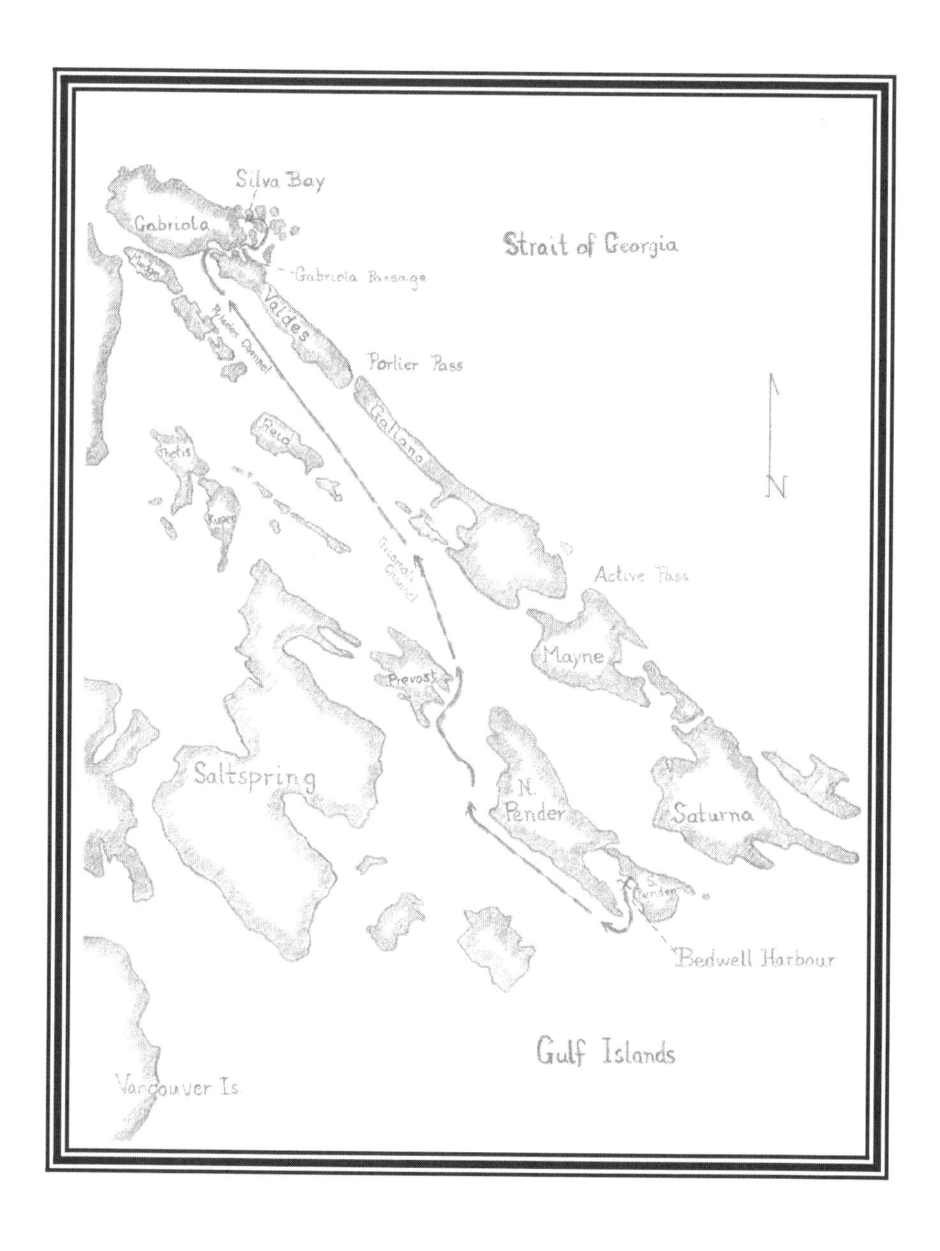
Silva Bay
Gabriola
Strait of Georgia
Gabriola Passage
Valdes
Porlier Pass
Gallano
Reid
Thetis
Kuper
N
Active Pass
Mayne
Prevost
Saltspring
N.
Pender
Saturna
S.
Pender
Bedwell Harbour
Gulf Islands
Vancouver Is

Day Two

Bedwell Harbour to Silva Bay
Or
Do They Really Want To Eat Us?

The morning sun crept over the horizon, emblazing the sky with a glorious display of pinks, purples, blues and yellows while extending promises of a perfect day to come. Nary a breeze stirred the water. Sea gulls wheeled slowly overhead. Humankind slumbered. All was well with the world. Or, at least that was the way I imagined it would have been had I been awake for the event!

It is both a blessing and a curse to be a sleeper in a universe heavily populated by those operating in a near-constant state of restiveness. Having been one who could curl up anywhere, anytime and within seconds fall into a blissful state of slumber, I have never been able to fully understand the market forces that drive the sleeping pill industry. There is no doubt that a strong demand for them exists and based purely on anecdotal evidence it would seem that a goodly segment of our aging population grows increasingly sleepless each day. But none of that really matters except as it touches on shipboard relations.

The wonderful woman I married suits me to a tee, except for one teeny, tiny, little thing! She operates on a 0500-2100 (military or Zulu time for 5:00 a.m. – 9:00 p.m.) schedule and I on one that is closer to 0900-0100. The astute observer might perceive that the four-hour time offset translates into a regular part of the day when one or the other of us comfortably could be either wide awake or sound asleep. Because of such differences, couples must learn to fit together. In our case we have managed over the years to reach a suitable accommodation that allows for a modicum of harmony relative to our sleeping differences. In return for going to bed a couple of hours earlier than my internal clock demands, my Shipmate generally refrains from awakening me until at least several minutes after her eyes pop wide open – an event that normally occurs some hours before dawn.

On vacations we relax the rules a bit. She awakens whenever the spirit moves her – I certainly do not want to know when that happens! – but instead of jumping up all bright and shiny, she snuggles in bed with a good book while I do more of what I do best (i.e., I continue to snooze!). Sometimes, when she can stand it no more she tortures me awake! Without going into personal details, this involves her sneaking out of our stateroom very, very quietly and then cunningly rustling up a steaming pot of coffee. I am not sure how she does it, but beyond just making the brew, she manages to cause its aroma to waft over me like a heavy fog coming in from the sea. It is probable that the average person finds nothing offensive in the fragrance of the coffee bean; the bouquet of this delight, however, so titillates my olfactory glands that there is little in this world to which I respond to more quickly or more favorably. So assaulted, I find this morning that even the lure of a few more winks cannot keep me abed.

Wiping the sleep from my eyes as I climb slowly up the ladder to the pilothouse, Cookie passes me my coffee cup – a container truly sized more like a bucket – and I sip and savor its pungent contents while surveying the anchorage. "Great," I think to myself. "Nothing had changed. No problems. No worries." I grin internally and reflect on how it really doesn't get any better than this! Still, life must go on so I don my best Captain Bligh command countenance – because good order is necessary on every ship – and advise The Crew that we would be getting underway just as soon as I could throw down a few more gallons of joe and maybe top it off with a Danish pastry or two. Sternly I added that when that moment arrived, there had better be no nonsense about turning to and looking sharp. Evidently that exceeded my charter and mutiny was only just averted with a reminder that was far from subtle that The Captain made a lousy pot of coffee and the cruise might be a long one should he be forced to consume his own work. Comprehending the seriousness of the situation, I quietly turned to the task of coaxing my eyes open by imbibing several more great gulps of fluid caffeine. With her Skipper productively occupied with that task, The Crew contentedly settled in to read another chapter or two of her book.

With no particular fanfare, but with exceptional efficiency, the Foredeck Crew slipped our mooring lines and The Pilot guided *Minstrel's Song* out of the sheltered waters of Bedwell Harbour. Ready though we were for the next part of our adventure, it was with a slight sense of sadness that we said goodbye to this fine little bay. Our stay there had been most pleasant.

The plan for the day involved running northward up through the full length of British Columbia's Gulf Islands to Gabriola Island, the last link in the chain. This archipelago stretches out in a southeasterly to northwesterly direction, with South Pender and Saturna Islands reaching their arms down nearly to the U.S. border while Gabriola Island, located 35 (67 kilometres) nautical miles to the north, lies just a few hundred yards east off the east shore of Vancouver Island proper. Because these dots of land roughly parallel the southeast coast of Vancouver Island, the slot formed between them and their big brother is protected from the windier and rougher seas frequently encountered on the open Georgia Strait. Thus, boaters who ply these waters are treated to a delightfully shielded cruising ground. Those who enter this realm can thrill to miles and miles of shorelines that mimic in beauty those of remote alpine lakes while finding numerous quiet anchorages to put into. Many people even stop and hike to their hearts' content up and down the hills and dales that make up this 15-island set.

To achieve his day's objective, The Pilot determined that once his little ship was clear of Bedwell Harbour, he would steer a northwesting course that bisected Swanson, Trincomali and Pylades Channels. Just south of Gabriola Island he planned to dart through the narrow Gabriola Passage on the slack tide and then put in for the night at Silva Bay. This destination, tucked into the southeastern coast of

Gabriola Island, looked to be both a nice day's cruise away from Bedwell as well as an excellent jumping off point for the next day's hop across the Strait of Georgia to the mainland. Additionally, it offered a variety of necessary goods and services and, being secure from the worst of the elements, would make an excellent place to spend a day or two should the weather turn sour.

DON'T KNOW MUCH ABOUT GEOGRAPHY...OR METEOROLOGY!

The North Pacific Current dominates the climate of the Pacific Northwest. A literal "river of water" that forms off the coast of Japan, this great, moving body arcs up through the North Pacific Ocean toward the Gulf of Alaska and the Bering Sea and then hugs the west side of North America on its way back south. It does not warm much on the trip across, regardless of season, and the anemic summer sunshine that infrequently bathes the environs of 49-51 degrees north latitude – B.C.'s southern extremes – does not raise its temperature by more than few degrees. Because of that, the Salish Sea remains very cold. On average it rarely exceeds 55 degrees Fahrenheit (12.78 degrees Celsius).

Across the great expanses of the North Pacific the prevailing westerly winds push slightly warmer air over the surface of the cold sea. Because of the temperature differential between the two, the breezes pick up extra moisture. That moist air rises, causing the formation of grey clouds. Those heavily laden air masses ultimately plow into the mountainous shores of the Western Hemisphere (including that area which now holds our attention). Without getting really technical – a possibility for which the author is wholly and totally incapable – the end result is that when this fairly continuous sky full of greyness runs into dry land, especially that having sufficient vertical reach to inhibit its free movement, then the heavens pour forth with plentiful amounts of rain. And, while this cycle is broken occasionally by unprovoked outbursts of sunshine, the appearance of the latter, especially during the summer months, tends to generate, out of clear, blue skies some really neat, dense sea fog!

It is worth noting too that although the rain and the fog turns everything it touches cold and clammy, the icy seawater that is the root cause of these atmospheric phenomena poses a serious threat to mariners of all descriptions. One unfortunate enough to forsake the comforts of their floating palaces for the briny home of Davy Jones – whether the exchange was intended or not – can anticipate an unredeemed life expectancy measured in mere minutes. Cold water kills and does so very quickly.

Although people take to boats for a variety of different reasons, we can be fairly certain that in the Pacific Northwest it is not for the rain, the clouds, the fog, the cold water or even the wind that stirs this whole pot. Why then? Because when the factors are taken in conjunction with landforms that rise quickly from sea level to mountainous heights, conditions become nearly perfect for growing trees! Trees? What have trees to do with anything you ask?

Just as watercraft of all descriptions love to wander, so trees have preferences too. But unlike our seaborne stray, give a seedling its choice and that sprout will forego all future movement for the opportunity to plant its roots deep in the soil, spread its branches way out, and soak up all the rain, clouds, fog, mist and other descriptions of nasty weather that the climate gods can dish up. Weird isn't it?

Bizarre though this whole concept may seem, it is just for this reason that the northwestern coast of North America, extending from Alaska south to central California, contains over half of the temperate rainforests in the world. Without belaboring the point, it is the crummy weather that washes ashore on this portion of the New World that makes trees settle in and grow like, well…like weeds.

Never having seen any comparisons on this particular point, a casual flip through my internal hard drive suggests that more prose has been devoted to things having to do with the sea than with things having to do with trees. Nonetheless, from somewhere under the smithy's spreading chestnut right on through Joyce Kilmer's thoughts on arboreal splendors, it seems to be well established that the sight of tall timber emotionally moves people. Multiply the inherent pleasure taken from the sight of a single specimen by no less than one million and we begin to appreciate what it means to gaze out over a forest that covers every inch of a hill or a mountainside, especially when it seems to stretch off to infinity, disappearing from view into a faint, distant horizon.

Herman Melville compared his white whale, Moby Dick, to a great, snow-covered mountain rising up out of the sea. How much more striking – and real – are the gigantic masses of snowcapped, tree covered heights that Nature has heaved up out of the cold Pacific? Whether admired as individual islands, as great island chains, or as coastal ranges, these natural wonders march in unbroken green and white phalanxes north to Alaska. Beginning along the shores of the Salish Sea these varied landforms define the incredibly beautiful Inside Passage. In a complex maze of fissures and islands that defies simple description, the tectonic action of the ages threw up dikes to calm and hold the greater ocean back while serving, too, as the source of infinite majesty. The hand that conjoined these blue-green waters, azure skies, snowy white peaks, and verdant woodlands, punctuating them all with grey-brown-red rock outcroppings, bubbling mountain streams, and tumbling waterfalls was that of a true master. It is to see his work, up close and personal, that so many pilgrims crisscross the waters of the wondrous Pacific Northwet.

B.C.'s Gulf Islands share the virtues and the splendors of their more northerly Inside Passage brethren. Hard rock, be it in layers, piles or jagged outcroppings, are their basic building blocks. A light soil stratum provides the essential footing for plant life. A natural blanket of green composed of trees -- primarily conifers – ferns and shrubs sit lightly on their landscapes. Although these isles include a few higher places, at least in the warmer months, all of their summits remain clear of snow. As if to make up for being "vertically challenged," however, Vancouver Island's loftier snow-bound mountains just to the west as well as those on the more distant mainland to the east thus creating the impression that the channels that separate each atoll cut continually through highlands. Thus, the the Gulf Islands rise up out of the sea against backdrops, both east and west, of great, white-capped massifs that tower above their own pale green bases.

Like Alfred Lord Tennyson's "The Charge of the Light

Brigade," entering the passages that lead to the interior of the Gulf Islands compels the newcomer to surmise that from there on all creation is made up of nothing but islands. So disposed, one is tempted to sing out,

> 'Islands to the right of us,
>
> Islands to the left of us,
>
> Islands in front of us,
>
> Volley'd and thunder'd...'

for at every turn, whether near or far, there stands another dollop of land set down on the great ocean bright. And because no two are alike, trying to absorb the grandeur that the slow-moving cyclorama presents to the casual boater becomes an absolutely enthralling task. Around each bend, across every inlet and bay, behind point after point, a new world opens. One is drawn simultaneously forward toward what is still to come while being pulled backward to explore what has already been seen. What a marvelous experience.

* * * * * * * * * * *

The First Mate perches atop the short bench seat on the port side of the pilothouse. This is her duty station. Alert, eyes straining to penetrate the distance, like the sweeping line of a radarscope she relentlessly scans the near and far shores and everything in between. At times she abandons her place and purposefully moves a few steps forward to reach the cabin door. She jerks the sliding portal open and braces herself against its frame, her body half in and half out, staring doggedly at the something that has piqued her interest. Quickly she raises her instrument and focuses it on the discerned curiosity. With deft, practiced movements she completes her task, closes the door and returns to her seat in a single motion.

Only marginally is The Captain distracted from his duties of keeping the ship on the straight and narrow by the engagements of The Crew; her activities have become a regular part of their daily routine.

Turning his eyes in the direction of her attentions, he approvingly takes in the scene. His thoughts, vying for primacy, vacillate between satisfaction with her ever-growing skill and relief that the chill from the morning air that flowed in through the open doorway already was starting to abate.

As these considerations press in on him, The Skipper becomes aware of The First Mate's immediate presence by his side. He senses, more than sees, that she has quietly covered the short distance that customarily separates their posts, taking delight in the slight rustle that brings her close to him. With soft voice and trembling fingers she inclines the device she carries and says, "See. Got another one. What do you think of this photo?"

While cruising the bounding Main, both The First Mate and I are ever watchful for that special picture. It is one of the things that we really like to do as we wend our way through the Salish Sea. My camera sits at the ready, tucked into the cushioned corner of the pilot berth (bench seat) located directly behind the helm; The X.O. usually rides with hers at the ready in her lap. In tandem or independently each of us moves at will and at leisure to capture some particular scene as it glides past the boat.

My attention shifts from the watery world ahead of the boat to the proffered screen The Second in Command now makes available to me. Being the senior partner in our photographic world, she is anxious to get my opinion, to win my approval. It is a bit of a ritual we have developed. And, like most similar ceremonies, the fundamental causes fade dimly into the recesses of memory. Peering at the object proffered, I intone, "Uh-huh...Sweet!" despite the fact that the one and a half inch screen I am looking at can barely convey color much less a complex image. Judging by the past, however, her shot probably is a good one – because most of what she takes these days falls into that category -- but that is not the point. It never was.

THE LONG AND WINDING ROAD

Long, long years ago, back in the ages of Kodak film and boxy little cameras with tiny inset lenses, I became fascinated with photography. My first experience with that art came, I believe, in the '50s. The occasion was a family outing to the Gettysburg Battlefield in Pennsylvania. How or why I was granted permission to use the clan's treasured still camera probably had something to do with the fact that my dad, having embarked on a near-frenetic quest to document our every experience in motion pictures, was so occupied with that task that he did not know what the kids were doing. Concomitantly, my mom probably thought that someone doing something that necessitated stillness was in fact doing the Lord's work.

Winding and hoisting the Kodak Brownie 8mm motion picture camera that was his pride and joy, The Old Man sought to immortalize everything and anything in sight – whether it moved or not. Being by nature a frugal man and a product of the Great Depression, his intention was to include all that the human eye could see – peripheral vision not excluded -- while not wasting a single frame of film. Thus, he swung his instrument from side to side and up and down at a speed approaching that of light. Lamentably, when the product of his efforts was projected onto a screen in a darkened room, what was visible to the audience was a black and white blur that conveyed almost nothing recognizable, but did manage to generate a feeling of dizziness that approached the level of active nausea amongst those treated to one of his private showings. It undoubtedly was the constant lampooning of his technique that ultimately led him to hang up his camera. That did not occur, however, before we had accumulated boxes of tiny reels the very sight of which, conditioned as we were like Pavlov's dogs, evinced immediate headaches and queasy stomachs.

Anyway, on this particular outing, with the patriarch of the family whirring away at Little Round Top, Big Round Top and the site of Pickett's Charge – all mostly at the same time, despite the considerable distances between them – it must have come to pass that both my mother and older brother had found something of greater interest than messing around with the box camera we lugged. Thus, despite my hierarchical insignificance, the precious black box along with a 12-shot roll of 110, black and white Kodak film made its way into my small, trembling hands.

With a not an inconsequential genetic pre-disposition toward photographic greatness coursing through my veins, I spent the afternoon carefully selecting the subjects of the dozen shots I was destined to make. Like my father before me, I wanted to commemorate everything, but waste nothing. And, like my father before me, I succeeded beyond my wildest dreams. That achievement was confirmed several weeks after the event when I tore open the envelope that contained my finished pictures and took stock of my work. Even though they lacked the fluidity of my dad's productions, in one fell swoop I had managed to capture in my very first snapshots the greyish, stomach-churning blur that had become the hallmark of The Old Man's labors!

The trusty family Brownie box camera came my way infrequently thereafter, but in 1965, in an unprovoked act of kindness, my elder brother bestowed on me a somewhat battered Petri 35 mm camera that he had acquired in a pawn shop while stationed in Japan. So fine was this machine, I was sure, that mere possession of it elevated me to semi-pro status. With its built in light meter and manually manipulated aperture and shutter speed controls circling the single, fixed lens, it was clear that pure magic was but a click away. I was overjoyed. (Upon mature reflection I am fairly certain that the senior sibling of the den presented this gift to me as a preemptive act designed to keep me far, far away from his beautiful Nikon F-1 35mm camera, the Rolls Royce of amateur photography back in the day.)

Trial and error learning can be slow and tedious and unrewarding as well. Weighted down then by the financial burdens of buying film and getting it developed, my progress toward artistic greatness was retarded at every turn by my very meager monetary resources. Although tightly confined by this economic straightjacket, I continued to snap as often as I could and within a few short years it was not uncommon for me to produce an image that was almost recognizable. Then, the cavalry came riding to the rescue.

Over the years I have come to value ever more the things that the U.S. Army did for me. One of its earliest acts of kindness was to school me in the dark science of capturing images on celluloid. When the great commanders of that martial organization thought that I had crawled my way through a sufficient amount of mud, spent the right number of nights sleeping in the open and had walked an acceptable number of miles burdened like a packhorse, they directed that I get a formal education in the art of taking pictures. Toward that end I reported to a nondescript NCO in a nondescript building at a nondescript post where I had to sign for a well-worn light meter and a over-used Graflex Speed Graphic 4X5" camera and a whole bag full of other stuff.

As always, my military training began with these particular pieces of antiquity – some of which likely came down directly from Matthew Brady – since they were the oldest, the most complex and one of the heaviest photographic outfits in the field at that time. (For the lovers of dated entertainment, the cub reporter for the Metropolis' famed Daily Planet, Jimmy Olsen – also Superman's awe-struck fan -- toted an instrument of this complexion.)

How anyone in his right mind could include "Speed" in the description of the device under consideration eludes me to this day. Unlike the Brownie, the 35mm single lens reflex, its range-finder cousin or most other period cameras, the "Speed" was anything but fast. This derived, mainly, from the fact that it did not use film on pre-wound rolls. Rather, it consumed, one at a time, single, light sensitive sheets of celluloid that measured a convenient 4 X 5". The consequence of this pleasant arrangement was that one piece of film equaled exactly one photograph (provided all of the stars in the universe aligned) and the camera could take only one shot before it had to be reloaded! Reloading the monster took a practiced cameraman somewhere between 10 seconds and thirty minutes, depending on how prepared he was for that particular endeavor. Thus, speed was not the "Speed's" long suit.

It is probable, however, that the Army selected the "Speed" to bolster its physical fitness program. The basic instrument weighed just slightly less than a .50 caliber machine gun, tripod included. Take along the camera, its massive flash unit, extra bulbs and batteries, some holders, a couple of dark bags (devices in which one could, in an emergency, reload film), a light meter, a tripod, and assorted other paraphernalia and the whole set up tipped the scale at a svelte 486 pounds. And at that you got to take, maybe, 12 photographs – if you had the space and the physical endurance to haul everything all at once.

To prepare for action when using the "Speed," one first had to load a thing called a "film holder". This usually was accomplished before starting out on a photo shoot because it could be done only in total darkness and thus, only by feel. Two sheets could be pre-positioned in each rectangular "holder," one on each side of the device; both of them were separated by a lightproof backing panel and both had their faces – as opposed to their backs – covered by a lightproof slide.

In condensed form, the process by which one actually took a picture with the "Speed" went something like this: 1.) Decide what to shoot; 2.) Dig the camera out of the bag and find someplace safe and dry to park it for a time; 3.) Take the light meter out of the bag; 4.) Use the light meter to determine the proper settings for the aperture and shutter; 5.) Make the necessary aperture setting by moving the ring on the lens; 6.) Select the shutter you wanted to employ – the "Speed" had two of them; 7.) Set the shutter speed; 8.) Drag a "film holder" out of your bag, taking care not to select one that contains celluloid that has been exposed already; 9.) Insert the holder into the back of the "Speed"; 10.) Pull the lightproof slide out of the holder and put it somewhere where you might be able to find it again in a minute; 11.) Raise the camera; 12.) Focus it using one of the two possible focal systems; 13.) Take the picture; 14.) Return the slide cover that you set aside earlier to its place in the holder and return the holder to its place in the camera bag. Follow these simple steps and, BINGO, you may have just taken one blinkin' picture! Mess up any of these acts or get them out of order and you will learn in the darkroom that you either did not capture anything at all or worse yet, what you did get does not rise to The Old Man's standards of excellence.

But wait! There is more! Once the shot was snapped, the finished product, suitable for framing, was still a ways off. The aforementioned holder had to be returned to the laboratory where it was to be unloaded in the dark, strictly by feel. The film then had to be transferred into stainless steel carriers, still by feel, after which it could be dunked, repeatedly, into open vats of chemicals. In this manner a negative was produced and from that, then, any number of prints then could be generated.

The Old Man, a World War II vet, used to say, "There is the right way, the wrong way and the Army way of doing things." At this point the reader needs to understand that the acquisition of the photographic skills Uncle Sam determined were necessary for soldiers like me remained, nonetheless, supplemental to the primary mission I had been assigned to perform: Military Intelligence. And, I expect that even those newer to the confines of the shadowy world of espionage can well imagine that there was little space in it for the likes of the "Speed." Thus it was that after forcing us to endure the trauma of endless weeks of work with that dinosaur there finally came a time when the powers that be executed a neat 180-degree turn. It was a glorious day, indeed, when we exchanged our funny green clothes for civilian duds, turned in our "Speeds" and were encouraged, nay even compelled, to spend all of our waking hours skulking around with tiny cameras, long, long lenses, night vision gadgets and a hoard of other spooky equipment.

During my years of soldiering I used a wide array of cameras and photographic equipment. Left in charge of my own laboratory and given free rein over all of the film, chemicals and cameras one could hope to have in a lifetime, I happily took and developed thousands of rolls of Kodak's finest, often while my tent-mates pursued less savory duties. Then, suddenly, my gravy train smashed into a brick wall.

Having made the decision to live life on the "outside," I was forced to give up the perks of being on the "inside." So it was that following these years of photographic abundance the civilian world I re-entered was one of photographic "cold turkey." In fact, it was worse than that. Whereas most of my friends in the military had scrimped and saved to buy their own cameras, I had not bothered. Thus, I found myself to be a poor, starving, struggling, helpless, homeless, wretched, undeserving, etc., etc...student, *sans* camera, and *sans* the time or money for this fine art...or for any others.

The natural passage of time, the expenditure of great effort and a modicum of progress up life's little ladder finally re-exposed me to the wonderful world of photography. My best efforts to the contrary sometimes notwithstanding, a degree of prosperity crept into my life that I was not able to shake off. Moreover, a multi-year assignment to the Far East found me knee deep in to some of the world's better camera equipment. True to my "Speed" roots, however, the gear I acquired tended toward the older, the bigger, and the less flashy. Even by the 1980s few serious practitioners of the art still carried, much less employed a hand held light meter, and most of them would have had a bag full of the latest, greatest, automatic, whiz-bang, my-word-can-you-believe-it does-all-of-that gadgets. I did not. I did not want them. I had been ruined.

By nature, the pictures I took for the government – while in the military and again in civilian service – tended to be bereft of artistic appeal. In most instances the emphasis was on clarity, rapidity and volume. Anything beyond that was wasted. My personal work, however, went just the other way.

After giving Dr. Jekyll and Mr. Hyde decades to play tug of war with my creative soul, I finally hauled them both off to the hills of Montana. Deep in a nearly inaccessible ravine cleaving a part of the northern Rocky Mountains I assassinated one of them and put the other on firm notice. "Henceforth," I advised, "I'll be shooting who, what, when, where, and why I want. Period. End of discussion."

Capitalizing on that liberating experience, I took my camera out when it could be used slowly, deliberately, and imaginatively. Stalking each subject, my approach was like that of a big game hunter short of ammunition. I did not care how long it took. I did not care how far I had to go. My single goal was to get a trophy every time out. The target: nature's landscapes.

Life might have gone along like that forever had it not been for the digital camera. Of course, from the first moment I heard about these abominations I did not want one. I did not need one. I did not like the idea of having one. In truth, I was uncomfortable around anyone who even suggested that he might get one. So how to explain buying one? Cows!

It took The Technical Officer and me nanoseconds (milli, milli, milli-milliseconds) to perceive how much easier it would be to market exceptional breeding cattle, when the pictures you took of them in the field momentarily could be dispatched electronically across the country or around the world with the push of a single button. From the first second we saw one of these devices in action, we knew we had to have one, but only for the cows!

Dependence, be it to chemicals or anything else, is still dependence and its an ugly load to have to cart around. Having gotten accustomed to the ease of our palm-sized, mega-byting, cow-picture-snapping wonder, hysteria all but overcame me when the sucker unexpectedly crapped out one afternoon. Sure, I still had my trusty film equipment, but that was reserved for serious photography. This was business and the question remained: How was I going to get the pics of those pricey yearling heifers I wanted to sell right away up to old Slim in Alberta this very day as promised? Always miles ahead of me, The Top Hand suggested we resolve the problem by going to look for a new business machine.

I should have seen it coming, but I did not. Before walking through the door of the photo shop there was some small talk of possibly upgrading from the base level camera we had been using to something a little more modern, a little more versatile. We strolled out of that pleasant establishment with a bag full of 35mm, semi-pro, digital equipment for my serious use – camera body, camera bag, quality lenses, filters, the works -- and the latest palm-sized beauty for her. The bill was…gulp…well, I would still rather not talk about that!

Since that life-changing moment, I have discovered two very important things: Number One, The Technical Officer really likes her pint-sized camera. She carries it everywhere and uses it often. Most surprisingly, she works to improve her technique, is finding her own artistic niche, and is taking some first rate pictures. Number Two, I fell in love instantly with my new toy. From the first moment I hefted it, my film cameras were relegated to Rip Van Winkle status; they have languished in their cases, literally untouched and unattended ever since.

It would be a mistake to think that I have embraced completely the high tech mentality. I still can see no need for shooting eight frames per second. Taking one shot at a time, carefully and thoughtfully, continues to sooth my restless soul. With visions of The Old Man's epics dancing through my head, I staunchly avoid anything resembling 'motion pictures.' And, I bristle a bit when I see someone indiscriminately clicking away, snapping hundreds of photos of everything in sight all with the hope of capturing something that is actually worth viewing.

I admit, too, to feeling a considerable sense of loss when considering what computers do to human art. Even truly gifted photographers no longer depend on an artist's eye and a lifetime's worth of experience to produce stunning photographs. In fact, at a recent small show I strolled past a category of pictures taken by children seven years of age and under! They were not bad. A couple of them bordered right on being good. But the disturbing question could not be shed: Were these things truly expressions of the human soul or were they cheap reflections of mere technology? Technology puts all of this within reach; sometimes that is good and sometimes it is not. As for me, well, the life of a Neanderthal really is not terribly unpleasant!

HAUNTING, HUNTING HOARDS

Ad we cruise this southern extreme of the Inside Passage two conflicting sentiments contend with each other. The islands that slowly move past our vessel appear concurrently to be wilderness-like and at the same time touched, heavily, by the hand of civilization. From any distance, the houses, roads, power lines, docks and marinas that are abundantly present magically disappear. The sense of virgin forests, untrodden hills and unexplored beaches pervades everything. Then blink and re-focus and the modern world leaps out at you like the cardboard scene in a children's pop-up book.

"Wow! Look at that one. The brown one over there, right on that cliff!" The Crew excitedly shouts to me. I turn my head in the direction indicated and take in a modern structure perched like a well-placed eagle's aerie on a rock outcropping.

"It's big, impressive and must have a view that goes on forever, but I'm not sure I want to be there in an earthquake," I return. "Looks to me like it could be splashing around in the water in a heartbeat." Having lived, worked and played at various points around the Pacific Basin's "Ring of Fire," that festering cauldron of volcanic/earthquake unrest that arcs out of Asia and then follows the west coast of the New World all the way to the tip of South America, I have been shaken too much to want to temp fate by balancing over a precipice. Besides, I hate heights!

"See that one over there? The one with the green roof?" The Executive Officer points toward the shore. "It would be perfect, except for those two other houses that sit right on top of it. Why would they do that? I wonder if those poor people in the center house can even squeeze past their neighbors to get down to the beach? Oh, and look! There is a road just beyond them and...Can you believe it? There is a regular subdivision crowding in right behind them. No...I'm thinking that's not my idea of a good time. I couldn't live there..."

The seconds, the minutes, the hours, the days, even lifetimes lazily can slip into a Never-Never Land-type of reverie out here on the water. In a bizarre, but delightful fashion, we pour our souls into this black hole of human consciousness, where fantasy and reality conjoin someplace between hopes, dreams, imagination and... "Holy Crap! That screaming ferry's headed straight toward us! Helm hard a port! Engines full astern! Lower the lifeboats! Dive! Dive! Dive!"

Hold it! "Dive? Dive? Dive?" This ain't no stinking submarine and we don't even have a lifeboat. Get a grip, Captain!

The banes of small boaters in the Gulf Islands and in many other parts of the Pacific Northwet are its ferries. Plying the waters between the mainland and the islands as well as connecting the islands to each other, these working vessels deliver the lifeblood of people, goods and services that support the roads, houses, schools, stores and general lifestyles of those who choose to populate the more inaccessible reaches of this domain. Each day they chug officiously from port to port taking on and disgorging passengers and cargo like bulimic pre-historic predators. And each day is a new adventure for recreational boaters.

Flat bottomed with squared double ends, these giants do not look much like most other sea craft. Their long, smooth, semi-open main car decks sit low in the boat, just a few feet above the water line. Like the gaping black maws of great oceanic nightmares, the opposing ends of these ships, where vehicles board and depart, form huge, wave-sweeping caverns that appear to be bent on vacuuming up any and every morsel that strays too close to them. It takes little imagination to see in the frothy white bow wave they push up the drooling lips of hunger-frenzied beasts.

Stacked above their car decks is a steel superstructure that adds one or two stories to the whole edifice. The many-windowed, slab-sided vertical surfaces that are tied together with a labyrinth of side decks and railings manages to form an exoskeleton so fashioned as to create a silhouette reminiscent of the sternwheelers of the riverboat days. That appearance is strengthened by the placement of two control bridges, one fore and one aft, each of which immediately overlooks either bow or stern. An exhaust funnel or two that might well pass for old-time smoke stacks caps that reflective row of domineering glass teeth that protects the pilots of these boats from the weather. With their gleaming white paint schemes, it would be easy for a daydreamer to conjure up cotton bales piled high on deck, southern belles in flowing pink dresses promenading, and black-coated gamblers sitting around a room full of green, felt-covered tables, were it not for the ever-present cold and damp of the north.

Having propulsion and steering systems that allow them to sail equally well either forward or backward, and not designed with a traditional bow or stern, at a distance and without binoculars it can be a chore to try to figure out whether a ferry is coming or going. The considerable speed at which they move tends to lessen that problem since they will either be down on the horizon or right up on top of the unwary in a very short time.

Ferries run between fixed shore points. They run on schedules. And, they run regular routes. They also get pushed and pulled considerably by wind and current; thus they frequently are hard to control and even harder to maneuver. By way of maritime rules dating at least to the age of Noah, boats suffering all of these maladies get special consideration. And whereas the letter of the law requires no more than that smaller and more capable vessels, especially those if the recreational category, whether under sail or engine-driven, give the ferries the right of way, tradition and a certain perverse playfulness generally conveys to the ferry captains the right to seek and destroy any non-commercial boat that dares draw too close.

Notice here that I say that ferry skippers only "generally" follow this delightful custom. While it is true that on any number of occasions, as I have been conveyed over the waters on one or another of these contraptions, I am certain that I have heard the gruesome thud and then the subsequent 'chop, chop, chop' of some hapless small boat being rammed and then ground to pieces by the unrelenting action of a couple of giant props, I cannot say for certain that this necessarily happens as often as it could. And, because anecdotal evidence has it that grinding up a few slow recreational vessels is just a part of any normal workday on the bridge of a ferry, it may shock some when I assert that there do seem to be exceptions to this unsavory convention. In fact, I am forced to admit to having witnessed, personally, the extremes to which one benighted captain apparently went to remain completely non-compliant with the usual-way-of-doing things. In that particular instance the faint-hearted master brought his vessel to a complete stop in a heavy fog to avoid pulverizing some fool in a 16' (4.88 metre) aluminum boat who was drifting and fishing happily, smack dab in the middle of the main shipping lane through which all of the commercial traffic into and out of Puget Sound and the Ports of Seattle and Tacoma moved. I cannot say what recriminations he latter suffered at the hands of his brethren for this action, nor can I even guess as to his current employment status; I can but speculate that he has lived a low and demeaned life ever since. I mention this only to underscore the point that even in this free-wheeling realm not all things are cut and dried.

The problem posed for the commanders of the boats that are on the receiving end of this entertainment stems precisely from the sources of the original entitlement that was granted to their adversaries. As mentioned, ferries run between fixed shore points. They run on schedules. And, they run regular routes. They also get pushed and pulled by wind and current; thus, frequently they are hard to control and even harder to maneuver. Let's examine these features one at a time.

Ferries run between fixed shore points. The truth of this is self-evident. These boats begin at Dry Land Point A and then go to Dry Land Point B, picking up and discharging all manner of things at both places. The space in between these disparate locations is nothing but water (the proof of which being that these vessels can neither fly nor operate on the hard ground). As a secondary verification we assert that when one is up on a dry part of the earth it is relatively easy to find out where ferries start and stop. After all, when the road comes to a dead end just at that place where the water washes up and a ferry docks, we get a pretty good idea that that might be a ferry landing. More apparently, they being toll vessels and with the government having an intrinsic interest in wringing as much money as possible from the unsuspecting public, no effort is spared for signage and other forms of advertisements that serve to lead the gullible and ill-informed down to the water (so to speak).

Unfortunately, determining exactly where the ferries put in and come out is not as apparent when at sea. There are no mid-bay billboards with arrows saying, 'Ferries this way.' Likewise, you cannot tune your radio to "530 on the AM dial" to get the latest ferry information. Sometimes, in some places, on marine road maps – we refer to these as charts –a little series of dots is included that is meant to represent pilings driven into the seabed next to the shore. Occasionally these are labeled – in tiny, faint letters – "Ferry." Failure to scrutinize every micron of every coastline, including all bays, inlets, arms, reaches, straits, harbors and ports, may result in the unwary being accosted mightily by a ferry as it blasts out from behind a headland intent on turning all the little 'boaties' that get in its way into fish bait.

We move next to the assertion that ferries run regular routes. This argument is both a tautology and the corollary to the fixed-point contention. No one is ever going to contend that ferries do not start and stop somewhere. Unless they have managed to unlock the secrets of perpetual motion, the laws of physics require that even this class of watercraft cease moving sometimes! The conundrum then arises not out of the question of whether they stop, but out of the question of where they stop. Even if we do identify correctly that tiny, faint print on our charts that tells us that a ferry comes to rest here, in most instances we have no way of knowing where the other end of her route lies. It could be a stone's throw across the water or it could be halfway around the world. The obvious rub is that just knowing that a ferry lurks in the general vicinity provides the average boater with little protection against the watery wrath of this seaborne terror. An understanding of a ferry's point of departure or even its destination is little better than being well aware of the location of a loaded gun. If you cannot tell where it is pointed, not much is gained by knowing where it is.

Being cognizant of the fact that ferries do operate at particular times is no more advantageous than knowing that the above-mentioned gun will go off at some precise moment. Without having a schedule at hand – and no chart, floating billboard or radio broadcast includes this information – the recreational boater can only hope that his number is not up.

Finally, the alleged difficulty of handling a ferry, while true in principle, provides Joe Boater with little solace and no protection. We assert that it matters not whether these floating car-haulers just are hard to drive or whether a fiendish civil employee brightens up his day by running over innocent vessels. After all is said and done, splinters are still splinters and the flotsam is still floating!

It is probably a bit of a challenge for the shore-bound reader to imagine why anyone would put themselves in this kind of harm's way just for the fun of it. As the entity legally liable for the safety of all those onboard my craft, I sometimes wonder the same thing. Suffice it to say that the willingness to endure these perils probably is deeply rooted in long-suppressed memories of the thrills taken from winning a grade school game of dodge ball.

* * * * * * * * * * *

Recall now that *Minstrel's Song* was quietly churning its way northward up the Swanson Channel when this ferry crisis struck.

Actually, it was not a crisis at all; rather, it was The Captain's adrenaline-driven reaction to the very sight of a ferry that pushed him into paroxysms of fear. Putting aside the urge to gulp a handful of Valium (Valiums? Valia?), and with the certain knowledge that The First Mate was watching his every move, the only real option left to our stalwart Skipper was to man up and face the music.

As if no memory now existed of the tizzy he had been thrown into just seconds before and with absolute nonchalance, The Pilot advised that a ferry had just cleared the headland bearing three points off the port bow and was proceeding northward at unknown speed, distance and course. It mattered not at all that he did not have a clue as to what any of that meant, but he had long since observed that speaking in nautical tongues had a soothing effect on those not schooled in the intricacies of the sea. In mistaking the bold use of the lingo for confidence, these poor souls usually fail to notice the real trepidation that enshrouds the leader in whose hands they have placed their very existence. Still, it works every time it is tried!

With the intensity of a season ticket holder at a championship game, The Helmsman studies the interloper, trying to determine if it hungers for fiberglass. It is with relief that he watches the seething monster slowly bear away from *Minstrel's Song*, turning northward, and exposing his enormous white flanks. But before he can breathe a long sigh of relief another attacker appears off the starboard bow and yet a third slides past a distant point, both apparently heading in the direction of our small craft. As the importance of these near simultaneous sightings sink in, the thought strikes The Captain again like a sledgehammer: "There is an entire pack of these fiends out here and they're on the hunt. Dive! Dive! Dive!"

Had he had the good sense to check the Internet for B.C. Ferry routes before this cruise, The Pilot might have known that he now was entering what rightly could be dubbed "Ferry Alley." Given this lapse in preparation, what he could not know was that he had been sailing blissfully into the Pacific Northwet's equivalent of the Devil's Triangle.

Neither a cursory look nor a close examination of the area's charts would have indicated that there was anything special about the communities of Fulford Harbour, Long Harbour, Sturdies Bay, Swartz Bay or Village Bay. That each was situated about equidistant from the mid-point of the northern reaches of Swanson Channel would not have attracted any particular notice. In fact, these mere names on the chart only gained value if and when one realized that each of these thriving destinations served as a terminus for the ferries that incessantly plied these local waters and all points east. Had that intelligence been at hand just then, the guiding hand on *Minstrel's Song's* wheel would have appreciated the fact that the upper end of the waterway he was navigating was nothing less than a labyrinth of randomly crisscrossing tracks. Had each specific pathway been drawn on paper in bright reds and greens, the product would have held a distressingly eerie similarity to the piercing red and green laser beams that the good guy/bad guy thieves on T.V. and in the movies have to pass through on the way to snatching the priceless jewels. Unsuspecting newcomers to this part of the world as they were, the stout little ship that carried our principals had blundered directly into a boating ambush.

While the phrase 'faster than a speeding bullet' cannot rightly be applied to a ferry, they do move along at a pace well above that which *Minstrel's Song* can attain. So outrunning these dangers is never an option. The only weapons that the recreational boater can use to defend against these great oppressors are stealth, maneuverability and a shallow draft. By choosing the right moment, by aggressively zigzagging all over the place and especially by hugging the shorelines, one usually can escape capture.

After recovering from the initial onslaught – but still not really understanding their plan of attack – I steered directly for the safety of a small bight and the shallow water that the chart told me I would find there. I was fairly certain that our antagonists would not dare to follow. Although a seeming eternity passed, it really was not too long before we were rewarded by the sights of two sterns disappearing around the point just north of us. That left only the one we had seen that was coming south.

As the jutting shoreline of Prevost Island forced us back toward the channel proper, our final tormentor came back into view. Hurtling along at 'hunting speed,' and constrained as he was by the rocky dangers of shallower seas, he opted to pretend not to notice us at all. In an effort to support this ploy, while undoubtedly hoping we would do something stupid, he stationed gaily dressed, cheerful passengers with cameras along his upper rails. They smiled and waved and took pictures of us; we smiled and waved and shot back, but still we knew the truth.

The excitement of these events caused us to veer from our original course and that, in turn, threw The Navigator off his game. Intending to be tracking along a particular bearing, we were now way off that line and in serious need of realignment. Despite the fact that The Navigator was totally unprepared for the Great Ferry Swarm-In, rare is the moment when he does not know precisely where on the face of the earth his ship is located at any given instant. That notwithstanding, and especially because careful piloting in coastal waters approaches an obsession with him, he now has to turn his attentions to the charts, establish his craft's present position and re-draw his course lines. While this task might strike many people either as drudgery or needless or both, some few perverse old souls – our Skipper possible among that group – might while away heavenly days nothing but that!

A BRIEF HISTORY OF EVERYTHING

In the darker, fainter recesses of human history, there was a time – before LORAN (LOng RAnge Navigation), GPS (Global Positioning Systems), AIS (Automatic Information Systems), FLIR (Forward Looking Infrared), satellite tracking, Google Earth, weather and broadband links, chartplotters, depth sounders, radar, cell phones, and "apps" for everything under the sun – when sailors crossed vast oceans utilizing little more than compass, clock and sextant to tell them where they were. A little tiny sliver of that era still is remembered by some rare few, and the mariners who continue to practice those black arts tend to fare a little better at sea than those who do not.

When just pointing the bow of the ship in a general direction proved unsatisfactory for getting to and from a particular place beyond the horizon, the search for navigational help commenced. Incredible discoveries were made and lost, terribly useful techniques proliferated here, but did not spread to there, and man's abilities to make his way far across the open seas ebbed and flowed.

The compass was known to the Chinese two millennia ago, for instance, but they used it for divination and not for guiding themselves from this place to that. In the late 1200s this handy little device showed up in Europe – whether independently "discovered" or brought there from the Far East is not known – but even at that it did not go to sea as an aid to navigation until the mid-1300s. In its very crude, early form, this instrument was novel, but in and of itself it did not represent much of a technological breakthrough. Due to the cartographic ambiguities of the day, the mere knowledge of which way was up (north) did not translate into locational certainty. What the ancient mariner still needed – and what the compass by itself could not supply – was the means of determining precisely which way he had to go from the ever changing "right here" so as to arrive on time and on schedule at an unseen "over there!"

Since the beginning of time man made pictures to describe where known places were. "See, Ooog I draw? We here at this cave (rock on ground) and big, ugly, mean things way over there by dark forest (clump of grass). No cross river (line in dirt) or no come back." By the Age of Exploration (starting in the early 1300s) European adventurers had learned enough about some great and distant parts of the earth to draw, by hand, a few primitive maps to describe them. These "eye-balled" charts became standard equipment on sailing ships. And when extraordinarily good charts were mated with especially fine magnetic compasses and boxfuls of other primitive, but useful devices, wielded by really talented sailors who possessed exceptional understandings of the movements of the sun, the moon and the stars, then and only then could someone like Christopher Columbus kind of, sort of, sometimes almost get to about where he wanted to go (so long as the East Indies and the West Indies could be regarded synonymously).

Over time, new inventions were made and the accuracy with which a capable mariner could record on paper where he was relative to where he wanted to go improved immensely. This act of keeping track of one's position at sea – part careful record keeping and part guessing – became known as "dead reckoning." (One need only contemplate that term for a moment or two to appreciate its full meaning!)

While the accuracy made possible by the improvements worked in navigational devices increased apace into the 20th Century, the truth remained that the modern seaman's 16th Century forebear would have recognized most of what he employed. The pronounced breakthroughs in this realm arrived with World War II (1939-1945) and followed in the decades thereafter.

The Great Wars of the past century catapulted mankind into a new navigational age. The advent of aircraft, especially the long-range, high altitude bomber, drove much of that change. To start, photographs taken from the heights that these babies could reach allowed man to craft maps and charts that for the first time reflected what the surface of the earth truly looked like as opposed to an artist's conception of the lay of the land.

Homo sapiens took another giant step forward when it dawned on them that in order to drop high explosives from the sky for the purpose of blowing some particular thing to smithereens, one had to be exactly over the offending piece of real estate. Leaving aside the problems created by the forward momentum of the airplanes that carried the bombs, the unpredictable winds aloft and the terrified boys in charge of these incredible flying machines, and considering only that these aeronautical wonders had to traverse great distances through a variety of meteorological conditions (e.g. clouds, fog, storms of all sorts), enemy aircraft and explosives shot from large guns located on the ground (flak) to particular bomb release points, it did not take a rocket scientist – oops, that comes later – to figure out that an old chart, a compass and a sextant really were not going to get the job done. To remedy this, and with varying degrees of success, huge air armadas began sweeping across the skies of Europe in order to get to specific targets by following, 'riding on' or "triangulating" radio waves broadcast on known frequencies from pre-determined positions. Via a number of extremely primitive mechanical devices, a skilled navigator could transform those radio signals into information that allowed him to direct the movements of his plane to a position that at the very least took him near the right country, mostly.

Radar (RAdio Detection and Ranging) was in the hopper long before WWII. Although a number of countries pursued it with greater or lesser intensity, by the early 1920s experiments by the U.S. Navy revealed that it could be used from shore bases to locate nearby ships even when they were obscured by clouds, fog, smoke, darkness, etc. The early 1930s found our naval researchers learning that they could "see" flying aircraft in like manner, but their work progressed at an unhurried pace despite impending world events. The devices they developed remained scientific curiosities right up to the first explosions of 1939.

It was the English who pried the radar out of the la**bor**atory – they still prefer the em**phas**is to go on that second syl**lab**le! – and planted them squarely up and down their eastern coastlines. It seems that once again they were in a bit of a tussle with their Teutonic cousins and in spite of the years of dire warnings pertaining to the impending catastrophe that they blithely ignored, they "suddenly" found themselves on the verge of losing the Battle of Britain (an airborne attack on the home islands) as well as the whole bloody war! Thinking that that was not very cricket, and desperate to gain some kind of relief from the schooling the Germans were giving them, Winston Churchill *et. al.* embraced the new technology wholeheartedly and did so just in time. The minutes of "extra" warning that radar afforded the plucky defenders of the Empire may well have saved the day.

It will not be lost on the thoughtful observer that the various crises the world has experienced over the ages tends to kick people directly in the seats of their pants and great leaps forward result. (Alas, we will have to leave for some other time the enthralling debate over whether they move ahead just because it is finally time to do so or whether they are thrown in that direction by the pummeling they receive from others.) Suffice it to say, however, that via the third Great War of this past century, the Cold War, civilization was forced to make a lot of progress.

Over a thousand years ago the Chinese invented gunpowder.

Apparently lacking the imagination of their (largely unknown) European cousins, these inscrutable keepers of the oriental arts first put their discovery to work as a medicinal product and then used it to entertain both royal courtiers and peasants alike. In particular, they liked to fill tubes full of this chemical concoction, carefully ignite said things and enjoy the fiery balls and tongues of flame that subsequently shot into the sky. This latter practice led to the development of the first primitive guns and the world was off and running.

It was only after the Europeans suffered the ignominy of having fallen light years behind their Asian brethren in this important field that they focused their attentions on the virtues of gunpowder and on developing guns. Undoubtedly fascinated by the idea of easily destroying nearly anything, the best Continental minds went to work to perfect the concept. Driven by the alluring thought that by the use of just a few common household chemicals, a tube and a spark one could fling deadly objects over great distances with acceptable precision, western civilization quickly outdistanced its rivals in what probably was the first great intercontinental arms race (a general competition that included contestants from north and south Asia, the Middle East as well as Europe). Their success in this sphere later allowed them to employ their technology to subdue most parts of the known world.

When the good folks of Europe were not using their early firearms to blast away at each other's ships, castles, armies and the like, they dabbled in rocketry. They might have derived great pleasure from these objects, as had the Chinese, were it not for the fact that our post-Dark Ages warriors seemed to have been consumed by the dream of turning these things into some type of 'super weapon.' (Sadly for them, until very late their obsession with that goal served mostly to disappoint and to drain their coffers.)

Relative to rockets, what probably frustrated our Western forebears the most was that despite the way they were able to surmount castle walls, cross great distances quickly and make a lot of noise, these nifty little devices could not be configured to do much damage or to hit anything with any accuracy at all. Trivial though it may seem in our modern times, these shortcomings were a source of constant irritation to those ancients who devoted their lives to the tasks of breaking things and annihilating people.

In one form or another rockets flew over, through and around the great military contests that so held the attention of European potentates and New World leaders from the 1600s onward. (To confirm this, we need only to ask ourselves what provided poet Francis Scot Key with the "red glare" he said lighted the night sky over Fort McHenry in 1814.) It was not until the 20th Century, however, that these munitions gained any real battlefield efficacy. And it was not until WWII that they made much of a difference one way or the other.

By the end of the Second World War, all of the principle participants had screaming, screeching missiles that warranted considerable respect. (Most of these were, however, of modest size.) As thankfully seems to happen in most tyrannies, the supermen of this past century came to realize that they probably had bitten off more than they could chew in challenging a great portion of the world to a fight to the death. Ultimately not possessing enough of all of the stuff they needed to reorganize the universe in the way that they thought most suitable, or in truth even having the wherewithal to counter effectively the forces they so thoughtlessly engaged at the outbreak of the conflict, they found themselves slowly being pushed toward defeat. And since nobody likes losers – or usually treats them particularly well – the maniac leading that particular pack believed he could engineer a last minute comeback by employing a number of "ultimate" weapons. These playground toys included incredibly large rockets, jet airplanes and, possibly, the atom itself. Thus, a capable and industrious people were sent by their leader to work out the details. One of the results of their endeavors was the "V2" rocket.

Even though German bombers carried more ordnance, were re-useable – when not shot down – had a longer range and delivered their payloads with greater precision, starting in mid-1944 the V2 rocket became the German weapon of choice for reaching out and touching people, especially those irritating islanders who imperviously were going about their ordinary lives across the English Channel. As often happens with madmen and megalomaniacs, the mustachioed house painter who claimed to be the brains behind the whole war effort convinced himself that adding a bit more terror to a scene that was grizzly beyond belief would turn the tide of events back in his favor.

The V2 was the world's first operational ballistic missile. When fired, it left the lower atmosphere, arced up to an altitude of about 128 miles (206 kilometres) and then descended back to earth where it went bang, loudly. Its range was limited, however, to no more than about 200 miles (320 kilometres) and it carried but a single warhead. Because there was no defense against it, and little warning of its arrival, it rained down terror – at five times the speed of sound -- on those it struck. Its virtue, if one may speak of such horrors in those terms, was to be found in the belief that it punished that group of smug Englanders not for strategic reasons, but for daring to resist the power and reach of the neo-Germanic barbarians. (The "V" in the V2's name, by the way, stood for "Vengeance.")

The Achilles heal of this weapon was its guidance system. In order to strike any given point with the V2 one had to know two things precisely: the place where it was when it started its trip and the place where it was supposed to be when it ended it. Additionally, one had to correct for a great many in-flight changes if there was to be any hope of getting it to fall near its target. Taken altogether, these obstacles were more than even the super-scientists of the Third Reich could surmount. Thus, the intrepid German soldier, charged with aiming and firing his deadly rocket might have been reduced to sticking a wetted finger into the breeze, stooping and squinting down the rocket tube and then yelling the equivalent of, "Yo! Hans! Cock it just a tad bit more to the left! O.K. O.K. That should do it!" Dispatched with this kind of meticulousness, most V2's managed to land within four to 11 miles (6.5 to 17.7 kilometres) of their designated targets. This was good enough to wreak havoc and destruction on something – almost always of a civilian nature – but useless when it came to delivering staggering military blows.

The emerging Cold War of the late 1940s warmed considerably when "Uncle Joe" Stalin joined the U.S. as co-proprietor of the atomic bomb. A decade later when Khrushchev's "Ruskies" surged visibly ahead of the Americans with the launch of Sputnik (1957), fear gripped the free world. It was clear that the atomic advantage the U.S. held in 1945 had evaporated and something had to be done about it. The best of the scientific minds in the U.S. were sent immediately to their drawing boards. The tasks that faced them were many and daunting, but the most important one was that of contriving the means by which a ballistic object could be guided down to earth so as to land smack dab on a given spot.

Because the Soviet's intercontinental ballistic missiles (ICBMs) were launched from hardened, underground siloes, the mere act of strewing bombs around them – regardless of how big a bang they made – provided no assurance that the targeted offender would cease to exist. In all likelihood, that scenario would wind up doing little more than making the earth's atmosphere very, very radioactive and the enemy very, very upset. What was needed was a way to "download" immense amounts of power to very precise locations. Adding to this challenge was the fact that much of America's nuclear might was delivered not just from fixed points but also via moving airplanes and floating submarines (referred to as the triad of nuclear deterrence for its reliance on missiles and bombs dispatched from land, air and sea). Thus, the trick of the thing was to find a way to hit not just anything or anyone when blasting off from a known point, as had been the case with the V2s, but to get that guy right there from anyplace on earth, whether the launch platform was moving or not!

Ironic though it may be, it was the study of Sputnik and other early "commie" satellites that led American scientists to the conclusion that one could pinpoint the location of any high flying object via multiple radio waves sent heavenward from the earth. (This required a combination of radar, radio direction finding, and geometric calculations that would have given Euclid a migraine. Fortunately, the concomitant development of early computers took some of the pain out of the mathematic gymnastics that had to be performed.) It was but a relatively small intellectual step from determining where a tiny sphere that was orbiting overhead was located at any given moment to being able to identify any spot on the globe by reversing the process (i.e., by broadcasting radio waves from satellites back toward the earth). Thus was born what we now know as the Global Positioning System (GPS).

At first the GPS was a highly guarded military secret. But over time the cat got out of the bag and technology overtook governmental druthers. Rightly understanding the enormous civilian benefits that could go with GPS accuracy – such as guiding things like airplanes safely through the sky and ships through stormy seas at night – Uncle Sam somewhat grudgingly released a dumbed down version of GPS for use by mere mortals. By fuzzing the signals from the satellites, civilian users could find their positions to an accuracy of a few hundred yards. Higher accuracies still were reserved for military purposes only. Nonetheless, even with a degree of precision that was sufficient only for a game of horse shoes or hand grenades, coming pretty close made getting people, goods and services from here to there a whole lot easier than ever before. Beyond whining about the expense, few complained about the early GPS machines.

Living as we do in an ever-deteriorating physical world, it was only a matter of time before the wall between military need and civilian wants crumbled. Over a couple of decades the GPS went from exotic defense establishment fare to ordinary household item. With the ability to "put" its user square on a mountain path, to backtrack precisely along a given route, even, ultimately, to "tell" a car where it is, where it is going and how far and how long it will take it to get there, a new era dawned. Can you say "Tom-Tom"?

With the atmosphere filling as it was with flying bits, bites and bundles of technological wonderment, it is no surprise that ordinary boaters began to load up on all of the benefits of modern science. As always, the pace of the changeover was established by the yachting set. ("The yachting set" is defined herein as a vague group of large, fancy boat owners who generally have more money than good sense. Collectively they have yet to meet a gadget that they did not want onboard their mega-cruisers NOW!) Dragging behind them, sometimes kicking and screaming because of the costs, came Joe and Joan Daysailor. Ultimately convinced that it would be O.K. to pay for their kids' college educations with government loans and second mortgages –

based on wildly appreciating home values and .com bubbles – they rationalized, 'Hey! What the heck! MasterCard will tote the note on this nifty gizmo!' So, about as fast as they could, they leapt at the chance to plunk down the relatively big bucks it took to buy a very limited amount of marginally useful electronic gear. Despite having to hope against hope that they could discern something, anything, on the miniature viewing screens then available in their price range, they dove right in anyway. After all, the point was to have it, not necessarily to be able to use it.

It was about this time that things began to change drastically. Providing the demand pressure needed to develop and then power an entire marine industry, it was not long before manufacturers of all descriptions were churning out more, bigger and better combinations of electronic goodies for marine use. After all, everyone just had to have them! Within this brave new world, the guy who yesterday could not find his neighborhood grocery store without asking for directions suddenly could rattle off his precise position in longitude and latitude – to the thousandths place -- with the certitude of an award-winning astronomer. With a radar dome twice the size of the average dinghy, our carefree mariner soon identified "bogies" at a distance that probably would have given the defenders at Pearl Harbor time for Sunday morning breakfast before manning their guns. Want to know what is going on under your boat? 'No worries, mate, this wizamagig will give you the depth in hundredths, the water temperature in tenths, can chart the sea floor to 2,000 feet and will share with you the size, species and sexual preference of the fish swimming beneath your boat!' The most up to date naval vessels or oceanographic researchers could not have produced any of that in a timely fashion just 50 years ago. Never mind that much of the information currently available is of little actual value; it is the having of it that really counts.

And, lest we miss an entire burgeoning segment of sea life, we have to include advances in communications while on the water. Satellite phones, automated tracking and messaging devices, emergency locator beacons, TV, broadband Internet, music, news and live weather, in short all of the comforts of home are at the Daysailors' beck and call.

And the best part of it is that their presence is not restricted to great ships or expensive yachts. At today's prices they can sit idling at the ready on even the lowliest trailered aluminum fishing boat. It's easy. It's no hassle. All it takes is cash or credit.

As this new world began to unfold, it seemed that the number of "essential" toys that could be stacked onboard any given craft would be limited only by the speed with which they appeared on the market and by the ability of the hull to continue to remain above water while under the load. Two factors, however, allowed history to keep advancing apace: incrementalism and miniaturization!

In days of old the basic principles of business and marketing remained in a rudimentary state. That condition cost a lot of people a lot of money. For instance, the guy who invented the gun clearly squandered a golden opportunity to build a commercial empire. Contrary to every tenet now taught in the classrooms of the finest colleges and universities across the land, he did not retain exclusive production rights, he did not control his market with franchises and he did not bother to work the whole spectrum by bringing out a full line of weapons. Oh, how much better off would he have been had he first introduced a "de-tuned" version of his invention, one that really only served to sting and annoy an enemy, while promising future buyers that the next generation would do much better. Incrementalism of this sort would have set him up for life.

Even well into the 20th Century we see brilliant minds and successful business people wasting chance after chance to stack up the greenbacks. Take the Wright brothers, for example. Gifted mechanics and men of incredible foresight though they were, they went full bore from wind tunnel to complete aircraft production in one giant step. It takes little imagination to see how much more lucrative that aviation thing might have been for them had they introduced controlled flight in tiny steps. They might, for instance, have started with, say, a wind up rubber band concept version and then slowly marketed bigger and better models over several decades. If they had done that, they would still be raking in the money!

Fortunately, most up-to-date producers of high demand items now understand how to squeeze every penny of profit out of their merchandise. At a teaser price set just slightly south of outrageous, they make the unwary think that they actually can get into the game if they just stretch a bit. Out comes the plastic WonderCard and the gullible happily head to their boats with shiny new Widget Mark I-s tucked under their arms. But, before they begin to paw through the 3,000-page instruction "booklet" included with every high-end, technotronic, gottahaveit piece of gear, the manufacturer releases the Widget Mark II. The Mark I is now not only obsolete, but within nanoseconds of the Mark II's introduction, the announcement comes that the company soon will stop supporting the Mark I altogether.

This really neat game of incrementalism can go on forever. Once the lights of the big city have been seen, it is really hard to go back to the farm. And, add to your boat just one box filled to overflowing with moving electrons, no matter how basic their functions, and you will be back weekly to take the next step up the onboard-goody ladder. Addicts are like that!

Compound incrementalism with the ability of man to make things ever smaller, and the consumer does not stand a chance. Not only does he now have to purchase the Mark II model – which only costs a couple of times more than the Mark I – but he is probably going to have to spring for the even pricier Mark II-B because that little number incorporates lots of incredible functions not available on the plain vanilla Mark II. But worry not, Bunkie, for the good news is that despite all of the improvements and the new, user-friendly features that are integrated directly into the super "B" model, it won't cost you a single dime more to install! With the aid of the ergonomically configured Class 14T mounting bracket – sold separately of course -- it'll slide right into the same old hole you made for your antiquated Mark I! By this time the buyer's only defense is a mumbled, "In for a penny, in for a pound." Scant solace.

Employing many of the advances perfected in the social sciences, entrepreneurs now know how to pack and then re-pack the latest and greatest electronic gadgetry onto vessels of all sizes without fear of glutting the market or of swamping boats. The number of pockets they can drain thereby is the ultimate measure of their success. That, in turn, is said to be very good for the economy! Thus, if possible, everyone seems to go away happy.

As any true financier will tell you, it is not enough to dominate a particular market. Real accomplishment demands that the size of the sales domain be ever increasing; otherwise what you achieve is but a drop in the bucket. Fortunately, the boating world provided a remedy for that eventuality even before most business people recognized the principle.

Snobbish though it may sound, but apropos of the above, I have always held that the innovations most costly to the recreational boater were the steering wheel and the key starter. Foregoing the full argument on this topic, suffice it to say that those devices, when included on small vessels, inevitably have had the effect of transforming a lesser watercraft into something that too closely resembled an automobile. And, because driving a motor vehicle is a common part of modern life – up on the dry land – everyone just assumes that the skills automatically transfer. "See, Ma? No Sweat. All ya gotta do is turn the key and steer. There ain't no magic to this boating stuff." As pertains to the subject under consideration, put a key and a steering wheel on a beach ball and in all likelihood you can document an otherwise inexplicable drop in the price of certain electronic equipment while noting what to the uninitiated might appear to be an equally puzzling rise in seashore fatalities!

Somehow, the mere acts of raising the sails, winching the sheets, grasping the tiller, even wrestling an outboard's handle or pulling its starter rope, tended to keep the mariners of bygone days in the proper frame of mind. While not mandated by anything but common sense, boaters in those days approached the water with awe and with a feeling of insignificance, even inadequacy. That such high regard was beneficial might be reflected by the fact that most political entities in North America have been forced to institute mandatory boater training and licensing to try to reduce the number of accidents we suffer each year on the water.

Historically, the arts pertaining to the tasks of getting from here to there in a watercraft were divided into two distinct categories: navigation and piloting. Navigation mainly pertained to that which was done to keep track of one's whereabouts when out of sight of land. Piloting mostly concerned itself with getting a sailor from hither to yon when in sight of land. The focus of navigation is on the question of 'where the heck are we' when there are no road signs or land marks to reference, while piloting concentrates on the, 'I think it's just around that bend,' and 'Look out for that rock!' parts of any voyage. The former necessitates putting little pencil marks on large sheets of empty paper (representing a boat's position on large, vacant oceans), while the latter demands that a spider web of straight lines be made all over the blue portions of nautical charts (which usually are those parts not representing dry land or hard things that can be dangerous to boats).

HOW DID WE GET HERE?

For as long as I can remember hoards of ordinary people have gone down to the water, twisted their starter keys and turned their steering wheels without much thought or further ado. Many of them even came back after doing so. Disdaining the pack, however, I locked my jaws around the past like a bulldog, studied the sea carefully, trained and took classes, read books and especially, learned from old salts. With unwavering determination I sought brotherhood with all those who rightly paid their dues to old King Neptune. Proudly I found shelter from the *hoi polloi* in my yellowing charts, my dividers, parallel rules, course plotters and the like; the world I lived in was founded on traditions that are wholly unknown to the denizens of the ski-boat and jet ski community.

A long and abiding love (and fear) of the sea made the rolling blue a special place for me. And while there was nothing I could do to keep those who were functionally illiterate in the sailor's arts from taking to the waves, I drew much solace from the knowledge that they barely could tell the difference between the pointy and the blunt ends of a boat! It somehow pleased me to think that they had only the faintest of notions – if notions they had at all -- of what a bark, a schooner, a picnic boat or a scow actually was, and I reveled in talking knot logs, azimuths and set and drift! My skills and preferences set me apart and I liked that.

Although somewhat painful to admit, many has been the time when I have smugly cruised by a boat left high and dry on a ledge by a skipper who did not even own a chart. (Naturally, I stopped to render the obligatory assistance tradition and sometimes the law demands. Yet I never expended a wit of true sympathy on any of those lost souls.) Twice, I even stood by idly – actually I was sitting both times – and said nary a word as two different "just start 'em and steer 'em" skippers drove their vessels – ones that I happened to be riding on at the time – straight up on the ground! In each instance I knew where we were. I knew where we were going. I knew what was going to happen when we got there. I knew that the men at their respective helms did not know what awaited them, but most of all I knew that both of these troglodytes had a history of not listening to anyone about anything having to do with piloting. Equally, I figured that if they had not taken the time to educate themselves, then they would have to suffer the consequences. There are no tuition discounts at the school of hard knocks.

And then my little world collapsed. It happened on that sad day when every boater in North America bought a trainload of exotic electronic gear and became instant experts. No kidding, they did! Worse yet, at exactly the same minute, of the very same hour of that dark, dark day, etc., etc., in unison, they switched on their electronic loot, threw their paper charts overboard and thumbed their noses at all of the "Old School" graduates.

This did not mean that "we" were wrong. There would be plenty of instances when these-latter-day "salts" did silly things. Who knows, for instance, how many times they pressed the "Go To" command on their shiny new GPSs only to learn the hard way that their high-priced devices could care less about the two peninsulas, three islands and four municipal docks that physically separated them from that cute little secluded bay they had heard so much about. Likewise, stories abounded of the newly minted yachters who had run amok because they thought that the press and forget onboard "Auto Pilot" was synonymous with an experienced, human helmsman with local knowledge and good judgment. Delighted though "we" may have been, the sad truth remained that when all of this new gadgetry was operating properly and when it was employed within the limits described by the manufacturers, then the tried and true means of the past could not keep up.

Bested by smooth-faced technology geeks and beer-bellied fishing buddies, wizened old salts soon were reduced to defending their turf with 'what ifs.' "That chartplotter is mighty nice," they might purr, "but what if on Tuesday next, right-smack-dab in the middle of the upcoming blue moon, while you're crossing the mouth of an estuary and your iPod is piping old Ricky Nelson tunes through your waterproof, 16 speaker sound system – with sub-woofer -- hydrophobic rats get loose onboard this ship and chew up all the copper wire they can get their little teeth into and then rip out the rest, just for spite, and throw it overboard? What if that happens?" Naturally, while delivering this elegant challenge they slobber some and leer a little bit more, all the while savoring what will be, at best, a pyrrhic victory. Sadly, I have done it myself.

Despite the fact that *Minstrel's Song* is nicely outfitted – but certainly not over-outfitted – with the electronic marvels of the age, I mumble my 'what ifs,' mostly to myself, and tend to my course, my charts and my logs just as if none of the advances in modern technology had ever taken place. The saddest part of it is that I know I am a sick puppy. That is right! Sick puppy! Sick! Those with this affliction spend all of their time out on the water with heads bowed down, shoulders shrugged, pouring over plots, making little marks here, a notation there, taking headland bearings with handheld compasses, drawing straight lines all over everything and sweating bullets when trying to factor in the effects of wind, waves, tides and currents on their ever-changing positions. And that is on a five minute run around the bay outside the marina.

Do we do it because we enjoy missing every interesting sight and scene available through a whole dang trip? Do we do it out of a sense of obligation to our forebears? Do we do it because we do not know any better? I submit that for most of us, it is just too hard to let go. Creeping out into the light is difficult after decades of living in the shadows.

During fits of that kind of youthful exuberance that arrives with less frequency each day, I set my sights on catching up with the rest of the world. Such ambition usually is both spurred and reinforced by on-the-water experiences. It is not uncommon for my obsessive checking-and-crosschecking-of-paper-chart reveries to be shattered by a boatload of 30 somethings partying on by with hardly a concern about where they are or where they're going. From afar one gets the impression that "Auto Pilot," "GPS" and "Go To" have been left in charge of these boats and that all together these electronic wizards take good care of their reveling owners.

It was not very long ago that I had the opportunity to pilot a small airplane over some very large mountains. In preparation for that act I laid in a basic array of the navigational paraphernalia that would have sufficed to get Admiral Byrd to the Pole and back, no sweat. And, for the first time I also took along a portable GPS. As we flew into the pass that would lead us safely through the high peaks, an argument broke out on board. GPS said that I had to fly south – directly into a mountainside – to reach my checkpoint; I said no I did not. GPS insisted. I demurred, loudly. GPS continued. So annoyed over his insistent insubordination did I become that finally I put the mutineer on a starvation diet and pulled his power plug. Ha! As time wore on and the miles slipped by the fact that the terrain I was flying over was similar to, but not an exact match with that which appeared on my trusty paper chart discomforted me considerably. The gap in the mountains through which I was flying kept narrowing. Increasingly its walls crept in until the little valley I was following began to look more and more like a box canyon. With less and less "wiggle room" on either side of the plane or in front of it for that matter, things started to look really wrong. By dint of circumstance I finally was forced to climb up out of this chasm and, upon surmounting the adjacent ridgelines, I finally glimpsed familiar landmarks in the distance. There, miles to the south, but just where GPS said they should be was the track I had intended to fly. I am pretty sure that I heard GPS chuckling as I plugged him back in and banked the aircraft to reestablished his course.

With this airplane experience under his belt, it was on *Minstrel's*

Song's 467th outing, when, like a nervous parent letting his teenager drive for the first time, The Helmsman let "Auto Pilot" steer a little all by himself. We were on a long straight run in deep water and the electronic miscreant could not do much damage no matter what. With the single touch of a button, "Auto" seamlessly took control. The Helmsman studied the little ship's wake and was impressed. It was straight as an arrow. With a few more touches of the controls, the course could be altered easily by single degrees or by greater increments. And, "Auto" responded flawlessly to these changing commands. He did everything that was asked of him so well, in fact, that it was not long before he had the helm for every event except entering and leaving marina slips. To the amazement of The Pilot, this marvelous coxswain proved cool, calm, steady and quick and showed that he could hold a better course even in a strong current or in rough conditions than most human hands. So beaten into submission, The Captain was forced to accept this new crewmember's competence.

"GPS" and "Go To," were likewise tested. Over very short courses of less than a half a nautical mile The Navigator found that "GPS" and "Go To" were slow to pass timely commands on to "Auto Pilot" and because of that a nearby mark might be missed. Over longer distances, however, those problems faded to insignificance. The remaining shortcoming of all of them, however, was that they could not recognize danger even when it was right there on the chart. Thus, The Pilot was pleased to be able to continue to draw lines on his papers and to worry, but not as much, about where they were and where they were going.

* * * * * * * * * * *

In her zeal to escape the clutches of the raging ferries, *Minstrel's Song* now was nowhere near where she should have been on the chart. "See?" The Pilot said in order to draw The Crew's attention to the paper laid out on the table between them, "We should be on that pencil mark just over there. Instead, we're here, on this vacant blue spot."

"Does it matter a lot?" she asked, looking around at the miles of empty water that surrounded them.

"Well, duhh. We're here and we should be there!"

"I can see that, but does it really make much difference?" she asked again. "After all, it looks to me like your "there" a perfectly decent place to be. It seems to have several hundred feet of water below us, no rocks or obstructions anywhere in sight and we can get to where we want to go by just changing course a little."

"But that's not the point! We should be there! Everything else is based on being right there!"

Alas, even when all the facts support your case it is sometimes hard to turn a loss into a win. In this instance I knew that nothing was to be gained by reiterating the obvious truth that we were well off course the planned course. Instead I took up my instruments, amended the chart and hoped that bad things would not happen because of it. These exertions seemed to satisfy The Crew completely. The Pilot pouted.

Closely rounding the light at Portlock Point on Prevost Island, it was time to start thinking about what we needed to do to make our run up Trincomali Channel. Although we were supposed to be making the turn that would allow us to accomplish that at least a half a nautical mile further to the northeast – a proposition that would have taken us straight up the slot past the Ben Mohr Rock buoy and almost all the way to Gabriola Island – the angles now had to be recalculated to compensate for where we actually were. By steering a little north of northwest we could make for the Ben Mohr Rock buoy directly. There we could turn westward and rejoin the sacred pencil line. And, although that event mattered not to "Auto Pilot" or to The First Mate, the thought did give The Pilot great comfort.

There was but one flaw in this strategy. We had been churning our way up to Trincomali Channel at 9 knots – a little faster than our most economical cruising rate of 8.5 – so that we would arrive at Gabriola Passage at slack water. Although I had calculated that we would be fighting a current for most of the way, literally swimming upstream, we were being pushed backwards faster than I anticipated. Worried that we would miss our appointment with destiny, we needed to shave some minutes off the trip. By leaving the Ben Mohr Rock buoy to the east of the vessel instead of the west as anticipated – passing it on the starboard side of the boat instead of on the port side –we could shorten our route enough to get us back on schedule. Moreover, this amendment had the virtue of expeditiously returning the boat to The Pilot's pencil line.

Disturbed minds often manage to weave great woes completely out of whole cloth. Equally, they rarely provide good solutions for simple problems. According to all information at hand, Ben Mohr Rock constituted a mere high point on the ocean floor. On average, even at low tide, it remains covered by 4 metres (13.12 feet) of water. It is marked as a danger area by a buoy because seagoing, deep draft freighters ply this Channel and they easily might draw that much water or more. *Minstrel's Song,* on a good day, loaded to the gunwales might draw three feet (0.9144 meters). But let us not allow mere facts to cloud our thinking.

In terms of getting from here to there, the choice was clear: Take the longer way and pass the buoy on the port side and possibly miss the start of the slack tide at Gabriola Passage or save time, cut the corner and pass the light to starboard. Well, duh…starboard it must be. "Auto Pilot, come to course XYZ if you will," I intoned in my best captain's voice. Well pleased, I leaned against the day berth behind the wheel and savored the joys of command. Then I glanced at the chart. "Wait one stinking minute!" I thought, stifling the urge to scream, "Belay that order, Auto!" For there on the parchment, in plain black and blue markings for anyone who ever bothered to read a chart was the 'Rock'…dead ahead…on our new track. And the buoy, well, it was not too clear where the buoy was relative to the Gibraltar of the undersea world that it was supposed to be guarding. It might have been placed a bit to the east of the high spot, or more to the south, or, perhaps even right on top of it. Who knew? Adding to the confusion, the chart had it positioned just over 'there,' while the chartplotter insisted that it was located over 'here.' And search the surface of the sea though we did, even the biggest boulder imaginable, when covered by four metres of ocean, usually is not visible.

At this point any sane person would say, " Who cares?" and just move on. After all, under the worst conditions the blinkin' pebble still should have been safely separated from the bottom of our boat by roughly, ummmm...three meters (9.87 feet) of brine! But unlike Auto, GPS, Go To and all of the other hardy electronic souls onboard, I had been conditioned for eons to never, ever run over any rocky kind of thing that appears on a chart. "Who knows?" we had all been drilled. And, "Suppose it's been mis-measured or mis-marked?" they would always ask. And finally there was the inevitable, "What if?" Panic filled my every pore as I started to spin the wheel to starboard.

"Why are you heading back that way?" The X.O. inquired. "I thought we needed to make up some time."

"We do," I replied, "but I'm just not that sure about that rock. I mean, well, is the buoy on it or just near it? Is it east of it or south of it? I just can't tell and I don't want to take any chances," ya-da-ya-da-ya-da.

As often happens, trials of this nature seem to speed time incredibly. Even though we had been a mile (1.6 kilometres) or more from the general area when the events just described began to unfold, by the time I had mulled, debated, made false starts and considered everything fully, we were right on top of the offending object. Having done nothing – by half measures to be sure – I had squandered every opportunity to maneuver and instead managed to guide the vessel precisely through the waters I most wanted to avoid! And then, like a WWII sub skipper awaiting the deadly arrival of the killer depth charges that the destroyers circling overhead were dropping, with each turn of our prop I anticipated the agonizing crunch and crash that would signify that we had smashed into that infernal obstruction.

Slowly we crept beyond the hazard and as the seconds ticked by normalcy returned. Soon we were reunited with my beloved pencil line. Turning slightly to a west by northwest heading, Auto was given instructions that would take us directly t up Trincomali Channel. From this point on, excepting for a minor adjustment near Pylades Island at the southeast end of Pylades Channel, it was pretty much a straight shot to the entrance of Gabriola Passage. The Pilot's task now was limited to keeping a sharp lookout for other boats and for unexpected dangers – especially the semi-famous floating logs of the Pacific Northwet – and worrying about whether that dim spot on the horizon actually was the anticipated Governor Rock buoy or just a small boat way out in the distance. With such good order restored, and with the ship running on track toward the next next navigational, and eating lunch became a priority.

As The Mess Steward served up chow and we sat munching in the warm sun that flooded in through windows of the pilothouse, we commenced a pleasant examination of our surroundings. The sky was a deep blue, accentuated by puffs of grey-white clouds that somehow underscored the brilliance of the day. It dominated both the land and the sea under it, transforming water that frequently has a greenish tint into a darker blue that blended perfectly whenever and wherever sky and horizon met. Concomitantly, the bright sun, the sparkling sea and the radiant heavens above, caused the greens, browns, greys and blacks of the islands, their trees, their rocky shores, even their cliffs and graveled beaches to pop out of their elements with a clarity and a beauty not often seen.

Whether true or not, the unfolding vistas that continually moved past the windows conspired to convince us that we were far from civilization. While logic told us that we were hardly beyond hailing distance of the charming city of Victoria, B.C. – a mere 35 miles (56 kilometres) or so distant – and still cruising within that which is referred to as "greater Victoria" and its 330,000 plus people (no conversion required here, thankfully), it did not feel that way. Even the cabins and houses that were visible on shore left the impression of being remote outposts. My Messmate and I dined, and marveled as we did so. This was what cruising was all about.

One of the oddities of life in the Pacific Northwest is the length of its boating season. With relatively small air temperature fluctuations from winter to summer – the difference of, say, 20-25 degrees Fahrenheit, at most – and with minimal water temperature changes, one might guess that life on the sea hereabouts only slowed during the darker months. But, if that were your guess, you would be wrong. The prime cruising season in these climes extends from June through August, with late May and early September providing most of what little shoulder season there is here. Before and after that, only a 'brave few' sortie from their marinas.

Out as we were now on a Friday in early-May, there was surprisingly little activity on the briny deep. Every now and then we caught the white flash of a sail raised far in the distance; on a few occasions we overtook sailboats that were motoring along. (This latter group tends to move even slower than the usual 8.5 knots made by *Minstrel's Song.)* Beyond that, we had Trincomali Channel to ourselves. Or did we?

Too often we forget that we are never alone. We somehow think that not seeing the telltale signs of humankind means that we are isolated. Certainly around the globe we can find plenty of places devoid of human beings – the proverbial desert island comes immediately to mind – but no matter how far we travel or how careful our search, the truth remains that we have always around us as much as anyone can ever have, even in the densest urban city at rush hour. Whether its rocks, bushes, grass, mountains, sand, trees, untamed beasts of one sort or another or people and concrete, our beings always are in close proximity to an infinite numbers of other <u>things</u>. The difference seems to be in preference only. (My mother, for instance, was terrified by the thought of living, as we did, in the wilds of the Rocky Mountains where grizzly bears roamed freely. She perceived no special threat, however, from the crime-haunted city that had been her life-long home. It seems, as always, that "One man's banquet…"). As it pertained to the complement of *Minstrel's Song,* wild and inanimate things were those that were much preferred.

Moving northwestward toward our day's destination, we had to traverse the western extreme of Porlier Pass. A somewhat nasty little strip of water separating Valdez and Galliano Islands, it is one of the several places in this vicinity where the entire ocean tries to fill or alternately empty these Gulf Island channels as the tides come and go. With currents that race back and forth through it at high speeds, it can create turbulence significant enough to ruin a small boat's entire day.

Against this backdrop, and in predictable fashion, The Pilot was all eyes, ears and charts as the boat approached it.

Both The Captain and The Crew casually watched a single small cruiser that had been running behind them, closer in toward Galliano Island, turn from Trincomali Channel and head east out through the Pass and into the Strait of Georgia. We did not envy him the transit, but maybe he knew something about it that we did not. Mentally we wished him a safe voyage and then immediately re-focused our attention on the handful of houses that appeared to have sprung directly from the rocks that lined both sides of Porlier. As if in a dream we wondered what it might be like to live in any one of them, what pleasures or concerns would come from being in them in foul and fair weather, winter and summer, and even what kinds of people preferred them? We also looked for the fixed lights and beacons that were there to guide mariners safely through the narrows. (The Pilot always likes to confirm his location via the presence of such things.) And, we scrutinized the writhing, surging, tumultuous seas that were locked at this moment between the extremes of Galliano and Valdez Islands. This living body of agonizing water heaved itself into visible contortions less than a half a mile from where we floated as if on a duck pond.

Amidst the gurgling cauldron I spied a standing wave.[3] As I was about to turn from the sight, being glad that we did not have to challenge that force of nature, something odd caught my eye. Before I could do anything else, the words, "Whale, ho!" sprang from my lips and with outstretched arm I excitedly guided the eyes of The First Mate to the find. What became immediately apparent was that the 'standing wave' I had seen was actually a small pod of killer whales making the trip through Porlier Pass from east to west. At a distance, their undulating backs created the impression of fluid motion and their black dorsal fins were lost against the dark water. The white of their sides and bellies,

---

[3] *These freaks of nature occur for a number of different reasons. Usually they are created when a large amount of fast flowing water is squeezed through a narrow neck or over a shallow bottom. These cuties can build to several feet or more in height and can rob a small boat of the ability to control its movements or, in the extreme, can capsize it.*

when visible, generated the illusion of breaking surf. With eyes glued to them we followed their movements for a minute or more and then, as quickly as they appeared, they were gone.

As mentioned earlier, things of interest are around us all of the time; usually we cannot or just do not bother to look for them. So this day was different. This day was special. This day brought a more unusual part of Nature's creation into our lives and The Exec and I beamed at each other because of it. Somehow, being able to take the time to look, and to take the time to reflect on our place in this universe was an experience that drew us closer to each other. We never are truly alone, are we?

The farther north we went, the prettier the scenery. There was no dearth of the telltale signs of human presence on the islands we passed, but there also was an amazing lack of human activity. This suggested that we were moving farther from civilization with each turn of our prop and that added to our pleasure.

Before we knew it, however, our next hurdle was upon us. To reach Silva Bay, our day's destination, we had to negotiate Gabriola Passage. This winding, narrow, watery thoroughfare divides Gabriola Island to the north from Valdes Island to the south. It also provides the small boater with access to the Strait of Georgia. But here too, just as occurs at the other passes in the Gulf Islands, all of the water from the Pacific Ocean tries to force its way into or out of the sheltered channels we had been cruising and because of that the small boater is advised to be cautious when moving through them.

To a large degree our day at sea revolved around the problem of getting through Gabriola Passage. While some people try to defy the periodic maelstroms that wrack this piece of water by depending on huge engines and great speed – with varying degrees of success – the more prudent amongst us wait for "slack tide" to make the attempt. Slack tide comes as the earth's rotation and the conjunctive lunar cycles cause the sea to either stop rising or to stop falling. At the exact moment that each of those conditions occurs, a state of stasis is achieved. This is followed by an ever-quickening reversal of the direction of the tidal flow. It does not take a brain surgeon to recognize that the best time to slip through one of these narrow openings is when nothing is going on. Thus, our morning's departure time, our track north and our speed all were geared toward putting *Minstrel's Song* at or close to the west end of this pass when that happy instant arrived.

We live in a delusional world. Few of us recognize that simple truth, but that does not change the reality of the matter one wit. Remember when everyone thought the world was flat? Ridiculous! Right? How about that joyous time when the sun revolved around the earth? Do you believe that anyone have fallen for that one? Or, have you heard of those golden days when the best cure for any serious disease was a "bleeding"? Ancient examples, you say? Well, the other day I read that the pre-historic creature that, for over a century, we had deemed the world's oldest bird – a fowl that according to some people may be 150 millions years of age – actually was not one of our feathered friends at all. It turns out that in our infinite, new-found wisdom we now know for sure that said beast belonged to some other group of creatures completely. Oops. Our bad!

Other examples? For decades we agreed with Smokey the Bear that forest fires had to be prevented. After massive amounts of research, however, we are finding that we have done great harm to our forests in pursuit of that noble end.

More? Sixty years ago we took it as absolute truth – purveyed by no less than the experts at the U.S. Park Service itself – that General George Armstrong Custer was the last soldier standing in the fight against the Sioux at the Battle of the Little Big Horn. The best historians of that day said that he died in the center of the defensive ring formed by his dismounted cavalry; based on modern science and the overwhelming evidence, it is clear today that Custer died in a running gun battle, probably while still on horseback, that extended over a distance of a mile or two!

Still more? Around the time that the first Sputnik went into space we were pretty certain that the smallest unit of matter was the atom. This interesting construct was imagined to resemble a ball (nucleus) surrounded by satellites (electrons) fixed in immutable concentric orbits. Ouch!

Think bigger now. Our whole world, our whole galaxy, even our whole universe is in a state of decay. How so? Well, we know, for instance, that a few billion years hence our sun will 'die.' And we also know that at this very moment, right now, a poor, unsuspecting nebula – way out there in that great unknown that engulfs our puny, earthly home – is about to be sucked into a giant black hole never to see the light of day again. Now that is decay on a galactic scale!

At a more mundane level, consider the grass clippings in your compost pile out back. With each tick of the clock that green-black putrid mass you have built all summer is transforming itself from blades of living tissue into...plain old, inorganic, dirt. And, by the way, the mountains are losing a little more of their stature even as we speak!

Yet out of the middle of all of this gloom and doom evidence that the world is going to end soon – perhaps in as little as a couple of billion years! – along comes brother Charles Darwin. This 19th Century gentleman has convinced us that the evolutionary process compels things to go from the simple to the complex and from the lower to the higher. Amazing! This line of thought, however, no matter how pure or liberating, puts us in a hard place. We wind up believing that everything that we can know immutably moves toward decay and extinction, while at the same time holding that everything around us is growing better and improving. Hmmmm... Fortunately, most of us, most of the time, are not bothered by these contradictions; rather, we happily cling to both positions, simultaneously, and get on with life. If these competing paradigms have any real effect on us at all, it is a practical one. For instance, they allow us to explain why our kids' performances in school continue to go from bad to worse, but assert with absolute certainty that the next generation will live better lives than we do! Comforting, isn't it?

The point of this is that we are sure that almost everything worth knowing is known now, even in the face of discoveries that prove that what we thought we knew just yesterday was not known to us at all. When compounded by the fact that our entire existence is organized around these various competing and contradictory theories, none of us would be able to get out of bed in the morning if we spent much more than a split second trying to analyze our true condition. To survive this morass we are forced to act as if everything were absolutely, unquestionably understood, from beginning to end, completely. That defense mechanism works pretty well as long as we do not succumb, simultaneously, to the notion that there is much yet to be learned about almost everything. Somehow, we love to imagine that the age of confusion, ignorance and dark curtains parting slowly belongs to other, much less fortunate people.

As asserted, our misplaced convictions seem to make little difference in the way that each and every one of us lives his life on any given day. We hang onto what we "know" and function accordingly. And most of the time it does not make any difference at all to us whether the atom, the electron, the hadron or the quark is the fundamental constituent of matter. What is important is that the grocery store is still around the corner and it continues to stock our favorite cereals, and that water still flows out of the tap when we turn on the shower in the morning!

There are times, however, when precision and certainty do make a difference. In those instances we do not wish to settle for theories; we want absolutes. Sadly, those things are harder to come by than most people think! For example, despite the fact that we can put men on the moon or gently land robotic "rovers" on the surface of Mars – my apologies to conspiracy theorists everywhere – it seems that we are unable to predict when slack tide will occur at any given point on the face of the earth. Granted, most of the time, for most of the world, this is an indifferent consideration. But when you are about to risk life and limb and an expensive boat by running Gabriola Passage, or a similar body of tortured water, it takes on a degree of practical, personal importance.

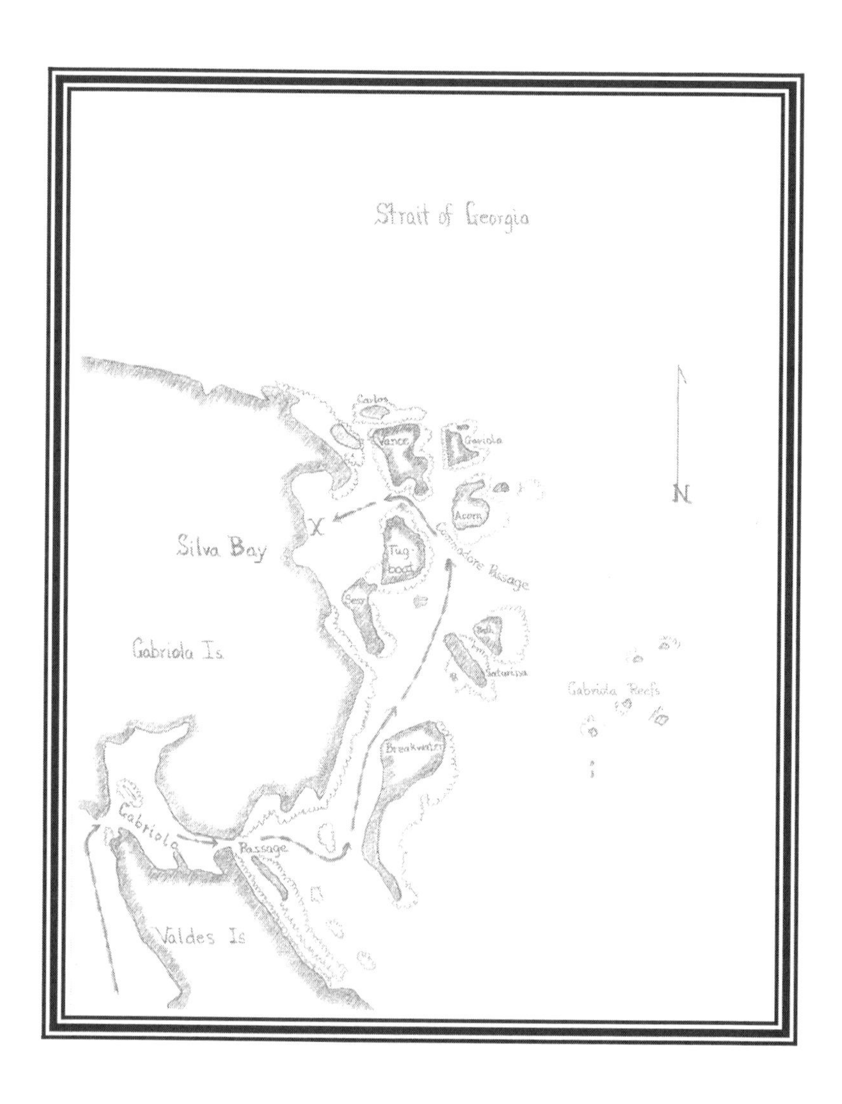
Strait of Georgia
Carlos
Vance
Gaviola
Acorn
N
X
Silva Bay
Tug boat
Commodore Passage
Gabriola Is
Gabriola Reefs
Breakwater
Gabriola
Passage
Valdes Is

As any good Boy Scout would have done, The Pilot prepared diligently for the voyage now underway. His planning included researching tidal activities so as to be able to transit tricky waters in relative security. Imagine his chagrin, however, when he consulted three different authorities on the subject – the U.S. Government, the Canadian Government and a private specialist – only to find that each of them had their own ideas about when slack tide would arrive at Gabriola Passage. In one instance, the proffered "estimate" – always shown with an asterisk and the disclaimer, "estimate" – differed from the others by over an hour!

So now what to do? Apparently that which would seem to be pretty basic (e.g. predicting the tides), is so fraught with variables and capricious events that even our leading scientists, armed as they are with thousands of years of data, with the reigning laws of physics well described and with access to supercomputers to collate and process it all, can only come close, kind of, to what actually will transpire. Without going into discussions of wobbly axes, elliptical orbits, asymmetry, gravitational anomalies, etc., etc., the bottom line is that the glorious moment when absolute peace reigns over the face of the waters of Gabriola Passage, on any given day, is anyone's guess. It seems that close now counts in horseshoes, hand grenades and tidal predictions! But, where does that leave yours truly, Joe Boater? As with most other things in life, he simply has to choose and hope.

The Pilot ultimately decided that since his ship would be plying Canadian waters, he should follow Canadian guesses. (That seemed, at the very least, to be the polite thing to do.) This preference had no scientific basis, but it did seem reasonable to think that the folks who owned this piece of real estate might know more about the things pertaining to it than those who did not. The problem that that particular selection presented, however, was that the conjecture formulated by the denizens of the northern portion of the Western Hemisphere was the one that differed most from the other two.[4]

---

[4] *After the fact, I stumbled across intelligence that shed considerable*

To the extent she could be thus forearmed and forewarned, the good ship *Minstrel's Song* gained the entrance to Gabriola Passage about a half an hour before the predicted event. A short time earlier, while we were still steaming north, we had taken note of a sailboat of considerable size that was lingering near the head of the channel. When we were a mile or so distant from her, this gallant lady stopped turning slow circles and purposefully steamed east into the Passage, disappearing behind the headland formed by Valdes Island. She clearly was going through the waterway despite the fact that her movements were premature. "Possibly," The Pilot thought to himself, "she's using one of the 'other' tide and current tables." Hoping that her skipper knew what he was doing, but also taking comfort in the fact that even if he did not his boat drew a lot more water and had a lot less engine power than did we, the decision to follow her was an easy one to make.[5]

In congruence with our experience at Bedwell Harbour, Gabriola Passage was nothing like we anticipated. Sure, The Pilot had poured over the charts. He also had read all of the written descriptions he could find and even had spent countless hours studying the overhead photos of the beast. But when the rubber met the road, he learned that all of those resources were about as useful as those titillating signboards nailed to posts at crossroad in rural villages that provide the confused traveler with the distance and direction to any number of the world's great cities. In short, none of them truly prepared him for the real thing.

---

light on the apparent discrepancy: Unlike the other entities, the Canadian Hydrographic Service of Fisheries and Oceans Canada does not adjust its forecasts to take into account time changes due to Daylight Savings! This tid-bit was buried so far down in the fine print of the Canadian Tide and Current Tables, Vol. 5 that I had to use a shovel to dig it out! My ego, however, was assuaged by the fact that none of my serious, seasoned, seafaring cohorts, even those with collective centuries of boating experience in the Pacific Northwest, knew about this either.

[5] *Ironically, not being aware then of the hour difference that our Canadian tables reflected, it turns out we both sortied nearly an hour late. Upon learning of our error, we took considerable solace from the fact that our leader, flying a Canadian pennant, was equally misinformed. When on the water, you take your little victories when and where you can!*

Size seems to be the biggest surprise we get at each new locale. I am not sure what we expected to see when we steered into Gabriola Passage, but what we got was not it at all. The opening that forms the western mouth of the watercourse lies between Gabriola and Valdes Islands. It is roughly 300 yards wide. Moving east beyond it, the land recedes on both sides to create small bays that flank the transit route to the north and to the south. The cove on the Gabriola side is larger than the one snuggling into Valdes and, unexpectedly, looked to have a mooring area, a marina and perhaps some private docks secreted within its depths. Thus, rather than the desolate, narrow chute we imagined that would have torrents of foaming water churning through it, we beheld a placid, somewhat open haven that appeared to be reasonably inviting and often used.

It may not shock the reader to learn that The Skipper started sweating bullets in anticipation of this moment about a week before the actual event. He is not terribly fond of the unknown and he especially abhors it when it comes in conjunction with things that can hurt him, The Crew and the vessel. Still, for the sake of The Executive Officer, he dons his best, seagoing happy-face and pretends to have not a care in the world. Wise beyond her years, The X.O. is not buying any of it.

Under these conditions the division of labor onboard is that I steer, run the engine and worry a lot about everything while she checks the charts and looks for anything around us that might be dangerous. This arrangement is an extension of that which we maintain when driving our car in unexplored areas. Having this second set of eyes focusing on the less mechanical aspects of the bigger picture allows me to respond instantly to her, "Oh, my God we're all going to die" moments! While not weighted down by the same level of responsibility, she expends, nonetheless, as much energy in pursuit of her duties as do I.

Gliding slowly through the water, *Minstrel's* Song easily transits the narrow west entrance of the Passage. Once beyond the extended points of land that serve to constrict that end of the waterway, we feast our eyes on the bright, sun drenched bays to left and right, note the plethora of boats stacked up just off the shores of Gabriola Island and look at each other as if to say: "Is that all there is?" But instead of collapsing with relief, we cloak our receding apprehension in merry chatter about how pretty it is, what a boater friendly place it seems to be and how we must have managed to come through exactly at slack tide. Good job, Crew!

While still basking in the warm afterglow of complete success, it slowly begins to dawn on us that although we have entered the channel without a hitch, the second half of the equation concerns getting back out of it. That problem, because it has to be resolved without benefit of exit sign, begins to trouble us. Looking dead ahead of our fair little ship all that The Pilot can comprehend is solid ground. Recognizing his dilemma, The First Mate chimes in with "I think it's more to the right, over there!" Not having the leisure to tell her, once again, that it is starboard when you are onboard a boat, my eyes sweep in that direction, hoping all the while to see something encouraging. About 1,000 yards distant, I make out what might be a slight parting of the land. I say it might be a slight gap because it might just as easily have been the mouth of a stream, a small inlet or even a mirage. I, mean, you never know!

The single place that holds my attention most is a bit of a low spot that may or may not have water running through it. It has land on each side of it for sure, and there seems to be something firm and low-lying beyond it. But does a channel that a boat can use cut through it? I squint. I consider. Finally I pick up my binoculars and give it a hard look. Yes. There, sure enough, is a small opening. The question now is whether it is the opening that will lead us out of the east end of the Passage. Given the dearth of other choices, The Helmsman swings the bow toward the crack and hopes.

It is true that we could have turned small circles in the water to kill time and contemplate the situation. That, however, would have been the aquatic equivalent of having to stop and ask for directions. No captain, and certainly no man, was going to do that, so onward we pushed.

Even with our trusty craft crawling along at a speed akin to that of an elderly man taking a long walk, we covered the intervening distance in what felt like a heartbeat. The closer we came to the opening, the worse things looked. We had anticipated a narrow passageway when the course originally was charted, but the conduit we were looking at was so slender that it might rival one of those 'Compact Car Only' parking spaces that dents so many door panels in underground garages. "We're supposed to get this through that?" I asked rhetorically.

Always looking on the bright side of things, The Crew offered several thoughts that did not increase the size of the needle we were about to thread. She was right when she stated that the big sailboat already had passed that way. She was also right when she opined that the total distance from land to land was about 150 yards. The two things she failed to factor into the equation, however, were critical. First, that there now was water visibly swirling through this constricted passageway at who knew what speed. This had the potential of making the boat difficult to steer. And second, that the measure of any channel was not what could be seen at its surface, but what was lurking beneath it. Further, experience dictated that the angle of the slope of land leading down to the water usually continued at about the same rate under it. In most instances, a shallow slope produces shallow water for quite a distance out; conversely, a steep incline generally equates to deep water immediately. We were coming up on two very flat points of land.

Holding to the middle of the channel – on the logical, but frequently erroneous assumption that it was deepest there – we plowed ahead, two sets of eyes glued to the depth sounder. The sea barging through this narrow neck – recall that we were actually about an hour beyond slack tide and the current was beginning to build – pushed and pulled the bow one way and then the other, but it failed to fling the good ship up onto the rocks. The seconds passed like eternities until, breathing audible sighs of relief, we gained the calmer water where the islands pulled back to north and the south and the seas broadened once more. In celebration of this monumental event I bark, "Arrgggg! Ahoy there Cookie! Step below smartly and serve up an extra ration of grog for The Captain and for The Crew. We've dodged shipwreck and disaster again this day!"

In the dark months of winter The Captain and The Crew devised a general plan for getting to and from Princess Louisa Inlet in the time allotted. The outline of that scheme included departing Sequim Bay, working northward through the San Juan and Gulf Islands and then popping across the Strait of Georgia to a landfall on the west coast of the mainland, somewhere along B.C.'s Sunshine Coast (north of Vancouver, B.C. and inside the Malaspina Strait). The primary challenge regarding this part of the undertaking rested on where to stop prior to hopping across the open water (Strait of Georgia) to the mainland. The thriving town of Nanaimo, standing on the eastern shore of Vancouver Island, just at the top of the Gulf Islands' Dodd Narrows – a body of water more daunting, perhaps than Gabriola Passage – had a good reputation, excellent facilities and offered all of the comforts of home. Its location, however, was a little too far north for our purposes and we kept looking for alternatives. At the last minute the small, well-hidden Silva Bay on the coast of Gabriola Island came recommended by a friend. Having a decent array of the things we wanted (e.g., food supplies, fuel and shelter) this watery mecca also was advantageously situated for the voyage across the Strait. Thus, with Gabriola Passage behind us, the last chore of our travel day was to pick our way into this snug little harbor.

All of "the books" advised caution when getting from the east end of the Gabriola Passage into Silva Bay. Guarded by such invitingly named places as Thrasher Rock and the Gabriola Reefs, this fine little anchorage is actually a small bight tucked into the southeast extreme of Gabriola Island. It is formed and protected by a ring of small islands, which in turn, are shielded by a number of submerged reefs, rocks and other obstructions. While there are a few navigational markers along the way, using them to get safely into this hidden haven is not like following the signs on the freeway. Because the waters can turn shallow and rocky quickly and because tides and currents can be a concern too, in negotiating this neighborhood care needs to be exercised from start to finish.

Creeping cautiously toward Breakwater Island, while being mindful that one must resist the temptation to cut the corner over Rogers Reef, the "grog" Cookie delivered at The Captain's insistence now cools unmolested on the chart table. The seas they were traversing were fairly shallow and The Pilot's full attention was needed in order to keep the boat off of something hard and nasty. "Easy…Easy…Steady as she goes…What's our depth, Number One?" he murmurs. "Six feet, eh? I'd like another fathom, mark twain at the least," he breathes.

Bending around Breakwater Island, we spy the mark that warns of the reef just southwest of Commodore Passage. The boat makes for that, leaving it to port and then rounds north into the Passage itself. This channel is narrow, sports some underwater high points and is subject to the swirl of tide and current. All of "the books" say to be careful here, but they include the proviso that it is still the safest way into Silva Bay.

Sweating bullets, as always, The Pilot strains every sinew and nerve in his body to guide them all safely through these unfamiliar waters. As *Minstrel's Song* reaches that point in Commodore Passage – an invisible spot on the water, midway between Tugboat and Acorn Islands – a precise turn to port must be made. Properly executed, this movement will put the boat on a line to split the waters that separate Vance and Tugboat Islands and thereby set the craft on final approach for the inner harbor. Concurrently reading chart, chartplotter, radar track, depth sounder and the water directly in front of the boat consumes most of The Skipper's energies. Slowly it dawns on him that The First Mate requires something. She seems to be saying, "What do they want?"

"Whadda who want?" I snap, hoping to achieve in one sentence that happy medium between an ugly 'leave me alone' and 'of course I'm listening, dear' reply that ultimately will allow me to continue focusing on the tasks at hand without actually responding.

"Those guys!" she says, pointing out the starboard door insistently! "Those guys right there!"

Engrossed in the varied jobs described above, I imagine first that she's referring to someone on shore and could care less about what they want. But The X.O.'s persistence causes me to glace quickly through the starboard door and to catch some movement out there. This then evokes the immediate – and retrospectively idiotic thought that "Someone is *running* alongside the boat!" (I did say that it was idiotic, didn't I?) By now perplexed, I turn more squarely to the right. There, not 10 feet away, sit two men in a rubber boat who are clad in some kind of semi-military garb (i.e. dark canvas shirts and trousers, web belts, black boots, etc.). Genius that I continue to be, I conclude instantly that they are not just sitting there, but they are motoring along side us. Moreover, given the short space between their boat and ours and the intensity of their stares, I figure they want something in particular. Duh!

In that infinitely miniscule part of my brain consigned to handling such sudden developments, an internal disagreement arises. One sub department of my mind says, "Are these guys pirates or what? Where did they come from? Why are they here? Are they dangerous? And, why are they wearing leather boots in a rubber boat?" while another part insists, "They look official. We had better stop."

Now, I am right is the middle of some work I consider fairly important: To wit, keeping us off of the rocks and getting us into the harbor in one piece. And, although I am reasonably certain that I know where I am, I am not so sure about where all of the dangers described in "the books" are living at this precise moment. Moreover, although the written word has promised me that there is safe water to float through all the way into Silva Bay, at this juncture Vance and Tugboat Islands are looking awfully close to each other and the bottom is shoaling up on us again. Thus, the reader must believe that at that moment, the mini-debate raging in my mind notwithstanding, attending to the druthers of our new-found friends was not very high on my "gotta do" list.

With her usual mental clarity, The Crew finally penetrates my miasma by saying, "I think they want to know if we have a Canadian entry number posted."

"Entry number? Entry number?" Frantically sorting through a plethora of unfiled mental trivia, I vaguely recall that yesterday, as we crossed into Canada, we received via cell phone an official clearance number of some sort. The mental fog that instantaneously enshrouds the thousand-and-one inconsequential details of any given day slowly begins to lift. Out of the greyness comes the faint recollection that we were instructed to post on the boat, where it would be visible from the outside, the number we had received. More clearly still, I recall now that in spite of having brought with us enough "stuff" to sink a proverbial battleship, we spent an inordinate amount of time the day before trying to find something onboard that would hold a piece of paper in place in our window. After much scrounging, a tiny scrap of an old, sticky label that had been languishing for months in the trashcan was pressed into service and by it we hung our official I.D. in the glass at the top of the starboard door. Apparently it was this that these keepers of 'truth, justice and the (North) American way' sought.

With as much attention as I dared devote to them, I politely pointed up to the roughly torn piece of lined yellow paper dangling from the door and hoped that that would suffice. With looks that said, "Oh, that's where it is!" our erstwhile guardians saluted and disappeared from view as quickly and unobtrusively as when they had arrived. 'Who were those masked men, Kemosahbee?' I was tempted to ask as they motored away.

Commodore Passage amounts to a small channel running northwest/southeast between five islands of very limited extent. The largest of these dots is about 30 acres (12+ hectares) in size. The Passage is roughly 1000 yards long, and it varies in width from 150 to 300 yards. [Herein and hereafter I will refrain from the dual listing of English and metric measurements. My brain hurts from trying to make the conversions!] "The books" on the subject underscore the need for caution when transiting this area because of the rocks and ledges that lurk just under the surface of the water. These helpful tomes spice things nicely by including, as always, statements to the effect that there may be dangers in the area that have yet to be pinpointed. Worse, they advise that not every known threat is included on the charts. In short, if you hit something that you have no way of seeing and no way of knowing about ahead of time, it is your fault anyway. We told you so!

Tugboat Island lies just south of Vance Island. One has to sail in an arc between the two when entering Silva Bay from the east as we are.

Midway along the 100-yard trek through the gap between them a white marker light sits atop a 10-foot tall structure that rises up out of the water. It is located a short distance off of Tugboat Island, but is even closer to Vance. Its purpose is to tell the prudent mariner, 'Don't cut this corner short!' And all of "the books" reiterate that special caution by saying that the only choices to be made in these confined waters are to stay north of the light or to run up on a ledge. The problem is that from 200 yards away the opening between the mark and Vance Island looks so slight that it is doubtful that a single scull, i.e. a sleek, competitive rowing boat, with shipped oars could slide through it. Contemplating the situation, The Pilot pulls the throttle back to an idle and nervously allows the vessel to edge forward slowly. With the marker coming up on the port bow, The X.O. intones, again, that the only safe channel into Silva Bay lies just north of the light. The Helmsman repeats, "Aye, north it is," but the sudden dryness of his mouth makes his words sound strangely muffled, as if filtered through a huge ball of cotton.

As they near the turning point, two things comfort The Captain and The Crew. First, the channel does seem to grow wider as they get closer to it and second, they see no wrecked hulks grinding on the adjacent rocks. Slowly *Minstrel's Song* slips past the light and with each unimpeded turn of her prop the confidence of the ship's complement rises. 'Piece of cake,' they want to yell!

Now, free to survey Silva Bay for the first time, we are startled by its size. In our experiences, things named "bays" are great bodies of water like Chesapeake, San Francisco, Tokyo, Biscay, etc. What spreads out before us suggests that mud puddles should be given titles too. Well, maybe that is a bit of an exaggeration, but that which we imagined would host several marinas, resorts, fuel docks, a restaurant, a grocery store, a liquor store, a yacht club, an air taxi service, a boat building school, a marine repair shop and something going by the name of "Silva Bay Kayak Adventures," did not cover nearly as much space as we expected. In fact, depending on how one measured it, the circular body of water we were staring at likely did not exceed in radius more than 275 yards. Making it seem smaller still was the great number of boats anchored willy-nilly all over the basin.

Having mastered the intricacies of Gabriola and Commodore Passages as well as having guided us safely into port, I now stand easy at the wheel. Prior study indicated that the marina where we planned to spend the night was dead ahead. With the jaunty air of a couple of old salts, we made directly for the quay and the safety of our slip. This last phase of our voyage was not as straightforward as one might imagine, however, since there were eight to ten boats of various descriptions swinging on the hook between it and us. Slowly we threaded our way through them.

The marina attendants -- Neil and his trusty dog Kona – apparently had spotted us as we came in, for they were standing at attention beside our berth, clearly ready to assist with our arrival. While the space in and around the dock was appropriately constricted – in keeping with the size of the Bay – I nonetheless was ready to wow the crowd with my boat handling skills by guiding our craft neatly into her slip. A quick burst of forward power followed by an equally short surge of reverse, both capped by exactly 1.38 seconds of push from the bow thruster and without banging or bumping anything we were stopped dead in the water, parallel to and six inches out from the finger pier. All that remained to underscore our competence was for The Crew to step ashore with the stern line in one hand and a shaken Martini in the other and not spill a drop of that precious liquid in the process. (This latter form of measurement is the standard for docking by which we judge all of our comings and goings.)

Secure in the knowledge that few seafarers could have brought their vessels to rest any better, and internally beaming like a Cheshire cat, I step casually out onto the our boat's foredeck and hand Neal the bow line. As he takes it, he says, "Bow thruster, eh? I guess that makes handling a boat this size real easy." Instantly I knew exactly what a deflated balloon experiences.

With almost 40 nautical miles of ocean behind us, our craft safely tied down, the engine and electronics switched off and the shore power plugged in, we were ready to survey carefully our surroundings. The altitude and perspective we gained after clambering up the steep ramp that led to the marina office gave us an unrestricted view of the

Bay. Although five distinct islands formed the harbor, the waterways separating each of them were so narrow or so contorted as to give the impression not of passageways out to the sea but of small arms or inlets that collided with dry ground. The net effect of this arrangement was to leave us not with the sense that we were standing on the shore of a briny harbor, but rather that we were looking out over a small lake.

The light from the afternoon sun drenched both land and sea with its soft, yellow rays. The fluffy white clouds that skipped across the azure sky, pushed by a gentle breeze, invited, even demanded, that those who beheld them relax, slow down, and enjoy. And though it is probable that many people within the confines of this microenvironment had to work through this afternoon, Nature's command would not allow that labor to turn to drudgery even for those performing it.

The circle of formative islands that created Silva Bay was draped in the varied, verdant greens of long-established fir and cedar forests. Gracefully arching ferns and low-lying shrubs filled every nook and cranny with their own special hues, helping to produce an array of soft brilliance that few artists' palates could ever rival. Punctuated by the deeper, darker shadows of their depths, these woodlands beckoned gently, asking only that the interloper tread softly and reverently on their red-brown, needled floors.

A straight line crisply running horizontally across endless outcroppings of rough brown rock separated sea from land. Neither purely rounded nor stratified, these hard reminders of the earth's attempts to claim dominion over the ocean reflected the never-ending war waged by the two opponents. Lighter in color further up their faces, these age-worn warriors are burdened by the ever-deepening shades of the semi-aquatic life that cling tightly to them in a vertical zone where the rush and rage of the advancing and retreating seas make their daily assaults on the seemingly impregnable redoubts.

Looking out over this vista, taking in man's works – the boats, the wharfs, the scattered cabins and structures – all the things that add their voices to the harmony that is Nature's, The Crew and I know for sure, through every fiber that is in us, why we go down to the sea in ships. What we do not know yet is the grandeur that awaits us still.

We had journeyed to this fine little harbor for two particular reasons: 1.) It was supposed to have a great grocery store and, 2.) It constituted the best departure point for crossing the Strait of Georgia. In preparing for our voyage we had discovered that one of the minor inconveniences relative to international travel between the two great North American neighbors was food. At first blush this would not appear to be much of a problem. After all, no matter which side of the border one calls home, there is a shared, truth: We eat food. They eat food. The corollary to that is that they eat what we like, and we eat what they like. So where is the problem?

As almost always seems to be the case in these situations, the rub comes when great bureaucracies manage to shoulder common sense aside. Whether protecting the opposing populations from the boundless, universally imagined, scourges resident only north or south of the border or whether to shore up commercial enterprises that might otherwise die peaceful, natural deaths, both governments stipulate what edibles can and cannot cross between them. Thus, the traveler may not provision as fully as he might wish to on one side of the line or the other and still remain within the confines of the law when the crossover is made.

This inconvenience would not be terribly onerous were it not for the indeterminate nature of the prohibitions. Indeterminate? How can a prohibition be anything less than dead-on specific? To prohibit something, by definition, is to bar some, one thing. And that cannot be indeterminate. Should the reader share this view of the globally accepted limits of language, he would be exactly right. Sadly, however, we must remind the more sheltered amongst us that here we are dealing not in clear thinking or even in basic linguistics, but in government logic. In that arcane realm the ordinary rules of rationality are held in abeyance.

In the case of the movement of goods back and forth between the U.S. and Canada, Canadian officials have very clear ideas about what they will allow into their country and what they will not. Fair enough! It is, after all, their country. Unfortunately, they have either read way too much Kafka, retain an adolescent attachment to treasure hunts or are wholly and totally oblivious to the ramifications of their actions. Whatever the reason, it is all but impossible to pre-determine what they will accept at any given instant. Call these authorities on the phone and the best advise they seem to be able to offer the law abiding sojourner is to study the list of banned items that they post on-line *each day*!

The quick-witted reader will take note of the last two words in the preceding sentence. For, the catalog (or catalogue if you are reading along in Canadian) apparently can change each and every diurnal without further ado or fanfare. Confirm what is legal on Monday, lay in your stores accordingly and by the time you cross the international border early Tuesday morning you may discover that overnight you have become a smuggler!

But wait, there's more! Should you be caught with a potato that was not purchased in Canada – do not ask me how anyone can determine the origin of a potato – not only would you then be a criminal subject to the full force and fury of the law, but – dig deep into the old memory bank here – you would lose your precious NEXUS rights and be forever bounced back into the cauldron of the unwashed and untrusted masses. Ouch.

Not being willing to put our new NEXUS cards on the line, before leaving the good old U.S. of A. we meekly stowed in our food lockers only those things that we were absolutely sure would not make the Top Ten Hit Parade of Things That Will Offend Some Government Official Somewhere! (We think it is better this way than the other way around.)

Having bid a fond farewell to our home country with just a few edibles that did not fall into the 'canned soup, 'ramen' or 'Chef Boyardee' category, accessing a grocery store within a fortnight or two became a priority. Anticipating significant grocery purchases at this stop, we even selected "our" marina because it was located closer to the building that housed the delicacies we sought than were the other available facilities. And, fearing a late Friday afternoon run on the local market, as soon as we were settled, Cookie and I grabbed some cloth bags and headed toward the building festooned with a large, descriptive sign that simply said "Store."

The targeted structure was but a couple of hundred yards away as the crow flies. The trip to it on dry land was the better part of a half a mile. But with nothing but time to kill we enjoyed the walk, the warm day, the new sights and each other's company. We were not ecstatic, however, about what greeted us upon arrival. The building was dark with no visible activity in or around it. Peering into the windows, hoping it was just closed for siesta or some other local event, we were greeted by the sight of a great, empty cavern. The walls contained no shelves, there were no checkout stands, in fact there was nothing inside except abject darkness! Before my racing mind could break the news to the rest of my body that collectively we all were going to starve to death, Cookie said, "Oh, well. No matter. I've got some stuff onboard we can have."

"Good old Cookie," I thought, "I'd walk a country mile for some of her stuff!" And taking her hand, we started back to the boat, wiser but just as happy.

We are not real big on sightseeing ashore during our boating adventures. Apparently many people approach these opportunities differently, however, since virtually all of "the books" that profess to guide the seaborne traveler spend an inordinate amount of time talking about the interesting things one can do up on dry land. But for us, our more narrow approach allows us to focus on the tasks we deem most critical on a decent journey of any consequence, like settling into the couch in the ship's saloon[6] with a good book or being lulled to sleep by the symphonic sounds of lapping water on a boat's hull! Besides, our enchantment with the Pacific Northwet stems not from an interest in what is visible from every village, hamlet and city on the continent, but rather from what cannot be seen from them! No. Our preference is for the briefest possible forays into the outposts of civilization – without schedule or demand. And those ventures, when necessitated, should be followed by an immediate return to the boat for serious reading, napping, snacking or a round of professional-level Spades.

---

[6] *Oddly, this non-traditional nautical term is pronounced like the word "salon."*

Glorious as this particular afternoon was, our intention beyond grocery shopping was to savor the immediate sights and sounds provided by the community surrounding Silva Bay – on the way to and from the store only -- and then to retire to our floating abode. The bright lights of greater Gabriola Island would have to remain unseen by us.

Meandering back toward our marina, we passed one of the local "resorts." Clean, tidy and well kept though it was, we decided that it more closely resembled a small, '60s-style motel – perhaps with a bit more lawn and a better water view – than it did a resort. But, given the diminutive size of Silva Bay and the age of the various establishments surrounding it, this slice of heaven was in complete congruence with local society.

In order to leave no (grocery) stone unturned, nor any pretty boat unviewed, we made a hard left turn into the resort driveway and then followed a public lane off of it down to a commercial building which was perched atop a ramp that led directly to a wharf that included a number of small boat slips. The aforementioned business space amounted to a nondescript wooden structure (commonly referred to as a "shack" in the American south) that was both well-weathered and assuredly a life-long stranger to the caresses of a paintbrush. Those things notwithstanding, the fading, notebook paper-sized, hand-scrawled sign on its door declared it to be the home of Silva Bay Kayak Adventures. Darkened, locked and showing little evidence of any kayaking activity – or even of any kayaks – we concluded that the "season" in Silva Bay had not yet arrived.

With the possibility of kayaking eliminated, we descended the incline toward the docks anxious to get a closer look at some of the wooden sailing boats that we had spied bobbing there earlier. With bright work shining everywhere, these jolly vessels could be nothing except the products of The Silva Bay Shipyard School, a living, working tribute to the older maritime arts. Styled as "Canada's only full-time, traditional wooden boat building school," we were certain that its location on Gabriola Island insured the kind of solitude that let its students concentrate solely on their work. Meandering past a forest of small, neatly hewed, wooden masts that were stepped lightly on equally golden-brown, sparkling hulls we opined that the work of these burgeoning craftsmen seemed to be first rate. We were glad to have been there and to have seen the fine little ships they fashioned.

Again wending our way back toward the marina, we strolled past a quaint Catholic Church. In keeping with everything else thereabouts, it was small, but inviting. We might not have paid much attention to it except for its "country chapel" appearance and because it seemed to have some kind of sculpture standing beside it. Untrained in architectural accomplishments though we are, we conjectured, at least, that the church had started life as something else, possibly a school. It was neat and white and was well suited to its environs. Off to one side of the building, nestled under some conifers, stood a sculpture that was quite interesting. Produced in a contemporary style – of 1990s vintage if memory serves – this piece depicted Christ on the Cross. It was about seven feet tall and was unique in that it appeared to have been carved from a single tree. It was modernistic to be sure, but it was striking for the character that it captured.

Turning at last toward "home," we checked in at the liquor store where we purchased some ice for our cooler. It turned out that the lady running that critical commercial hub was the wife of Neil, the marina attendant. Like everyone else we encountered in Silva Bay, she was friendly and accommodating. Also, she had under her control that which constitutes the candy equivalent of catnip for me: Necco Wafers. Knowing that opportunity knocks but once, we trundled back to the boat under the weight of a fortnight's supply of the New England Candy Company's finest.

Happily back onboard *Minstrel's Song*, the residents turned to two undone chores. Setting up their folding chairs in the open air of the cockpit, The Captain and The Executive Officer embark immediately on their long-neglected reading regimen. Given the advancing hour, however, the former concluded that the only way he could have a decent go at that and still have a chance to complete the other pressing task would be by combining the two. Thus, with a light breeze and the warm sun bathing him in soothing freshness, he settled into his cozy corner, opened his book and let his head drop onto his chest. So positioned he dove into the second job at hand: the afternoon nap. Success would have been his in mere seconds if the Bay had not come under attack at that precise instant.

Having just re-read the same sentence for the 14th time – a sure sign that an excellent catnap was in the offing – The Skipper's serenity was shattered by a raging, diving, roaring kind of airplane noise that rivaled that which must have preceded the assault on Pearl Harbor. "What the heck is that?" he asked nobody in particular. Spinning in his seat, while simultaneously trying to shake his slumbering mind back into semi-functional condition, he craned my neck in the direction of the sound. As he did so, a brightly painted aircraft shrieked overhead at an altitude that should have worried even the Bay's smaller sailboat owners. Pulling up just over the trees to the north, it banked hard right and then commenced a long, 180-degree turn that took it out of sight again. "That's one very lost crop duster!" he thought to himself.

The growl of its engine faded in the distance and then grew once again to a throaty rumble. Scanning the southern horizon so as to draw a bead on the varmint, it finally re-appeared, floats and all, coming in low over the trees, with every apparent intention of either making a landing on the Bay or completing a kamikaze attack on one of the yachts anchored out in it. And from where our heroes sat, it was not apparent which was most likely.

Slowly the scene unfolded. The plane came down the slot between Tugboat and Sear Islands, all but clipping the adjacent treetops with each wing tip. When finally it cleared the forest and was fully over the edge of the harbor, the pilot cut the engine, rapidly lost altitude and touched down on the water mid-bay. Had he missed his target by fifty feet in any direction he would have taken out half the fleet; as it was, the air jockey nonchalantly taxied up to the fuel dock – just 50 feet or so from *Minstrel's Song* slip – and tied up to it just like any other arriving boat. It was learned, later, that the uncovered end of the pier the flying boat occupied served as the air terminal for the scheduled flights that arrived and departed from Silva Bay each day. (So astounded by this intelligence was The Captain, that at the time he completely failed to inquire as to the whereabouts of the metal detectors, body scanners, security agents, etc. that are standard fare at all of our commercial airports these days!)

It turns out that our host, Neil, once had been a seaplane driver. As always happens when a couple of fliers meet, he was more than happy to regale me with tales of the perils and the joys of island hopping. More importantly, he sang the rightful praises of the small planes and the skilled aviators who added a lot of value to these isolated communities. In the process he did opine that in tourist season landing room in Silva Bay was at a premium, but he said too that the local air-jockeys were innovative and usually found a wet place on which to set down. Usually. With the eye of an aging aeronaut, I surveyed once more the forest of masts bobbing on the water in this, the off season, and at the treetops swaying all around in the breeze, and all I could think was that this definitely proved the truth of the old adage, 'Ignorance is bliss.' Were it not so, nary a passenger, ever, would board one of these little birds here!

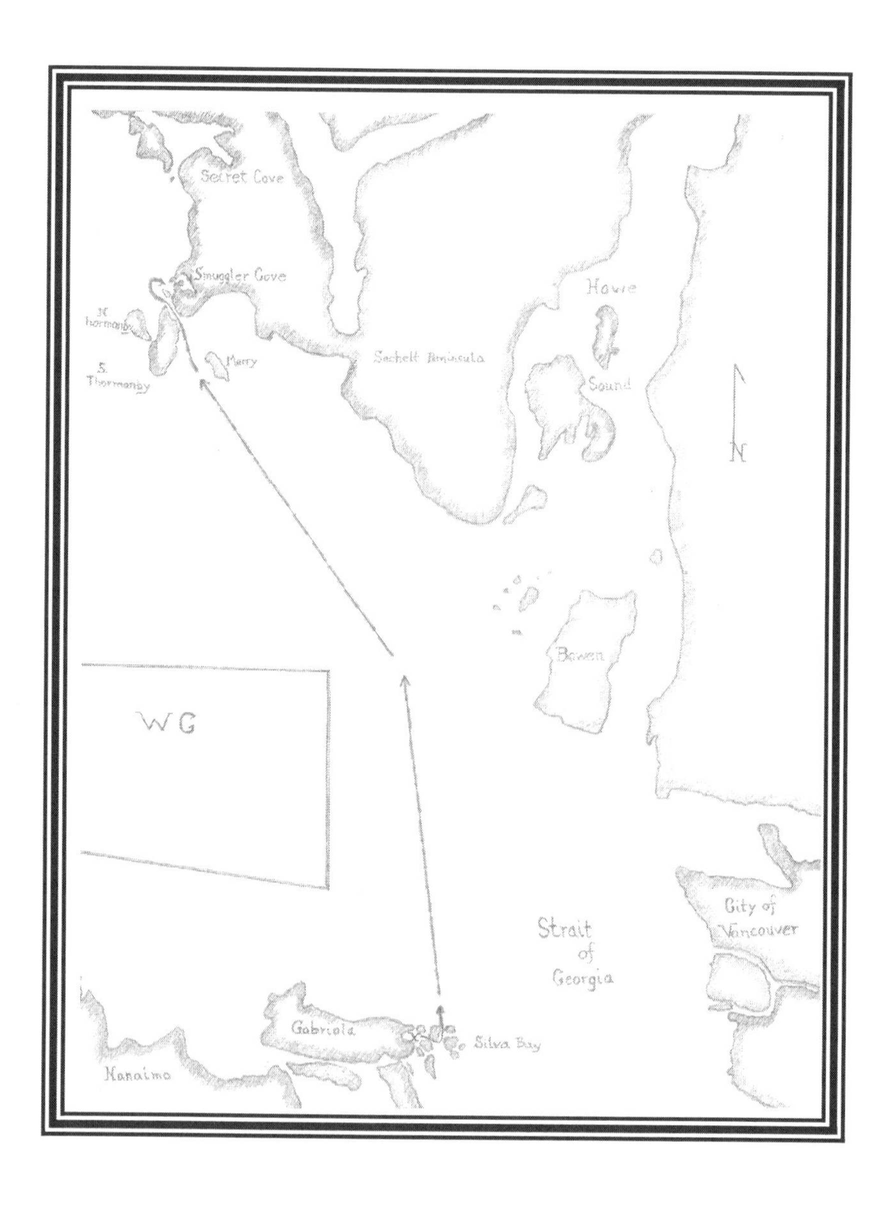
Secret Cove
Smuggler Cove
N
hormanby
S.
Thormanby
Merry
Sechelt Peninsula
Howe
Sound
N
Bowen
WG
Strait
of
Georgia
City of
Vancouver
Gabriola
Silva Bay
Nanaimo

DAY THREE

Silva Bay to Smuggler Cove
Or
"Don't Worry! The Book Says It Will Fit Through There

Under the blanket of low-hanging clouds that managed to turn the water beneath them into a flat, cold, steel grey, sheet, we threaded our way out of Silva Bay. Gone was the warm sun and blue skies of the day before. Gone, too, was the lovely snug harbor we had enjoyed. In its place was a dull, lifeless expanse of flat water surrounded by equally flat-green trees and muddy islands.

Before putting to sea, The Pilot once again had the opportunity to demonstrate his boat-handling prowess. A few moments before The Crew was ready to cast off the lines that held *Minstrel's Song* in her slip, a couple of larger boats came in and made fast to the fuel dock just behind her. Tied perpendicularly to the little ship's stern, they were less than a full boats' length distant from her. With little room for error, The Pilot worked his charge slowly backward and forward until his vessel was out of her berth and pointed toward the center of the Bay. Engaging the engine at all ahead slow, he centered the helm and left the confines of the marina without bump, thump or further ado. As he did so, it was difficult to resist the urge to yell back to Neil, "Did you see that? And I didn't use the bow thruster!"

The Skipper had spent the evening before poring over his charts, drawing course lines this way and that and listening intently to the weather reports. The Strait of Georgia is another one of the Great Northwet's many waterways that can take advantage of the unwary. Rarely wider than 20 miles and protected from the storms of the open ocean by Vancouver Island, this piece of brine suffers from a number of defects that are not readily discernable. Primary among these is the fact that the topographical features of the barrier island conspire to transform the breezes coming in off the Pacific into northwesterly blasts that roar straight down the slot that separates the island from mainland. This means that even in good weather, when the skies are blue and the zephyrs romp gently over Vancouver's hills and valleys, they may be churning violently down the 65-70 mile, northwest to southeast, extent of the Strait.

Based on a forecast that favored an early morning crossing, we slipped around Tug Boat Island and turned hard to port into Commodore Channel. Anxiously, all eyes were focused on what lay ahead, straining to see what the open water a few hundred yards distant would look like. The hot coffee Cookie brewed for our early departure tasted good and it gave us something to do with our hands as we picked our way carefully between the barrier islands.

The plan for the day was to run across Georgia Strait to a tiny backwater known as Smuggler Cove. Smuggler Cove was a safe haven on the west coast of the mainland – situated on what is known as B.C.'s "Sunshine Coast" – that we had only read about in the guidebooks. If all looked good when we arrived there, we would drop the hook and spend the night. Because it was a mere 30 nautical miles distant, barring unforeseen incident or inclement weather, we anticipated a short cruising day – barely four hours at our usual 8.5 knots – with the added benefit of stopping at a point that was no more than a hop, skip and a jump from our next port of call, Pender Harbour. Having built some "extra" days into our schedule to accommodate Nature's moods, we had the luxury in this instance of not being pressed for time. We were, after all, cruising for pleasure.

As the reader may remember, Vancouver Island sits off the west coast of North America. Conversely, the bulk of British Columbia lies east of that same island. Ergo, one's knee-jerk reaction is to think in terms of going east when traveling toward the mainland. Such thinking would work just fine if one intended to go from Gabriola Island to the city of Vancouver, B.C. If, however, one seeks the solitude the Sunshine Coast, as we did, then that reckoning has to be amended radically. Specifically, to cross the Strait of Georgia directly from Silva Bay to Smuggler Cove, one must take up a heading that is somewhat west of north!

One of the maxims by which The Skipper now lives is, "Nothing is ever as easy as it looks." Whether it is solace or delight that he takes when making this observation – and his humor generally alternates between the two, depending of who's ox is being gored – he trots it out and waves it around like a signal flag whenever he comes near a task that should be simple to perform, but somehow is not. In this instance, the straight-line course that should have been set for Smuggler Bay was about 330 degrees (magnetic). The fly in that ointment, however, was that that heading took the boat directly through the dreaded "WG Area" (a.k.a. "Whiskey Golf" to local mariners). Whiskey Golf consists of a few lines drawn on a sea chart that delineate a Canadian military exercise zone. To the extent that these things can be divined at all, what The Navigator had learned about Whiskey Golf was that from time to time Canada's Navy uses the region to practice its dark arts. Rumor had it, too, that periodically not one but both of their ships could be found operating in WG![7] (Why they fail to take make use of the entire, immediately adjacent, Pacific Ocean for this purpose is a subject best left for the experts.) At least according to the scuttlebutt on the American side of the border, these intrepid warships steam from one end of Whiskey Golf to the other for the express purpose of causing the water to make great booming sounds and large schools of fish to float to the surface. The latter aspect of this occupation is said to be excellent sport and those who have observed it first hand opine that it far surpasses

[7] *While spoken of in jest, the Royal Canadian Navy has a long and distinguished history. Whether protecting Canada proper or defending her interests abroad, the world would be a more dangerous place without the men and women who serve so gallantly in this small, but excellent fighting force.*

catching big ones with an ordinary rod and reel! Be that as it may, however, the participants seem to be a little possessive about their fishing grounds and demand that civilian interlopers stay off of their court when they intend to fill their lockers with fresh salmon and halibut.

Since retiring some years ago from that alphabet agency alluded to previously, The Skipper has made it a personal rule to never enter military exercise areas. They actually exist all over the place, on the ground, the sea and even in the air, and it is possible, at times, to pass safely and legally through them. It is just as possible, however, that without much forewarning – yea, verily I say unto you that there may even be times when no advance notice is given! – the defenders of a nation may swoop, roar, dive, march, rumble, sail and otherwise make life unbearable for the precise purpose of raising as much cane, havoc and general destruction as is possible with the wondrous tools of modern warfare at their disposal. Knowing well the potential effects of these shenanigans and understanding that they often are inimical to the ordinary bystander, our hero makes it a point to keep clear of these playgrounds, even when "they" say that nothing is going on within them.

Further, in days of old these exercising warriors were not nearly as touchy about intrusions as they have rightly become. It used to be that if some regular Joe just happened to wander into one of these sites at the wrong time, everything would come to a screeching halt and the offender would be shooed away before he could come to much harm. But these days, trained personnel with real guns, real ammunition and real reasons to err on the side of prudence may well pounce on anyone caught within their purview. We have it on good authority that such encounters rarely are pleasant from the civilian perspective.

Unfortunately, while restricted areas on land can be physically designated and even separated with relative ease, to the best of my knowledge we have yet to come up with a way of permanently painting lines on the surface of the sea or of suspending them in the air. This means that those who travel on those amorphous mediums (i.e., in the air or on the sea) have to *inform* themselves as to where they can and cannot be at any given moment.

As a species we do not seem to excel at that *inform* thing. In truth there are some, possibly even many of us, who have never tried it at all or who have only given it a half-hearted shot before they have moved on to something really enthralling like "Angry Birds!" An example of this might suffice. A 75-year-old pilot recently flew into airspace that was temporarily listed as off limits to civilian aircraft in order to accommodate the travel of the President of the United States. Said criminal had not checked with anything or anybody before her flight, so she knew nothing about the restriction. Without boundary lines hanging in the sky, she did not even know that the familiar air through which she was passing was closed to her. Worse yet, so uninformed was she of the current state of aviation and the types of aircraft that could take to the friendly skies on a moment's notice, that she thought that the two F-16s buzzing around her – both fully armed with air-to-air missiles – were just there to admire her airplane!

So instead of pointing the bow of *Minstrel's Song* directly north-northwest, we set off on a course that carried us considerably east of north. This would serve to keep us running well clear of the guys with short fuses and bad tempers. I simply cannot stand testy people when I am on vacation!

Instead of taking the straight-line route north-northwest through Whiskey Golf, The Pilot decided to take up a northeasterly heading first, an act that would have the boat passing about a nautical mile to the west of the Halibut Bank buoy, before hooking back toward the west to reach their destination. Carefully he had drawn his line northeastward over the empty expanse of the chart to the equally empty spot he had chosen for his turn. There, and exactly there, he would put the helm down and, hooking northwestward would make for Merry Island. Despite all of the luxuries of modern electronics, our Skipper still prefers to steer from point-to-point. He knows there are lots of corners that could be cut and that not doing so adds time and expense to the trip. Still, he does not care. Dinosaurs are like that, you know.

The day before, while still back at the slip in Silva Bay, the marina attendant, Neil, related an incident wherein a fellow "driving" an open pleasure boat containing his four young grandchildren flew into Silva Bay seeking directions. Said adventurer pulled out a tattered Texaco road map of British Columbia and asked quite seriously where he could find a good place to spend the night on the mainland's Sunshine Coast. He roared off in a cloud of foam and spray and to this day no one knows for sure whether or not he reached the other side safely. The world is full of that kind of sailor, too!

There are a plethora of reasons why The Navigator uses pencils by the gross to mark charts, make notes all over the lines he draws on them and ultimately why he produces a product that seems to pursue the most pusillanimous of paths. The short answer is: self-preservation. When a heavy fog suddenly descends, when we tear off the bottom of our boat impacting a semi-submerged object (like an errant shipping container or a water soaked 40' log), when someone aboard keels over with a heart attack, or when we experience any one of a thousand other emergencies, it is probable that what will be wanted most will be to get to the nearest point of safety quickly or to get someone rapidly and directly to us. The middle of a crisis does not seem to be the time where one ought to be fumbling around in the proverbial dark, playing blind man's bluff over empty square miles of cold, cruel, moving seas. More *Titanic* passengers might have been saved had she not broadcast erroneous position reports. So, we steer toward Merry Island via the Halibut Bank Buoy and we are happy to do so!

The Strait of Georgia is a large body of water. It feels much like an ocean because it is much like an ocean. Although mountains line its shores, their presence does not mean that the intervening sea is the equivalent of a big lake. In fact, when one stands on one shore and gazes across to the other it is likely that the impression they come away with is that the imposing heights are locked in a life and death struggle with the watery deep and it is not clear which one of them will win the battle. Instead of standing tall, dominating everything around them as they usually do, the towering peaks of these ranges seem to struggle to free themselves from Poseidon's deadly grasp. Thus, even in a stout boat one does well to respect the forces at work in such an arena.

As *Minstrel's Song* chugs away from the western shore of the Strait, we are reminded that the greyish waves that lift, roll and carry us along in a wallowing kind of a way ought not to be our only concern. For we had hardly started across when, around the northern end of Gabriola Island, there ranged one of our perennial nemeses: a ferry! Connecting the town of Nanaimo on Vancouver Island with the city of Vancouver on the mainland, these uncaring beasts blithely churn a straight line between the two places that will waver nary an inch from start to finish. As always, they care not for small chum like us! Consulting the AIS, while carefully studying the radar "blip," and simultaneously eyeballing the heck out of this unwanted interloper, we determine that he will pass well ahead of us. This is so pleasing that I cannot help but shout, "Cookie, more coffee!"

I worry a bit about The Executive Officer when we are on the open water. She has a checkered past when it comes to tolerating turbulence. Spurred as much as anything by a lack of experience and the confidence that comes with it, even when aboard oversized, stabilized cruise ships, she has been known to pass up exquisitely prepared and presented chow in preference of an extra hour or two in her bunk. Knowing this, I always try to make the ride as smooth as I can. That, of course, is pretty much an impossibility, but spinning the wheel this way and that gives me something to do and it makes her think that somehow I am in control. It is especially pleasing, then, when she passes up the coffee – and a warmed Danish as well – and happily plunks herself down in her watch seat with her own cup of Java and a sticky bun on a napkin. This means that in all likelihood the only "green" I will have to contend with this day is that of the seas around us!

We chatter away as we move across, keeping a close lookout for shipping and for other dangers in the water. A ferry running out from Vancouver lies low in the southeast, too far away to threaten us. A tug dragging a barge churns its way slowly down from the north, but again, it is of no concern. Beyond the philosophic questions of the day that we almost always manage to explore, my primary interest now is to pick out the Halibut Bank buoy.

It is a strange thing. You can see a small boat on the water from miles away. You can perceive seals, dolphins, even the odd whale from considerable distances. Ships may reveal their presence at 20 miles or more out, but a 15' buoy, numbered, fixed, known to be in a single location – more or less -- is one of the harder things to identify while at sea. I am not sure why that is, but it is normal for me to have to be within a mile or two of even a big buoy before I can actually spot it, and that is when I am using powerful binoculars and know about where the danged thing should be.

One of the oddities of the Strait of Georgia is that the side that remains in the lee of Vancouver Island – the west side -- tends to have the roughest seas. Whether caused by the vagaries of the bottom, the tidal flows, the winds or any combination of those or other factors, it is true that the further east we move, the smoother the water gets. Equally delightful is the fact that the clouds look like they are ready to break. Both events reduce The Pilot's workload to little more than sitting back, sipping his coffee and holding up his end of the conversation.

Decades of experience have taught me two important lessons. First, that the only law really worth knowing is Murphy's (i.e., "If something can go wrong, it will go wrong."). And second, that Murphy was an optimist! Predisposed like that to finding trouble lurking everywhere, it is tough to relax. Instead of enjoying an ever-brightening day on a calming sea, I divide my attention between listening intently to the throb of the engine, studying the ships gauges, scanning the electronic gadgetry and keeping a sharp eye peeled for anything that might be in the water in front of us or coming up around us.

Fretfully I peer through the windscreen (a term used in deference to our international readers) looking hard for the elusive buoy. Our plot says it should be coming up soon. I take up the binoculars and vainly peer into the hazy grey. I murmur something inane to Number One so as to keep her distracted, and then start the whole process all over again.

By nature, obsessions become the sole focus of the mind. I know I am fretting over nothing. I know it doesn't make a bit of difference if I see the stupid thing or not. I know exactly where we are. I know where we are going. And I know that even if the silly buoy did not exist at all, nothing in the world would change a whit. Still, I stare, pace and speculate.

But wait! What's that over there? Is that a boat? No! It is the Halibut Bank buoy! Hooray! And amazingly, given the size of this whitish-metal contraption and the way it now pops out against the dull, grey sea like a character in a 3-D movie, I wonder where it had been all this time! As off-handedly as possible I advise The Crew, "Well. There it is. Just where it should be." Making the planned course correction now, I order "Auto" to "Come to course 330." And then, finally, I sink back into my seat, enjoy the sweet warmth of the coffee I had been ignoring for too long and bask in an undeserved sense of self-satisfaction. Adding to my general delight is the fact that I already can see our next waypoint.

Passing Halibut Bank marks the beginning of a new phase in our day's travel. Literally as we clear that milestone, the clouds overhead give way to blue skies and a warm sun suddenly drenches the sea for miles in every direction. Almost instantaneously the ocean turns from the surly, steely gray aspect it has maintained all morning to a cheery green-blue color. The rolling chop of the water we traversed on the Vancouver Island side of the Strait has grown calmer with each mile and we are now plowing through a medium that more closely resembles that which might be found on a duck pond. Ahead of us lies Merry Island, Halfmoon Bay, Welcome Passage and the end of this phase of our voyage. Better yet, as if entering the physical domains of such pleasantly named places was not enough, we have reached the southern extremes of B.C.'s Sunshine Coast. With such wonders ahead and our trip across the big water mainly behind us, we are as excited as two little kids on the way out to recess.

Welcome Passage is fairly wide, about a third of a mile at its narrowest, and only slightly more than a mile and a half in length. It has good depth – hundreds of feet of water that continues in that condition almost up to the rock-strewn shorelines that mark its outer limits – with no obstructions that need concern small boats. There is a well- charted ledge about a half mile northwest of the northern end of the waterway and a couple of named, but not exposed rocks, to the southwest of its southern terminus. All of these things are covered by sufficient water at all times to keep pleasure boaters happy. The channel itself, running southeast to northwest, separates the Thormanby Islands (both north and south) on the west side from the mainland (Sechelt Peninsula) that lies to the east. Welcome Passage literally greets those running northwest up the east side of the Strait of Georgia from the vicinity of Vancouver, B.C. or the Bellingham, Washington area. Its northern terminus opens onto the southern reaches of the Malaspina Strait. The large and northwesterly oriented Texada Island, a towering mass that separates the Malaspina Strait from the Strait of Georgia, helps funnel marine traffic north up the coast of the Sechelt Peninsula toward Powell River.

So situated, Welcome Passage provides both the casual cruiser and smaller, commercial vessels with several nifty benefits. First, it is not customarily ravaged by fast moving currents. While one may have to 'go against the current' to get through it, the risk of the loss of a few knots of speed is of little consequence when compared with other passes that routinely come with more dangers. Second, maintaining steerage along the way is not a concern since the deep water that flows through it precludes the formation of the kinds of swirls, eddies and overpowering currents that can be problematic. Thus, one may make take advantage of this passage at any time and on any tide. Next, especially when moving north up the seaboard, the Thormanby Islands, aided by the curve of the coast, serve to shelter these waters from the fury that can be found on the more open seas of the Strait of Georgia. Of further note, Welcome Passage serves as quick conduit for craft transiting this part of the coast. With bustling Vancouver, B.C. little more than 30 miles to the south and with the wonders of the Inside Passage beckoning from the north, it is not surprising that plenty of pleasure boats fill this channel through the summer months. Larger commercial vessels use it too, but generally not those of an ocean crossing variety. The best part, though, is that despite the fact that they roam further north and further south each day, B.C. ferries do not take advantage of Welcome Passage. Yes!

From six or eight miles out, and just a point off our starboard bow, we watch as Merry Island rises up out of the sea. It is a pretty chunk of rock that is festooned with a bit of finery in the form of a few shrubs and trees. Being brown-grey in overall tone, the green of the flora joins the white splashes of the surf to create a truly gay scene. The addition of a white navigational tower perched on an eastern outcropping moves the mind of the viewer to see not an ordinary shipping marker, but an old time lighthouse. Nineteenth Century watercolor artists produced many a fine canvas that was not as charming as the seascape that spreads out before us on this fine day.

A few miles off to starboard, but closer in to shore we note a solid line of small boats marching steadily northwest up the mainland coast. It is clear that they will pass east of Merry Island while we intend to slip by it on the west. All of us seem to be making for Welcome Passage, and all points north, and in all probability each of us only recently embarked on their adventure. Rare is the day that is not made better by becoming an integral part of a fine little parade. Sadly, this particular cavalcade was to prove the exception to that rule.

Suddenly and without warning the crackly sound of our marine radio shatters our joyous mood. "*Cupcake 6*. This is *Pork Chop Too*. Can you hear me? [Pause.] *Cupcake 6*. This is *Pork Chop Too*. [Pause] What's going on back there? *Kool Aid* wants me to tell you that he thinks you should change your burgee. Everyone else is flying the green and yellow one."

Momentary silence.

"*Cupcake 6*. This is *Pork Chop Too*. [Pause] Come back *Cupcake*?"

More – but not nearly enough – radio silence.

"Well *Cupcake 6*, this is *Pork Chop Too*. If you can hear me, *Spitball* advises that we need to put in somewhere soon because he doesn't have anything for lunch and he forgot to fill the cooler with ice before he left. What do you think?"

Listening to these exchanges makes me feel like I have been

caught in a time warp and set down in the middle of an old Abbot and Costello movie. Apparently unaware that Channel 16 – the frequency these mariners are blathering away on -- is a hailing frequency reserved mainly for emergencies and Coast Guard communications, these Pilgrims chatter away like teenage girls at a pajama party. Oblivious to the fact that their homey exchanges could be 'stepping all over' real life and death radio transmissions, I long for justice and at least a Coast Guard admonishment directed at these ships of fools. Sadly, there is never a cop around when you want one.

Resisting the temptation to grab the mic and 'advise' *Pork Chop Too, et. al.,* that no one anywhere gives a fish's flipper about whether *Cupcake 6* hears anything; that no one cares if the burgee of the day is barnyard brown; and we would all consider it a blessing if poor old *Spitball* had to eat dirt and die, iceless, this very day! Instead, I leave the mic on its hook and launch into a diatribe, directed at no one in particular, about boaters who know nothing about radio procedure. But before I can empty my spleen on the topic, the drama begins again:

"*Cupcake 6.* This is *Pork Chop Too.* If you can you hear me, good buddy, give *Witless One* a shout. He wants to know what you're going to do. He's thinking that because the weather is so nice we can get further up the coast today. What are your plans?"

Plans? PLANS? My <u>plans</u> at this point are to try to get my hands on these bozos so I can strangle the life out of all of them. Wisely, I keep those thoughts to myself, too. And the fly in the ointment is that it is really difficult to determine who is doing the talking, because the radio waves remain pretty anonymous. The offending transmissions could be coming from that clump of boats over there, but just as easily they could be coming from some group we cannot even see. Gathering what few facts are available and analyzing them in an attempt to discern what is at this point indiscernible, I begin to plot exquisite punishments for my high frequency tormentors. Sensing the malice that is forming in my soul, The Executive Officer takes the precaution of reminding me that the flare gun we carry – in Canadian waters it must be referred to as a 'signal launcher' – is for emergency purposes only. Likewise, she casually mentions that the bow of the boat is made of fiberglass and not the steel required for a true ram. (I hate it when she knows what I am thinking.)

Meanwhile, the fun continues. "*Pork Chop Too*, this is *Witless One*. I think *Spitball* wanted to talk to the guys on *Going Down Slowly* and *Where Am I Now* before making any final decisions about where we stop for the night. Have you heard anything from *Bottoms Up?*"

"*Witless One,* this is *Pork Chop Too.* Haven't heard a peep from *Bottoms Up* but I think that *Cupcake 6* told him a while back that *Where Am I* was out of touch again and that they both should try to catch up. *Kool Aid* mentioned last week that *Where Am I* hadn't treated his fuel or serviced any of his filters for years. He did say that his engine had been running a bit rough and he thought he might have a little water or some dirt in the system. Can you see him? By the way, are you guys up for some beer and cards tonight?"

Left with no other reasonable (or legal) recourse, I reach up and turn the volume on the radio down to next to nothing. The law requires that I run with the squawk box on; it says nothing about how loud it has to be when in that mode.

Passing Merry Island to starboard, we begin our mental preparations for putting in at Smuggler Cove. We review the cruising guides, the charts and the *Canadian Sailing Directions*. Being conveniently located just around the northeastern extreme of Welcome Passage's mainland side, we have learned that this small, safe harbor requires a very careful entry. As often is the case, however, this inlet is such a tiny backwater that the charts are of little real use and ultimately nothing but caution and good judgment will get a ship safely into it.

Beyond being popular with boaters in the summer months, Smuggler Cove's main claim to fame is that it was a starting point/hiding place for bootlegging whiskey smugglers during the 1920s and 1930s. These rumrunners would stage out of this tiny anchorage in dark, foul weather for a fast trip down to the States in order to deliver tax free boatloads of booze to their thirsty neighbors! That these entrepreneurs did not achieve the notoriety of Al Capone and Elliot Ness may be a testament to the seclusion of this little cove as well as an indication of how impossible it was for peacekeepers south of the border to uphold a crazy law that only a few truly wanted.

With our destination nearly in sight, we have but to make our way up through Welcome Passage and then jog east to the entrance to Smuggler Cove. Thus, The Pilot swings the bow of *Minstrel's Song* a couple of points to port in order to split the waters of Welcome Passage. As he did so, his fair craft fell into a gaggle of sailboats motoring along in the same direction. These pleasure sailors were moving at a pace somewhat slower than that of *Minstrel's Song,* so safely getting around and through them would require some care.

Even though the lower end of Welcome Passage is about a half a mile wide, the channel narrows to roughly a third of a mile before reaching Malaspina Strait. With a steady line of vessels ahead of us as we churned our way into this "funnel" it was necessary to bear two things in mind: 1.) Because there might be ships coming down the pass that required an unobstructed lane in which to navigate, we did not want to veer too far to port; and 2.) We should favor the starboard shore since we would be turning that way for our scheduled stop at Smuggler Cove. Further, since our speed was greater than that of the boats around us, we would either have to slow a little or undertake a passing maneuver. In short, if we did not want to poke along at 4 or 5 knots, did not want to impede southbound traffic by being too far over on the west side of the waterway but did want to be in a position to bear off for Smuggler Cove, then we had some adjustments to make.

The problem, really, was quite like the one often encountered on a freeway. Knowing that soon you will need to exit to the right, you have a decision to make: 'Do I putter along behind the slowpokes for the next 40 miles or do I put the pedal to the metal in the fast lane and hope I do not cause a 16 car pile up when I shoot across four lanes of bumper-to-bumper traffic to get off on the road I want?' That is the question.

Mulling the options, I decided that since there was no oncoming shipping and we could increase or decrease our speed to create the space needed to make our final turn safely, I would leave some or all of the line on our starboard beam, with my green light to their reds. I reached for the marine radio's mic while simultaneously studying the craft immediately ahead of us. I was looking for the vessel's name so I could call her and advise her of our intentions. It was then that I realized that there, less than a quarter of a mile away from us, was the now-despised *Pork Chop Too.* Instantly my hand shot to the throttle and shoved it hard forward. As my focus narrowed and the throbbing diesel engine roared to life I shouted, "Ramming speed!"

With equal alacrity, The Crew gave me one of those, 'What the hell do you think you are you doing,' and, 'You had better get yourself under control, boy' looks which stopped me dead in my tracks. By the time I recovered, the "moment" had passed and so I meekly dialed the engine back to its normal cruising setting. (The First Mate's quick thinking probably saved another life at sea!)

With no reasonable alternative in the face of this psychological onslaught, I reluctantly, but dutifully, called *Pork Chop Too, Cupcake 6,* and the whole darned pack on the radio to give them the information they probably did not even know they were supposed to have. I might have signaled my intentions by horn and not radio, but I was sure that doing that would have elicited little more than smiles and waves or perhaps even curses, so I said my piece and hung up. Ugh…greenhorns.

In all probability had I been born a dog I would have been part English bulldog and part Irish setter. For as quickly as my blood gets up and I am all in for justice, I can let go of the darkest vengeance schemes and get on with my life. In this instance, however, I could not let pass the opportunity to roast my fellow seamen. Beyond favoring The First Mate with a series of scathing critiques on the sizes, shapes, colors, conditions and sailing qualities of each of the accursed craft as they came abreast of us, a rather transparent, but tremendously satisfying thought struck me. It was nothing more and nothing less than that although the vessels we were passing all were sailboats, none of them were sailing. Each and every blighted one of them was motoring! And motoring, as anyone can tell you, is the bane of all true sailors!

ANCIENT DREAMS

"Sailing…sailors…hmmmmm…sailboats," I think to myself. And as I do so my mind races back over a lifetime of seemingly discreet events to ponder the psychological amalgamation that produces the current set of thoughts on the subject.

I grew up on a farm that was not too distant from the Chesapeake Bay. But it was not too close to it either. And regardless of its physical location, the truth about the old homestead was that it was light years removed from world of sailboats and sailing. Despite including a small pond and a couple of streams that ultimately made their tiny contributions to the maintenance of the seas, there was nothing and no one on that land that knew or cared a wit about the pleasures or the challenges of a life afloat.

For reasons unfathomable even today, my interest in things nautical dated from an early age. As best I can remember, from about my seventh year on I began hoarding the "egg money" that passed through my small hands for the purpose of going to sea! Egg money was the meager recompense I received for the shelled product of the noisy, stinking, feathered flock of wretched birds for which I had become the sole, unwilling guardian. In exchange for running our family's chicken business, an entrepreneurial opportunity that included feeding, watering and ministering to the health of the birds, cleaning the coop, collecting the eggs, washing, weighing, sorting and boxing each of those edible orbs, and then operating a 24/7 store for everyone and anyone who happened to be in need of a dozen or two of these "farm fresh" delights, I received a portion of the proceeds. The implicit expectation in this mandatory arrangement was that the pirate's ransom thus being amassed, one egg at a time, was going to result in a startling super fund – after having been laid aside for decades – that would be incredibly useful the moment the world ended, or I needed to buy a house, or I decided to purchase a wife, or I saw fit to gather a gaggle of kids, or any other number of "reasonable" things deemed by me to be equally ridiculous. Being opposed from the start to this squandering of easy money, but powerless to resist the force of The Old Man's logic, I nonetheless went quietly to work on my own objective: I would save to buy a boat!

If memory serves, a 10' aluminum jon boat could be had back then, were one inclined to believe what appeared on page 237 of the Sears and Roebuck catalogue, for the modest sum of $69.95. plus shipping. The gargantuan nature of such a rebellious acquisition might be put in perspective by the fact that the goods I was dealing in netted me a tiny percentage of the 19 to 29 cents per dozen, U.S. coin, that we grossed for every set of 12 eggs sold…when prices were up.

Circumstances, The Old Man and hard times never allowed me to place with Sears the order for my boat. I always felt a bit guilty about not being able to support that great company with my business since about that same time it entered what remains to this day its long, slow death spiral.

Denied the dream of becoming a shipping magnate by age 15, I was able to catch occasional glimpses of the sea from time to time and that was enough to keep the internal fires burning. On rare occasions The Old Man would take us out on "the Bay" for a day of charter fishing. Equally joyous were those infrequent instances when one of my friends, whose families had summer cabins and boats on the Chesapeake or other large bodies of water, included me in their activities. Twice, that I can recall, "we" had exclusive use of our own runabout, rented for a week at a time, when our family vacationed near sizeable lakes.

Perhaps it was because I never enjoyed fishing or maybe it had to do with my lack of interest in water skiing or in driving noisy boats around in big circles, but whatever it was doing anything that involved powerboats was always my second choice. Sailing, despite the fact that I had never done it, was what rang my chimes!

I was well embarked on the voyage through life before finally getting an opportunity to hear the wind in the rigging and to feel the exhilaration of slicing through the water without any accompanying engine noise. It came in the form of a half-day outing on a rented 15' sailboat. Although young adulthood found me strapped sorely for cash, I calculated that if I split the cost with another guy and did not eat lunch for at least a month, we could hire a fine little boat for a full three hours at sea! Moreover, my partner in this small crime said he was an experienced sailor and would teach me everything I needed to learn for nothing. The only fly in the ointment was that his wife, who was noticeably pregnant, would have to come along with us.

I remember everything about that day quite vividly, but especially the part about having hardly reached the open water before she needed to return to use a restroom. In my mentor's zeal to get his suffering wife back to the dock quickly, he cut the corner around one navigational marker just a bit short. And therein I received my first lessons relative to running aground and the importance of reading your charts beforehand. By the time we reached shore, still dripping wet from the salvage operation we were forced to undertake in waist deep water, our three hours was up and I had done scant little sailing.

As a result of active duty time in the U.S. Army Reserves in the '70s, I had access to the Navy's recreational facilities at Long Beach, California. After some snooping and poking I learned that the naval stronghold there had a fleet of sailboats that any active duty military person could use IF they jumped through a few hoops. These low cost hurdles included taking some basic sailing courses and passing both a swimming and a sailboat-handling test. Gleefully, after making this discovery I whiled away many happy off duty hours that summer in conforming to the Navy's requirements. As a result, I got a "ticket" from them – which I still have – that authorized me to rent and use any of the sailboats in their flotilla. Thereafter, nights, weekends and any time in between that I could spare found me happily cruising the busy waters of the Port of Long Beach in a Navy pleasure boat.

Some years later, while working in the Far East, I re-connected with this fine military organization. Once again I was able to use, at minimal cost but with great happiness, any of the many 14'-36' long sailboats they kept there. Concomitantly, I began to read everything I could find on the topics of sailing and sailboat design. I also took courses to improve my maritime skills and, most importantly, I discovered the wonderful world of sailboat racing.

To the best of my knowledge the old adage, "There is no such thing as a free lunch" holds true absolutely except for when it comes to securing a berth on a racing sailboat. Latch onto that choice billet and you get the best of all worlds. If a racing crewman has a modicum of talent, shows up on schedule – in nearly any weather – and can take instruction, then he/she will be rewarded with a lot of free sailing time along with the opportunity to learn the finer points of the art from excellent seamen. Beyond supplying his own food, drink and personal equipment the only thing this freeloading marine hitchhiker has to do is to be willing to work the boat for the duration of the event. Meanwhile, the poor schmuck who holds the title to the vessel must worry about paying slip rental fees, insurance, maintenance and upkeep, equipment upgrades and any all of the not inconsequential expenses that go with boat ownership. (On a lovely, very expensive and very competitive 44-footer I served on for a couple of years, The Crew installed a brass plaque over the navigation table that read: "The job of the owner on this vessel is to remain below decks and to write the checks!" Cheeky, yes, but we never lost a series.)

In days gone by I raced as much as I could, sailed casually and often and finally acquired several fine little sailboats of my own. In these I cruised bays, inlets, channels, straits, reaches, large and small lakes, followed long coastlines and sometimes went offshore into blue water. I did so at every chance I got. Occasionally I rubbed shoulders with the luminaries of the profession and once, but only once, I almost bought a sailboat-building company!

The point of all of this is that beyond those childhood dreams of a jon boat, driven as they were driven by egg money and an abiding hatred of chickens, and excepting later in life, when The Old Man took up residence on a neck of the Chesapeake Bay and I shared with him, in the final moments of his life, many delightful hours on his flat-bottomed crabbing skiff, I never, ever had any interest in a boat that was not propelled by the wind. In fact, the list of derogatory appellations I amassed over the years to describe anyone with a vessel dependent on the internal combustion engine would run to multiple volumes. There was nothing about the "dark side" that intrigued me; I did not even want to be around those "stink pot" jockeys.

To demonstrate the depth of these feelings, one has but to know that I single-handedly destroyed over 4,000 budding friendships by tediously setting upon those who had ANY kind of an engine strapped to their boats. Inboards, outboards, gas, diesel, electric, jet, mattered not at all to me. As far as I was concerned there were only two absolutes that pertained to watercraft: 1.) Only boats with sails were real boats; and 2.) If your vessel had sails you had better know how to use them. From this outdated perch I constructed a moral imperative that insisted that because man had been traveling the Seven Seas for thousands of years without wasting any time, money, energy, or thought on motors, those who did so demonstrated nothing less than their own genetic incompetence.

To avoid the charge of being a hypocrite, I do admit that some of the boats I raced did have engines...but some of them did not. And, in the spirit of full disclosure I concede that once I too owned a sailboat with a motor. Once. The offending hunk of metal came into my possession as part of a package deal. It arrived in the form of a faded green, 1946 Johnson six horsepower outboard that would only start on days that began with the letter "B." I do confess, too, that I failed to drop it overboard despite ample opportunity.

Sometime within the first lustrum of our matrimonial association I discovered one day that the blood drained from my Messmate's face and she turned a shade or two of bright green about the gills whenever we set out in a sailboat. Worse, while she never complained about our sailboat(s) or discouraged me in any way, shape or form, I noted that the hiatus between the sorties we conducted together grew ever longer. Being the intuitive, sensitive type of man that I am, I finally screwed up all my courage and asked, "Don't you like sailing with me anymore?" And being the intuitive, sensitive type of woman that she is, she responded "Heck no!" (Or words to that effect.)

Only fleetingly, and then after a visit to my favorite boat builder's shop – an event that was followed immediately by a chance encounter with a charming sailor who was working feverishly to complete a vessel in which to enter an around the world sailboat race, solo – have I ever given much thought to putting to sea alone. After carefully studying Captain Joshua Slocum's groundbreaking efforts in that sphere,[8] it just did not strike me as a particularly healthy thing to do.

When you know that you do not want to spend your time wandering the oceans blue solo, and you know that your Messmate has no passion whatsoever for cruising under sail, then the wise man discovers that the shortest distance between two people and a happy relationship leads directly through a boat broker's office. There he will divest himself of all things floating and put his dreams away with the memories of his egg money. Rightfully pursuing this course my transition from sailor to landlubber was complete when we re-located to that notable maritime bastion, Montana. With big skies, big mountains and long-horned cattle surrounding me, I was sure that my sea days were behind me forever.

What most of us do not know about things oceanic and the love that goes with them is that it is a disease. Much like malaria, if left untreated it can be fatal. Like malaria, too, there is no cure for it. Even when the patient appears to be doing well, he can and probably will suffer periodic relapses. For the mariner, this translates into a lemming-like march to the water. In my instance equal doses of hard work, intellectual engagement and physical adventure usually are sufficient to keep it at bay. However, when my defenses are at their weakest, the urge to get to sea in a small boat, and fast, becomes overpowering.

Well do I remember when my most recent descent began. It was on a sunny afternoon when my Shipmate and I were sitting on the balcony of a cruise ship that was wending its way up the Inside Passage to Alaska. As was not terribly uncommon, we passed a small craft that was emerging from a remote bite carved deeply into an otherwise inaccessible wall of mountain and trees. Together we noted how freely she was able to put in here, there or almost anywhere, wherever and whenever its master inclined, and we also agreed that she was in a perfect position to pursue anything that interested her for as much or as

---

[8] *An incredible read is contained within the pages of his Sailing Alone Around the World.*

little time as she liked while she just meandered along. This, naturally, was contrary to the determined schedule of the vessel we then were aboard and the contrast made me start to itch something fierce. Wisely, though, I held my piece.

Following that voyage, or maybe it was the next, it occurred to us – slow studies though we might be – that the one week grand tour on the big ships to Southeast Alaska was all well and good, but the only real way to see anything approaching all that the Inside Passage offered was either by small boat or float plane.

Like rust eating through ancient iron, time eroded my resistance to the call of the sea and the long-dormant malady I thought I had beaten began ravaging my psyche once again. We were sitting in our library in Montana one gloomy December afternoon, years removed from our first discourse on the general topic, watching the snowflakes laze their way down out of the sky and pile up on the driveway where I would have plow them with the tractor first thing next morning, when the Librarian casually asked, "Would you ever consider getting another boat and cruising to Alaska?"

"Really! Consider? You've got to be kidding!" I thought to myself. But fearing some sort of cleverly camouflaged ambush, I innocently held back and feigned ignorance by mumbling, "Huh? What? A boat? What do you mean by a boat?"

"Well," she replied, "do you have any interest in buying a boat and taking it to Alaska?"

"But I didn't think you really liked boats," I replied as casually as I could.

"Well…For reasons I still can't explain, I didn't enjoy our sailboats, that is true, but I've been thinking that maybe if we had a motor boat it would be different. Is that something you might like to try?"

Her words were still lagging some distance behind me when I reached the computer to research the possibilities on the Internet. More incredibly, The First Mate darn near fought me to a draw over who was going to get to sit in the chair in front of the screen! And, if I experienced any yearning at that time or later for another vessel that only came equipped with mast and sails, I have repressed it completely. What I do recall is that my Crew, my First Officer, my Messmate, my Finance Officer and my guiding star all thought it would be O.K. to get a boat again! When one hears words like that, it is well not to quibble.

Within the month we had consumed massive amounts of information about all kinds of different cruising craft and then we braved the January roads through the northern Rocky Mountains to make the 500-mile trip west to the Seattle Boat Show. By the time we got there we knew that what we wanted was referred to in modern parlance as a "trawler". Such little ships tend to be seaworthy, economical, comfortable and roomy. They are fully enclosed, heated and sport all of the comforts of home, as long as it is a small one! What they do not have is great speed. We opined that when it came to considering a vessel that would allow us to cruise in sparsely populated waters when surrounded by little more than the incredible natural beauty within the Inside Passage, the one property we could compromise on was "fast."

Although we went to the boat show to see as many modern cruisers as possible, there was an old friend of sorts that we especially wanted to visit. Decades earlier, in absorbing as much as I could about sailboats, I picked up a volume called *The World's Best Sailboats.* The author of that tome, Ferenc Mate, included descriptions of many wonderful sailing craft, but for purely sentimental reasons he snuck one little powerboat into the mix: it was a Nordic Tug 26 (26' from stem to stern). Our inquiries into the 21st Century trawler world led us to discover that an entire line of Nordic Tugs had burgeoned over the decades since I had read of the "26," and even better yet, they had become a well respected line of pleasure craft.

After dreaming a lot of dreams, looking at a lot of pictures, visiting a lot of boats and crunching a lot of numbers we concluded that by virtue of their only being astronomically more expensive than anything we could ever afford right off the way, a good used one, with at least 10 years of previous life on her hull, might be what we should try to find.

We purchased *Minstrel's Song* some time thereafter and never regretted it. It is true that every now and then I do think that I would like to have another sailboat, but the persistent object of such dreams, these days, measures something under 10' in length, weighs less than a 100 pounds, performs nicely under sails and oars, will slide neatly into the bed of mypick-up truck and can replace, absolutely, the ugly grey RIB we carry on the stern of our otherwise beautiful floating home.

O.K., I admit to the reader (only) to having felt rare pangs of guilt when I have been required to fess up to a sailboat owner that my Nordic Tug carries no cloth aloft. For quite a while I was at a loss as to how to explain to these prior soul mates how I had fallen from grace and had been brought down, taken under the spell of the 'dark side.' And then suddenly the mental fog cleared. This happened exactly when, as things often do, it was least expected. The epiphany came as we were working our way up Welcome Passage, gliding past that offensive line of sailboats formed by the likes of *Pork Chop Too, Kool Aid* and all of his other little buddies. Clothed in casual slacks and tee shirts and warmed by the yellow rays of the sun that poured in through our windows as well as by the soft heated air spewing from the wheelhouse heat vents, sipping hot coffee, snacking on delectable morsels and delighting in the 360-degree view greeting us everywhere, we noticed something very odd. Virtually all of the sailing vessels we were passing or had seen on our trip shared a common set of attributes. The cockpit of each was filled with one or more humanoid forms bedecked in full foul weather gear (i.e., heavy wool watch caps, tough, waterproof and insulated coats and pants usually worn over layers of synthetic undergarments all graced by tall rubber deck boots and sturdy gloves) and looking about as happy as a bathtub full of cold, wet cats. Undoubtedly seeking to ward off hypothermia, these benighted souls clump together like dried raisons in a can. They spend their every minute simultaneously working to find a modicum of shelter from the wind that blows constantly over their flat, open decks while trying to maintain a watch ahead sufficient to keep their vessel off of the rocks. As if frozen to their hands, these wretches inevitably grip coffee cups in their poor, gloved paws and each and every one of them looks, well…they look miserable.

Laboring along at the low rate of speed that the small engines, the misaligned drivetrains and inefficient props they sport can muster, these bare-masted conveyances look lost, out of place. Festooned with furled or bagged sails, coiled sheets, halyards, downhauls, outhauls, reefing lines, topping lifts, stowed whisker poles, covered winches, etc., etc. and guided by hooded, faceless beings who must stand shivering watches exposed to the elements, we begin to think that this seems to be a poor way in which to have fun. It is true that there is nothing like surging along in a sail-driven boat in a fair wind on a pleasant day. The trouble is that what these stalwarts of the great Northwet are doing most of the time is nothing at all like that! In fact, contending with the hellacious tides and currents, the fluky and unpredictable winds, the narrow channels and the naturally cool, cloudy environment that define the southern reaches of the Inside Passage, even when the planets align and all is right for a day of travel without an engine, pressing sailboats into service as sightseeing platforms or even pleasant conveyances is, at the least, a problematic undertaking.

Armed with this sudden insight it becomes frighteningly apparent that except for those with great skill and tremendous determination, sailing these inland oceans is a fools mission. Whatever the hopes or dreams of these boat owners are, in most instances they have been hoodwinked. At considerable expense they have acquired what may ultimately be excellent sea craft, but vessels that are inferior *in these environs* to the "stink pots" they probably distain.

Waving and smiling heartily as we pass each benighted member of *Pork Chop's* plodding flotilla, I slide the pilothouse door closed, turn the heat up a tad, sip my hot coffee and casually say to The Crew, "Don't you wish you could be having fun like that?"

She answers, "It just doesn't get any better than that, does it?"

There are some things in this world that are true, simply. Having apologized too often to too many people for not having a sailboat, we suddenly know that the smiles we shared with our fellow mariners just then reflected a new certitude that was dished up with a bit of poetic justice. This revelation was made the sweeter, still, by the fact that no one except the two of us would ever know what had transpired. Smiling and waving like royalty in a motorcade we slipped past the final two sailboats and turned *Minstrel's Song* hard to starboard to begin the process of guiding her into the shelter we have chosen for the night.

* * * * * * * * * * *

Pulling the throttle back to a fast idle, both The Captain and The Crew scan the shoreline for the opening to Smuggler Cove. About a mile or more off to the east The Skipper espies a small grove of masts that rise above a forest of fir trees that sits atop an intervening rocky strand. At the same instant, he identifies a tiny break in the coastline that assuredly constitutes the channel leading into the inner harbor that protects the boats that are supporting the copse of masts. "Thar she blows," he sang out as he spun the wheel to take up the new course.

"No. I don't think that's it," The Exec dissented.

"Well sure it is," The Skipper insisted. "Look at the chart. See? It is not very far beyond Grant Island. It surely is a harbor and I don't see any other openings between here and there. Done deal!"

"I don't care," she resisted. "It doesn't look right to me. Besides, there is supposed to be a white sign on the west end of Isle Capri marking the extreme of Smuggler Cove Marine Park. I don't see anything on that shore that looks like a sign."

"Well I don't see anything else, anywhere, that is not doing a first-rate impression of a rocky shoreline," I responded testily.

"Humor me and just steer south for a time. The chart shows and 'the books' say that it should be just behind Grant Island. And Grant Island is best identified by the red school bus perched on its northern end. There is the school bus."

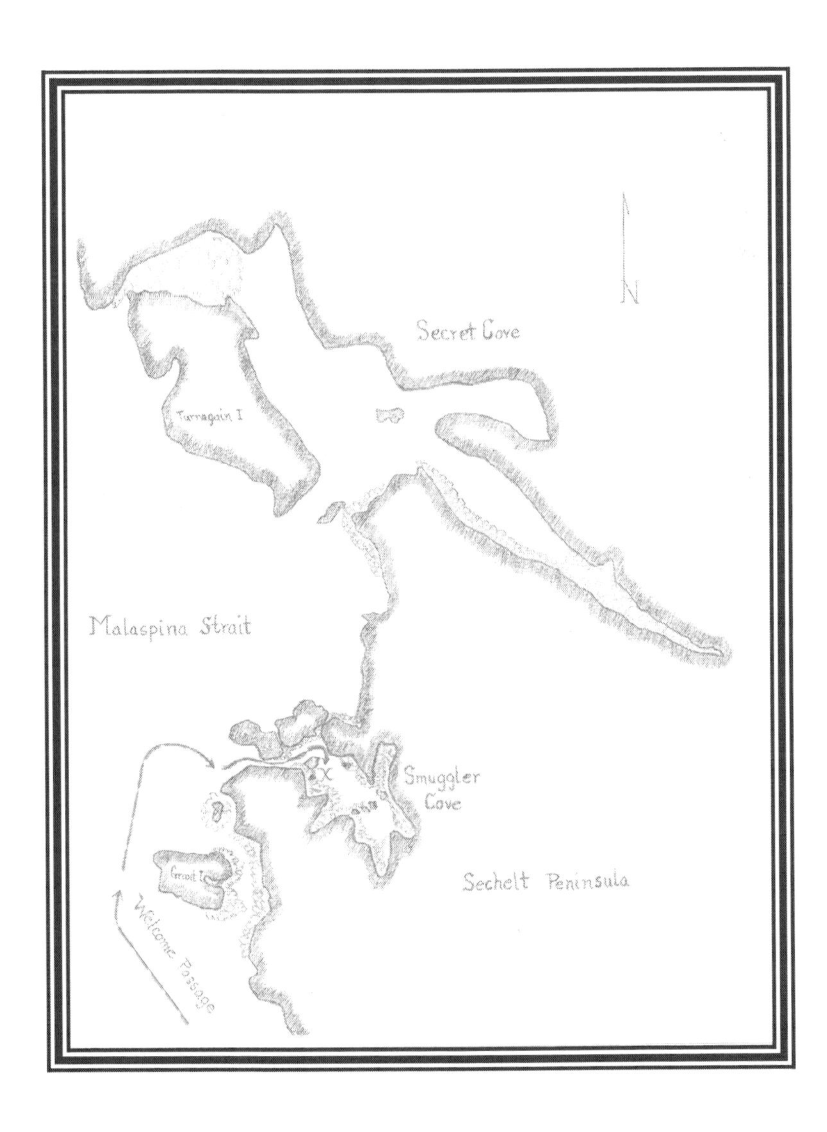
N
Secret Cove
Turnagain I
Malaspina Strait
Smuggler
Cove
Sechelt Peninsula
Grant I
Welcome Passage

Mutiny is an ugly word and in the beginning even Captain Bligh comprehended the wisdom of giving Mr. Christian a chance to speak his piece. Thus I told her, "I'll take her down there, but I'm not sure exactly why!"

Pressing slowly forward, The Lookout shouts, "I see it, I think. Look off at ten o'clock…At that rounded point just there…It looks to me like there is a small plaque or sign posted up on that headland."

Grabbing my binoculars I study the place she indicates and sure enough I agree that there appears to be something there with writing on it perched some 10' above the water. Even with the assistance of eight powered lenses, however, I do not see anything except solid rock stretching away on both sides of it.

Very cautiously we creep forward at our 'all ahead slow' setting – an absolute idle of the engine – but it still propels us at over four knots. This is a speed way too fast for my liking just now, so I nudge the transmission into neutral periodically so as to progress more slowly. I keep my hand on the throttle as we move ever closer to the rocks and to the mortal danger they can present. With only a few hundred feet or so to go, I worry about the effects that an unexpected current might have on us, but my real concern is for uncharted boulders, covered by minimal amounts of seawater, that could loom darkly under us.

Just as The Pilot looses his courage and moves to reverse course, The Lookout points to a place about a hundred yards well off the port bow and cries out, "There. See it? There is water between those two outcroppings."

I squint. I stare. I reply. "You call that water? I've seen more water in a thimble! We're looking for a channel. That can't be it!"

"Why not," she asks.

"Because," I snap, "a mud puddle and a channel both have water in them, but only one of them has sufficient breadth and depth to float a boat! And whatever that thing is, it's not a channel!"

"Yes it is."

"No it isn't..."

"O.K., look, if it makes you happy I'll inch my way over there, but keep your eyes peeled for dark, UNDERWATER objects lying in ambush! I'll humor you for a moment or two more, but then we are getting out of here before we are so far in that if attacked there is no possibility of retreat."

Alternating between moving forward at an idle and losing way in neutral, I have *Minstrel's Song* slowed to a veritable crawl; still we are going faster than I want. With the chart and the chartplotter showing a bunch of nasty submerged things hereabouts and with the numbers on the depth sounder falling into single digits, the truth is that I really do not want to be moving ahead here at all. As our way carries us closer toward something that looks a lot more like a crevice in a cliff than it does like a channel dividing two rock walls, The Lookout tells me again, "This is it for sure. See? The sign is over there. The passage turns back that way and then it looks like everything opens up a smidge, as it should, just around that bend."

"Do you really think that is it?"

"Absolutely."

Suddenly I find myself between the proverbial rock and a hard place: She insists that this is the way we have to go to get into Smuggler Cove and I am not sure that our boat can even fit in the narrow opening ahead! Because uncertainty generally retreats in the face of confidence, I defer to The X.O. and devote my attention to the task of trying to make what may be impossible actually happen. As carefully as I can I aim the bow of *Minstrel's Song's* toward the middle of what lies directly in front of us. As I move the wheel gently one way and then the other to keep the little ship centered, my most fervent hope is that there is no current flowing in any direction that might push or pull this ship of fools toward either of the granite walls that we must bisect. The whole business is made the more exciting by the knowledge that because we are moving at less than the speed of a dead idle, our ability to turn (steerage) is limited severely. That means a timely reaction to any unforeseen sideways forces probably will be of the too little, too late variety. So, as we enter this mini-canyon about all I can do is sigh, 'In for a penny, in for a pound.'

"'The books' say to favor the port side here," Number One advises.

"Favor the port side?" I repeat sarcastically. "If I favor the port side we'll take all of the paint off of it. Still, if I do not favor that quarter we will probably put gashes down the length of other side when we grind past the boulders that are sticking out over there!"

Slowly we creep forward and almost imperceptibly the walls widen and we gain a little breathing room. This is, for certain, the narrowest channel we have ever traversed.

"The books" claimed that this pass was a full 15 meters (13.67 yards or 41.01 feet) wide! They do not bother to say when that measurement was made, whether at high, low or slack tide, but assuming that it remained the same regardless of the ebb and flow of the sea – and that would be nearly impossible -- and allowing for our 11+ foot beam, we have an "excess" of about of 30 feet of width in which to play. That, of course, is provided that the rock walls that define this opening are perfectly perpendicular – and they're not. It also presumes that there is nothing that protrudes dangerously up from the bottom for the length of the entire watercourse – and there probably is. So, based on those numbers and accepting all of our assumptions as spot on, then a few simple calculations tells us that in the best case scenario we have a margin of error of 15 feet on either side of the boat. Given that water and the air above it moves unpredictably and that all vessels are subject to the forces of either or both, successfully navigating the entrance of Smuggler Cove might be likened to driving a tractor-trailer through a toll booth at 60 mph. It is doable, but there sure is not much space left over. Scary!

Once through the gates of the Cove, though, things become much tamer. The confining dimensions immediately grow larger, but before we get carried away with the idea of size, we should add that everything at this instant seems much bigger than it truly is because of the preceding experience. Having passed through the eye of a needle, even a keyhole looks huge by comparison!

To give the reader some idea of the world we had entered, it might be helpful to envision a satellite's view of Smuggler Cove. What we would see would be something that resembles, vaguely, a European-style "7." (The Europeans tend to add a horizontal line to this numeral about midway up the stem.) Letting our imaginations run wild, we might offer that the top piece of our figure is oriented southwest to northeast and is formed in the main by the small channel that led us into the Cove. This part of our numeral is about 200 yards long. From its northeastern terminus, the stem of our fictional number angles southward, avoiding an intruding island that occurs just southwest of its crux, to an end point about 650 yards distant. The "cross" of our "7" is formed by a chain of low-lying islands – oriented mainly southwest to northeast – which give way, for but only for a brief moment, to a narrow and relatively shallow passageway that allows our "stem" to continue to its full length. Although this description is neither exact nor perfect, especially because this area is punctuated by a myriad of nooks and crannies, islands and outcroppings, it may suffice nonetheless for the formation of a mental picture.

Passing around the aforementioned island, near the apex of our "7," The Captain and The Crew decided to anchor in the tiny bay that occurs between it and the make believe bar of the "cross" of our number. They found this puddle of water to be more or less round, having a radius of about 65 yards. Its depth was sufficiently shallow to make anchoring easy, but deep enough to allow for safe movement through its full extent. According to the charts and "the books," a high spot in the middle might, at extra low tides, be a concern, but located as it was more or less midway between everything else, it was easy to avoid since it served as that invisible point around which one naturally turned. Picking a spot at the western end of this bay, our intrepid mariners readied themselves for the trauma of anchoring.

As discussed in a previous chapter, boats instinctively tend to wander. And, to remind those less inclined to hold onto arcane details, the most unreliable method for putting an end to this wanderlust is to chain the prodigal beast to the bottom of the sea using that hook-like weight we like to call an anchor. We say this is the least effective means by which to tie down a boat simply because everything from the composition of the ocean floor to the size and shape of the anchor to the length, strength and weight of the tether – referred to as a rode – to the prevailing winds, tides, currents and sea conditions impact the viability of this maneuver. Worry over the interaction of the aforementioned factors conjoin to keep anyone having good sense at all in a constant state of agitation and that, in turn, robs them all of a good night's sleep! One slip, one bump, one misapplied tug and the result may be a boat that is left free to pursue its own, dark ends. Worse, having unencumbered hours, even days, to swing idly around a single point – time spent mainly without close or immediate human supervision – provides the errant craft with ample opportunity to work out its escape plan. Knowing this, the savvy mariner only deigns to anchor when absolutely necessary, preferring any of the other means of stopping his boat to this one.

Sadly, few who have spent any time on the water have done so without watching boats of every description hurtle freely past them when a hard blow or an unanticipated current sweeps through an anchorage and liberates a willing hull or two. And while some captains will claim the contrary, few of the good ones sleep with more than one eye closed when hanging on "the hook" in any but the quietest, most accommodating waters.

Despite the fact that The Captain has anchored boats many times without ill effect, The Crew has not. In reality, while she has watched her Skipper toss small hooks into minor backwaters and streams so as to spend lazy hours together happily turning round and round, those days were in the distant past, long before she signed her ships' papers. And, whether from prudence or cowardice – I leave it to the reader to determine which – through their previous adventures on *Minstrel's Song*,

The Skipper previously managed to halt the movement of that vessel in every conceivable manner except by way of dropping the anchor. But having no other options in Smuggler Cove, all agreed that this would be an excellent place for The Crew to come to grips with the intricacies of this essential nautical art.

With The Crew standing on the foredeck peering into the dark green water, the windless (anchor winch) at the ready and the anchor unshackled, The Pilot strove to bring his craft to a stop over the holding point of choice. Studying the depth sounder, he rounded up above a likely place, gently slid the transmission into reverse, allowed the prop to make a couple of turns backwards until the ship lost all way and then leaned out the pilothouse door and said, "Let her go!" Dutifully, The Crew stepped on the black rubber button mounted on the deck that controlled the electric windless and the anchor splashed down as the chain attached to it began to rattle noisily out of its locker. When 25' of chain rode – marked by a swath of bright orange paint emblazoned on the steel links – Number One let up on the button to rest the electric motor and simultaneously shot a quizzical look toward the bridge. Reversing the engine, The Pilot eased the boat slowly astern while signaling The Crew to let another 25' of chain run out. They continued this process until 100' or more of rode had gone overboard. Thereupon The Crew secured the chain to the boat's sampson post while The Pilot again guided the boat slowly backwards. Biting into the bottom as it set, the anchor caused the chain to straighten horizontally until the rearward progress of *Minstrel's Song* came to an unceremonious halt. At precisely that moment The Pilot shifted the transmission back into neutral and yelled to The Crew, "We're there!"

As the engine ceased to make its low rumbling noise and the world became eerily quiet, The Crew flashes a weak, drained smile toward the bridge. She knows it is over and she knows that from that moment on her Captain personally will tend to all of the trifling final tasks associated with setting the hook. Having dreaded this exercise for years, she is both relieved that it is behind her and equally surprised at how easy it was. "Is that all there is?" she seemed to be thinking, almost aloud.

With the anchor holding nicely and the diesel, the radar, the radio, the chartplotter and all of the other whiz-bang gadgets onboard now set to the off position, we finally have a moment to survey our surroundings. Gone is the worry about crossing the Strait; gone is the pressure of passing into the Cove; gone is the concern for finding a safe shelter for the night; gone is the anxiety of anchoring. After all of these apprehensions, we are now free to experience a Disney moment!

Some few hours before this luxurious time we had steamed out of Silva Bay under cold, steel grey skies that were being pushed by a chilly, freshening wind. With pilothouse doors closed, the heat on and with fleece jackets zipped all the way up to our chins, we had then cared as much about the warmth of our coffee as we did about its flavor. On the way across, even after the weather had broken and we were passing our friends in the sailboats, we had commented on how glad we were that we did not have to work out on deck. That was the world we had left. Yet here on the Sunshine Coast, only a turn or two more of the minute hand on the ship's clock removed from all of that, we were living in Fantasyland! In this new domain the sun casts its bright yellow rays warmly on everything. The crystal blue of the cloudless sky above us arcs overhead in perfect symmetry with the land below. And the lazy air that barely bestirs itself to welcome us with its soft kisses, promises that nothing but absolute sensory pleasure follows for the remainder of the day. In fact, every detail of the scene is so perfect that we wonder whether the whole thing might not be a dream or a mirage. Should we have wanted to test that perception seriously we might have done so by pinching ourselves, but we did not want to ruin it, so we did not.

There seem to be two kinds of people in the boating community (and perhaps around the entire planet): those who want to get away from it all and those who want to take it all with them. Our ship's compliment definitely falls into the former category and sometimes it lives a hard life because of it.

An inordinate number of boaters are flocking creatures. They spend their days, whether ashore or out on the bounding Main, seeking out the company of others. Their comfort zones reflect the motto: 'The more the merrier.' They join yacht clubs, service organizations and any number of other groups so as to be with like-minded souls, frequently. They come together at every opportunity, even when boats aren't involved, and, like the great migrating herds on the Serengeti Plain, they travel from place to place *en masse*. For these mariners, the apparent object of every activity seems to be to meet as many people as possible, to remain forever in the company of others, and to leave no marina (with a decent restaurant) unvisited.

Cohabitating in roughly the same space are the independents. Friendly enough and willing to join the odd company here or there, they prefer the freedom to march to the beat of their own drums and to whimsically and willfully pursue their own destinies in solitary splendor. These folks generally hang around long enough to find out where the crowd is headed and then set course in the opposite direction.

Neither set of the species truly understands the other, but they do manage to coexist. The one limps along wondering why their gracious invitations are rebuffed continually while the other cannot understand why the first wants company to start with. The truce between them is a fragile one and remains in effect so long as neither side crosses the red line in the water.

Watching as we have many times while the empty miles of the Inside Passage and the waterways of southeast Alaska slip by the sides of a cruise ship, we take to the water in our own boat in pursuit of…nothing, absolutely nothing. More properly stated, we put to sea in a small vessel to escape the confines of human life; we search for those few places left untouched, if only for a moment, by the presence of others. Because *Cupcake, and Kool Aid, and Pork Chop Too, et. al.* seem intent on filling every nook and cranny known to mankind with the vibrant products of eight-speaker sound systems, RIBS on the fly and jet skis of all sizes and shapes, and since those having those inclinations seem to far surpass those of us who prefer wandering solo, the numbers of the quiet, even lonely destinations available tend to be miniscule by comparison. They are available mainly in the desolate, hidden or hard to reach places that are so far removed from the hustle and bustle of every day life that one must work to identify them.

Shocked we are, then, to look around Smuggler Cove – located less than 40 nautical miles from the bustling City of Vancouver – and see…no one. No one! And based purely on that delightful discovery, we would have screeched "hurrah!" continuously for the next two hours had we not known from long experience that it was early in the day and empty anchorages can fill quickly as evening approaches. Our jubilation was checked too, by the knowledge that Smuggler Cove, being situated just off the major north-south route between Vancouver and the rest of the Inside Passage, was the aquatic equivalent of a Motel 6 situated at the end of the off ramp of a busy interstate highway. Still, there was no one there at the moment and hope springs eternal.

Given the limited size of Smuggler Cove, particularly that part in which we had taken up residence, and accepting that we probably would not be its sole inhabitants for very long, we decided that the polite thing to do would be to limit the swing of *Minstrel's Song* by tying down her tail.

On anchor, any vessel can run freely around and around the circular limits established by the combination of the fixed holding point and the rode linking it to the boat. This has the benefit of giving the craft lots of extra exercise without letting it go off on it own. As should be obvious to the reader, the radius of the imaginary corral we create for our ships in this manner comes somewhere near the amount of rode we stretch out. It is not an exact figure because the tether never is perfectly vertical or horizontal and we have to factor in the depth of the water too. Always being something less that the full extent of the rode and suffering from varying degrees of curvature due to the ever-changing pull exerted on it, we use the length of the rode nevertheless for rough calculations. Having allocated about 100 feet of chain this day, the diameter of the circle we can inscribe on the water is 200 feet. If anyone else stopped off in our small pool (diameter roughly 400'), they would need to set their anchor and rode carefully to avoid a potential tangle. We knew that hogging an anchorage would be rude, so we sought to avoid doing just that.

We forestall any problems of the nature just described by stern tying *Minstrel's Song*. If put to a vote, we would choose to spend the rest of the day enjoying the sights and sounds of our delightful little cove, reading or napping, or just sitting out in the sun and fresh air – and I definitely would prefer to be eating lunch – but first things first, so it is on to this final chore we move.

Down off its davits swings the dinghy and into the brine it goes. A precautionary painter (a light line tied to any small boat that serves to keep it from disappearing) is secured to its bow ring. Next, we wrestle the new outboard engine carefully off its perch on the ship's rail and endeavor to secure it to the transom of the RIB without letting it take a swim first. Successful at that, I start the little motor, receive from The Crew one end of a long, stout line that is wound onto a reel fastened firmly to our boat, and set out for shore. My chosen landing spot is only about 75' away, but with every square inch of the bottom – visible through remarkably clear water – populated by prop-busting rocks of considerable dimensions, I spend my time looking for a route through them that will keep me from rendering useless our new outboard. Ultimately I must settle for just getting the inflatable close to shore. By taking advantage of what little forward momentum the RIB can muster, I swing the outboard up, let the raft run in until it bumps on something hard and then jump out it into a couple of feet of icy water. Cold and mostly wet from the waist down, I drag my transport up onto dry land.

Although I had chosen what looked like a good place to get ashore, I soon found that in order to reach a good area for tying off the stern line, a climb up a rock wall that would have made a mountain goat proud was required. Grunting and groaning and only slipping to bark my shins four or fine times, I finally reach the summit. It is there that I triumphantly wrap the stern line that is still gripped in my teeth around a 20,000-pound boulder that I fancy might keep the stern of *Minstrel's Song* from swinging through for the night.

The return trip to our vessel varies only in that instead of falling up the rock face as I return to the "beach," I am able to fall down it.

Thinking, too, that worrying about what the prop of outboard is going to hit is more trouble than it is worth, I take up a paddle and use it to compel my floating brick back toward the boat. It only takes a minute or two for me to make my way to the stern line I had just laid out and then I take that hand-over-hand back to the mother ship. With a quick motion I throw a bowline in the painter, hook it through one of the davits on the swim step and climb back aboard. In just a few moments I play out a sufficient amount of stern line to hold *Minstrel's Song* in place and finally the workday is over. No longer needed to perform her cheerleading duties and drenched through though I am from the waist down, both The Crew and I smile expectantly. We are ready now to receive our "Good Citizen's" award from the crowds that we are sure will push into Smuggler Cove later.

The confines of the tiny harbor we have settled into wrap around us like a snug blanket. Or, more like candidly, the ring of rocks, small islands and tidal flats that form our miniature bay hug us closely, making us feel safe and secure. From the deck of our boat we can just see the open water of Malaspina Strait a half a mile or so to the northwest, but there is no direct route out to it. Beyond the sun, wind and sky, our world consists of six elements: tall green conifers pushing up out of every crack and crevice imaginable, reaching as if to touch the heavens; great grey rocks scattered randomly, as islands and as landmarks, through the confines of the reservoir that is formed by the arcing stone cliffs that rise up and circle around the pocket of water they strive to secure; pebbled tidal lands and beaches; wild grasses that dance and sway against an unmoving backdrop of brown tree trunks and a plethora of metamorphic boulders; lapping, clear water; and the fauna of this pint-sized microenvironment.

The great, hulking sarsens, the rocky islands and the cliffs that form the bedrock of this world conspire to present a vision tinted in all imaginable shades of grey. From light, almost white, to dark, almost black, every conceivable tone is at hand. Surprisingly, instead of creating a flat, drab environment, this greyness compliments and brings out the vibrant colors of everything near it.

The trees that wedge themselves into rock crevices, cling

precariously to the nearly vertical faces of stone walls or sit jauntily atop every landform capable of amassing soil, form solid green, conifer walls that shelter and define the spaces they fill and encompass without stifling or constraining. Spear-like, each member of this army of giants, immobile and rooted in the molten earth that hardened eons ago, stretches upward as if to become a part of the firmament, melding simultaneously into an unbroken, verdant curtain that denies individuality to anyone not intent on carefully identifying the individual threads of the whole fabric. The less diligent surrender to the notion that they observe not established forest tracts having length and breadth, but rather that they stand in the midst of a great emerald cyclorama. The domain so established becomes both infinite and infinitesimal at the same time.

Interspersed haphazardly about the scene are great, jagged piles of lifeless grey-brown rocks that were thrust up out of the bowels of the earth eons ago. These behemoths cleave both land and sea and seem to be straining to reach ever higher as if, somehow, seeking to touch for an instant, the green of the moss, the ferns, the grasses and the trees that live and breath on top of them. Binding these parts together are the tidal lowlands and the sand and pebble-strewn beaches. These loop round and round the core of the cove, forming a continuum that ultimately conveys to the observer an undeniable sense of timelessness.

Nature's unwavering hand adds brush strokes of interest to the dominant greys, browns and greens with a touch of tan here, a bit of black there and a splash of bright yellow from those flowers trying to hide behind that brown-black stump. The reflecting pool that lifts and gently rocks our boat back and forth captures and re-captures all of the visual delights that surround it, adding depth, contrast and interest to every vista. This tiny world of light, texture and color becomes a personal kaleidoscope.

Since the creation of all things progressed in a dictated order, it is fitting that we take in first the heavens, then the sea, and finally the dry ground. Thereafter our senses inform us of the vegetation that clings to this rugged scene and then and only after all of that do we perceive the living creatures.

As noted, we are ecstatic to find our anchorage devoid of our fellow man and perhaps because of that we feel unconstrained in our examination of the teeming world that lies almost within arm's reach. Sammy the Seal, ever-present, shoves his head up out of the water to see what we are all about; we wave at him and send our smiles his way. Grey, white and speckled gulls wheel and soar and dive overhead, making, well, making their usual gull racket. Forest birds flit through the trees more felt than seen. A silver streak flashes in the water to tell us that we have company under us as well. Finally, the stars of this day's show appear: a gaggle of Canada geese and a bald eagle.

Off to the left, at a distance of little more than 100 feet, stand a pair of Canadian geese. Unperturbed by our presence, they ruminate together atop a rock just barely awash. Apparently this perch allows them to keep their feet in the water, but their feathers dry. They seem to desire little more than to be left alone so as to absorb as much of the warmth of the sun as possible. Periodically, however, they set up a terrific, long-necked, trumpeting din that surely is audible in the States. As newcomers to the neighborhood who did not wish to seem impolite, we posed no objections to their intermittent outbursts although we did not fully understand them. In fact, we tried at first to pretend that their clamoring was an ordinary part of our daily experience. Despite those efforts, however, the racket began to wear thin. And the more we noticed it, the more we realized that the hullabaloo was anything but normal. As our attention was drawn toward the pair of offenders we discovered that their throats were not the only ones filling the air with sound. From several different directions at once we noted a veritable symphony of goose complainants; we noted too a correlation between the cacophony that flowed out of the uncounted number of goose necks and the swooping and screeching of the gulls above them.

THE GREAT GOOSE WAR

I cannot advise the reader as to when or where it hit us, but the truth of the situation ultimately settled in and provided much amusement. Unbeknownst to us, we had apparently set up shop smack-dab in the middle of the primary battlefield of The Great Goose War. As best we could discern, the geese considered the islet a few feet distant from us to be their exclusive domain. Apparently they had inhabited it seasonally for many centuries. (Whether they actually held legal title to the rocky protrusion remained moot, for in their eyes possession of it clearly was 90% of the law.) The gulls, for their part, disputed the assertions of the larger grey fowl, contending that as year round residents – who forcibly were displaced each summer by the gaggling goose hoards – they had the more valid claim to the real estate. Moreover, they argued that it was size discrimination solely that denied them the use of their property during the warm months. Regardless of which group had justice on its side, open hostilities between the parties had broken out and a civil resolution of the dispute was unlikely.

Although smaller in stature and not terribly well suited for direct conflict with the geese, the gulls were aviators extraordinaire. Quick and nimble in flight, they circled high above their adversaries, waiting for the chance to swoop down on them and peck their heads unmercifully. Usually they attacked in waves and their effectiveness was abetted by a sophisticated system of communications that sounded, to outsiders such as, like little more than a series of eardrum splitting screeches.

From personal observations we concluded that in an effort to dislodge their enemies, the smaller birds preferred to make quick, harassing air assaults rather than try to mount full frontal charges. With wings swept back to maximum angle, they would dive from the heights, hit about Mach 2.8 and then, at the last possible instant – pulling at least 11 Gs – they would flatten their trajectories and blast just over the heads of their adversaries. As they did so, they would use their long, sharp beaks to strike at the crowns of any goose not paying close attention. The slightest error in judgment or timing, however, could end in gull-tragedy since the geese countered these depredations by snapping their wide bills upward in an effort to snatch the smaller birds out of the air and fling them to their deaths on the rocky ground – an end too grisly to be contemplated.

Much larger and much slower in flight, the geese employed a different strategy. They fought only from the ground and only from behind well-defended natural bulwarks. Serving as their castle keep, the long-necked combatants had taken up a nearly impregnable position in a depression perched nonetheless on the edge of a small cliff. This fortress – for surely that is what it resembled – was surrounded by a wall of skyward-pointing rock outcroppings that resembled either a circle of jagged dragon's teeth or, perhaps, the upper ramparts of a medieval citadel. This imposing defensive position was backed by an adjacent stand of tall trees that limited the arc of air attacks the gulls could press to something under 150 degrees. Thus ensconced, the dispositions of the geese militarily were sublime.

Hunkering safely behind their battlements, the long-throated gaggle divided themselves into two phalanxes. The first division, clearly made up of the quickest and the bravest, took it upon themselves to extend their long necks above their secure parapets and snap their bills viciously at any gull that swooped too close. Danger lurked in every part of this mission since even the slightest miscalculation might find them on the receiving end of a gull's unmerciful beak. Meanwhile, the second group apparently was charged with thwarting the intruders' formations via concentrated sound. With a plethora of geese all directing their voices toward a single gull, all available throats would let loose with a honking roar that might, in other venues, have stopped a clock. It would be disingenuous to suggest that this bray had no effect on the gulls' morale.

The forces of good and evil raged against each other off and on throughout the sunny afternoon. At times the field was empty and still, the gulls' assaults giving way to foraging expeditions and the geese being content to sun themselves or pick through the nearby meadow grasses for culinary treats. But suddenly, for reasons unidentified, the serenity of the scene would be broken again and in would come a squadron of gulls with death and destruction clearly in mind while the geese hustled back to their battle stations.

It was late afternoon before a fragile truce between the sides took hold and further conflict was averted. The gulls, for their part, relinquished their airspace and the geese ambled out from behind their walls. All was quiet on the western front.

* * * * * * * * * * *

Despite the intensity of the conflict that seethed just off our port beam, we managed, after lunch, to while away most of the afternoon. With no wind and a bounty of warm, yellow sunshine washing everything, it was perfect for sitting outside reading, snacking, sunning or just ruminating on the nature of being. Looking back, it is hard to say how many hours we spent thus unemployed; it might have been five or six, but equally, it might have been 500 or 600. Time passes that way in places like this.

Periodically one or the other of us would make comment about something. We would engage in conversation for a few moments and then return to our reveries. The concerns of daily life hang heavily and constantly on most of us. Every now and then, however, we have these idyllic moments wherein all seems right, nothing presses and a deep, pure contentment sets in. This was Smuggler Cove at that instant.

Lost in inner space, one or the other of us would emerge occasionally from the delightful stupor of well being that we each enjoyed only to blissfully lapse back immediately without further fanfare. Thus, for instance, despite being engrossed completely in a section of a good book, we might look up for no apparent reason and conclude with surprise that there still was an entire universe lurking just beyond our fingertips. Or, our mental capacities might become fully fixated on the fascinating movements of a wayward insect that had alighted on a nearby panel of bone white fiberglass either a second or two before or, perhaps, a few eons previously. Alternatively, our attentions might seamlessly give way to unprovoked and extremely intensive cerebral dissections of the tonal variations found in the voices of the woodland birds then populating the depths of the forests surrounding Smuggler Cove. Periodically, we might even find ourselves sitting up for no apparent reason, blinking once or twice in the bright light, while attempting to separate reality from the soft murmuring dream we might have just had. Perhaps, then, it was a shadow passing overhead that pulled us both into a different realm; perhaps it was the sound of air slipping over wide, feathered wings; perhaps it was just time to look up and find an eagle soaring in great circles above us. Perhaps it just was.

As if the majestic creature now turning slowly overhead perceived no hostility in our world, or possibly, for a split-second, we his, he slowly spiraled down and gently alighted on the top branch of a nearby tree. There he perched in proximate splendor while casting his sharp eye on us as if to say, "Look ye, earthbound mortals. Look ye at ether's prince! Behold my magnificence, my grace and my beauty. Loose your thoughts, your hopes and your dreams and let them soar with me. Watch and wonder and find in yourselves a shade of the marvel I reflect."

For many long minutes we exchanged considerations. He seemed to find in us a fascination equal to that which we discovered in him. Then, without warning, he spread his great wings and glided steeply down toward the water in the cove, picking up effortless speed as he went. Shifting his upper body backward and churning the air with a horizontal flap or two of his outstretched wings, he extended his talons forward. In a single roiling movement, his claws broke the surface of the sea while his body lurched forward and upward in a mighty effort to regain the speed he had lost. A fine, wriggling slash of silver was held tightly in his grip. Quickly regaining his aerodynamic efficiency, our friend climbed regally through the clear air until he came to perch in the top of a stand of trees across the small bay. Thereafter, he watched us eat a snack as we watched him eat his.

Late in the afternoon we heard the distinctive chug-chug-chug of a boat. Looking toward the cove's entrance – a few hundred feet away as the crow flies – we watched as a sailboat motored into our domain. Without apparent hesitation she passed through the gates of hell, steamed around the central island of the upper cove, shot through a narrow pass to the southeast of us and disappeared from sight, except for the top of her mast, behind the marshy spit that separates the upper section of the harbor from the lower. Their rate of progress and their lack of hesitation suggested that they were veterans of this area. Thankfully, they settled in quietly and intruded not at all on our serenity.

LOST WITHIN SPACE

After dinner, as the shadows grew long all about us, I remained in the saloon and amused myself by alternately feasting on the book I was reading and by observing the Canadian geese who were dining on the succulent grasses nearby. It was a serene time of no consequence, but of great pleasure. Out of this tranquility a nagging thought pushed its way into my consciousness. Where was The Crew?

As I am wont to do, I tried to stuff this mental interloper back into its box and go happily on my way with the indulgences I had been enjoying. As almost always, the beast was four sizes too large to return to the deep recesses of its container. Soon I was forced to surrender to it and consciously break my reveries. Thus drawn out, I was compelled to contend with the situation. According to the facts at hand, I established beyond all doubt that I could not see my Shipmate, and through the lack of any rocking of the boat that I felt as it sat quietly on the still water, it was clear to me that she was not temporarily out of sight by virtue of relocating from one place to another. Adding fuel to the conceptual fire I was building, it occurred to me that I could not remember when last I had noted either of those two events. My next thought, then, was that she was lost, as in not found. The thought right after that one, the more rational one, cancelled out the first. After all, it is really hard to get lost on a 32-foot boat!

This caused my anxiety meter to race from zero to a thousand instantaneously, while my internal "black box" began to record all of my actions and considerations as they developed throughout the crisis. A later review of that evidence revealed a sequence that went something like this: Reflection A: When sitting in the central part of the boat I cannot see her. Reflection B: The vessel is not rocking the way it would if she were moving from one place to another onboard. Reflection C: My underpowered brain cannot recall precisely when last it was conscious of her presence, but it has been a while. Logical Conclusion: She is not on the vessel!

Thereupon all of the internal warning lights, buzzers and bells I possessed went off simultaneously. Without retracing the route my thoughts took through all of the dark possibilities, suffice it to say that I realized immediately that not having The Crew onboard the boat was a particularly bad thing, especially since *Minstrel's Song* was surrounded wholly and totally by deep, frigid water. From that intellectual pinnacle I had but two other options to explore: 1.) She had taken the dinghy and gone somewhere; or 2.) She had fallen overboard and drowned.

Since the human mind will do cartwheels to avoid dealing with unpleasant realities, I found myself desperately praying that The Crew has taken the dinghy for a quick run to the 7-11 Store for a quart of milk. This, of course, was beyond ridiculous since it required that I ignore two gigantic facts: 1.) That The Crew had never, ever, taken that boat anywhere by herself; and 2.) We certainly did not need any stinking milk! (The reader might understand that the pressure of the moment kept me from adding a third factor to the list: to wit, there probably wasn't anything even vaguely resembling a 7-11 within 50 miles, nautical or statute, of Smuggler Cove.) But even with the weight of these proofs in hand, I did all that was possible to cling to the hope that she had gone away somewhere and that she was not just gone (as in over the side).

Again, against this backdrop the reader may feel some sympathy when I confess I began to contrive alternative explanations that satisfied my immediate needs. That was not very easy, however, since by now I was standing in the middle of the saloon looking out through the stern windows at the picture of our RIB bobbing quietly on its painter, just where I left it tied some hours before. And, a quick trip forward to our stateroom told me that that was empty too. Beyond the saloon, the stateroom and the empty pilothouse, there really were no other spots onboard for her to hide. "Where in hell could she be?" I frantically asked of no one in particular.

As if to reassure myself, or at least to fend off the unthinkable, I reviewed everything carefully once again. And once again I said, "No! She couldn't be overboard because I would have heard a splash and her calls for help."

"You would have heard the splash and calls for help if you hadn't been so self-absorbed in what you were doing! Oblivious to everything outside of you, You, YOU, as usual, YOU missed the whole show, Bub!" intoned the angel who sits haughtily on my right shoulder at times like these.

"No! Enough!" I shouted to myself. With no further debate, I rushed forward again to check physically that the head is empty, the stateroom is clear and the foredeck unpopulated. Then I move smartly to the cockpit to see what I can see from there. Looking 360 degrees around, my eyes suddenly lock onto her familiar form. "She's not overboard. She's not dead. She's carrying out her duties as Ship's Photographer. See, she's right there, sitting on the pilothouse roof, with dangling legs kicking back and forth lazily while she occupies herself with something that must be important," I sigh with relief!

"What are you doing up there," I ask casually, trying my very best to stifle a fear-invoked snarl.

"Oh, just enjoying the evening and hoping to get some pictures of the sunset."

I climb the ladder, step across the sun deck and take up a place on the pilothouse roof beside her. There I savor her presence and I bask in my burgeoning sense of relief. Although darkness is not far away, the waning moments of the evening serve to reinforce the grandeur of the day. We wait and watch as the fire-red sun, as if fatigued by its exertions since dawn, falls heavily into the distant sea and is extinguished slowly. The Photographer takes her shots. We sit side-by-side, hold hands and marvel. And then it is over. Could life ever be any better?

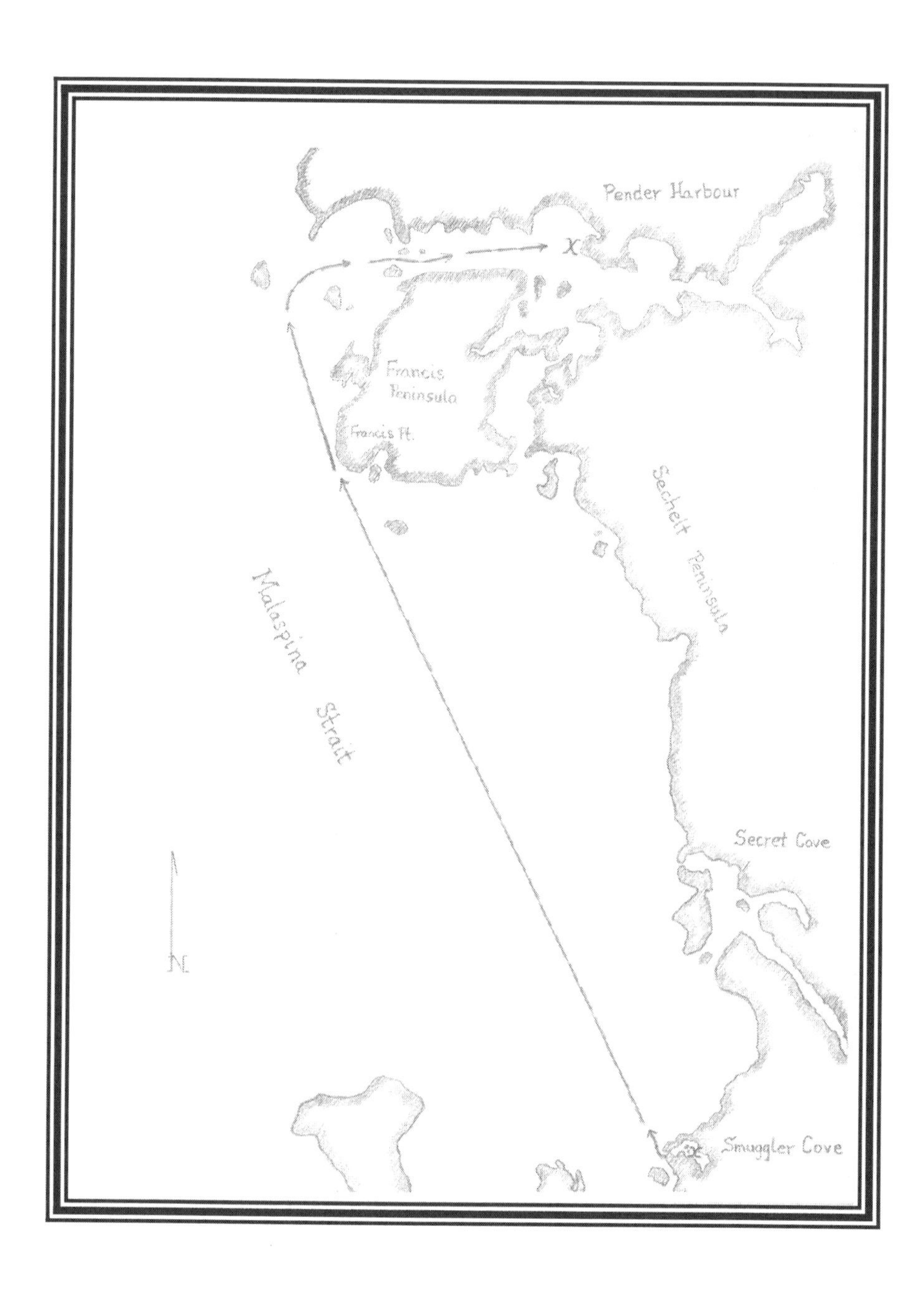
Pender Harbour
X
Francis Peninsula
Francis Pt.
Sechelt Peninsula
Malaspina Strait
Secret Cove
N
Smuggler Cove

Day Four

Smuggler Cove To Pender Harbour
Or
How We Lost The %#@&% . . . and Other Salty Tales

And then the honeymoon ended! Sometime during the night the earth stopped spinning in a counter clockwise direction and reversed course. Out of the fog of deep sleep, along about 4:00 a.m., just as the sky starts to lighten in these latitudes, I stumbled up the ladder (steps) to the pilothouse to take a look around. *Minstrel's Song* was bobbing and weaving like a heavyweight prizefighter and my half-functioning mind sought vainly for a rational explanation. All had been so peaceful, so serene when we turned in. Why the change now?

Peering into the semi-darkness, expecting to look out over the placid tidal pool swaddled by stately trees that had been our home the evening before, I beheld instead a grey, unsettled scene of swirling movement and dusky turmoil. The waters of our tiny bay, though protected through 360 degrees, were racing northward frantically as if to escape the lash of an unseen whip. The picturesque rocks, shelves and islets I anticipated had turned black and had assumed a hulking, surly complexion that commanded respect if not outright fear. The elegant firs and cedars that had provided an artist's backdrop for a pastoral scene were bending, twisting and sweeping wildly in grotesque responses to the blasts of Aeolus' cold breath. Even that warm, blue umbrella sky that had arched protectively over us reeled as if under the blows of some great hammer. It had been flattened, beaten down almost to the sea. Its azure essence pounded into an unrecognizable, steely-grey sheet that now careened recklessly just above the ship's antennas.

I considered this tempestuous milieu with detached curiosity. From the low, scudding clouds, to the howl of the wind through the rigging, right on down to the dark, soulless water that now cradled our boat, it was hard to grasp the magnitude of the transformation that had taken place. Philosophically I asked myself, "Which is reality?"

If blame could be assigned and apportioned based on a lack of preparation, it would have to be split 50-50 between the weatherman and The Skipper. Caught up in the idyllic scenes of the previous day, the latter mentally projected that picture to infinity and beyond. Thus, in his incredibly tiny brain, Smuggler Cove was and always would be exactly as it had experienced the day before. Based on that assumption, the preparations our gallant commander had made for the day's onward journey up the coast had not included *any* thoughts about a possible change in the weather. In fairness, it must be added that the prognosticator apparently had been operating in about that same mode, since his broadcast musings, sent out on the airwaves mere hours before, included *nothing* about the typhoon that had dropped in like unwanted weekend guests.

With this new situation all neatly sorted out, explained and catalogued in my mind for future reference, I made a lap around the boat to affirm that all was as it should be. Being satisfied that *Minstrel's Song* was safe and secure, I descended the ladder from the bridge and happily dove back into my snug cocoon, knowing that we could sleep as long as we wanted because we were not going anywhere in this weather. Through the semi-darkness my Shipmate's voice reached my ear. "Is everything O.K.?"

"No worries." I responded, "It's blowing a gale and raining some, but we're snug and safe here. Doesn't look like a good day for traveling, so go back to sleep and I'll see you when you wake up."

By the time we sipped our first cups of coffee, the weather, if anything, had taken a turn for the worse. I listened to the forecast, looked at the sky and at the sea in the cove and opined, once more, that we probably would stay put for the day. As if to second that sentiment, the wind howled louder and the raindrops pounded harder on the cabin roof.

Being betwixt and between is the bane of my existence. Go? Stay? Go? Stay? These words plague me relentlessly. Despite having built time into our schedule for the likes of this morning, not moving ahead with the plan seems too decadent, even borderline cowardly. Prudence, however, screamed, "Are you nuts?"

In situations such as these I tend to settle, absolutely, on the right course of action and then spend all of the rest of the time available second-guessing that decision. As happened on a Caribbean sailing adventure a couple of decades back, abetted by a crew that focused exclusively on schedules, I allowed myself to be pushed from the right side of the decision making process to the wrong. Not only did the trip turn ugly, fast, but also the punishment Poseidon dished out for not heeding the wisdom of the ages stopped uncomfortably shy of the loss of the vessel or worse. Having made that mistake once, I tend now to ere exclusively on the side of caution, yet the voice of male machismo still taunts me unmercifully.

As the storm rages outside, we are comfy-cozy inside. Thanks to the steady flow of warm air wafting from the heater vents and the soft, yellow light of the oil lamp that converts the saloon into a romantic chamber, our circumstances could hardly be better. Adding to the ambience, The Mess Steward keeps the coffee pot full and our table well victualed. We sip, we snack, we read our books, we chat, we marvel at Nature's fury from safe behind our windows and we want for nothing. But I still feel like a caged animal. Emotionally torn, each gust of wind assures me that we are exactly where we should be, while each lull causes me to wonder. Periodically listening to the latest weather broadcasts, it seems that even the forecasters stoke the fires of my indecision. Their mechanically generated voices – whether male or female, speaking in English or in French – suggest, but only just, that things might be getting better later in the day.

Shortly after 2:00 p.m. I stop reading, put down my book and get up from my burrow in the saloon. Nervously, I begin my 112th survey of our little world. I listen to the wind, look at the sky, note the action of the waves on the water, watch the trees bend, and again attempt to effect a change via telekinesis.

PLEASE PASS THE CROW

Making the rounds of the vessel, I climb the ladder to the wheelhouse and peer through the windscreen to ascertain the angle and condition of the anchor rode. I look at the battery gauges and make a mental record of their indicated power levels. I pull up the deck hatches and stare down into the engine compartment to affirm that all is safe and dry. Descending the ladder to the saloon, I take a step or two aft to glance out of the stern door and am struck dumb, as if by lightning! There, not ten feet off the swim step, is our dinghy, untethered, and merrily floating away!

Preceded by a cry that was somewhere between a gasp and a scream, I fling the door to the cockpit open and race to the back of the boat. Startled, The Crew instantly musters alongside of me awaiting orders. My first inclination is to dive into the water in order to retrieve the ungrateful deserter. The distance between it and me, though widening, is still but a few strong swimming strokes away. This impulse is fortified by two brutal truths that whip through my mind at the speed of light. First, as the careful reader will recall, attached to the aforementioned miserable hunk of air-filled rubber that serves as our tender, is our new outboard motor. It had been employed only twice: once in Bedwell Harbour and once here, in Smuggler Cove, for the 89 second one-way trip it had been forced to make in order to deliver our stern line ashore. My razor sharp faculties calculate that floating away is a piece of nearly new equipment that had, so far, rendered service at an amortized rate of approximately $9.00 a second. Concomitant with that thought comes the realization that our sole source of transportation from *Minstrel's Song* to shore, anywhere, has just taken off on its own. Thus it seems right and just that the perpetrator of such ingratitude should be pursued relentlessly and punished unmercifully when caught.

Despite the strong case made by these considerations, my second set of reflections on the topic completely nullifies my first. Carefully processing the data, I observe that the distance between the runaway and our boat grows wider with each passing second. And, while the gap does not seem to be great, I have no direct knowledge of how my body will respond to a full immersion in the intervening water. The ice-cold sea might immobilize me before I can propel myself to the raft or it might make it impossible for me to climb into it once there. And, we're pretty much alone out here. Any necessary emergency assistance would require long minutes, if not hours, to arrive on the scene. Lots of bad things can transpire in that amount of time. Thus, The Crew and I stare in frozen disbelief as our RIB defiantly bids us a fond adieu.

The dinghy's first port of call is the rock ledge directly astern of the boat. Maybe it is 50 feet away, but maybe it is only 30 feet. Whatever the actual distance, it seems content to settle there for a time and while it does, my mind starts turning. "If I attach a line to the handle of the rubber cleaning bucket, I might be able to toss it into the dinghy. The weight and shape of the bucket should be enough to let me coax the raft back to us. Hmmmm."

As if it could read my mind, and before we could begin to set this retrieval scenario into motion, the vagrant took off again. Driven north by the gale, it bumped its way along the eastern extreme of the ledge – a distance of 30 feet or so – and then rounded its northeastern tip only to turn westward down the narrow, shallow channel that separated the rock shelf behind us from "Goose Islet" (of The Great Goose War fame). With that slight body of water draining into the Smuggler Cove pass, it was clear that if the RIB kept up its nerve it was almost as good as gone. For once it began a cruise down the channel leading out of Smuggler Cove, the next stop was the open water of Malaspina Strait. Seeing this The Crew wails, "It's making a run for it!"

"I know," I moan. "And if that stinkin' piece of rubbery, silvery junk gets out there amongst those gray rollers and whitecaps, both our shore transportation and our new little outboard will disappear forever."

It is for crises like these that captains spend years preparing themselves. Cool. Calm. Collected. They stand on the bridge and bark precise, unemotional orders to achieve the only possible outcome that could save the ship. Afterward, the crew marvels at the genius of their leader. (At least that is the way it works in the movies.)

Stumbling through the saloon toward the helm, I grab the trusty sailing knife I keep there. My thoughts race, but the primary objective now is to take in our gear and get *Minstrel's Song* underway post-haste. The vague plan forming in my beady little brain requires that we yank the anchor, disengage from shore and quickly motor the long way around "Goose Islet" so as to be in a position to head the dinghy off at the pass (or someplace thereabouts). The first link in that chain of events amounts to cutting the stern line and hence my desire for the knife. (Of course, the reader knows full well that the conveyance designated for taking parties ashore to do things such as properly freeing lines tied around large boulders has jumped ship. What he may or may not recall is that the line in question is a part of a new, 600-foot spool of a really splendid rope that is attached to the ship's rail. The option at this juncture is either to sacrifice a shorter length of the cord or just to pitch the whole reel into the sea!) Emerging from the interior of the boat into the cockpit again, ready to slice and hack at any and all restraints encountered, The Lookout conveys game-changing intelligence. "The dink," she reports, "does not seem to be making for the open sea. When last I saw it, it was just there, on the western end of the island [Goose Islet] but it seemed to be making its way back toward the northeast, back into the cove. It disappeared a few seconds ago behind the island and I still can't see it."

The import of this tid-bit makes no impact on my adrenalin-addled brain. But before I can brush this interruption aside with the terse "So what?" that my slow-moving intellect always produces without thought or notice, she points and emphasizes, "I think it went *behind* the island."

I choke back another "So what" and this time try to comprehend the significance of her words. Then it hits me. "If our rubbery agitator turned to starboard instead of to port as I expected it would when it got to the larger channel, then it would be moving back around the islet and ultimately would be re-entering our little bay. And that would be the cat's meow."

Charging her with keeping a continued sharp lookout, I run forward to our bow pulpit. From that perch I expect to catch the next glimpse of the RIB as it makes its way back home. My agitated mind works while I stand there, producing full-blown sets of plans for retrieving the fugitive when it is at hand again. Meanwhile I wait. Then, I wait again. And then I wait some more. Nothing.

I call back to The Lookout for a report. She sees nothing there either! Not believing my ears, I scramble back to the cockpit via the pilothouse and saloon in a flurry of idiotic activity that allows me accomplish nothing except barking my shin on a rung of the ladder and then reading The Crew's lips as she pronounces the word, "Nothing."

"How can that be?" I wonder. Annoyed and perturbed, I mentally construct an aerial view of Smuggler Cove and then ponder it. From this lofty perspective I can reach only one conclusion. Provided that the RIB is constrained to move only by way of the force of the wind and the currents acting on it, and provided that there was but one way in and one way out of the cove, and provided that no one blinked and missed its escape to seaward, then the dinghy, though temporarily hidden from view, must still be close at hand. Moreover, given that it did not re-enter our little pool, it had to be in hiding on the far side of "Goose Islet."

"O.K., O.K., this is good," I think, as a new plan emerges. I brief The Crew and she turns to, heading for the windless while I make for the helm station. My strategy now is to fire up *Minstrel's Song*, yank the anchor, snip the stern line and convert the mother ship into a rescue vessel.

Milliseconds after the diesel springs to life, my brain screams, "Whoa, big fellow. Whoa! What are you doing? Setting our craft free in these windswept, tide plagued, constricted waters with the idea that somehow we will be able to motor right over there, retrieve the dinghy without even getting damp – because it will be waiting quietly for us, mid-channel – and then live happily ever after is nuts! What is more likely is that either the winds or the tides or both will drive our precious *Minstrel's Song* directly onto the rocks or, if we are really living right, we'll discover the dinghy taunting us from some inaccessible nook on the far side. Then, there we will sit, with two boats ready to wander separately around the world and still no effective way to bring them back together." Other possibilities did occur to me as well, but none of them were nearly as good as these.

At The Captain's direction, The Crew stands down from her station at the bow and returns to the warmth of pilothouse. Despondently The Skipper professes that we now are in need of a Plan E. Having failed in every way possible so far, he is running short of nifty ideas and is reduced to asking if she has any.

"What about the other boat that came in yesterday? Maybe they could help us somehow." I mull it and know that the odds are way against us, but when you are down to your last bullet, you are not above hoping for that incredible shot that will save the day – even though you know that only John Wayne actually ever made it.

Taking mic in hand, I switch on the VHF radio and make the call, repeatedly, to the unknown sailing vessel in Smuggler Cove. Reflecting the common practice of most sane sailors, their lack of response probably means nothing more than that for reasons pertaining solely to personal tranquility they have turned off their noxious noisemaker while swinging quietly at anchor.

At risk of putting my growing sense of desperation on public display, I resorted to trying to call, literally, our neighbors via bullhorn. The quarter of a mile or more of distance that separated us, the reedy, marshy lowlands betwixt our positions, the wail of the wind through the rigging and the wild thrashing of the trees around us all were conspiring, I was sure, to preclude any contact in this manner. Nonetheless, there was not much else to be done. Thus, I turned up the volume and made my plea, repeatedly. As expected, I got in return no human sound.

Defeated, I slumped over the chart table wondering if there was anything left to be done.

"Can we call the Coast Guard?" Number One asks.

"No," I mumble. "The Coast Guard monitors Channel 16 continuously. If a single radio wave had escaped the black hole we're parked in when I called the other boat on that channel, they would have contacted us to ask if we were in need of assistance. Besides, this isn't an emergency and they certainly have better things to do in this weather than to fix my rookie mistakes. Losing the RIB wounds my pride deeply but it doesn't impact the safety of our boat or of any others."

As these words died away, my gaze dropped to the clutter on the chart table and my mind went back to work again. My mention of the Coast Guard led me to wonder who might provide assistance in a situation like this if the Coast Guard did not. With my eyes wandering aimlessly over the papers spread on the table in front of me, I suddenly remembered the tree farm of tall masts that I had mistaken for Smuggler Cove only the day before. Searching for that spot on the chart, I found the words "Secret Cove" imprinted on the paper. A quick calculation told me that that place was not more than a single nautical mile – as the crow flies – from us. Simultaneously, I recalled that many entrepreneurs located in ports throughout the region made exorbitant sums of money by dispatching small, high-speed vessels to help the boating public when they do dumb things. These business people operate – for cash or credit, paid in advance – like a waterborne AAA. Mulling the possibilities, I wondered aloud if there was any way for us to contact someone in Secret Cove who might then be able to tell us if any of the kind of people we needed had set up shop over there.

In a single bound The Crew shot down the ladder to the saloon. In seconds she was back again with a file folder and a cruising guide. Our original itinerary had not included, specifically, a stop in Smuggler Cove. Rather, we anticipated pulling into an inviting looking place somewhere on the Sunshine Coast, more of less as the spirit moved us. One of the prospects we had pre-identified for that was Secret Cove. Being an organizational genius, Number One was rarely caught short of information. Pawing frantically through her stash, she emerged triumphantly with the phone numbers for two Secret Cove marinas. The only question now was whether we could raise them via cell phone.

"Hello," I said. "Yeah...Hi...How's it going? Well, it's been better before...Hey look, I'm over here in Smuggler Cove and I've got a bit of a problem and I wondered whether there might be someone over there who could give us a hand." Relating the crux of the difficulty to the she girl on the other end of the line, I learned that she could not help us. Her marina just provided slips, fuel and groceries. But, as my hope was fading, she added that there was someone, somewhere around there, who might be of use. The rub was that she was not sure she had their phone number. Long, anxious moments passed as she made her search.

"Hello," I said again. "Yeah…Hi…How's it going? Well, it's been better…ya da, ya da, ya da…" With the social conventions finally out of the way I dive in once more. "Hey look, I'm over here in Smuggler Cove and I've got a bit of a problem and I wondered whether there might be someone over there who could help." And again, I start the humiliating process of describing the stupid thing I have done and the consequences of it. Concurrently, I have to exert all of the self-control I can muster to keep from falling to my knees and pleading – unnatural and unworthy of an old Sea Dog as that would be – that they send relief ASAP (as soon as possible). My reward for that gargantuan effort is a flat, normal sounding voice that gives me a very positive response to my inquiry. Bursting with excitement I all but yell, "You could? He would? On the credit card? Here over the phone? No! No problem!" By now it's all I can do now to keep from jumping up and down and shouting into the phone, 'Would you like my first born son too?' but I resist that temptation as well.

When I finally hang up, I turn to The Crew and deliver the news. This action is redundant given that she was standing next to me during conversation and was watching my reaction to it, but it is a formality I think best retained nonetheless. As nonchalantly as possible I advise her that some nice man from Secret Cove is going to be over shortly to rescue our bacon and it is only going to cost us an arm and a leg to get him to do it. Putting a happy face on this last piece of news, I underscore the sad fact that replacing the outboard and RIB together would cost us about ten times as much as the outrageous price I had just agreed to pay to the person who was lacking sufficient good sense to know better than to go out on the water in an open boat in this kind of weather. It is always good to provide perspective when delivering news of this kind.

Now there was nothing for us to do except sit, wait, pace, and hope that the guy who now had all of our credit card information showed up before the dink high-tailed it to more distant climes. Tick. Tick. Tick.

We passed a nervous half an hour before I could hear, above the natural din, the high-pitched sound of a hard working outboard motor. My ardor was dampened, some, by the fact that the noise was coming to us from the wrong direction. Since there was but one way in and one way out of Smuggler Cove, I could not understand the discrepancy. Peering through the raindrops in an effort to get the rational world back in focus, I spied a rubber dinghy laboring out of the south end of Smuggler Cove and into our bay. In it were four people, dressed in foul weather gear, who could have come from nowhere except the boat that joined us last night. They waved. They smiled. They pointed cheerily to the other side of "Goose Islet." Then they disappeared behind it.

Virtually the same moment they vanished, a throatier roar reaches our ears from the other direction (i.e., from the right direction). Into Smuggler Cove careens a single man standing spread-legged behind a wheel in the middle of an aluminum skiff. He looks much more like a surfer on his board than a serious marine salvager. With his arrival we find ourselves suddenly awash in a sea of would-be Good Samaritans. Mere moments before we were on our own to conclude this sordid matter as best we could and then within nanoseconds the cove was crawling with assistants!

Although provincial (state), local or other coastal regulations make a tangle of everything, basic maritime law says that anything abandoned or adrift on the surface – even when not on purpose – and anything that has found its way to the ocean floor – even when not on purpose – belongs to the one who finds it (the salvager). And, anyone can be a salvager. Thus, the two craft we know to be converging on the scene of the crime potentially could come into conflict with each other. If our boating neighbors snag the dink first, it is theirs. That act, however, might seem to rob the hired service provider of his commission. And while we are certain that in either case the wayward craft would come back to us, we fear a confrontation. And, the fact that we now have two sets of rescuers at hand makes us feel even dumber than we did before.

In a few short moments our sailing neighbors motor around the east end of "Goose Islet" and steer toward *Minstrel's Song.* Passing on our port beam they slow just long enough to tell their tale and receive our heartfelt thanks. It seems that they had been ashore, hiking around the cove (!), when they heard my bullhorn ring. From their vantage point on land, once alerted, they saw our RIB. Hustling back to their ship, they jumped into their gig and set off after ours. Thus, when they passed us the first time, they knew what they were seeking and they knew where it was. They also recognized the monetary interest that the other guy had in collecting our dink, so they deferred to his expertise in vessel recovery operations.

After accepting our bountiful gratitude – they would take no more than that for their kindness – our compatriots went on their merry way. Before they left, however, they told us that the other guy would be bringing our dinghy around shortly.

It was not long before our pre-paid knight in shining armor rounded the point, leading a much subdued, even contrite, prisoner. Coming alongside *Minstrel's Song* he handed me the painter and I thanked him profusely while sheepishly trying to explain how such a thing could have happened to a seasoned mariner. He accepted the former, but clearly was skeptical about the latter assertion! In our brief exchange, I learned that the storm "outside" had abated some and that conditions were not as bad as they had been.

I opened and closed my investigation into the root cause of this sordid escape effort in around 10 minutes. The day before – you know, the one that was warm and calm with nary a ripple to stir the water – I took a length of new, nylon line and quickly crafted from it a painter to use whenever the RIB needed to be secured to something. I attached one end of this to the dink and looped the other end through a davit clip on the mother ship. In both instances, the sailor's best friend, the bowline knot, was employed. The virtues of this knot are that is easy to make – once the art is mastered – it does not slip and even when wet or under great strain, it comes free with minimal effort. (I especially prefer it because most 'lubbers' cannot tie it!) Not intending to hold the inflatable through hell and high water, what I jury-rigged the previous afternoon using stiff, slippery new line should have been used only temporarily. One might liken it to throwing the rein from a horse's bridle over a hitching rail; it was sufficient for keeping a tired beast in place on a warm day, but totally inadequate when the gunfight broke out!

The after action report I verbally conveyed to The Crew included the facts above, but in it I mentioned that I had never had a bowline fail. After a close examination of the available evidence, however, I was forced to admit that this one had given way, most probably because of the combination of new nylon rope – notoriously slippery – and the prolonged, counter opposed rocking endured between the two boats. What I did not tell her, but which we both knew, was that like the greenest apprentice seamen, we neglected, individually and collectively, to check this connection repeatedly and often. Worse, instead of putting the dink in its onboard rack where it could not have caused any trouble at all, we had let it float aimlessly around on its light tether, succumbing as we did to the fantasy that the interminable pleasure of our snug, sun-filled little lair would go on forever.

* * * * * * * * * * *

When first we sailed into Smuggler Cove our plan included an overnight stay followed by a leisurely run up the Sunshine Coast to Pender Harbour. At something less than ten nautical miles distant, it would be an easy cruise that would reward us, on arrival, with a night on the grid (plugged into shore power at a marina), fresh water, hot and cold to spare, restaurants, grocery stores and all the other delights of civilization.

As previously indicated, all day I had waffled on leaving

Smuggler Cove. Throughout our little adventure with the RIB, the weatherman continued to insist that conditions would be getting better as the day wore on, and perhaps just to humor him I persisted in embracing his version of reality every time the wind fell off a trifle. There is no doubt, too, that the declaration sworn to by our dinghy's

rescuer, i.e., that the seas were not as bad as they had been, when allied with my absolute mortification, conspired to drive me straight over the brink. Having eaten more than enough crow for the day, I directed The Crew to make preparations for putting to sea. A little blow was not going to keep us in port!

Quickly, efficiently and in a seaman-like manner – at last – I drop into the RIB for a fast trip to dry land to retrieve the stern line. Not bothering with the outboard, I pull myself hand over hand to shore. With the tide in, I hop from the dink directly onto the plateau where the line is secured, free it and head for the barn without even getting my feet wet. The Crew then pulls me back to the boat when the job is complete. After stowing everything properly back onboard, I make my way to the helm station and order The Crew up to the bow in preparation for retrieving the anchor. Within a short time that device is free and off the bottom, up, lashed into place and we are ready to get under way.

That whole operation would have gone swimmingly had not The Executive Officer acquired a bad case of target fixation. So intent was she in cleaning the chain and anchor – achieved in this instance by using the winch to dip the rode up and down in the water and by manually scrapping the muddy clay from each and every chain link as it came into reach – that she forgot completely that once the hook was free from the bottom, so was the boat! Meanwhile, I work the engine, the rudder and the bow thruster feverishly to try to keep our conveyance reasonably stationary. This required more than a modicum of concentration since the wind seemed intent on blowing us onto the nearby rocks. Moreover, because I had not the slightest a clue as to where the anchor, now dangling at some unknown depth and/or angle beneath the boat actually was, I was loathe to move too much in any particular direction. The only thing I knew for sure was that at that very instant all of the gear we had underwater undoubtedly was working desperately to foul itself irretrievably on something we either could not see. Getting things sorted out required that The Captain address The Crew, firmly. And although that facilitated the immediate retrieval of our wayward gear, i.e., the anchor and all of its rode, and led to its proper and precise storage, it also generated another prime example of winning the battle, but losing the war. By its nature, command is a lonely position; despite the warmth that the heaters were adding to the pilothouse, as The First Mate returned to her duty station on the port side of that enclosure the air in there seemed especially cold to The Skipper.

I was not sanguine about the prospect of running the channel out to Malaspina Strait again. It had not grown any larger since we came in and now the wind was howling. It nonetheless is remarkable to observe how an event or two can change perspective and how, in turn, that new mental picture can make that which had been difficult seem to be effortless. Despite conditions that were anything but ideal, we slipped effortlessly out through the tiny opening in the rocks. Whereas the day before it seemed that *Minstrel's Song* was destined to lose paint on one side or the other, she now had leagues to spare in all directions. Amazingly, The Pilot did not even break a sweat!

The wind outside was making up from the southeast, blowing a steady 25+ knots, or somewhere between Force Five and Six on the Beauford scale. The Captain surveyed the grey and white expanse of water that stretched out toward his next landfall, Francis Peninsula, about seven nautical miles off to the northwest. The scene was not one that caused him to feel warm and fuzzy about the crossing. The "salvage guy" had said that it was better out here now than it had been, and he may well have been right about that. The question facing our stalwarts, however, was not how it was now compared to how it had been, or even how it was here, in the lee of the land, compared to how it had been somewhere else, but 'Precisely how is it out there, right now,' with the 'there' being that empty stretch of ocean that separated *Minstrel's Song* from Francis Point. It was, after all, not what was going on in close to a lee shore, but what was happening a couple of miles out in that area where the wind could get a good bite on the sea and pile it up to the sky that was of greatest interest to them just now.

Having survived the Smuggler Cove passage for a second time, I was not yet anxious to make a return appearance there. That left us only two options. We either could slog directly northwest up the Malaspina Strait, where there would be no shelter until we could make the lee of Francis Point, or we could duck into Secret Cove, a destination that was only a nautical mile or so away through the relatively protected waters of the coast.

Aristotle taught that the good life was one properly lived between the extremes of possibilities. In modern parlance, he might have said that too much of anything – except absolute good – always causes us trouble. A small dish of ice cream eaten on a warm Sunday afternoon, for instance, adds to the joys of life. A large dish taken everyday, however, simply adds to the waistline and benefits no one except, perhaps, cardiologists and Weightwatchers. There is no doubt that this is the wisdom of the ages. Unfortunately, the trick of the matter is not in understanding perfectly the virtue found therein; rather, it comes from trying to achieve the proper, but obscure middle, when called to take some specific action.

To wimp out or not to wimp out! That now is the question, again. Whether 'tis better to suffer the slings and arrows of fellow mariners, tucked safely abed this afternoon, and run for immediate shelter, or to man up and point the bow northward in spite of what might await? My answer, to paraphrase Popeye the Sailorman, was 'I've had alls I can stands. I can stands no more.' So I turned the wheel and pointed *Minstrel's Song* toward Francis Point.

STORMY WEATHER

The hue of the gunmetal grey sky dictated the tone of all that lay under it. The ocean that it dominated exhibited a particularly cold shade that was not quite grey, not quite green and not quite black, but an impossible combination of all three of them at once. Moreover, despite the fact that they were a product of a medium enjoying the absence of a definable color, the frothy heads of the whitecaps that marched across the sea's surface added not a wit of light to the somber scene; rather, they served only to darken it further.

Dull, roiling and illuminated solely by the dusky residue of the light that filtered through the thick blanket of the fast moving clouds overhead, it was impossible to tell what the surface of the water was doing more than a few hundred yards out in front of our boat. There was no doubt that it was wild. Or even that it was rough. But the answer to the question that previously could not be answered, to wit 'how bad is it out there?' remained somewhat elusive. From where we sat, we could not tell whether the seas making up on the way to Francis Point would be of the five foot or of ten foot variety? It just was not possible to say.

Even though what I could see was not encouraging, based on the weatherman's predicted southeast winds, I counted on running most of the way up the coast in what I hoped would be waters that formed in the lee of the land behind us and to our south and east. It would be a rough, bumpy ride, no doubt, but at least the voyage would be quick and tolerable. Everything I could know at that instant affirmed that these expectations were reasonable. As usual, it was not what I knew, but what I did not know that hurt the most.

Minstrel's Song is a stout little ship. Built strong and true, she likely will take much more than either The Captain or The Crew care to. As master of the vessel, however, my job in situations like this is to consider the capabilities of the boat *as well as* the limits of those onboard. As pertained to this day's travel, the first concern has to do with the size, speed and direction of the waves we have to negotiate. A head sea, one coming toward the bow of the boat, is always preferred. With the bow nosing into the waves, the boat will hobbyhorse or pitch a good bit – especially if the seas are choppy – but this orientation puts the vessel in the attitude for which it was designed. A beam sea, however – with waves coming in at an angle perpendicular to the side of the boat – will roll everybody and every thing unmercifully. A following sea smashes into the stern, lifting and pushing the back of the vessel willy-nilly while restricting the effectiveness of the rudder. Steering in a following sea is, at best, a chore. In stormy conditions none of these possibilities will put a smile on anyone's face, but the first option remains the preferred one. Thus, in judging the wisdom of making the trip north, The Skipper has to weigh the size, direction and speed of the waves (and also like aspects of the wind and the currents) against what seems to be prudent under any given set of circumstances. He also must take into consideration how much The Crew will tolerate before asking to be put ashore.

Working our way northwest up the Malaspina Strait I am chagrined to discover that the prevailing wind has veered from the southeast to the southwest. This, of course, means that the waves now are running before the wind in a northerly-northeasterly direction. This unanticipated shift in wind direction neutralizes any benefit we might have had from being in the lee of the land since remains, unchanged, off to the south and east of us. So much for the flatter waters I expected.

As we begin to slog toward Francis Point, we fall in with an assemblage of six to eight foot rollers that are marching smartly up the Strait. From the looks of them, these briny-demons appear to have formed up somewhere just north of San Francisco Bay and they leave on us the strong impression that they have no intention of stopping before they get to Prince Rupert, B.C. or possibly even Juneau, Alaska. Unimpeded by anything solid – like land – for who knows how many miles, they are able to get up a tolerable head of steam before slamming into our stern quarter. I neither wanted nor appreciated their help.

Knowing that the combination of green water flinging itself up on the rails of the boat and The Crew turning green around the gills because of it could bring his second nautical career to a screeching halt, The Pilot did everything in his power to smooth out the ride. He supplemented that work by craftily engaging The First Mate in the kind of scintillating conversation that could only help to keep her mind off of the unpleasant sea conditions. The cat was out of the bag, however, when a particularly large greybeard ran up under the stern of the boat, lifted it out of the water and then slewed it sideways, hard. The brute force of that act caused the bow of *Minstrel's Song* to swing wildly to port. Her port beam then was parallel to the crest of the next wave in line and before The Pilot could right that wrong, the salty bad boy slammed hard into the little ship. Beyond just causing the boat to roll heavily, this collision set the dining table in motion.

Under normal circumstances we do not fetter the aforementioned, freestanding piece of furniture so as to make it remain in any particular part of the saloon. Thus, when the need arises or the mood strikes us, we move it hither and yon to suit our tastes. In this instance, however, Mother Nature decided that it would be better for this wooden helpmate to ride out the storm not on its feet, but on its side, and in close company with the deck. The first we heard of this decision came with a crash from below that was loud enough to conjure up images of a perforated hull. Springing instinctively into Damage Control Party mode, The Crew quickly reported to The Skipper that there was no harm and no foul: the saloon table had just hit the ground. We knew from past experience that it was prone to doing so whenever the weather outside got a little moody; we regretted, however, not rigging for rough seas by setting it down gently before this inauspicious table-flinging event took place.

The Pilot did the best he could to keep the tossing seas from treating those onboard too much like the numbered Ping-Pong balls at a BINGO tournament, but, alas, indecision struck him again. The course lines he had drawn the night before took the cruiser through a shallow stretch of water. This area provided plenty of depth for a safe passage, but the fact that the seabed quickly rose from several hundred feet down to about 30 feet could be a problem under weather conditions like these. Without having to detail what little The Pilot knows about wave action and hydraulics, suffice it to say that when a taller pile of liquid gets pushed up by something like winds or tides onto a place that supports only a shorter one, bad things usually happen to the surface. Compared to what happens to the surface of the water when it is over greater depths, over shallower places the norm is to have a rougher, more confused cauldron wherein the waves become higher, steeper and choppier. Because neither The Captain, The Crew, nor even their little vessel really needed any more thrills on this outing, the proper way to avoid additional turmoil was to avoid the place most likely to encourage it. Thus, the course should be altered so as to run around the high spot.

As usual, doing the right thing necessitated making a difficult decision. Should The Pilot choose to steer a course that would let the prevailing eight-foot seas slap them directly on the beam, or should he adjust their direction of travel in such a way as to allow those same trouble makers to get directly under the stern. In the first instance, the ship's roll would be extreme, but in the second, steering would be a nightmare. As too often seems to happen, his lack of foresight and/or indecision gave all of those involved a healthy dose of both possibilities as he managed to find a course that took them almost over the high spot and sort of around it both at the same time!

* * * * * * * * * *

Finally making Francis Point, we began to luxuriate in some of the lee conditions that The Pilot had hoped they would have all the way up the Strait. Cruising along almost due north now, they hugged the coast as closely as caution would allow. Amazingly, the relative extravagance of having to contend only with three to four foot waves put both Captain and Crew in a holiday mood.

For the neophyte, the entrance to Pender Harbour can be perplexing. Very loosely speaking, the sea cuts into the mainland in this vicinity to form an inlet almost 3 nautical miles in length that runs mostly on an east-west axis. The mouth of this mariner's haven is to be found at its western end. Guarding this ingress are a series of haphazardly strewn islands, submerged rocks and other natural delights undoubtedly placed there to charm the itinerant voyager. What makes the approach to the harbor especially interesting is not that it is terribly tight – the two main channels are each about 500 feet wide – but that any number of false passages beckon the unwary. These pseudo-channels call to the inexperienced sailor like the proverbial Sirens did to Odysseus. From the surface, they look to be absolutely safe; in reality they constitute a quick road to self-destruction.

Excepting with the use of electronic chartplotters loaded with state of the art topography, identifying this or that particular rock or unnamed islet as it appears on the harbor's charts requires considerable attention to details when arriving. Even from less than a mile away, one can spend inordinate amounts of time comparing the squiggly little lines on the paper that are said to represent hard things that are more or less dry and rise up above the surface of the water with the reality of what one can see looming ahead. Even for the well trained, this chore can be daunting and fraught with error. Knowing, too, that deceptive routes and opportunities abound, one tries not to make too many mistakes when considering when to make the turn into Pender Harbour.

Easing our way into this place, The X.O. and I studied the chart, a variety of books that addressed the subject, the chartplotter, radar, depth sounder, but most of all we referred constantly to the limited amount of common sense we kept onboard for just such occasions. We surely would have consulted the Encyclopedia of Britannica or any other reputable source had we had them with us, but we didn't. Likewise, had there been any other people foolish enough to be out on the water this day, we might have considered following their example. Alas, there were none, so we were on our own.

Doing the best we could, we zigged and zagged our way into the protected waters, passing islets, exposed rocks and the odd day marker along the way. When we had run past all of the perceived obstacles that guarded the mouth of this harbor, we finally were free to visually explore the fine, strikingly large anchorage that now spread out before us. Boats of all descriptions were dispersed widely around it. The even mix of pleasure and working vessels conveyed the feeling that here was a solid, year-round, shelter.

The shores of the bay were dotted with view homes and private piers separated one from another by dark green patches of forests that sometimes climbed to the tops of the hills that encircled the sea below them. The water of the bay, although still rippling under a fresh breeze, somehow managed to shake off the surly greyness that defined it when out in the Strait. Here it sported a lighter, brighter green hue that complimented the ubiquitous flora that crept down toward the beaches. Even the rain that drummed lightly on the pilothouse top conveyed a cheery, pseudo-Caribbean beat that lifted the spirits of those within it. Having come in out of the storm, we found the whole place wonderfully calm and inviting. We agreed that it was good to be home even if it was just for a single night.

Unlike what we had encountered at our other landfalls, Pender Harbour was of such considerable size that identifying our final destination was not as easy as usual. We had reservations – absolutely unnecessary at this time of year – at a local marina. We knew where the guidebooks said it should be, but the hand drawn charts from them that we used to find it did not seem to match the landmarks we could identify.

"Could that be it over there?" I would ask.

"No." The Crew would answer, "It sits more in a cove."

Finally we locked onto our target and made straight for it. The Skipper used the VHF radio to let the dock attendants know we were on our way in and to ask where we should berth. The voice emanating from the speaker said that we were free to pick any spot we wanted. Moments latter we were running toward a line of empty 'drive-straight-in slips' that stretched perpendicularly to our left and to our right. The Pilot drew a bead on one of them, opting not for show, but for 'easy.' And, all dockings should be like that one! Pull the throttle back to idle. Slide the transmission into neutral. Add a touch of starboard rudder. Guide the shifter back into reverse. Let the screw turn round, twice, and then The Docking Gang steps neatly ashore with nary a drop of her martini spilled! Ahhhh, home sweet home!

Dave, the marina owner, and his trusty dog Rosie make their way down the ramp from the beautiful house perched on a point above the harbor that is both residence and office. I begin to think that Canadian marinas must, by law, have one of man's best friends on the premises, but being a canine hound myself, I put it down to another one of those quaint aspects of life up here that I like so well. We chat for a time, getting instructions on where to find groceries, real sit-down food, ice, fuel, etc., etc., and enjoy the interaction. It seems that our host originally came from the British Isles. I think, but I am not sure, that he said something about settling in Pender Harbour because of the way they spelled things there and because of the measuring system they used, but my memory is not terribly clear on that point!

Contrary to expectations, The Skipper finds that despite his recent victory over Poseidon, he has a scurvy and mutinous Crew aboard this evening. Captain Bligh never dreamed he would have problems like these! White sand beaches lapped by the warm waters of corral reef-guarded lagoons, populated by free, dark-skinned maidens, all drenched in tropical sunlight was as nothing compared to The Master's worries. For, right smack-dab in the middle of the day's sail – which happened to be somewhere near the middle of the Malaspina Strait – an ultimatum had been passed up from the fo'c's'le's rabble: "Make for a marina with wi-fi or else! And, oh, yeah, be there by 1630!"

The source of this conflict, incredible though it may seem, stems from the fact that The First Officer is moonlighting as an executive something or the other while making the passage with The Captain! Thus, she states in no uncertain terms that she has to Skype her other master or The Commander will have real trouble. The option, she informs him, is to do precisely as she directs or to never, ever think of having enough money to fill the ship's fuel tanks again. Perceiving the virtue of giving a little to get a little, The Captain wisely places the entire ship and all within it at her beck and call. Speaking with the authority of a Fleet Admiral, The Crew informs The Skipper that he is required to clear the chart table, provide pen and paper and generally stay out of the way while his teak-trimmed pilothouse undergoes conversion into a floating office. Retreating quietly to the saloon with book, he pouts in solitary splendor for the next hour and a half while she solves the problems of the world.

Finally freed from the chains of pecuniary servitude – the very enslavement that pays most of our bills – the ship's complement headed up the dock in search of the grocery store. Although ready to take on supplies of all kinds, we pare down our shopping list sharply when we get a look at the posted prices. Recognizing that the establishment we have entered is stuck way out in the middle of nowhere, and bowing to the fact that they cater to a seasonally limited cruising clientele, our mental defenses of 'Mom and Pop' collapse nonetheless when we ascertain that an ordinary sized bag of potato chips, still reclining comfortably on its dusty shelf despite being many days beyond its listed 'best if used by' date, is going to cost us upwards of $10.00 U.S. The resultant near fatal case of sticker shock that I suffer so nearly incapacitates me that I am reduced to thinking that the boxes of Mac and Cheese stacked three deep in the boat's food locker might keep us going for a very long time. Demurring, the ever-thrifty Cookie selects an array of less expensive items that she later transforms into culinary delights.

After a quick trip back to the boat to stow our loot, we make our way again onto dry land. The rain has stopped and the evening is turning pleasant. We enjoy a stroll through Dave's well-kept front yard – the only way out to the street anyway – and then continue traveling in the only direction that seems to lead anywhere. We are hungry and ready for food, but we are also voyagers in a strange new land with no real idea of what lies around the next bend.

Following a narrow, blacktop road devoid of traffic, we feel like we are hiking down an old country lane instead of meandering along a street in a seaside village. We pass two large, ancient structures both of which seem to be closed or abandoned. The paint peels from their sides and the foliage around them presses right up to their doors. We wonder what they are or at least what they were. Tall, dense stands of trees straddle our highway and limit our view. A few hundred feet on we get our first glimpse of returning civilization as we bend around a corner and spot the greasy spoon that our host suggested had good eats. Surrounded immediately by a small, gravel parking lot, the structure seems to be waging a losing battle against the creeping might of the darkening forest that ranges nearly up to its doors. We do not bother to cross the road to get a better look. Even from a distance we can read the sign hanging at an angle in the dirty front window: "Closed."

Following our noses we make a couple of turns onto unmarked avenues in what we hope will be a productive direction. The last of these course changes dumps us into a smallish, nearly empty, dirt parking lot that sits at the end of a dead in street. Said vehicular resting zone appears to be in mortal danger of succumbing to the predations of the vegetation pressing in on it. From our vantage point we opine that the true purpose of this clearing is as much to hide a kind of dilapidated, wooden, pub-like structure that sits partly out over a small arm of the bay as it is to provide vehicular access to it. Walking past what ought to have been the back of this largish shack, but is not, we glean a little something of the building's primary purpose by virtue of the dusty, neon Kokanee Beer sign that illuminates a small window set next to the only door we can see. We discover no other identifying marks, symbols or cyphers on the edifice and thus remained in the dark, more or less, about what lurked within.

Not knowing what to expect, we cautiously nose our way though the solid wooden portal and peer inside. Our eyes are drawn into a large, darkish cavern full of tables and chairs – mostly empty – set around in such a manner as to provide what must have been a long-since departed hoard of clientele a panoramic view of the water through either of the two long, salt-encrusted glass windows that made up half of the four sides of the rectangular room. The old linoleum flooring that accented everything added a degree of dinginess as well as a level of audio reverb that would be hard to replicate outside of a laboratory.

Taking another tentative step or so further into the room, we are able to discern a small bar set way back in the darkest corner of the chamber. Four or five stools sit in front this gathering place. The usual kinds of non-descript revelers occupy three or four of those seats. A surly looking bartender moves lazily around in the space between the patrons he attends and the mirrored wall set with booze bottles that seem to hold their rapt attention. A TV, blaring across the expanse from the opposite corner of the room – affixed high in the junction formed by the two glass walls – attracts considerable, over-the-shoulder consideration from this same group.

Exchanging the quizzical glances that amounts to a formalized vote, we quietly, if somewhat cautiously, move forward. After a trying day we are hungry and given that we had yet to encounter any other prospects, taking advantage of the eatery that the Lord had just placed in our paths seemed to be the right thing to do. With no one too interested in our presence, we pick out a shop-worn table that had but two features to recommend it: a remarkable view of the bay and a location about as far from the T.V. set and the bar as we could get.

A plump, but haggard looking woman, who might have stepped

directly out of the pages of an updated version of one of Dickens' squalid tales, emerged from the kitchen through the swinging doors that opened beside the bar. She plodded toward us, two plastic menus and a fistful of silverware in hand. While I occupied myself by wadding a napkin to form a wedge that I hoped would still the rocking movement caused by the inevitably shortened leg on our table, she shuffled back toward the bar to retrieve our drinks. We studied the bill of fare like a couple of hungry wolves and found that despite the fact that it was limited both in scope and in grandeur, its prices were reasonable. Not ones to stand on ceremony or to expect too much, My Messmate picked something simple from the menu that she thought should be O.K.– the fish and chips – and I, ever the carnivore, went straight for the steak sandwich.

Despite being nearly empty, the interior of this glass-sided grotto reverberated with the harsh din of a T.V. sound system pushed well beyond its design limits. That cacophony was fortified by the occasional whoops of those loafing around the bar. The X.O. and I tried to converse, but the competition was fierce. We finally gave up and settled for quietly enjoying the view.

After a wait sufficient for someone to run to town – wherever that might be! – and ick up our order, our meal finally arrived. We noted that at least it came out steaming hot. Not expecting much more than that, we went to work on the plates set before us and...Holy Mother of Clementine!...was it ever good! Fresh, fluffy cod graced The Crew's perfect bun and a one-inch think slab of hot steak, smothered in crackly fried onions, oozed its juices into a soft, fresh-baked roll. Giving our best impression of two old mariners who had been eating nothing but moldy hardtack and salt pork for weeks, we all but fell face first into our plates. This was the kind of "sleeper" restaurant that everyone dreams of, but few ever find.

It is interesting to note how perceptions can transform themselves. All we had hoped for when we entered this eatery was a decent meal at a reasonable price without fear of ptomaine. Nothing that we encountered before the food arrived gave hope for anything beyond that. The pleasure we derived from the excellent cuisine, however, adjusted our attitudes and put us in the mood to re-evaluate our surroundings. Soon we were enjoying both an excellent dinner and getting an education to boot. As our victuals slid down, we noticed a correlation between the racket on the TV and the roar that went up from the patrons at the bar. Given that except by sign language we could not communicate with each other anyway, we entertained ourselves by trying to discover the relationship between the two disparate events. Suddenly the truth of it hit us: ice hockey!

Babes in the North Woods that we are, we neither knew nor appreciated the importance of the evening. With the patience of a kindergarten teacher conveying the fundamentals of the alphabet to a dim-witted class, our waitress provided all of the instruction we required. It seems that we had arrived on site at that precise moment in time when the Vancouver Canucks – apparently not a slur when related to the beloved, local team – were locked in mortal, play-off combat, with their arch nemesis (some crew from California). Groans and moans from the gathered fans indicated setbacks; whoops and cheers accompanied approved play. By degrees the volume and elation of the crowd grew until even we were vocalizing our support. Having been inducted into this fanatical fraternity by dint of our participation, politely restrained though it was, we later were pleased to be recognized positively as fellow travellers by one of the customers we happened to pass on the street as we made our way back to our floating abode.

With full stomachs, a true sense of accomplishment and a little greater appreciation for the place that hockey plays in the hearts of our Canadian neighbors, The Crew and I clamored back aboard *Minstrel's Song* seeking the comforts of our bunk and the reassuring rocking of a boat safe and snug in a fine, friendly harbor. Another glorious day was done; another wonderful adventure logged.

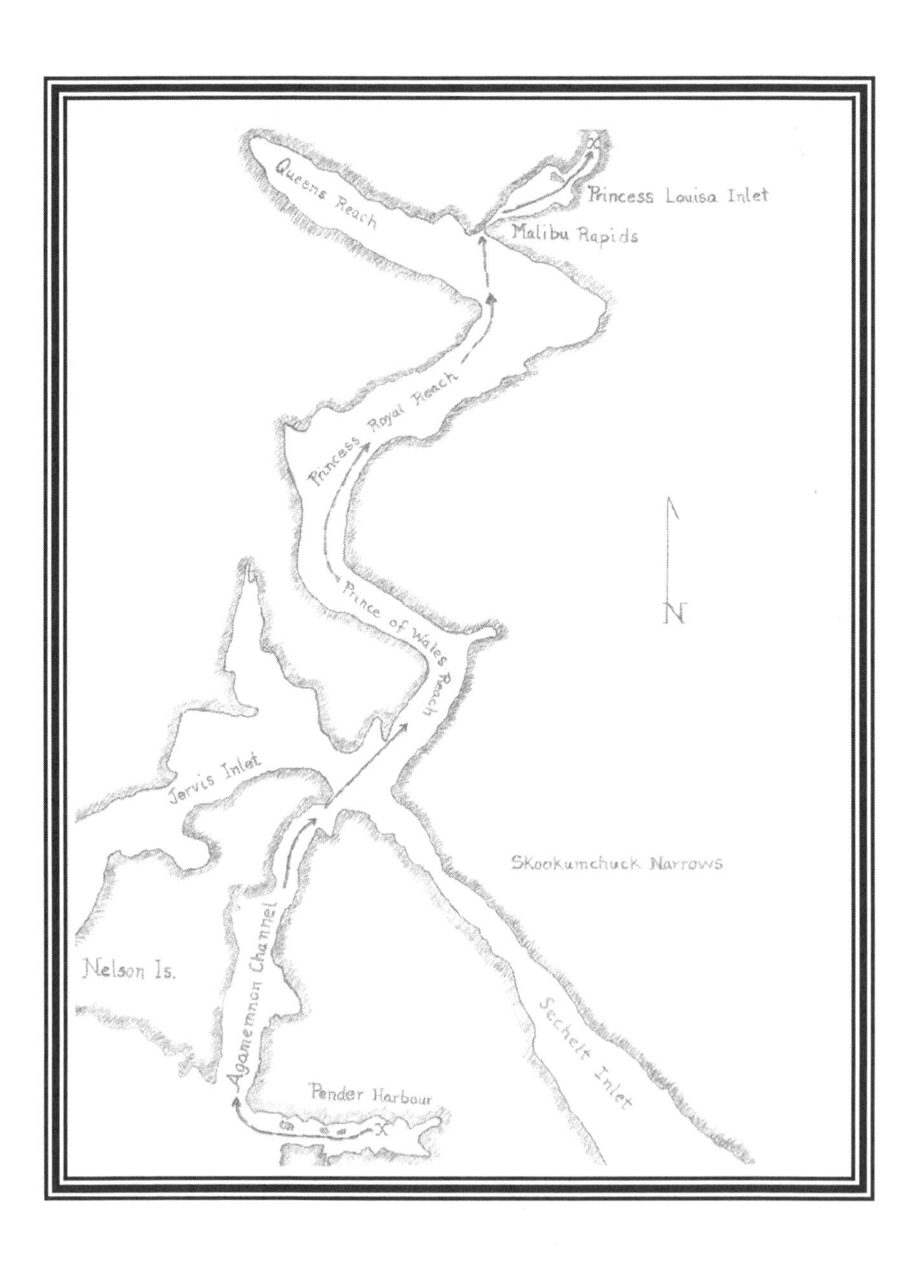
Queens Reach
Princess Louisa Inlet
Malibu Rapids
Princess Royal Reach
N
Prince of Wales Reach
Jervis Inlet
Skookumchuck Narrows
Agamemnon Channel
Nelson Is.
Sechelt Inlet
Pender Harbour

DAY FIVE

Pender Harbour To Princess Louisa Inlet
Or
Finding Fathoms In Foggy Fjords

Our preparations for departing Pender Harbour were made leisurely. The irony of our situation was that despite the 40 or more nautical miles we had to cover to reach our day's destination, we could not go too fast in getting there. As in Goldilocks and the Three Bears, the time at which we arrive at the entrance to Princess Louisa Inlet has to be just right. The reason for that is a thing called Malibu Rapids. Sounding either like something out of an old Beach Boys album or a rafting attraction, the place is neither. Rather, Malibu Rapids is a narrow, saltwater passage that connects one body of the sea (Queen Reach) to another (Princess Louisa Inlet). This charming little slot functions both as the only way into and out of Princess Louise Inlet and, when the tide is running either way, as a place to satisfy thrill seekers who use its standing waves for purposes of surfing or white water kayaking. Except at slack tide, attempts to pass these rapids in any conveyance that does not routinely require the wearing of a wet suit are ill advised.

Our planned day's travel has us motoring into the interior of British Columbia. Following departure from Pender Harbour, we intend to run north through the Agamemnon Channel, cross the confluence of Jarvis Inlet and Skoockumchuck Narrows, and then cleave the waters of Prince of Wales Reach, Princess Royal Reach and Queen Reach to wind up in front of Malibu Rapids. Immediately following the negotiation of that challenge, we will proceed to the northeastern end of Princess Louisa Inlet where we will spend the night.

Princess Louisa Inlet differs significantly from other places most North American boaters might understand or visit. Although linked immediately to the ocean, it is roughly 35 nautical miles directly inland – either east or north depending on what part you reference – from the main trunk of the Salish Sea. At about four nautical miles in length, this body of water does not seem to be anything special. If one were to locate it on a chart, it might appear to be just another saltwater cul-de-sac at the end of a long, winding channel. No roads lead in to it and it has no shops, stores, hotels, motels, fueling stations, marinas, tee shirt stands, tattoo parlors, golf courses or any of the other modern necessities. The Inlet can only be reached by aircraft, floatplane, helicopter, boat or by that which The Old Man's used to refer to as the "ankle express." The employment of the latter method gives the adventurous trekker more than sufficient opportunity to contemplate the true meaning of backcountry command, "pack it in, pack it out."

To get to Princess Louisa Inlet via watercraft the anxious seafarer must pass up a series of reaches – long necks of water set off by sharp bends at each end – that zig-zag in a direction best described, loosely, as northerly. Few reliable anchorages occur along the way, so practically speaking the entire distance must be covered in one continuous leap. Given these considerations, one would be justified in asking, "Why go there?" The answer to that question is twofold: First, by virtue of its geographic isolation – although still only a straight line hop, skip and a jump north of Vancouver, B.C. – it is a place of wonderful serenity. Of equal importance, however, is the fact that Princess Louisa Inlet is a classic example of a fjord, an especially beautiful one, and one that is situated at an easy cruising distance from virtually all parts of the Salish Sea.

Fjords occur in Norway, Iceland, North America (Puget Sound to Alaska), South America (the Chilean coast down to the Strait of Magellan), and in New Zealand. Our friends at Wikipedia describe these phenomena simply as long, narrow inlets with steep sides or cliffs. One might elaborate a bit on that depiction by including that fjords flow, river-like, through valleys carved out of high landmasses by ancient glaciers many eons ago. To fully appreciate their wonder we need to emphasize that although they may look like long, narrow lakes nestled in the valleys of snow covered mountains, they remain, nonetheless parts of the sea. Fjords are strikingly picturesque precisely because the tree-covered, snow capped peaks that rise up around them are 100% alpine in appearance while the water that runs through them is absolutely oceanic. In essence, fjords combine two elements of the natural world that logically should not occur together. The result is breathtaking.

At a civilized hour we motor out of Pender Harbour and turn the bow of *Minstrel's Song* north up Agamemnon Channel. The day is dark and threatening and a crisp wind sweeps across our decks. Rain-laden clouds scuttle low and fast overhead and a light, but steady drizzle beats a symphonic rhythm on the cabin roof. Despite what might otherwise seem an inauspicious day for travel – a near carbon copy of the day before – we are in high spirits with few worries about the weather!

Beyond the short distance we have to cover between the mouth of Pender Harbour and the southern terminus of Agamemnon Channel – an stretch of less than a nautical mile over water that is swept but not roiled unduly by the remnant of yesterday's storm – the route we plan to follow gives us excellent protection from almost everything Mother Nature might hurl at us. Provided we do not encounter williwaws, powerful and unpredictable microbursts of wind most often found in proximity to seas adjoining mountainous terrain, there is little by way of natural adversity that should trouble us on our run up to Malibu Rapids. The relatively narrow, twisting and turning fjords we will traverse do not give the seas much room to build and concurrently offer a myriad of lee shores in which to take shelter should that become necessary. And, unlike those who would be traveling in sailboats, our warm, snug pilothouse keeps both the sky's deluge and the cold that comes with it on the outside of the cabin where it belongs.

Making our way along the brief bit of southwest facing coastline that separates Pender Harbour from the lower end of Agamemnon Channel, we marvel at the steady parade of beautiful homes, perched high on the rocks, that slide slowly past our windows. These magnificent edifices of wood, stone and glass remind one that while the feel of the area is remote, wealth is no stranger to this part of British Columbia. Oddly, however, the image of opulence vanishes almost immediately as we turn the corner and begin to make our way north up the channel itself. In what seemed to be nothing more than an instant, man's great monuments were gone, replaced by tree covered mountainsides. The fir and cedar forests on the steep hills that plunged down to the water on both flanks of *Minstrel's Song* appeared to exist in a land that was beyond human reach. Although little more than a stone's throw from the quiet bustle of Pender Harbour or even the McMansions that lined the rocky coast outside of it, the new world we were entering seemed wild, remote and full of wonder. It made us smile because this was, after all, the reason for the voyage.

Once well within the confines of Agamemnon Channel, my Shipmate and I relaxed and settled in for a substantial cruise up what was looking a lot like a grand, lazy river. Gone was the sea chop; gone were the frothy whitecaps; gone were the great rolling waves pushed up by a howling wind. Placid waters that barely were rippled by a very slight breeze had replaced them all. And while it is true that others might have described the day itself as grey or wet or dreary or even bleak, it is one of those strange twists of life that some of our best times are those spent locked inside a place that is safe and warm and protected from the assaults of Mother Nature. Thus, we luxuriated in a smooth ride, the steady throb of our diesel engine, the rhythmic beat of the wipers on the windscreens and the warm air wafting from the heater vents. Concomitantly, we chatted happily, studied the outside vistas intently and slurped prodigious amounts of hot coffee.

Steaming steadily northward though the watery, half-mile wide valley that was our thoroughfare this day, the only manmade creations we observed, rarely, were ramshackle wooden structures built out over the sea on pilings that were adjacent to the shore. Most of them looked to us to be ready to drop into the ocean on a moment's notice. A few of them were identified on the charts as fish farms and a few others seemed to be habitations of one sort or another, mainly of the just barely remaining above the water variety. We entertained ourselves by wondering what it would be like to live in such places. More importantly, we expended much effort trying to discern the circumstances that would incline or even drive people to make such choices. As the varied, isolated structures slid by, left and right, we cast judgment on each of them. In return they gazed blankly back at us. Despite seeing few signs of life, we deemed it likely, even probable, that these shanties harbored souls who noted our passage from inside their darkened windows and repaid the favor of judgment back to us somehow.

Twice in our eight nautical mile trip up this channel we sailed under sets of high voltage power lines that, held up by giant steel-armed monsters, linked the mainland to our east with Nelson Island to our west. These misplaced apparitions reminded us that no matter what we thought or how it looked from the water, the conveniences of society were not far removed. Twice, too, did the icy fingers of dangers wrought by humankind encircle our hearts and burst in on our natural reveries.

The Pilot had just ordered a slight change of course to avoid a charted rock near the middle of the channel, when, peering into the gloom ahead he spied something a mile or two distant that seemed to be moving his way. It looked to be favoring the east side of the waterway and since there was no shortage of room to let both vessels get by each other, he swung the bow of *Minstrel's Song* more toward the west to make the passing both easy and obvious. Although the intruder was coming directly toward them and there was no question as to her course or bearing, there was something very odd about her character. This inclined The Pilot to undertake a determined study of this newly discovered species. Look and conjecture as he could, however, the exact identification of this oncoming specter eluded him. Even when he placed her under magnification using powerful binoculars, he drew a blank. The contrivance seemed to have a normal sized bow, a regular pilothouse and the standard proportions common to a craft in the 60-80 foot range. What baffled The Pilot, however, was why the stern of the vessel spread out all over the sea! (The reader should understand that we are not talking about a beamy boat in this instance. Instead, we are discussing one that looked to brush the mainland side of the channel with its port flank and Nelson Island side of it with its starboard. This constituted a distance of over three-quarters of a nautical mile!)

"What do you think that is?" I asked The Mate.

"I don't know," she replied. "But is sure does take up a lot of the water."

"Yeah. Too much for my taste."

The combined speed of our two ships was causing us to close with some rapidity. It was incumbent upon The Skipper to figure out what was going on and then to make a decision. If it was a commercial vessel he was obliged to stand clear. But given that the monstrosity seemed to be taking most of the channel, the question was how or where? Should they run for shelter close in to the Nelson Island shore or should I they just run?

Staring through his binoculars, which are staring through the raindrops on the windshield, which is swept only periodically by an anemic wiper, The Captain catches an occasional, distorted glimpse of the frightful invader. Long minutes pass before finally, on the verge of a sustained panic attack, he discerns the truth. Coming around the bend ahead of them, making a turn to her port (to her left) is a tugboat pulling a raft of logs. Attached by cable, and just marginally under anything even vaguely approaching control, the timber she is dragging reacts to the tug's movement toward the east by heading directly in the opposite direction, toward Nelson Island in the west. Viewed from the distance down the channel that we are, the lash-up creates the illusion of a gargantuan something spread evenly over the entire waterway.

GREEN, GREEN, IT'S GREEN THEY SAY

Some of the most productive forestlands in the world can be found in the Pacific Northwest. In a great swath that stretches from northern California all the way up to Alaska and then from the spine of the Rocky Mountains north of the Great Basin west to the Pacific Ocean, trees in this domain grow like proverbial weeds.

When fur trapping and trading, the force that lured U.S. and European explorers, adventurers and treasure seekers alike to the wilds of the Far West, had run its course in the 1840s, a more stable industry that could sustain a developing society was sought to replace it. While ranching and farming caught on in some places – and the rush for gold was great sport – the rugged nature of much of the Pacific Northwest turned those not seeking additional hardship away from this part of the continent. Some few, however, thinking that they might find wealth in the mountains that seemed to stretch to infinity or in the lonely, unnumbered valleys that penetrated the interior deeply, took to the hills with sharp, cutting implements in an effort to wrench great rewards from mere wood products.

Since the beginning of time man has transported his commerce and his culture by water. The streams, rivers and oceans of the world were and still are the real highways of human intercourse. From Mesopotamia to the Mississippi drainage, civilization is both created near and spread via the water. The great societies of antiquity, both East and West, were built on the rivers Yellow, Yangtze, Ganges, Nile, Tigris, Euphrates, Rhine, Danube, Thames, etc., and/or were firmly planted on the shores of the globe's oceans. They sprang up in such places precisely because water allowed the populace in one place economically to bring in and take out the things that others, elsewhere, either had and did not need, or wanted to have and could not get on their own. It is no accident, then, that the great cities of North America – New York, Montreal, New Orleans, St. Louis, Chicago, Los Angeles, San Francisco, Vancouver, etc. are port cities. Mankind flourishes in proximity to the sea because his trade does too!

Interestingly, although modern man thinks in terms of superhighways, jet aircraft, FedEx and UPS, and possibly even trains, when it comes to hauling goods over long distances, the most cost-effective way of getting stuff from here to there still is to pile it on to ships. In fact, roughly 90% of the world's commerce continues to moves by sea despite the aforementioned supplemental means of distribution.

The hallmark of the Industrial Revolution was the machine. Of course, that is not to suggest that the earth had no mechanical devices prior to the late 1700s; it only means that man's great mechanical leap forward began during that age. But even with the help of the marvelous labor saving contrivances that were ubiquitous by the waning days of the Industrial Revolution, getting large, heavy things from one place to another continued to be a constant chore. When it came to wood, although extremely valuable in bulk quantities, the exertions required for moving it from where it grew to where it was needed made the old task of shipping mere hogsheads from London to San Francisco look, by comparison, like a simple warm up exercise.

Contrary to much popular thinking these days, trees actually grow and even thrive in the wild. That fact does not contradict the converse, that they do fine too when domesticated and farmed. Thus, we need not lament the plight of the stately elm that lines the streets of quaint New England villages or the maples that grace the landscaped exteriors of homes around North America. Instead, we need to remind ourselves that Nature seems to do just fine with her products when left to her own devices.

And that brings us back to the extensive forests of the Pacific Northwest. For it is there, clinging to the untrammeled slopes of millions of square miles of rugged, nearly inaccessible mountainous terrain, the barky treasures of which we speak flourish both naturally and most happily. And it is precisely because of that that the perennial problem for those who would reap a profit from woody things, from beginning to end, was, is and probably always will be, how to get the great trunks of these huge plants from where they like to live to where someone will pay good money for them.

When the first American and Canadian pioneers established themselves on the northwestern extremes of the Western Hemisphere, a few visionaries understood that, lacking anything else of particular value, the standing timber that extended in all directions, for as far as the eye could see, potentially represented vast sums of money that was just hanging around on top of big stumps and root systems. From the earliest days these people knew exactly where the wood was and they knew precisely where it had to go in order to transform it into gold. The rub was that those two places rarely, if ever, coincided. Thus, a system of transportation had to be devised if profits were to be made.

Being in something of a lather to build their fortunes and retire in luxury, the earliest timber barons were unwilling to sit idly by in hope that some unnamed philanthropist would run a railroad – the most modern form of heavy transportation in that day – into the interior of their mountainous and far-flung forests. They were equally unwilling to remain on hold while the great minds of the age invented the heavy excavating equipment needed to cut roads through the highlands or even to slow up long enough to allow Henry Ford, the Wright brothers and a hoard of others to put the automobile, 18-wheelers, helicopters, and paved, all weather highways at their disposal. Given the rush they were in to make themselves fabulously wealthy, the only possible way to move the huge stacks of logs they anticipated cutting off of the slopes of the distant craggy realms was to do it the old fashioned way: with manpower, horsepower and waterpower.

Although men were needed to cut the trees down and then whack them into pieces, and both horses and men were essential to the task of dragging the felled timber away, both could be in short supply, expensive, difficult to handle, and virtually worthless when forced to travel over rugged, undeveloped terrain. Only water could move the harvested timber efficiently and inexpensively across the great distances that separated the wood product's point of origin from its end user. Fortunately, if there was one thing that the Pacific Northwet had in abundance, it was water.

If the reader would be so kind as to engage a mere handful of the grey cells that have been collecting for some odd number of decades in your personal memory bank, it is likely that you will be able to stumble upon a general file entitled "Old Time Woodsmen," or something similar. Open it and it is probable that in your mind's eye you will be able to "see" gangs of rough looking men, captured in stark, greying splendor, wielding saws and axes and other instruments of destruction staring out at you from the depths of their dusty, glossy, monochromatic, paper abode. Let just a few more neurological synapses fire once more and stark images of long chutes and sluices carrying logs down mountainsides to deliver them to the partially hidden lakes and rivers below their heights should appear. (You will know the ones that I mean when you can mentally "see" the geysers that are thrown up as great lengths of wood pass down the rough sawn-slides and drop without fanfare into the water below!) Exert barely any more effort and the smiling faces of another set of long-departed time travelers, balancing precariously on floating logs, should come into focus. This group can be identified by the long pikes in their hands and by the hobnail boots on their feet. They will be observed wrangling huge herds of tree trunks together so as to form rafts of timber that they intend to send to the distant mills downstream.

Harvesting nature's bounty has never been easy. The work tends to reward those who persist and who are efficient as well. With the myriad of topographic hurdles always faced and now, also, with ever growing demographic and ecological impediments, the old ways of doing things – with minor adjustments here and there – in many instances remain the most cost efficient way of getting the job done. This is true in general, but is even more so when it comes to trees.

Today, whether up river or up the coast, trees felled by mechanical giants, with hardly a man and nary a horse in sight, still are pushed, pulled and otherwise conveyed to the nearest body of connected water and therein dumped. Graded, marked, sorted and collected into manageable groups, this market timber, when ready for transport, is corralled within a simple contrivance called a boom. Booms consist of a series of logs chained together, end to end, so that they form something that resembles a long, rough necklace. When wrapped around a mass of free-floating wood, the product is both confined and ready for transport. Thereafter, a powerful engine, usually in the form of a tugboat, has but to attach a cable to some convenient part of the boom and tow the whole shebang away.

It was just such an apparition that was now bearing down on *Minstrel's Song*. As mentioned, when the towboat changed course to its left, inertia caused the boom to continue along its original track and that meant that relative to the tug, the logs appeared to be swinging to its right. Once the line leader straightened its tract and got some tension back into the boom, the timber slipped back behind the vessel where it belonged and it looked like everyone would live happily ever after.

* * * * * * * * * * *

If nothing else, pop culture has taught most of the known world one important lesson about seamanship: if you do not want to lose your love or your life, *a la* "The Titanic," keep a sharp eye out for floating objects that can punch holes in the side your boat.

The incredibly beautiful lands and seas that stretch from Puget Sound to Alaska are accessed only with a degree of real risk. Mentioned already have been the tides, the currents, the eddies, the rips and the winds. Logs need to be added to that list. And they should appear way up near the top of it.

As with almost everything else that floats, logs are preordained to try to run free. Lash them, tie them, and anchor them, encircle them with a boom if you wish, but they will be gone in a heartbeat unless great care is taken to secure them. And where do you think these crazed fiends go when they are out on their own? Hunting, that's where.

Knowing that the great commercial ships they encounter can suffer little more than a marginally bent prop from their shenanigans, these prowling predators hold themselves in abeyance in order to seek and destroy the most vulnerable victims: pleasure boaters. Lying low in the water with just the suggestion of their dark, barky tops bobbing above the surface – in reasonable imitation of the semi-submerged snout of an alligator – these ecological battering rams are especially effective during hours of darkness or in a fog. Add wind and waves to the equation and they take on a form of invisibility on par with that of the latest stealth aircraft. Throw in a distracted or an oblivious skipper, like the one who just nips below for a moment to fix himself another martini, or the speed demon whose upward canting foredeck blocks completely the view ahead of the boat and what we have is a vision of 'log heaven.'

Being forewarned is forearmed and when under way, the bridge of *Minstrel's Song* never lacks a posted lookout. Regardless of what else we are doing, whether talking, drinking coffee, eating lunch or just sightseeing, both The Captain and The Crew constantly scan the seas ahead for predators. It is healthier that way. And, in passing the tug and its boom of logs, we make a mental note to be especially careful. Ship jumpers from that procession undoubtedly lie in wait!

As we approach the northern end of Agamemnon Channel we enjoy a sense of anticipation. When we attain Prince of Wales Reach – just a nautical mile or two past the upper end of the channel – we truly enter 'fjord land.' All of the miles we have logged on our journey so far have been preliminary, even secondary, to this last stretch of water. The fjords are what we came to experience. The fjords are the main event. Now the fjords are directly ahead!

Staring through the windscreen, we strain to catch a glimpse of the future. Across the mixing bowl of green-grey water that brings Agamemnon Channel, the Jervis Inlet, Skookumchuck Narrows, Hotham Sound and Prince of Wales Reach all together in one place, we see mountains, real mountains. Cutting slightly through them, but only just slightly, lies a flat, silvery ribbon that we know can be nothing except the sea. Our eyes follow that dull surface out until it blends into the foundations of the great masses that rise sharply up to form ridgelines that at 5,500' in elevation dominate the valley below. Then, as if by magic, those ridges visually meld into to ever more distant undulating folds that appear to be marching in close formation off to rendezvous with an unseeable horizon. Their presence dwarfs everything else. So massive are these climbing landforms that despite the fact that the slot between them widens ahead to nearly two nautical miles, the great Oceanus appears to shrink in trembling deference, as if in fearful awe of the majesty of the granite kingdom he deigns invade.

Passing Agamemnon Bay to starboard, the last gasp of the like-named channel, I happen to glace to the right and am stopped dead in my tracks. There, not 300 yards off, looking just like a crouching tiger, sits a Canadian ferry! Its great white hull looks to be full of cars; crew swarm over its decks as if preparing for the attack. Too late we realize its presence. We weigh our options. The point we just passed is now too far behind us to provide any shelter; we might be eaten alive before getting back to it. Making a run for the safety of Nelson Island, off our port beam, and the shallower water it offers suffers the same defect. Our only hope, then, is to plow forward boldly so as not to look too much like easy prey.

As any fighter pilot will affirm, there is a heavy price to be paid for target fixation. We had been so narrowly focused on the splendor ahead of us that we failed to notice the danger lurking much closer. By the time the threat was identified, there was nothing for us to do except sweat through each passing second of every following minute in hope either that the crouching beast would not attack or at least that it would spot a more attractive morsel in closer proximity to itself. Eying the menace closely – but not aggressively, for such a belligerent act could goad the beast into a charge – our prospects grew better with every turn of our prop. The 2.4 feet we moved forward with each revolution meant that we had put another 2.4 feet between it and us.

Miraculous though it seemed at the moment, we were shocked by the fact that the beast never left the dock. The only explanation we could provide for our good luck was that the monster had gorged itself with small boats on its run in to its lair and was not yet ready for another meal.

Getting up the fjords leading northward out of Agamemnon Channel is a simple business. It amounts to little more than connecting the dots. The walls of the valleys – 1.75 nautical miles maximum width in the south, narrowing to a uniform 0.75 nautical miles as one progresses northward – provide the boater no room for directional confusion. He either can proceed forward or return from whence he came. As to water under his keel, so steeply do the mountains drop down from their peaks and so quickly do they continue their plunge toward the bowels of the earth, that grounding is never a concern. With soundings approaching 2,500 feet in places and with no exposed rocks or shallows to avoid along the way, the sojourner need not deviate a single iota from the straight and narrow. Additionally, the speed with which the bottom drops away from the shoreline means that recreational boats of almost any size can closely approach dry land without much fear.

The final check mark to be entered in the plus column relative to getting through the preliminary fjords and on to Princess Louisa Inlet derives from the fact that, although the track leading to it is fairly long and twisty, it terminates in a cul-de-sac near Malibu Rapids. This means that missing the inlet through a piloting error is nearly impossible. Thus, like a marble propelled through a pipe, those who start at one end of this waterway most assuredly will wind up at the other end of it. And, they are most likely to get there both in reasonably short order and in one piece.

Based on these considerations, The Pilot's chore in planning this part of the run the rapids is but to lay out straight course lines with an eye toward guiding his vessel most efficiently through the dog-leg turns of the three reaches north of Agamemnon Channel.

And all of that is the good news. The bad news is that because of the extreme depths everywhere along the way, there are virtually no viable anchorages between the lower end of Prince of Wales Reach and the entry to Princess Louisa Inlet. So, for a distance of about 30 nautical miles, one way, the wise boater will not schedule any "potty breaks," medical emergencies or incapacitating mechanical incidents that might require a stopover.

All human relations are political. Despite its negative connotations in American thought, politics is nothing more than the art of each person getting along with everyone else, everywhere. By way of example, think back *Robinson Caruso*. Therein, the shipwrecked hero established a happy, though solitary, life that remained *sans* politics until the moment he saw a single human footprint in the sand. Thereafter, everything changed. He established a standing army (himself); he set up laws to regulate the citizenry (Friday); he taxed the local population (by enslaving Friday and taking from him all of the fruits of his labor); he established territorial boundaries (the entire island) and he developed a foreign policy (unrestricted warfare against the cannibals who periodically invaded his turf). The essential lesson therein is that whenever you get two people in proximity to each other, then like it or not political life necessarily ensues.

Based on observations gathered over many long years, I have concluded that the democratic nature of our world – currently described, I think, as being neo-post modern, but a newer moniker already could be in style – is just too much for me to fight. Despite holding multiple, higher degrees attesting to many long years spent in the close examination of things political, of having under my belt decades of practical and scholarly inquiries on the subject, of laboring some years within the hallowed halls of ivy in pursuit of an understanding of the particulars of the topic and of having immersed myself for another score or two of years in the theory and practice of the statesman's art, I find nonetheless that the value of my views on things pertaining to governance is exactly equal to that of the humblest and/or the most ignorant societal misfit!

If you contract pneumonia, you go to a medical doctor for help. If you wish to save a lot of money for retirement, you employ a financial advisor. If you need a loan, you call on your banker. If your car is not running smoothly, you stop it off at your mechanic's shop. But when the welfare of our great and small villages, towns, cities, states, provinces, nations and even our regional alliances are at stake, we turn without further ado to the opinions of millions of do-it-yourselfers. Thus, scarier than a loaded gun could ever be, should be the thought that we let, nay, even encourage, almost everyone over the age of 18 to go into a voting booth and seize control of the levers of governmental power. And we allow each and every one of them – even crazy Uncle Fred – to take on that responsibility all alone, unsupervised, and in absolute secrecy. Frightening stuff, that!

Plowing northward into the Prince of Wales Reach, I supply live entertainment by way of scintillating chatter relative to the general state of the world. As always, The Crew is my audience. It is a joy to share my musing with her especially since she encourages and applauds these performances. The issue I take up this day, as only it can be, is politics. Within the snug confines of the pilothouse I shower her with my peculiar views and insights and she happily responds with her own. She is bright and quick, even for one who suffered the ravages of a thorough course of study leading to a bachelor's degree, with honors, in economics. Whether because of that or in spite of it, we both delight in these exchanges.

Today's inquiry concentrates on the history and purpose of Amendment X -- better known as the Tenth Amendment – to that part of the U.S. Constitution referred to as the Bill of Rights. Fascinating fare though this exploration may be in its own right, my intention in presenting it serves as much to mask my growing concern for the weather as it is to bring The Executive Officer up to speed on a critical aspect of our system of government. For, the further north we progress, the lower the rain-filled clouds overhead descend. Gone are the snow-capped summits we had glimpsed as we passed out of Agamemnon Channel. Gone are the few rays of sun that briefly brightened our day. Gone, too, are the stately green forests that climbed high up the walls of our moving valley. Increasingly, flat, dull, greyness dominates the view in every direction.

CUTTING THROUGH THE FOG OF TRUTH

We departed Pender Harbour confident that we were immune to most of what Nature could throw at us this day in terms of the weather. We were dry. We were warm. We were inside. And the possibility of having the kinds of high winds or waves that could impede our progress or make us really miserable was almost non-existent. What we had not included in our thinking, however, was fog. Low, thick, soupy, dreary, cold, grey, disorientating, fog. (To my chagrin, I left this meteorological phenomenon out of the atmospheric equation because it is May. I did so on purpose, for, as we all know, May only contains three letters. And, it is simply understood in the Pacific Northwet that any calendar month having just three letters in it is *not* a part of the normal, 11-month long fog season! So, the reader will appreciate and forgive my omission; if feeling generous he might even applaud the decision under the circumstances.)

Anyone who has ever driven a car in a heavy fog or wandered aimlessly in the famous pea soups of London or San Francisco will grant that when the clouds occur at ground level – for whatever reason – they turn the surroundings, even when very familiar, inside out. That which was customary yesterday cannot now be recognized at all and that which was not known previously becomes wholly indecipherable.

At sea, the basic problem presented by fog is far worse than it is on land. Without viable references – excepting exposed rocks, beaches, reefs, breaking waves, and dangerous shorelines – an infinite expanse of undulating grey-black water provides no clue as to where a mariner may be. The are few situations in boating more harrowing than bobbing quietly along in a thick shroud of grey only to hear breaking waves, a nearby bell or horn or, worst of all, the sound of mighty props cleaving the gloom from somewhere nearby.

When visibility drops to nothing the mariner must rely on skills that are not intuitive if he is to avoid trouble. The compass will tell him which way is north and which way he is heading. If he has carefully tracked and recorded his positions he can continue to plot his approximate progress on his charts using speed and distance computations. With access to the right references, he can estimate what the tides and currents are doing to his vessel. All of this – known by the discouraging name of "dead reckoning" – can get a sailor close, *if* he has paid attention, and especially, if he has practiced these arcane arts.

The addition of modern electronics (i.e., GPS, depth sounders, radar, etc.) allows those not quite so attached to the old ways to move more confidently toward their objectives even in low visibility. In most instances, when all of the stars have aligned properly, when nothing transpires too quickly, when the on-board gadgetry works as advertised and is spot-on accurate, then any given vessel should be able to get pretty close to its destination safely. But getting close to one's target at sea can be as disastrous as missing it altogether, for rocky shores, obstructions and a plethora of other things often are collocated close to perfectly safe waters.

Being enveloped in fog in the relatively narrow fjords leading to Princess Louisa Inlet is not something we embrace cheerfully. Because of the depths of these waters, anchoring or holing up until the clouds deigned to lift was not an option. But conversely, running semi-blind was problematic as well. When visibility is reduced to a range of a few yards, floating hazards, including other boats, may not be identified soon enough to allow for evasive action, even when idling along. Likewise, just the slightest inaccuracy in our radar, our GPS or our chartplotter and the first indication that we are getting dangerously near something unpleasantly hard might come in the form of a grinding, scraping, crunching sound. So, earlier in the day when we voted on what kind of weather we wanted for this outing, neither The Crew nor The Skipper chose fog!

One of the most important functions of a ship's captain is that of worrying. The responsible skipper bears that burden so others do not have to. Knowing that there is nothing less effective than a frightened crew, I pretend for her sake that the descending clouds do not concern me. Whether or not it comes as a form of divine retribution for the happy face I pretend to wear, visibility falls from four nautical miles to about three. Then it drops to two. Finally, the flat, grey ceiling that has been distressing me is a hundred feet or so overhead and but a half-mile distant. The sweat that is now running down my brow is proof that I am meeting or exceeding the high standards of command I set for myself.

Cruising past Moorsam Bluff, just south of the point that marks the lower end of Princess Royal Reach, we are surprised to see, charging out of the gloom, a 25 foot aluminum skiff doing about 20 knots and coming straight for us. Apparently apprehending our presence through the mist, the craft bore off slightly toward mid-channel and passed us closely on our port beam. With the rock face of the bluff close off our starboard beam there was little we could do anyway beyond wave. In the grey twilight the apparition was there one moment and gone the next. We imagined that someone inside the shiny metal deckhouse waved back to us, but we really could not see anything. Even as we surmounted the wake it left, the returning fog shrank our little world back into its former, introspective confines.

Although we are about halfway up the slot leading to Princess Louisa Inlet, it occurs to us that while we have been steaming into the interior for quite a while now, we have seen few signs of humankind anywhere. Certainly the fog has not helped change that perception, but even allowing for it and including the silver aberration that just shot by, it occurs to us that we have seen no boats, no houses, and no manmade structures since clearing Agamemnon Channel. In fact, we have not even heard the marine radio crackle. The emptiness is palpable and unexpected. It feels like we are alone in a virgin wilderness.

Most of the pencil lines that The Pilot drew on his beloved charts the night before were arrow straight. His course changes came exclusively where a significant turn had to be executed in order to follow the waterway. As mentioned earlier, the depths of the sea under the keel of *Minstrel's Song* allowed him to cut these corners tightly. As The Pilot now spins the wheel to alter his track by almost 90 degrees, the beam of the boat swings around and past a 20-30 foot high, craggy outcropping. As he does so, The Crew wonders aloud what would happen if the engine failed. This causes The Skipper to run through his long mental checklist of potential boating calamities and their possible remedies. He keeps this compilation handy for occasions such as this one. As he completes the general diagnosis, he also weighs the virtues of reporting with absolute clarity all that he concludes or whether the preferred option should not be that which is often pursued in the advertising and marketing domain. His intention is not to deceive The Crew, exactly; it is only to come down more heavily on the 'happy face' end of the scale than on the 'we're all going to die horrible deaths' extreme. Thus he begins with a drawn out, "Well…" and then follows that with an amorphous, "It would really depend on where we were."

Not to be put off, The Crew asks, "What if it happened when we were right over there?"

Hmmmm. Looking in the direction indicated, I see that 'right over there' features the bluff face of a solid rock wall doing a wonderful imitation of a sheer, 50 foot cliff. Based on experience, I am pretty sure that that granite exposure does not gently level out and turn to sand just under the surface of the sea. I am all but certain, in fact, that it continues to drop like a rock (?) to who knows what depth. With the current pushing in toward the flat side of this piece of real estate and without the usual growl of the engine working to keep us off of it, I surmise that we would be up the proverbial "#?&!% Creek" pretty fast. But I really do not want to go there with The Crew!

Still, the withering intensity of her stare allows me to kill only so much time before I have to offer something reassuring. The best I can do is, "Ahhhh…Well…Let's see…O.K…Ahhhh. If we were really lucky and someone was around we might call them on the radio and have them pass us a line. Even a small boat could get us out into the middle of the channel, no sweat."

She does a 360 degree scan of our little grey world and reminds me that I had opined not half an hour past that the radio probably wouldn't transmit more than a mile or two, given the steep canyon walls that surrounded us. And then she adds that the aluminum skiff that sped past recently was surely long gone by now.

With this I know she is playing hardball and so I have to produce and produce fast. "O.K., O.K. What we'd have to do is to drop the anchor and run out every inch of rode we have in hope that it would find a piece of bottom to grab before the rocks consumed us. [Ridiculous as this may sound well after the fact, the reader should keep in mind that I was pressed for time and under the circumstances no straw was too thin to grasp.] Immediately thereafter we would launch the dinghy and use it as a large fender to keep us off the hard stuff and to try to guide the boat a bit as it drifted up or down the shoreline. Beyond that, we would have to await the arrival of a really great Samaritan…Oh! Did I mention that we have wonderful insurance?"

The Crew shifts her weight from one foot to the other and then inquires, "Do you think the dinghy's outboard would move us at all?"

Suppressing the urge to roll on the floor laughing, I consider whether our tiny, 2.5 horsepower outboard, sporting its 1.5 inch prop, strapped to our worthless rubber inflatable might ever move our 16,000 pound boat. Not wanting to burst any bubbles I said, "Sure. It might…a little…if there was no current, no wind and we had a flat calm…Maybe. Well, we could certainly give it the old college try couldn't we!"

She fell silent, asking no further questions. That thankfully kept me from having to make up any other preposterous answers. I sensed her discomfort a while later, however, when after we passed a headland she suggested I might not want to cut the corners quite as close as I had been. Rarely does she tell me how to set a course or where to steer. Good communications being the key to successful command, I read her loud and clear and lay the boat out an extra hundred feet or more, just because.

* * * * * * * * * * *

The rain came down harder as we turned 60 degrees to starboard and began the trek up Princess Royal Reach. We traded the heavier precipitation, however, for higher clouds and increased visibility and thought we got the better part of the deal. As the sky lifted and brightened some and the greyness ahead dissipated, we watched in pleasant fascination as one silvery ribbon after another, streaming down the sheer mountain faces we could now see off to the right, revealed themselves to us. We had not expected these springtime waterfalls, but we marveled at their beauty nonetheless. Rarely were we able to penetrate the misty grey enough to identify the origins of the streams, but there was something magical about the way they seemed to come out of nowhere in order to romp and frolic merrily as they fell down toward the sea. It was remarkable, too, that over the growl of the engine, the beat of the rain on the pilothouse roof, the din of the heater fans, the slap-slap-slap of the wipers, and all of the other noises associated with a moving boat, the clean, fresh, sprightly sound of splashing water cascading down rock walls penetrated then closed doors of our snug little house. They penetrated our souls too! Without a sign of civilization in any direction, it was as if God wanted to share something special with only us. And He did.

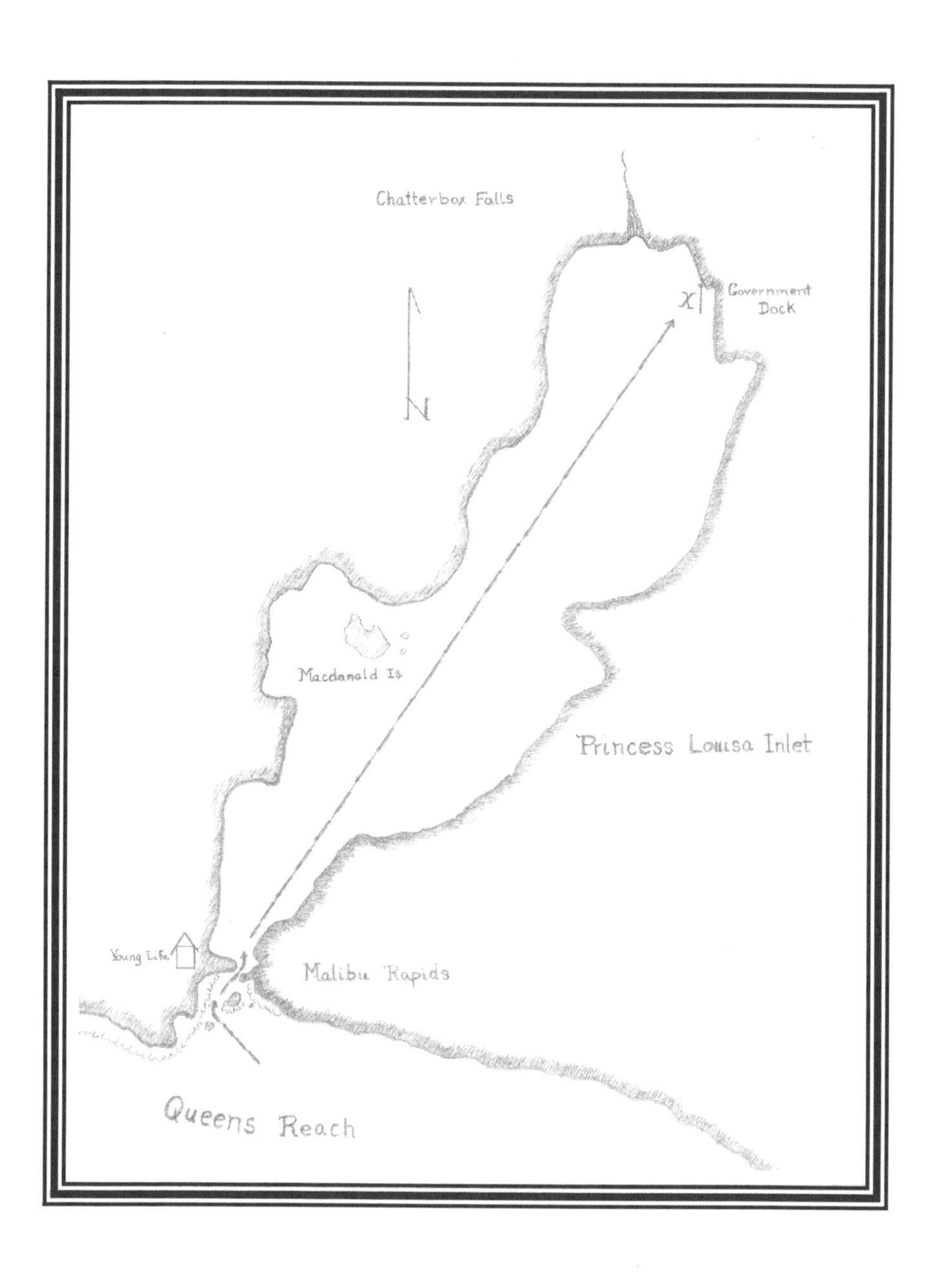
Chatterbox Falls
Government Dock
X
N
Macdonald Is.
Princess Louisa Inlet
Young Life
Malibu Rapids
Queens Reach

Snapping pictures, pointing, laughing and generally behaving like a couple of school kids on a class trip, we gleefully cruised up Princess Royal Reach. With each passing minute the clouds lifted a little more, the sky brightened a few extra shades and the water, mirror flat and calm, turned a deeper, darker, and a most elegant emerald green. All cruising should be like this!

With almost unlimited visibility now, we are struck by an unanticipated incongruity. For miles and miles we have seen nothing manmade – in fact, through the fog we have hardly been able to see anything at all! During that time our psyches adjusted to and even embraced the reality of having exceeded the clawing reach of civilization. To the extent possible, we had become one with wild, untrammeled Nature. We savored it; we drank it into the depths of our very beings. And then, in the distance, something metallic, something shiny crashed in on our solitude. Through our glasses we observe a small freighter of about 200 feet in length anchored off a distant shore. We could see no movement on her decks. There were no tenders, no docks, no piers, and no buildings anywhere near her. Why was she there? Was she a derelict? Had she escaped from some cruel master only to be marooned in these distant waters? The miles that separate the two of us, absent any further clues, allow for no apparent answers.

While searching for an explanation regarding the commercial vessel we spy, at an even greater range, some heavy earth moving equipment parked in a clearing up on a mountainside. They seemed to be waiting to meet someone or something. But piling mystery on top of mystery, we can detect no roads leading to them and no camps or human habitations anywhere around them. Who brought them there? How? Why? We sail beyond these oddities without ever learning anything more about them. But like passing shades in a graveyard, we feel more like interlopers in a strangely forbidden, even alien landscape, than carefree ocean cruisers.

At Patrick Point we make a 75-degree turn to port to enter Queens Reach, the final leg of our journey. Diagonally across this body of water is Malibu Rapids, the single opening that leads into Princess Louisa Inlet. Queens Reach is oriented on a southeast-northwest axis. We entered it from its southeastern end and are steaming northwest. Malibu Rapids occurs about two-thirds of the way up (northwest) Queens Reach, on the northern shore. Beyond it lies Princess Louisa Inlet. It extends on a southwest-northeast line away from the Rapids.

We are delighted by the fact that we have almost reached our destination, but minute by minute our spirits are dampened, literally, by the heavy clouds that descend again on us, bringing with them with the likelihood of more rain if not another dose of fog. We like rainy afternoons as much or more than those filled with sun; in this instance, however, the short clearing period we enjoyed gave us a taste of the splendor around us and the spirit-lifting power of the scenes we beheld briefly were awe inspiring. We longed for more.

Because a ship's operation continues despite the sights and sounds around it, a flurry of activity now broke out on the bridge of *Minstrel's Song*. The Skipper scanned the distant shore with binoculars to confirm the vessel's destination and The X.O. pulled out all of the "extra" charts and reference books she could get her hands on so as to assemble the clearest picture possible of what lay ahead. Meanwhile, The Pilot nervously checked and re-checked his clocks for the proper time of day and then compared the results to the tide and current tables that were spread out before him. It was his job to make sure they arrived at the Rapids at or near slack tide.

The entry to Princess Louisa Inlet is not too hard to identify. Getting through it can be more difficult. The preferred channel is clearly recognized by the fixed white marker that resembles a miniature lighthouse at its western extreme and by a small, rock islet jutting up out of the water less than 200 yards northeast of the beacon. Lying to the north beyond these references points, but only a couple of hundred feet distant is the mainland shore and lots and lots of sharp, gougy-looking rocks. Favoring the lighthouse side – to avoid some potential dangers to the east of it – one carves a sweeping arc clockwise around the backside of the aforementioned islet, taking care to stay off of the boulder strewn coast, before reversing the turning radius in order to get centered in the narrows through which one must pass to get into the inlet. This latter feature, a waterway of about 40 yards in width, on a good day, is festooned liberally with large, boat wrecking, submerged masses undoubtedly placed there just to make the transit interesting.

In addition to the currents that can whip through Malibu Rapids at speeds approaching 10 knots, the most curious feature of this opening is not the constricted, treacherous waterway, the rocky shores, the submerged impediments or the surrounding mountains, or the peaks or the glaciers that flank the whole thing; rather, the most riveting aspect of this bit of real estate is the modern, cedar and glass lodge complex that sits immediately northwest of the channel as if tucked in next to a freeway exit. Fronted by a swimming pool that gives the impression of having been blasted out of a chunk of solid rock – with a stingy 50 feet separating its chorine-laden water from the sea washing back and forth through the Rapids – this ex-luxury resort *cum* Christian youth camp provides its inhabitants with a grandstand view of all the vessels that struggle to safely reach the confines of Princess Louisa Inlet. It would not surprise me if the managers of this unique facility did not post the tide schedules prominently around the grounds just so the inmates could gather at the appropriate moment to watch all of the fun.

Our experiences with the tight approaches to Gabriola Passage, Silva Bay and Smuggler Cove stood us in good stead when it came to making our way into Princess Louisa. We arrived at the Rapids just at slack tide, and slowing to a mere crawl, we wended our way carefully, but uneventfully, into the calm waters on the interior side. It was not without concern that The Pilot spun the wheel this way and that to follow the channel, but he was relieved to note in passing that the rain had kept the crowds inside the buildings. No one on *Minstrel's Song* really needed an audience.

HOME AT LAST

Whether a topographical or a psychological barrier had been passed, the world beyond Malibu Rapids suddenly seemed different. On the outside the sea was roiled by wind and chop and its aspect had returned to that cold, grey that sent shivers through one's soul. On the inside tranquility reigned. The water's surface was mirror flat and calm and it took on the warm, dark green hues of an alpine lake. Out in Queen's Reach the boat's bow worked to drive the ocean back onto itself, pushing it up into frothy waves that allowed only for the grudging passage of the craft. Once inside inlet, however, the crystal clear sea opened so gently and with so little disturbance that it revealed to us the secrets below its surface down to 20 or 30 feet or even more. The massive raindrops that bludgeoned and confused the outside ocean here kicked up small, silvery geysers that plopped delightfully back onto the mirror-like surface of the water in a way reminiscent of millions of tiny wedding fountains. The nearby trees, just barely out of reach as they overhung the shoreline to starboard and warmly spread their boughs like the open arms of a welcoming committee, had been just moments before distant, receding forests. Not to be outdone by the flora, a small flock of tufted puffins bobbed in the cove abreast of us as we idled respectfully into their domain. Swimming along slowly on a course parallel to ours, this avian parade, most striking for the amusing shapes and bright colors sported by its participants, seemed to be saying, "Hello. We're glad you made it."

Even though we reminded ourselves, repeatedly, that we continued to sail on the high seas, everything we saw contradicted our experiences. Surely we were way up in the Swiss Alps, floating on a crystal clear lake. Because of that sensation, neither of us would have been surprised had we spotted a lovely Swiss chalet perched on high and looking down on us. We had entered a land of natural charm and unimagined fantasy.

Princess Louisa Inlet is about four nautical miles long from start to finish. Its general orientation is southwest to northeast, but because it arcs from northeast to north over the last mile of its extent, one end cannot be seen from the other. From start to finish this body of water barely reaches three-quarters of a mile wide at its widest, while the bulk of it manages to hold the neighboring mountains in abeyance for less than half a mile.

With no break in the weather, a thick blanket of low clouds obscured most of the heights that formed and shaped this paradise.

Everywhere lower down, however, dense forests of firs and cedars, broken only here and there by green-grey-brown rock outcroppings and cliffs, rose up the precipitous slopes they clung to only to be swallowed forever by the hazy swirl of the soggy sky above. Meanwhile, the myriad silver-white streams that plunged down the inclines crashed into the sea as if gratefully returning home after a long journey. Limited though it was, the scene was breathtaking.

The mountainsides run so sharply down to the surface of the sea that in many places putting even a small RIB ashore is difficult if not impossible. Great chunks of granite and bluff cliffs frequently supplant the white sand beaches associated with the oceanfront. The dominating hillsides above the shores form great walls of timber, but in numerous locales massive faces of naked, grey rock separates the forests one from another, both horizontally and vertically. Appearing as silver ribbons, phalanxes of small streams follow well-established beds down from the heights only to turn themselves into suicidal rivulets as they hurtle ever faster toward the waiting ocean. When considered as a whole, the combination of these divergent features is stunning.

Cut through the hard rock by glacial action, Princess Louisa Inlet resembles a kind of a box canyon. The salt water here is bounded by two sets of parallel ridgelines, punctuated by four major peaks. One ridge stretches along the southeast coast of the inlet and one follows the northwest. These mini-ranges pinch together in the north to block the ocean's progress further inland. The highest prominence immediately adjacent to the fjord is over 7,200 feet in elevation; three lesser peaks all of which top 5,500 feet rise up along its shores. Because each of these is measured from sea level up and because all occur within the relatively short horizontal distance of 1.5 to 3.5 miles from the ocean, they seem to reach astounding heights, much beyond their actual dimensions.

The crowning features of this landscape are the creamy white glaciers that cling to the peaks and highland valleys. They cap these wondrous summits as if placed there by a skilled ice cream parlor attendant. It doesn't take much imagination to transform the vast glacial spreads from snow-laden heights into monstrous, oozing vanilla cones on a hot summer day.

The focal point and the "destination" of the inlet is Chatterbox Falls. Fortuitously positioned at that very end of the fjord, its presence draws visitors to its freshwater pool like flies to honey. Although it is not Niagara Falls, due to the hundred-foot vertical plunge this river takes over its rocky bed, splitting the verdant forests that flank it, this marvel attracts a small army of beauty-seekers during the summer months. In a crashing, churning, mist-spitting display of unconcealed glee, the granite chute that contains the stream conveys a river of fresh, clean water – bouncing, bubbling, and babbling – down to a rock-strewn, gravel delta that spreads out at its base. From there it gently glides the few additional feet that separate it from its maternal source.

Man's visible presence in the inlet is limited to the Christian Camp at Malibu Rapids, an adjunct of that same establishment nestled snugly behind MacDonald Island[9] – about half way to the falls – and a government dock. The latter extends several hundred feet out from the inlet's terminal shore and is a like distance removed from the bottom of Chatterbox Falls. Due to its deep water and the limited number of viable anchorages elsewhere in Princess Louisa, the government dock becomes prime real estate when the crowds arrive. This floating parking lot allows boaters to enjoy a continuous view of the falls while they luxuriate within earshot of their sound and fury, 24 hours a day, all without the worries of trying to find a place to hold their hooks.

In spite of the rain and the low clouds that cut visibility greatly, we marvel as we slowly cruise toward Chatterbox and the dock. The engine is set to idle, our slowest forward speed, to maximize our exposure to our magnificent surroundings. Everywhere we look there is something else of interest and we are interested in looking everywhere we can.

It is very early in the cruising season and we are lucky. Perhaps the rain and the chill also have worked in our favor. As we make the last turn up the inlet, we are relieved to see that only four boats are tied up to the dock. Later in the summer, finding a spot on the wharf or laying claim to one of the few places that will hold an anchor will be

---

[9] *On some older maps, this speck of land is known as Hamilton Island.*

problematic. The pier itself might accommodate 12 or 14 average sized boats, singled up, and another group of about that same proportion may be able to set their anchors, but in July and August twice that number may show up looking for a night's lodging.

In preparation for arrival at our final destination, The Crew dons her foul weather gear and then begins to deploy our fenders to starboard. Thereafter she takes up her post in the open cockpit and prepares to handle the stern mooring lines. Meanwhile I make myself psychologically ready, all safe, dry and warm in the pilothouse, to wow the crowd with my boat-handling prowess. Guiding *Minstrel's Song* to a point more or less parallel to the wharf, I give the bow thruster a quick touch and then dial in a few turns of reverse prop while holding the helm hard to port. Within magnificent seconds we are there, stopped dead in the water about six inches off the pier and just ahead of the next boat astern. In such a position and without apparent wind or wave to change anything, our little tug might have spent the rest of the afternoon and part of the evening fixed right on that spot without moving a millimeter one way or the other. So well and so easily had this been achieved I am inclined to spend the rest of the day simply sitting back and admiring my own perfect work. None of that was to be, however, since the couple from the vessel behind us kindly braved the chilly rain to lend us a hand at the dock. Under those circumstances, and with The Crew sloshing around somewhere toward the stern of the boat, the only decent thing for me to do was to leave my shelter and pass our bow lines to our helpmates and then thank them profusely for helping us tie off the boat. Acts of such generosity must be accepted warmly even when they conflict with the demands of unalloyed egocentrism.

Although keen to send out a shore party to explore the wilderness, pragmatism and a refined sense of self-preservation prevails, especially since it is raining cats and dogs, so we decide to have lunch first. Cookie rustles up her usual array of exceptional fare and we settle in to savor her offerings and to enjoy the feelings of satisfaction that go with having arrived after a goodly day's cruise. Like dry sponges, we sit in our little nest, look out of the large saloon windows and soak in as much of our surroundings as our mental faculties will allow. The majestic scenes presented in 360-degree, IMAX 3-D with full Dolby Surround Sound, if one includes the beat of the raindrops on the fiberglass and the unceasing roar of the falls in the distance, is a balm for our souls. Nothing more in life is wanted or needed.

The rain continues to fall, hard, throughout the afternoon. Somehow the warmth of the cabin, the grey daylight penetrating the saloon – softened and supplemented by the yellow glow from our oil lamp – and the attractions of a couple of good books manage to keep us at home. We curl up on the couch, breath deeply, barely move and consider not at all the soggy perils of an expedition.

Late in the day, however, conscience gets the best of us and we convince ourselves that the rain has abated enough to make a trip ashore something less than absolute insanity. Pulling on our oilskins – Gortex for modern mariners – and arming ourselves with cameras, we carefully hop onto the ice-glazed dock and then slip and slide up the ramp that leads to the only identified path in the area. At the top the wooden incline we step onto a wet, needle-strewn brown carpet and follow it toward the sound of great quantities of water tumbling over rocks. Concomitantly, we assess the weather situation and agree that it is not raining nearly as hard now as it had been… as long as you discount the big drops that fall from the overarching cedar branches to pelt us unmercifully and, as long as you pay no attention whatever to the little drops that fill in the gaps that separate the bigger ones. But, we figure, 'In for a penny, in for a pound,' so we check to make sure that our cameras are still riding above the waterline and then slog off in search of the falling river.

We have hardly started down the trail before we realize that an amazing microcosm beckons from all sides. Large, old cedar trees with trunks the sizes of SUVs encircle us. They tower over our path. They block out the distant world. Their great arms droop under the weight of the rain. Their lacy sprays transform the light of the departing day into something darker, greener and, remarkably, soft. This is their domain, their home, their only place in time or space and we their insignificant guests. It is probable that some of them have been standing here, alone, for a thousand years awaiting our arrival. They welcome us and we bow to them.

Draping over the lower limbs of the cedars are long wisps of grey-green moss. Moss clings thickly to the trunks and branches of the trees too. The ground, the rocks, the occasional fallen limb or the old stump – almost anything solid – is covered or wrapped in soft green blankets made of this natural unguent.

The shadowy darkness wrought by the leafy upper realm serves to protect and enhance the lower one. Ferns with uncoiling fronds arc up here and there. Blooms and blossoms from lesser plants unobtrusively dot the landscape as if afraid to proclaim their own beauty too loudly. Decaying wood and peat host multi-colored fungi of myriad sizes and shapes. Mushrooms and toadstools sprout randomly on the dark, dank forest floor.

Our on-board Botanist is in her element here. Despite deep agrarian roots, for me flowers come in three basic varieties: roses, pansies and daffodils. And while The Botanist may not profess to know either the common or the scientific name for much of what she encounters, her thing, her real THING, is close-up photography of any and all of the wild flowers that cross her path! Never has the wiliest old hog sniffed out truffles any better than The Botanist discovers flowering things that need to be recorded for posterity.

My picture-taking interests lie in the broader world around me. Particularly, the lights and the darks, the abundant green-brown-black tones and the overall texture of the panorama enthrall me totally. Unfortunately, I am also interested in keeping my electronic camera and myself (in that order) reasonably dry. So, with these chores taking up most of my attention, I have little time to devote to the kinds of artistic composition I enjoy most.

Meanwhile, The Botanist stumbles onto a treasure-trove of likely looking subjects. Bending close to her targets in order to fill her frames with droplet-covered flowers, so fixed is she on her specimens that it seems that she has forgotten the rain that continues to fall in torrents. Snap, flash, move, re-focus, bang – she makes her way along with the careful, but methodic step, of a fire team leader. All the while she reaps a bumper crop of digital delights.

Being prevented from a like occupation by the precipitation pelting my head, and by the darkening gloom that robs me of the requisite illumination – really, friends, a built in flash will NOT light up a mountain side or even a football stadium! – I am reduced to entertaining myself by surreptitiously taking scrapbook quality pics of The Botanist as she works her way through the flowering flora of the forest.

Few things I can do are more likely to spark a mutiny than photographing The Crew. In order to cop my candid shots I have to use all of my military and professional skills and then get lucky to boot! Carefully I line up my subject and then I depress the shutter. Sadly, the dreariness of the lengthening afternoon coupled with the light-eating properties of the wet cedars that encircle us, demand that I use a flash if I want an actual image when I get home. Even when bent double and gazing intently toward her feet, and even with her own flash going off periodically, The Botanist senses as much as she sees that something untoward is in the offing. When I release my shutter, a simultaneous ball of white light arcs across the landscape like a bolt of lightning. "What was that?" she barks.

"What was what?" I innocently reply.

"You know…that," she insists.

"Oh. You mean that flash? Oh… just me taking pictures."

The enormity of my crime either eluded her or she was determined to finish her own work before the conditions got worse. Whatever the case, she returned to her flowering subjects, but her mind was on me as much as on them. Moments later I flashed again. Within nanoseconds she was on it! "Were you taking pictures of me?" she growled. (Some people think that women cannot growl, but they are dead wrong.)

"Uh…well…you might have been in the frame, but not because I was taking your picture...exactly." The instant I said that I knew I had chosen the wrong road. My intention was to give her the small lie to try to weasel out of the situation. In so doing, I had proved Hitler and his National Socialist Party (Nazi) friends right again! People recognize small lies for what they are. Conversely, folks work to accept the big lie as the truth, the whole truth and nothing but the truth precisely because what they hear is so preposterous that they think it could not possibly be false! Trying desperately to save myself, I changed the subject and said, "Let's go over and check out the falls before it gets much darker."

It is not a great day for exploring. It is not the best day for taking pictures. But it is a grand day for being out together, for drinking in the beauty all around us and for relishing the sense of isolation and freedom we find everywhere we look. Everyday we face problems, challenges, hurdles, obstacles, hurts, pains and general sufferings. All of them are gifts unwanted. Without them, however, days like these would escape our notice. After a quick visit to the falls, we ambled, wetly, back toward the dock and a warm change of clothes. Quietly we contemplated how much joy we missed, every day, when we chose not got out in the rain.

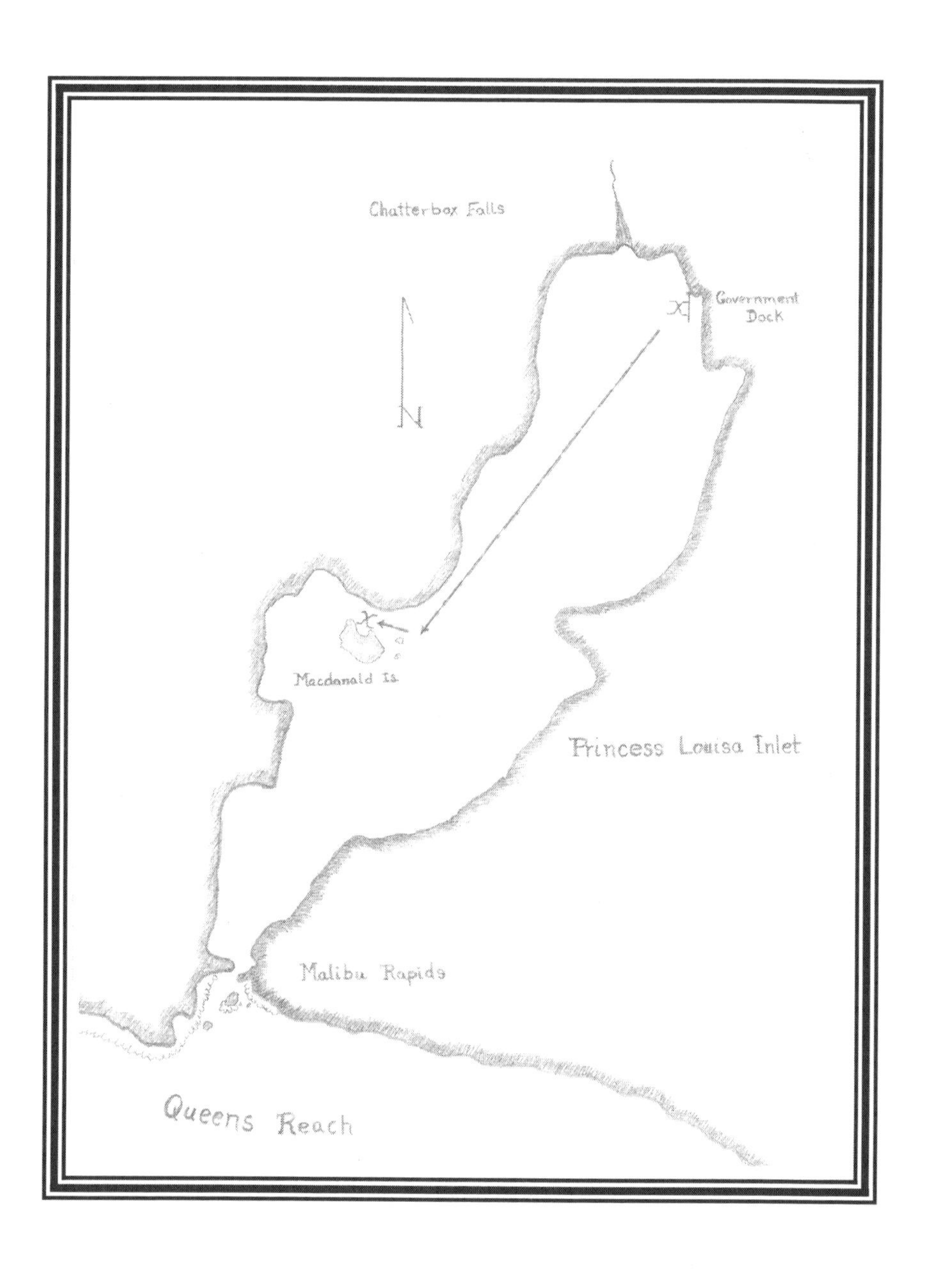
Chatterbox Falls
Government Dock
N
Macdonald Is.
Princess Louisa Inlet
Malibu Rapids
Queens Reach

DAY SIX

Princess Louisa Inlet Refrain
Or
Is That The Sound of Music?

The day dawned, bright, clear and marvelously crisp, or at least I am sure that it must have. With the sun pushing itself up over the eastern horizon before 5:00 a.m. at this time of year, it was unlikely that I was going to be there to greet it. Given that we were in a bowl surrounded by high, steep mountains, I figured that the orb actually cleared the peaks at about 9:30 a.m. I did not take note of that august event either, but when at last I deigned to make my first appearance of the day, it was a rested and especially pleased citizen that set foot on the deck. While alacrity has its place, it probably should not be a part of a visit to Princess Louisa Inlet.

As we fortified ourselves for the trials awaiting with large doses of Cookie's fine coffee and an infusion of fruits and vegetables – meeting 36% of our average daily need so long as one counted the berry goo smeared on top of the Danish as a serving of fruit and the grain in its body as a vegetable! – we surveyed our surroundings with quiet satisfaction. Happily, what seemed to be present on the other side of the saloon's fogged windows was NOT what we had left there the evening before! The flat, grey, wet, cloudy, dull gloom that dominated this tiny part of the earth just 12 hours earlier had disappeared completely. To the extent that we could identify anything through our hazy glass, we marveled at the artist's palette of bright greens, browns, blues, whites and a complete range of other natural hues and tones that encircled our vessel. Although we had spent lifetimes believing that only little girls named Dorothy who were featured in children's stories could be swept up out of Kansas and taken to magical worlds, we were ready to reassess that position based on this simple transformation!

By smearing ShamWow!s all over the windows of the pilot house and the saloon, we were able to clear and dry them enough to assure ourselves that we were seeing reality. Where it had attained sufficient altitude, the sun was pouring its yellow rays down the slopes that lined one side of the inlet and was infusing the forests, the rocks and even the streams of water that cascaded gaily through and down them toward the sea, with its golden beauty. Instead of the dark, flat, low ceilinged panorama we anticipated, everything popped out in 3-D brilliance. Looking up, one almost got dizzy following the terrain ever higher into the blue heavens above; gazing straight across the water, the distant shores, many miles away, seemed to be but an arm's length removed.

With the art of a skilled draftsman, a perfect horizontal line had been inscribed upon the sides of all of the hills above us. That which was higher that this divider had been dusted white with snow; that which was below it, had not. Massive rock faces that overlooked the sea from thousands of feet up sparkled under a coating of ice that, when gently touched by the sun as they were, quickly became the essence of the shimmering waterfalls that streaked the steeps below.

The great wrinkles in the earth's crust that formed the sides of this oblong valley in no longer made any effort to remain hidden from our view. Instead, these fractured, rocky fragments of tectonic plates that were driven upwards eons before, underscore their own magnificence by donning regal robes of ancient greenery. A quick glance at the rising mountainsides might convince even the most skeptical that the tops of the trees that extended to the very heights did little more, in appearance, than mimic the triangular teeth of an old wood saw left leaning against a workman's bench. So precisely did each "tooth" fit its assigned space and so exactly did it continue the same angle up as the one before it, that believing that this order came randomly out of chaos would have been the essence of irrationality.

When considered from sea level, i.e., when staring directly down the inlet from the deck of a boat, one easily could imagine that Paul Bunyan had passed through this land, furrowing its surface deeply as he drug his mighty ax behind him. It required no inspiration at all to see how the trench thus made had filled with the water that in spring and summer flowed down from the icy, snow capped mountains above.

The effect this imagery had on our souls was magnified many times over by the unusual sense of visual depth created by the contrast between the nearby slopes that surrounded this great geologic crease, as compared to the duller, greyer ones that marched in mute formation far behind them. Human hands and human art are incapable of fashioning such striking magnificence.

With a burning desire to take in as much of this new world as possible, I ordered The Botanist to fall out immediately and accompany the ship's complement ashore. The chill in the air that greeted us as we emerged from the warmth of the boat reminded us that we were but frail interlopers on a beautiful, but strange, alpine sea. The slippery frost that coated the dock tried to make fools out of each of us, but its efforts were thwarted, mostly, by the caution it demanded and the slow speed it required. Eventually we made dry land unscathed.

We followed the path we had taken the evening before back into the forest, but instead of the darker, wetter realm that had greeted us then, we stepped into a sun-drenched wonderland. Penetrating deeply through the cedars and the hanging moss, the bright light randomly touched places here and there, having the same effect as do professionally controlled stage lights when they draw one's attention to some particular part of a playhouse. Delighted, we took picture after picture of forest monsters that seemed to hold their ghostly, moss-draped arms out as much to dry as to frighten. The Ship's Botanist chirped and squealed as she discovered new delicacies to record for posterity that were dripping wet with rain, dew and sometimes frost. I looked for contrasting lights and darks, opposing textures and incongruous foregrounds and backgrounds. The hunting was particularly good and neither of us was disappointed.

Travel by foot in this hinterland was limited to a few paths of no more than a half a mile or so in total length. We did a bit of bushwhacking through the ferny forest, but the going was tough and really wet…from the chest all the way down. I followed a rough trail a hundred yards or so up a tiny streambed to get a feel for the climbing conditions. The Crew had the good sense to wait for my analysis. It did not take me long to conclude that lacking serious hiking gear, an ascent to the top of the closest summit was not in the cards this time around. I accepted that reality stoically; The Crew greeted the news with disconcerting enthusiasm.

After poking and prodding to our hearts delight, an effort that netted us many fine digital pictures and a couple of different view of Chatterbox Falls, we returned to the boat for rations and rejuvenation. The other vessels we shared the dock with had sent out parties of their own, mainly via outboard driven RIBs, and though there were only four or five of those creations abroad, the water seemed abuzz with activity.

Having taken in the main attractions ashore, we determined to survey more carefully the remainder of the inlet by water. With *Minstrel's Song's* shallow draft – less than three feet – and the tremendous depths almost everywhere to be found, we saw no need for getting the dinghy down. Instead, without fanfare we cast off from the government dock and began lazing our way back toward Malibu Rapids. With neither discernable wind nor apparent current, I felt comfortable taking our craft close in to shore when something interesting was spotted. At idle speed or less, we moved along easily, barely rippling the placid seas with our passage. Studying our surroundings intently as we went, our primary entertainment consisted of crawling all over the boat, inside and out, in search of just the right place from which to capture any of the many photographs we could not live without.

How does one describe beauty? Whether it's Michelangelo's masterpiece "David" or the Grand Canyon or even the heart and soul of the love of one's life, what words do you use to reproduce a canvas that cannot be seen, to rival a hand that can have no equal, or to share what cannot be divided? Even as their eyes, their ears, their minds fixed concurrently on the same things, neither The Captain nor The Crew had the same experience. They could point and comment and wonder and enjoy together, but even to them, the commonality of the splendor they discovered remained, as ever, individually exclusive. Thus they cruised and marveled and tried to remember the blanketing silence, the infinite colors of the blue sky, the texture of the water, the feel and the smell of the air, the white of the mountain snows, the greens of the trees, and, no less, the yellows of the sun, all with the vain expectation that it would remain theirs to keep and to give to others long after the day had become but a fleeting shade passing quietly over the pages of the book of life.

FOR SALE

As we crept past MacDonald Island, a small spot of land on the north shore of the inlet about midway between Chatterbox Falls and Malibu Rapids, we simultaneously let out a, "What the heck is that?" Off to starboard and up toward the top of one of the glacier-covered summits floated an otherwise nondescript bright, orange dot. With hardly any more substance than just a bubble in the air, it seemed to be moving slowly and deliberately. But the questions were: What was it? Where was it going? Why?

To recap, we were, most accurately, at least 50 miles from anywhere. We were, with equal accuracy, completely surrounded by wilderness. Although it was true that there were four or five known boats within a couple of miles of us, we doubted nonetheless that any of them could fly. Likewise, we discounted the idea that the Young Life Christian Youth Camp had launched anything into deep space!

Not yet convinced that we were under attack, I resisted the temptation to beat The Crew to battle stations. Instead, grabbing my binoculars, I focused every optical fiber I owned on the intruder. Being many thousands of feet above sea level, even when magnified eight times by powerful lenses, it was still impossible to tell exactly what it was. I stared. I looked. I wondered. I postulated. The X.O. did the same. Following nervous minutes of intense analysis an identifiable image slowly began to push its way in on my senses. "I think it's a helicopter,"

I blurted. We both stared at it again.

Almost on cue the speck in the sky began to grow, to descend, to become larger and to take shape. We watched in fascination, offering alternative explanations for its presence. By now there was no doubt that it was a helicopter. But the question we jointly posed still remained: why?

In rugged country – and the mountains around Princess Louisa Inlet certainly qualified – logging frequently is done with helicopters. When the slopes are too steep, the environment too fragile or the cost of building rough logging roads is prohibitive, a common fix is to put cutting crews with chainsaws on the ground and, by way of cables, to let the working choppers haul the harvested logs off to a more accessible place. Thus, an otherwise extreme sport – logging – is made all the more interesting by trying to meld with it air travel, aerial lifting and low level mountain flying all at once. There are few more deadly combinations.

Flying anything manmade in or close to the mountains is not for the weak of heart. The ranks of its practitioners do not include many old pilots. Suffice it to say that thrilling though this activity may be, the perils are great and even small errors can be very costly! Although the possibilities are legion, the two most immediate natural dangers that threaten anyone flying in such an environment comes from air movement: updrafts and downdrafts. These invisible forces can be powerful enough to drive even the largest and strongest aircraft to ground, and that is just a less gory way of saying straight into the side of a mountain.

In the field of aviation, we identify mechanical failure and "pilot error" as two of the primary sources of accidental death. Thus, anyone wishing to successfully challenge nature with their own mortality requires, at a minimum, an absolute knowledge of the weather and of local air currents, great skill, good judgment, courage and the absence of mechanical problems. When it comes to logging, we need to include the notion that a ton or two of dangling, swinging, and otherwise uncivilized wood products serve only as multiplying factors when something starts to go sideways. Taken together, we find that the chances that any particular log-hauling sky jockey will enjoy a hot meal at home after a hard day in the woods, in terms of percentages, is nearly on par with the number of servings of fresh vegetables I willingly consume at each meal.

So, as this flying contraption continued to descend, our first inclination was to say that they were logging way up on the hill above us. What else would impel any sane pilot to be flying a perfectly good helicopter in such close proximity to those peaks? That conclusion made some sense given that the bird seemed to be hugging the face of the mountain as though it were coming down to pick up a new load of logs. What kept the scene from neatly complying with the dictates of reason, however, was the fact that we could see neither a logging site, the usual lifting harness, nor any dangling wood.

Once our curiosities had been satisfied in this matter, our interest in this aerial anomaly waned and we happily returned to the studied enjoyment of the rest of the alpine panorama. But, before we had time to say, "Look at that waterfall over there," our thoughts were yanked back to the helicopter and we had another "What the heck is that" moment. For instead of working away thousands of feet above us, where it might drop the occasional log on an unsuspecting boater, the helicopter continued to descend. When it was less than 50 feet above the waters of the inlet, its downward movement slowed to almost nothing. Hovering there in a nearly stationary position, apparently content to let its rotors blow concentric circles of wavelets in the water, the beast seemed to be scrutinizing the shoreline.

Then, we watched in fatal fascination as it sank, ever so slowly, toward the sea. Since it did not have floats, we knew it could not land on that medium, but we could not understand why it had had approached it so closely. Was it out of control? Was it going to crash? What was it going to do?

The helicopter stabilized its descent again at about 25 feet above the surface of the water. It was about 200 yards off shore. Then it began to inch its way in toward the land while simultaneously losing what little altitude it had left. At a speed much slower than a walk, the machine required several minutes to cover the distance to the tree line.

Mesmerized, but equally baffled, we watched and waited.

For what seemed like hours this spectacle commanded our attention. With every passing moment the bird got closer to both the land and the sea. By now its skids were just a foot or two above the ocean and it continued to creep forward. From a mile or so away, it began to look like the main rotor was going to clip the trees. What was it doing? We waited for the disaster; it didn't happen.

Like a butterfly gently settling on a flower, the helicopter landed lightly on a tiny tongue of grass-covered sand that was virtually invisible from our distance. The rotors steadily spun to a stop and soon people began to exit the hull. One, two, three, four, five... out they came.

With binoculars glued to these interlopers – they could not have been more interesting had they been genuine aliens – we studied them intently. The first soul to hit the beach shouldered a daypack and headed straight for the trees. The others gathered more casually near the tail of the aircraft. The original explorer returned some minutes later only to lead his fellow travelers back into the forest.

In consultation with The X.O., the ship's compliment agreed that we had stumbled on to a party of foresters who had just flown in to examine the crop. That explanation, however, held up for milliseconds only, as we determined that our group of "foresters" actually consisted of two couples, the principals of which were barely ambulatory. Judging by the way they moved, we guessed that the youngest of the bunch was aged well into his or her mid-'70s!

Riveting our binoculars on these enigmatic figures, we followed them into the woods with our eyes and then again we started postulating. What had they come for? What were they doing? Why were they there? And how could a gaggle of people that could hardly cross the beach unassisted expect to surmount the precipitous mountainside that backed up to it? Hmmmm.

It was at that moment that The Crew spotted something very out of place in this environment. Just to one side of the landing zone she saw a large, billboard-like thing apparently attached to one of the trees.

Following her point finger and putting my optic nerves through their paces, I could just make out, I thought, the largest of the words. They were, in bright red, "For Sale."

"Give me a break," I breathed more than said. "They're here in the wilderness, with hardly a human being for hundreds of square miles for the purpose of looking at real estate. Now I've seen it all!"

"Wow," was all The X.O. could muster.

* * * * * * * * * * *

Finishing our tour of the inlet, I steered *Minstrel's Song* back toward MacDonald Island. This small, rocky, fir-covered atoll is separated from dry land by about 100 yards of ocean. It sits just southwest of that point of land where the northwest coast of the inlet, having turned sharply to the southeast for a short distance, bends back to the north for its final run up to Chatterbox Falls.

Based on our studies of the charts, we had developed a vague plan that included spending the night off of MacDonald Island. As we motored by it the day before we appraised it for suitability. Our survey suggested four strong reasons for spending at least one night there. First, located as it was behind the aforementioned protrusion of the shoreline, the government dock, the enticing Chatterbox Falls and especially all of the boats and people that are drawn to them were out of sight (and out of mind!). That was a definite plus for us. Second, the Young Life lodge at Malibu Rapids – a couple of miles to the southwest – was obscured from view by the trees of the island. Third, there were some walking paths on shore that looked inviting. And the last reason for positively assaying the scene was that four of our favorite boat-retaining devices, mooring buoys, were fixed there, free for the taking. With all of these advantages calling, we anticipated passing up this little piece of heaven only in the event that the small shelter there was crowded i.e., that it contained another boat!

The white floats set behind MacDonald Island arc along parallel to its northeast shore. Approaching the island from the southwest, it was only slowly and bit by bit that we could confirm that each one bobbed invitingly in the channel between the island and the mainland, unattended by any other vessels. Easily dodging a couple of submerged rocks as we made our way into this tiny harbor, we selected the buoy that seemed just right to us and tied up to it. There wasn't a breath of air moving. The surface of the water was like a mirror. The thermometer hovered around 70. And, excepting the screech of an odd gull and the high-pitched scream of the occasional bald eagle, we were surrounded completely by the sounds of silence.

After the exertions of the morning The Crew was anxious for shore leave, so we got the RIB down, attached the motor and crossed the short distance to the mainland. We landed at the dinghy dock that was located conveniently there, tied up and quickly scrambled up the large rock adjacent to it that served both as a landing ramp and a sunning perch. We observed from its top that we were at the southeast extreme of a point of land that was remarkably flat, but tree covered. Our little "plain" extended about a quarter of a mile both to the northwest and to the northeast. Where the flats ended the terrain almost instantly transitioned to nearly vertical mountainsides. Speculation led us to conclude that this geographic arrangement was the product of an ancient rockslide.

It was a perfect day for doing nothing. The sun was out, the wind non-existent and the temperature was just cool enough to make walking a pleasure and just warm enough to make sitting equally delightful. We poked and prodded and wandered aimlessly for some time, enjoying the sunshine, the solitude and each other's company. Here was a tiny sand beach. There was a marsh. Look how clear the water in this salt pool is! And while dense forests surmounted the surrounding hills, cedars and small hardwood trees that were much less densely arrayed dominated the level areas.

Young Life had a number of cabins and support buildings nearby, but they clearly were closed until summer. We probably were trespassing horribly, so we tread lightly and hoped we might be forgiven by virtue of being there in the off-season. The snow-capped peaks around us looked down mutely on our meanderings; we interpreted their silence as tacit approval for us to be there. Sitting on an old wooden bench in a small grassy meadow we sunned ourselves, talked incessantly and returned the favor bestowed on us by the towering heights by looking back at them, appreciatively.

OF WARS FOUGHT AND WON

Despite the serenity of the afternoon, the needle on my anxiety meter began to climb as we returned to the dinghy. While standing atop the rock that would lead us back to the dinghy dock, we took a few more moments to admire the day, the mountains, the sea, the trees, the inlet, MacDonald Island and the jaunty way *Minstrel's Song* snuggled in next to it. As we did so, something intruded upon the idyllic scene. With the low profile and with all of the stealth associated with a large, old crocodile, a huge log, mostly submerged, was working its way into our anchorage. Even though there was no wind and hardly any current running, I knew this turn of events could only spell trouble.

Concerned about where this beast was going and what it might do when it got there, we boarded the RIB and motored quickly back to our ship. Once there, between grateful bites of a freshly made sandwich and a few handfuls of potato chips, my eyes surveyed the battleground while my mind contemplated our potential foe. The massive battering ram I scrutinized showed no emotion as it stared vacantly back at me. Locked together thus, we circled each other like two heavyweight champions, with *Minstrel's Song* pivoting round and round on her tether and the monster free of all constraint. Although our fragile hull was not plowing through the water at over eight knots, I still did not want to collide with a ton or more of semi-submerged, waterlogged wood. So I stood at the ready, key in the ignition, boat hook nearby, disposed to instantaneously dodge or parry his best shot. He appeared to do the same.

Most of the rest of the afternoon passed in like manner. Every few minutes I would gauge our opponent's changing tactics and his progress. Sometimes he moved closer and then sometimes he would back off. Slowly he twisted this way and then he reversed course. He remained, always, just distant enough to keep me from lashing out at him, but too close for comfort. Round and around each other we went, both seeking an advantage. My chance finally came toward evening. He apparently did not know the waters very well.

In 480 B.C. a vastly superior Persian army set heavily upon an unholy alliance of numerous Greek city-states. The former swept west across modern-day Turkey, crossed the narrow Dardanelles (Hellespont) and then turned south to ravage Greece. Under their king, Xerxes, the warriors of the ancient Persian Empire smashed everything in their way. At Thermopylae, a small band of Lacedaemonians (Spartans), taking advantage of their knowledge of the terrain, courageously held back the onslaught for a time. But the tide was rising and the great city-states further south, especially Athens, were in peril. Benefiting a second time from their familiarity with local geography, a much inferior Greek naval force was able to lure their Persian counterparts into a melee in very constricted waters. This robbed the invaders of their ability to maneuver, and caused them to lose much of the 3:1 advantage they enjoyed over the Greeks. The result was the stunning Greek victory at the Battle of Salamis. This win ultimately marked the turning point in the war; because of it the Persians were sent packing, empty handed.

Tearing a page out of history, I decided that the best way to defeat a superior naval force would be by putting geography to work for us. As later became clear, the great ram that swam menacingly around us knew little of the local depths, tides or currents. Understanding these forces much better, I disdained meeting him in a head on attack; rather, I kept the brute at arms length while nature did its work. The circles it kept inscribing around us took it close to the MacDonald Island shore. I encouraged that action since the afternoon's falling tide effectively brought that rocky beach ever nearer to our boat.

By early evening the trap was set and then sprung. I all but cheered as first I saw one end of the threatening behemoth bump onto the rocky bottom and then the other end of it do the same. Within a moment or two it was apparent that this natural dreadnought had run itself hard aground! Sharing the excitement with The Crew, the reader can imagine the delight felt onboard as the trace of current that was a constant on this side of the island pushed through the channel with sufficient force to ease that massive timber higher and higher up on the rocks. By bedtime, it was teeter tottering precariously on an exposed boulder, starring inanely out at us while undoubtedly wondering how it had so ignominiously lost both the battle and the war.

Through the night I checked periodically the condition of our opponent. Obviously, it did not take a rocket scientist to figure out that what goes up, must come down. I knew that a higher, high tide than the one just experienced, especially if coupled with a reversal of the current's flow around the island, would make it possible for that that sulking giant to come back at us with a vengeance. Fortunately for us, those things did not come to pass and so, all remained quiet on our western front.

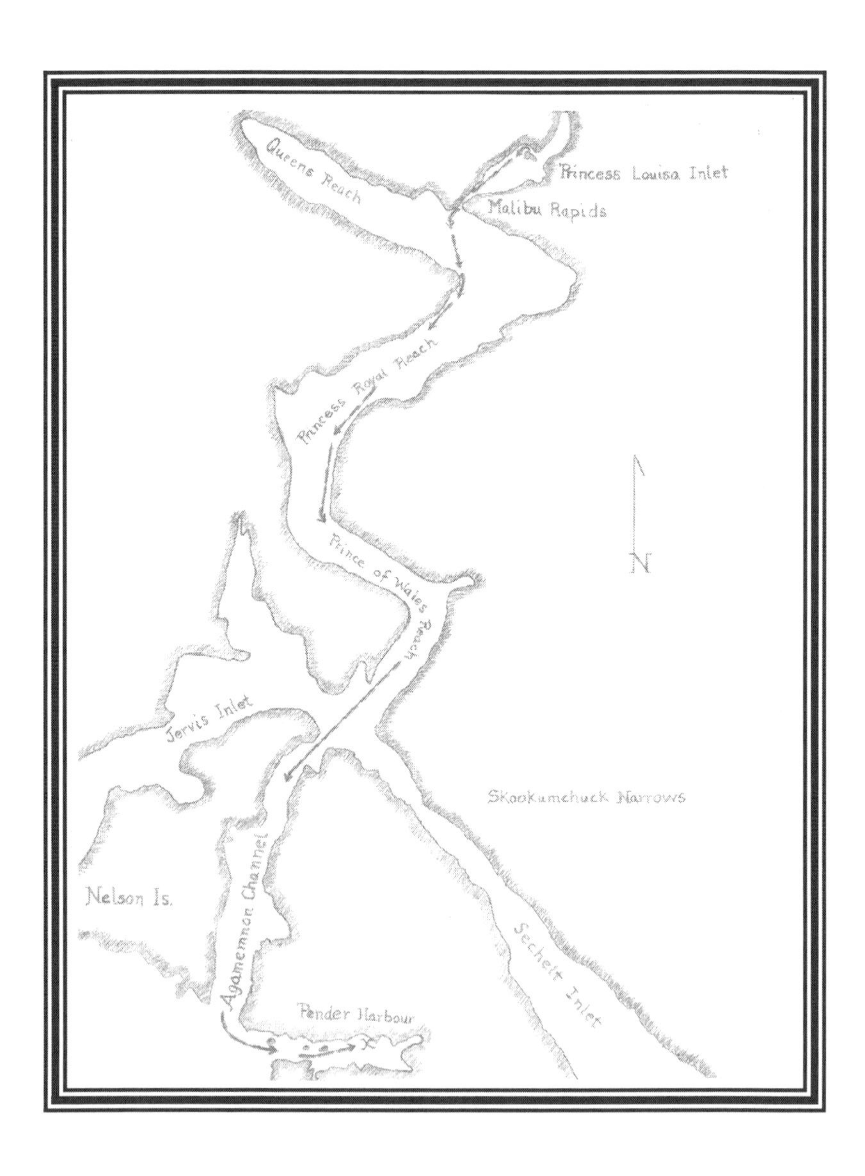
Queens Reach
Princess Louisa Inlet
Malibu Rapids
Princess Royal Reach
N
Prince of Wales Reach
Jervis Inlet
Skookumchuck Narrows
Nelson Is.
Agamemnon Channel
Sechelt Inlet
Pender Harbour

Day Seven

Princess Louisa Inlet to Pender Harbour
Or
Back to the Future

We did not have to hurry to get underway this morning. Neither did we have much to worry about in doing so. The log stayed where it belonged. A gorgeous, carbon-copy day seemed to be in the offing. And the slack tide necessary for passing Malibu Rapids arrived at a civil hour. Moreover, the coffee was hot and delicious, the Danish were, well…just like always, and the cabin, snug and warm, warded off the early chill. Topping everything, the entertainment, provided courtesy of some nearby Barrow's Goldeneye ducks was pleasing. The only fly in ointment was the realization that the apogee of our voyage was behind us. It was time to start home.

Slipping our mooring lines we slowly glided around the north end of MacDonald Island. The surface of the sea continued to do its impression of a mirror. The Pilot eased the boat ahead at the slowest possible speed, trying to keep from marring the scene with even the tiniest ripples. There was something magical about the way the sky, the glaciers, the mountains, the trees, the rocks and the water all came together there; it seemed disrespectful to disturb any of it.

Striving ardently to capture the best shot of the grand panorama that nature provided, The Crew and I once again crawled all over the boat, hanging here and balancing there, giving the shutters of our cameras an excellent workout. Midway through this exercise, The X.O. suggested we sail past the "sign" just to confirm that we were not nuts.

Favoring the northwest shore of the inlet anyway, it took little amendment in course to leave this anomaly close off our starboard beam. Coming to within a few hundred yards of it, we sadly substantiated its contents. There it was, in stark black and white – actually it was emblazoned mainly in red – "For Sale – 1,700 acres – Call..." I looked all around, ran my eyes up the pristine mountainside to its glacial snowcap and then just shook my head slowly and muttered, "Is nothing sacred"?

Without the rain and the slap, slap, slap of the windshield wipers that we had experienced two days before, getting through Malibu Rapids was almost anti-climatic. The only real challenge – and this one was completely psychological – derived from the presence of numerous 'judges' randomly posted along the decks and walkways of the nearby Young Life lodge. These gawkers had not been present on the run in, but the warm sun brought them out in droves and it was certain that they were there to assay our seamanship as we made our way through this tight bit of water. Whether the elders of the group kept a running tally for awards presentation purposes at the end of the season is hard to say, but we were pretty sure we saw a number of signs go up with 9.8s and even some 9.9s on them as we cleared the last obstruction. The Captain and The Crew were well pleased by their performance.

The ancient Greek philosopher Heraclitus once said, "A person cannot descend into the same river twice." Our run back down the various reaches and channels toward Pender Harbour required that we travel, in reverse, the very route we had taken two days earlier. This caused us to test Heraclitus' timeless assertion and ultimately to substantiate its validity.

Upon re-entering Queen's Reach we were astounded by the view. Great mountain summits majestically adorned with ageless snows looked down upon us. Vast highland ranges stretched out in every direction. The blue sky seemed endless. What had been hidden previously under a low-lying blanket of clouds now was joyfully revealed in its fullest by the brilliant sun that spread its yellow warmth over everything below it. Even the ocean – which still resembled most a long, narrow lake – had shrugged off its dark, brooding mantle of grey in favor of a lovely blue-green aspect that encouraged nothing but frolic and play.

We had not been out for more than 10 or 15 minutes when, zoom, zoom, zoom, one fast aluminum skiff after another shot by us. "Must be rush hour," I thought. This activity was striking in that within the space of just a few moments we had been greeted by more human hustle and bustle than we had seen since leaving Pender Harbour three days before! Our surprises were not to end there.

Making our way south, it was hard to believe how much we had missed in the drizzle and the semi-fog that dogged us on the trip north. Had we been asked to describe what we had experienced on that journey, we would have answered, unanimously, wilderness and desolation. Now, just a few days later, our eyes were opened…to the truth?

We marvel at the number of commercial fishing boats we see. Each seems to be working alone, plying the waters in close to shore, steaming back and forth while scooping up the sea's bounty in nets. Surely they are not just sunshine sailors, we think, but as we count – one, two…eight, nine – we cannot help but wonder where they were when we were going the other way? Did fishing season just open today? Or were we legally brain dead?

Distant groupings of sheds, buildings and even what might have passed for small communities occasionally dotted the shorelines. Hello! Anyone home? Have we been caught up is some kind of a time warp? Where did all of this come from?

Rounding once more the point off the lower end of Princess Royal Reach – the one just north of Moorsam Bluff where we encountered the only other moving craft we had seen as we were heading north two days before – we all but ran into a flotilla of sail and power boats. Stretched out in a line that extended for a mile or two to the south of us, we were surprised by a parade of all manner and shapes of small pleasure boats. Whereas previously we had peered through the rain and fog just to keep our bearings, we now seemed to be cruising through a zone defined by some kind of a tickertape-style celebration. In fact, so congested had the way suddenly become that The Pilot had to take the wheel and steer a course around the oncoming hoard. "Must be the day shift coming on," he observed. The Crew just stared in amused disbelief.

As we begin the task of re-adjusting to this day's new world, The Mess Steward serves up sandwiches and drinks and we chatter about all that we had not seen before, but did now. In the process, it occurs to us that this happens as we move through life too. In a way, experience seems to be little more than seeing clearly what was missed the first few times around. The question is, of course, which is reality, really.

With our bow easily cleaving the water leading back toward Pender Harbour, our lives begin to return, somehow, to what might be deemed 'normal.' It is a bittersweet event. With each passing mile the ruggedness and the serenity of the great northern wilderness gives way to a tamer, more civilized south. The VHF radio starts to crackle as it picks up parts of distant conversations for the first time in days. The appearance of a group of Pacific white-sided dolphins romping alongside *Minstrel's Song* is a further reminder that the alpine fantasy of just hours before must defer to the natural rhythms of the ever-broadening ocean. Homes begin to pop up on shore. As usual, we wonder what it would be like to live right over there, or how you would ever get your groceries ashore at that place. Pressing questions like 'do you think people live there all year round' and 'why would you paint anything that color' mingle with commentary about what is right and what is wrong with the planet in general. Somehow, without knowing where or when, we have passed back over the threshold of a magical land that might never have been anyway.

Working our way southward into Agamemnon Channel, we are relieved to find that the Ferry Monster is in hibernation. We see no activity in or around the tall, white ship lashed in its berth there, so we breathe a sigh of relief, hold course and continue our trek down the channel.

Steering now becomes a bit more challenging, as the waterborne traffic in the area grows heavier. Frequent course changes and adjustments must be made to accommodate the myriad of vessels we encounter that are moving in both directions. And, the further south we run, the greater the number of houses we see along both shores. By the time we reach the lower end of the channel, we discover that some giant hand has set down a goodly number of McMansions we had not seen when outbound. It is hard to believe that in just three days time so much could have been built on this wild and barren waterway!

Even the trip into Pender Harbour is different. Without the wind, the clouds and the rain, the entrance seems especially wide, open and easy. The islands and submerged obstructions that had been a concern on our first entry suddenly look inconsequential, even familiar. As we work our way in, the only challenge we face is that of maneuvering between the boat that precedes us, another that's on its way out and a third that is racing up from astern. All four of us look to be on schedule to arrive at or near the narrowest point of the pass at the same time. It would be no big deal were it not for the fact that the vessel bringing up the rear appeared to be intent on splitting the rest of us like pool balls. At the last instant, she throttled back and got in line properly. You have got to love being back in civilization!

An easy course that took us almost due east delivered us back to Dave and Rosie's pleasant marina. As it had been, most of the slips still were empty and we were told that we could drive straight into the spot we had occupied previously if we so desired. The Pilot's initial reaction was to do just that, but on second thought he decided to bear off to port to top off the diesel tanks at the local fueling station.

IT AIN'T EASY BEING GREENE

To reach the service dock it was necessary to work one's way carefully down a fairly narrow, dead end channel that was formed by two parallel finger wharfs each of which extended about 75 yards out from the shore. Separated by roughly 25 yards of water, these piers were oriented northeast to southwest, with the shore end being at the northeast extreme. Accessing this area required that the boater leave the marina close on the starboard beam, then once past it, jog immediately to starboard for a few yards and then square up right away so as to come to a stop near the pumps. It was no big deal beyond the fact that a freshening breeze and the waves fleeing from it were coming straight down this manmade slot and they seemed intent on hustling any vessel therein right on up onto the shore.

We prepared for the passage and docking as always: Bow thrusters on. Check. Starboard pilothouse door open. Check. Bow line from forward cleat led back to within grabbing distance of pilothouse door. Check. Fenders deployed. Check. Aft lines ready to deploy. Check. The Crew at aft docking station. Check. All was in order.

Anticipating the weatherly push from astern, I brought *Minstrel's Song* to a stop slightly short of the pump. The Crew stepped nimbly onto the dock and, selecting a nearby cleat, began to tie us off. At about the same instant, I jumped down with the forward line in hand and passed the order back to The Crew to ease the aft some so we could slide the boat forward enough to position it next to the fuel pump. Unfortunately, a piling of substantial height and girth was so located on the wharf as to separate effectively our boat's bow from its stern. And, because The Crew was on one side of this huge creosote post, and The Captain on the other, the former did not hear the order. Oblivious to this disconnect, I tug on my mooring line, but nothing happens. Our little ship does not budge. I call back again for some slack, louder and annoyed. The Crew, now privy to my desires, springs into action but the intervening column requires that she free the line from its cleat and then inch her way forward with it, past the great, tarry post. This, in turn, requires her to balance precariously on the narrow sliver of dock that separates the obstacle from the sea. With her stern now loose, with me pulling on the bow, and with the wind and the waves doing their small bit, our craft perceives this to be be the perfect time to take a tour of the harbor and so she commences to do just that by swinging her aft end out into the fairway. This spurs The Skipper to pass further *instructions* to The Crew. While this noble soul is doing acrobatics trying to get her lines passed around the black-oozing pillar without ruining her new tee shirt, the best I can do is to pull the boat's head back toward the pier. Unfortunately, given the one-way nature of ropes, I can do nothing to influence the whereabouts of its hind parts. At last, The X.O. completes her circumnavigation of the piling and taking the slack out of the line she still holds is ready to get the ship strapped down. Our Chinese fire drill comes to an end as she pulls our wandering craft back toward the dock.

Mortified by these antics – for only the crew of a nearby commercial vessel, the fuel attendant, the patrons of the ship's store at the head of the ramp and most of the rest of the known world had been able to observe our machinations – I may have articulated a degree of mild displeasure concerning the recent performance of The Crew. That clearly was a mistake, because no sooner had those words cleared my tongue than mutiny broke out! Citing the lack of a prior briefing for the purpose of going over the anticipated effects of the wind and the waves on the boat, and precise training on how best to handle the vertical obstruction that became central to the drama, as well as registering a high degree of dissatisfaction with the wimpy command voice employed and with the general incompetence of The Captain – or words to that effect – The X.O. suggested that if her work was not up to The Skipper's high standards he could...well...he could darn well do it himself the next time. Touché!

There is nothing worse, whether at sea or ashore, than a rebellious crew. And now I had one. The Captain always walks a fine line between too much and too little. The good ones manage to balance like a feather between the dictates of good discipline and slovenliness. Once the equilibrium has been lost, however, it is difficult to regain it without jeopardizing the command structure. Thus, it was imperative that I do something quickly to avert absolute disaster. But what? "Groveling usually works pretty well," I thought, "but with the fuel attendant on hand, the three or four commercial fisherman watching from just across the channel and a store full of shoppers, I don't think I can pull that off right now." Knowing that my pride, a hot dinner later this evening, and perhaps even coffee and a Danish on the morrow were at stake, I had to do something right away. So, I muttered a few banalities that were intended to be a kind of quiet apology…kind of! That was not the best idea I had had that day either, I understand now, but it was the only one available at the moment! Unfortunately, as I should have known from past experience, muttering only begets more mumbling and The Crew was already way too heavy into that. I was just pouring gasoline onto the fire!

I bought a little time by pumping the fuel as slowly as I could. The Crew conversed with the guy taking the money. That is usually a good sign because if she will talk casually with someone else, it is possible that eventually she will talk to me too. Possible.

As we readied for departure, I took another shot at setting things aright with her. As quietly as I dared I suggested that maybe I could have done a better job at conveying my wishes to her. I even went so far as to opine that I was sure that the departure would not be the disaster that the arrival had been! Wilted by the glare I received in return, I succumbed to the obvious and uttered the dreaded words, "It was *mostly* my fault, you know." Good intentions are great, but sometimes too little comes too late. Rather than lighting up and becoming her usual good-natured self, The X.O. stomped off toward her post at the stern and prepared to take in the line when ordered. I was left to wonder how cold my crow dinner was going to be that night.

With mooring lines in hand, it was time for me to focus exclusively on the job ahead. The tight quarters we were in first required that the boat be eased out from the dock in such a way as to keep it parallel with that structure. At the same time, due to the narrowing of the waterway and the shoreline in front of us, our vessel could not be allowed to move any farther forward than it already was. Once sufficient distance away from the wharf had been attained, *Minstrel's Song* would have to spin like a needle,180 degrees within the confines created by the fuel pumps on one side and the fishing boat across the way. Subtracting our boat's length – dripping wet at plus or minus 36 feet – and allowing a foot or two at each end for buffer, we would have about 20 feet 'extra,' fore and aft, to use in performing our pirouette. That space would have been ample for this undertaking had not the press of wind and wave turned it into a sporting event. The smirking countenances of the various members of the commercial fishing crew that had found a long list of compelling chores to attend to on the starboard deck of their boat at that particular point in time added no pressure whatsoever to this workaday undertaking.

Maneuvering a single-screw boat takes a bit of practice. In reverse, the torque developed by the spinning prop pushes the stern in one way or the other (depending on the boat and the direction in which the screw turns). Because the movement of the water is reversed over the rudder, and because the rudder is effectively located at the wrong end of the vessel – as compared to when moving forward – directional control over the craft can be very limited. Without continual compensation by the use of thrusters and/or engaging the forward gear, it is all but impossible to back such a ship in a straight line.

Conversely, to make a single screw boat turn when it is underway, the wash of the water over the rudder forces the stern to one side or the other. This, then, causes the bow to head off in the opposite direction. Thus, while it feels like the front of the boat determines the direction being taken – like the front wheels on a car – the reality is that the stern is doing the bulk of the moving.

At sea, no one cares if a vessel will not dance backwards in a straight line, or if its stern swings widely to take up a new course. In constricted areas, however, it makes all of the difference in the world because the preferred manner of boat handling does not include crashing into and bumping off of all of the hard things in sight! Avoiding those potentialities is exactly what makes the art of close handling particularly interesting.

Thrusters came to recreational vessels a decade or so ago. The idea behind them being that if one built a small, reversible, fan-like device into the hull of a boat and oriented it crossways so that its blast went out toward either beam, it could shove that part of the ship in one direction or the other. A vessel with a thruster fixed in the bow – like *Minstrel's Song* – benefits from the ability to apply independent, sideway power to that end of the boat. The effect of this applied force, for instance, when one is next to a pier, is to cause the front of the craft to swing away from the structure while the stern pivots, more or less in place.

To get off the aforementioned fueling station, we could not just retrace, in reverse, the course we had taken when we arrived. Because our stern 'walks' to starboard when backing up, doing so would just drive the aft end of the boat directly into the wharf. To get where we wanted to go we first needed to drive the bow out to port a few feet. We did that with a burst of bow thruster. Then, by holding the rudder fully to starboard, a very quick shot of "forward" would get the stern moving in the opposite direction, to port. If properly executed, both bow and stern would be pushing themselves more or less equally away from the pier and no headway would be generated. A cycle or two of this dance should find *Minstrel's Song* 15 or 20 feet off of, but still parallel to, the fuel dock.

Once gaining the middle of the channel, we had but to back and fill a number of times and we should be turned around. Backing and filling involves, in this case, putting the wheel hard to port and then allowing the prop to turn over several times in the forward direction. This action will cause the stern to begin to swing to starboard and the bow to begin to go to port. In and of itself, that would be enough for getting us turned around in a large space. Sadly, what we had to work with was a small space.

To achieve our goal within the close confines allowed us, we need to creep forward enough to get the stern moving to starboard and then shift into reverse long enough to hold the boat in position while encouraging the bow to continue its arc to port. This will serve the dual purposes of keeping us from ramming the nearby fishing boat as well as of letting us to retain the inertia developed when the stern first headed to starboard. (The thoughtful reader will recall that *Minstrel's Song* backs to starboard). As long as wind and wave action do not negate the effects of this ritual, and it usually does, the expectation is that the boat will spin around like a weathervane on a central axis while not actually leaving the middle of the channel. Laboring under this delusion we enjoyed what Alexander Pope described when he wrote, "Hope springs eternal in the human breast."

Scorecards in hands, the fishermen next door pressed their bodies into their ship's rail, jockeying for the best spot from which to see what they seemed to imagine would be a train wreck. (Nothing warms the cockles of the hearts of seamen faster than watching someone else making a mess of things with a boat. It is even better if the victim is an amateur. Our performance on the way in did little to disabuse them of their preconceptions!)

With The Crew still looking mutinous, I gave the order to cast off, loudly and clearly. Taking in the bow line myself, I stepped aboard and prayed that I would not tangle things too badly. My ego gauge was resting squarely on empty.

Assuming my usual position at the helm, I spin the wheel full to starboard. Leaning forward I press the button that activates the bow thruster and hold it there until the front of the boat begins to move away from the dock. Sliding the transmission into forward, I let the prop turn over only until the stern walks away from the pier. Going back into neutral, I repeat the process. When finished, we are about 15 feet off the wharf.

Next, I spin the wheel hard to port and ring up slow ahead on the throttle. Just as the stern starts to swing to starboard and the bow to port, I called for all engines stopped and we wait for the drift to cease. As it does, I begin the drill again. By now, we are perpendicular to and about equidistant between the fishing boat and the fuel pumps. Gaining courage, we press on and our little ship continues to respond nicely. The wind and waves, however, were beginning to shove us around and we were starting to drift toward the side of the fishing boat. Immediate action is required.

Damming the torpedoes, The Pilot goes for the *coup d'grace.* With the bow still working its way to port, instead of letting the prop take a couple of easy turns in reverse, he applies half power. This either will jerk the stern around – thereby forcing the bow over into exactly the right position – or it will run the ship, backwards, into the side of the commercial vessel. There are no other alternatives. With all eyes glued on the actions of The Pilot, observers would have noted the beads of sweat that were forming on his brow had there been time for them to develop.

Amazingly, all happened as predicted. The ship turned around neatly and was pointed toward the open sea, standing in the process a reasonable distance off the side of the nearby fishing vessel. Now, the only thing left to do is to stop the nuclear chain reaction that has been set in motion. With a coolness that even he could not have anticipated, The Skipper spun the wheel to amidships, pushed the tranny into forward and throttled up a few extra horses. Incredibly, our trusty craft stopped turning in its circle exactly as it should have and it ceased its drift back toward the fishing boat too. Without further fanfare it began churning its way straight as an arrow right out of the channel. I never did see what numbers our on-lookers ultimately recorded on their scorecards, but in one quick glace astern, I did see smiles, nods of approval and a quick thumbs up. Boating really does not get any better than that!

We made our way back to the slip at the marina and communed for a time with the owners, Dave and Rosie. As we watched them head up the ramp for home, The X.O. opined that we had made neat work of our retreat from the fuel dock. This reduced me to such intellectually laden ripostes as “Ah, gee...”, “Do you think so?”, and “Shucks, mam, I couldn’t have done it without you…”

Guided by the wisdom garnered from my time at sea, I seized the moment and said, “How about I buy you some fish and chips at the ‘Cannuk’ bar”?

My whole being fell when I heard her reply “No thanks.” Savoring the instant, she adding, “But I would like one of those steak sandwiches they serve there.” Chastised, but with the crime clearly now forgiven, I took her hand in mine and we strolled happily off in search of the perfect meal. Life, sometimes, is just so simple.

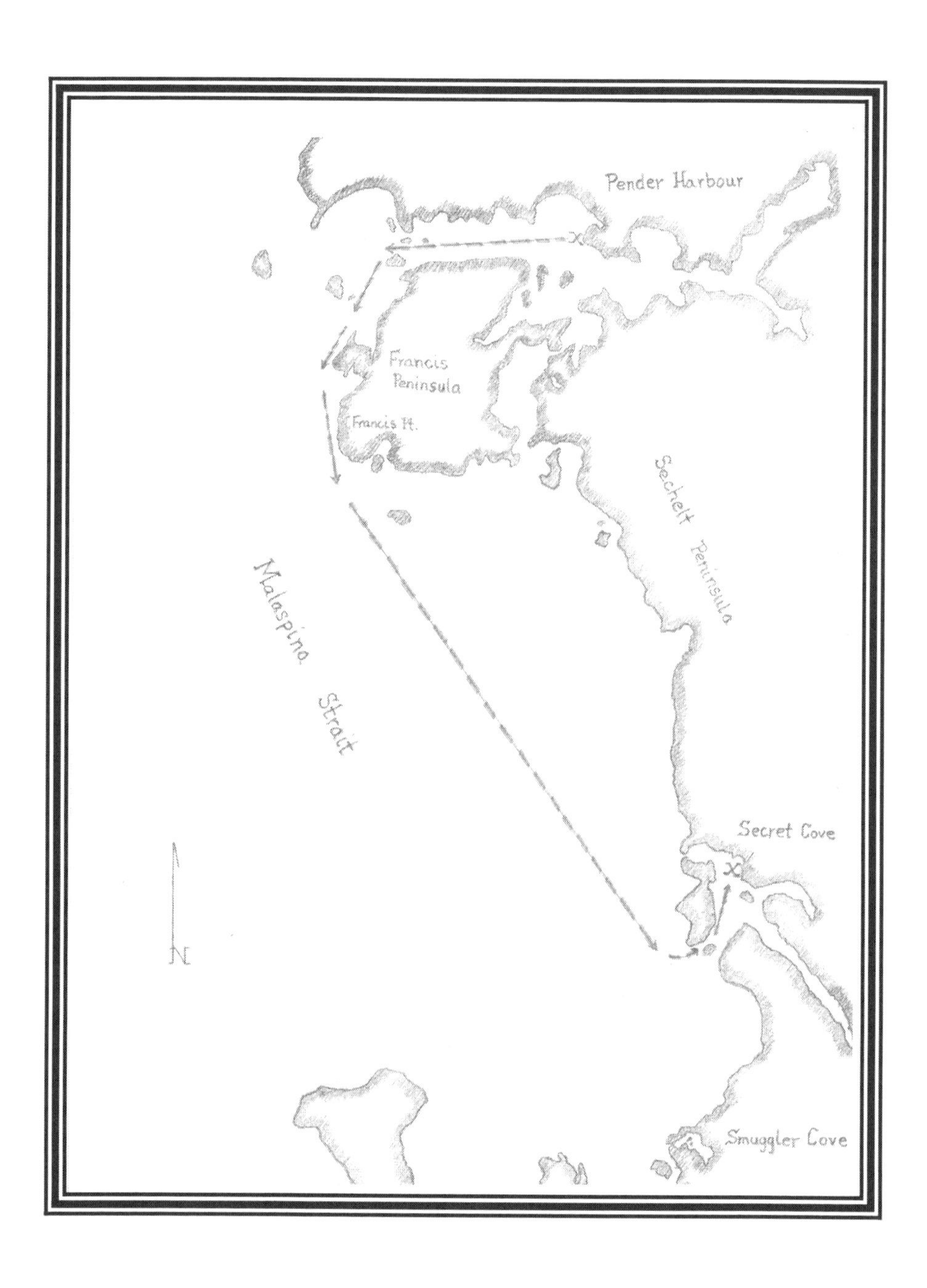
Pender Harbour
Francis Peninsula
Francis Pt.
Sechelt Peninsula
Malaspina Strait
Secret Cove
N
Smuggler Cove

DAY EIGHT

Pender Harbour to Secret Cove
Or
Is the '53 Chateau Lafite Still Available?

Plans are the things you make to pass the time while waiting for the real stuff to happen. The plan today was to shoot down the Malaspina Strait, squirt through Welcome Passage, dodge out toward Halibut Bank in the Strait of Georgia – to miss the Canadian Navy and the exercise area "Whiskey Gulf" – and then to hole up for the night in Silva Bay.

But when we awoke low clouds hung over Pender Harbour. It was early, but not at the crack of dawn, and after glancing around the anchorage, we decided that the things that had to be done immediately were coffee, Danish and a listen to the latest weather forecast. After that we would see.

The most recent weather update, from 0430, called for conditions that were O.K., but just. "The wind is up a bit," the voice crackling through the radio said, but it was supposed to drop by mid-morning. Later it would pick up again and then the skies would start to clear. From our snug berth in the marina we really could not tell anything about what the wind outside of the harbor was doing. We could see the tops of the trees sway occasionally and noted the ripples on the bay's surface; the only thing that was patently obvious from where we sat was that given the solid grey blanket we had over our heads it was likely that any "clearing" one was likely to find out 'there,' in the Malaspina Strait, was that which existed in the short vertical distance that separated the sea from the thick, low overcast that scudded just above the antennas on the pilothouse of *Minstrel's Song*. Black and white decisions are easy to make; grey is always, well, grey.

"Let's go," I said. "We can see what it's like 'out' on the run down to Welcome Passage and make a final decision based on that. If it doesn't look good, we can duck into Secret Cove and wait it out." The Crew concurred.

As always, the anticipated trip across the Strait of Georgia was worrisome. The crossing is fairly long and the Strait has a reputation for getting worse the further west one goes. And while no ship's master ever wants to be seen as timid, there is no sense fighting Mother Nature tooth and nail when you are on a vacation cruise.

A few drops of rain started to splash down as we slipped our dock lines. Making our way slowly west, out of the harbor, we sipped our coffee, studied the clouds and tried to guess what the winds, tides, currents and seas were doing outside of these sheltered confines.

Clearing the mouth of Pender's fine little anchorage and bearing south for the trip around Francis Peninsula, we got our first glimpse of Malaspina Strait. I was not comforted by what I saw; at best it looked borderline. We kept the coastline a half a mile or more off our port beam as we ran toward Francis Point and conditions got no better along the way. The heaving, grey sea and the whitecaps it was sporting did not give either of us any warm or fuzzy feelings. Looking like a re-run of the trip north, The Skipper told The Crew, "You may as well set the saloon table down on its side before it falls over, and go ahead and secure anything else that's liable to be tossed around. This isn't going to be too smooth."

My Spanish never was all that good and my Latin next to nonexistent, but I knew enough to know that the combination of "mala" and "spina" could translate into 'bad spine.' Despite the fact that this part of the Salish Sea actually was named for an Italian, Alessandro Malaspina, who explored under a Spanish commission, my translation seemed more appropriate. Given its surliness on the two occasions we had transited part of it, we were learning to expect only bad things from this piece of water.

After passing Francis Point we came around toward the southeast. The lonely greybeards that embraced us there, like long-lost cousins, had by that instant covered a distance of over 10 nautical miles of open sea. Driven by a Force 5, or maybe Force 6[10] breeze on the Beaufort Scale that was coming out of the northwest, these rollers had had plenty of time to work up a tolerable head of steam. Thus, the trip to the southeast toward Welcome Passage was about like the one we experienced going the other way. The only real difference between the two, if one can call it such, was that the weather this time came roughly 180 degrees off from where it had been last time. Translated that meant that although we were headed in the opposite direction, we again were able to 'enjoy' a following sea all the way.

Dodging the shoals that plagued us going north, I stood in closer to the coast than before. With the land running away to the southeast there was no need to stay out; doing so would only give us more of the abundant rolling chop that the strait seemed to like to dish out to us. Equally, there now being no doubt that we would be putting into Secret Cove, we could save a little discomfort by following the short-line course direct to that haven's entrance and benefit, slightly, from the lee of Francis Peninsula. Although gratuitous, I advised The Crew that the plan now included hanging out in Secret Cove until things calmed down outside.

The wind sang its eerie song through our rigging, buffeting us with its periodic blast. We rolled and wallowed along, heading in what generously could be deemed the right way most of the time. Our progress seemed snail-like due to the optical illusion created by having everything around the boat moving at about the same speed and in the

---

[10] *The Beaufort Scale measures wind and sea conditions. It evolved over several centuries, but its use did not become formalized until the early 19th Century. Force 5 represents a 'fresh breeze' of 19-24 mph with waves about five feet high; Force 6 consists of a 'strong breeze' of 25-31 mph that raises waves of roughly 12 feet in height.*

same general direction. It is a disconcerting sensation nevertheless.

The entrance to Secret Cove is nothing special. The rocky, southern tip of Turnagain Island defines the northern extreme of the channel leading into it while a small, unnamed islet, distinguished only by the presence of a white marker light perched upon it, is situated a hundred yards or so off to the south. That defines its other side. After the narrows of Gabriola Pass, Smuggler Cove, Malibu Rapids and even the west end of Pender Harbour we anticipated no worries here.

The "books" said to favor the light side of the passage some, so I aimed for a point in the waterway that was just south of its middle. Doing so required that we take up a northeasterly heading and that put the wind and the waves on our port beam. The closer we got to the opening the more I had to correct and then re-correct the course to compensate for the 'push' we were getting to the southeast. "Auto" was actually doing the driving, so all I had to do was push a button to add a few degrees to port to bring the boat's head up. I did this a time or two in two-to-three degree increments with virtually no result. Because we were drawing near the coast, I pressed a pre-set button that upped the ante to 10 degrees all at once. To my chagrin, with wind, wave and current working against us, Nature saw my puny 10 and raised me 12. Instead of being on a course near the centerline, we were being swept uncomfortably close to the marker islet. I doubled down, twice more, with "Auto," and then had roust a goodly number of horses out of the barn to get *Minstrel's Song* back on the strait and narrow. With 12 knots of speed and over 35 degrees of 'extra' course compensation working in our favor, finally we passed safely into Secret Cove.

Since childhood I have reveled in tales of the sea. In my pre-sailing days I could not fathom how a ship manned by professional sailors could go aground. Our entry into Secret Cove reminded me, once again, that in boats bad stuff happens fast. To quote my Army instructors, "In battle there are only two kinds of people: the quick and the dead." The same pertains to the ocean. Nothing there ever should be taken for granted.

Secret Cove consists, very generally, of three arms of water.

Two of them are located to the south of the entrance and one of them is to the north. We sailed north, intending to tie up for a few hours at the government dock that we had read was located there. With most of the space available at that pier already claimed, we reverted to Plan B, opting to loiter at a marina, cum grocery store, cum restaurant, cum fuel and pump out station. We idled across the hundred yards of bay that separated the two places and gently came to a parallel stop in front of the store that was built out over the water and marked the south end of the marina. The planking that separated *Minstrel's Song* from the business' entrance did double duty as a front porch. The restaurant, heralded in several large, brightly painted signs, was a flight up over the store and the various pumps that were available sat on the same dock but were another 30 yards further north. A nice kid came out of the store, took some of our lines and helped us tie up.

The plan, as will be recalled, was to put in only until the weather abated as forecast. So, we were not interested in renting one of the marina's slips for the night, did not need any fuel following the 10 nm run down from Pender Harbour and had more than enough groceries to keep us going for weeks. Moreover, as always, no one onboard really wanted to go through an anchoring drill in the middle of the cove. But not wishing to say flat out that we were there only to mooch freely their dock space, I asked the girl who was assisting us if the restaurant was open. It was, after all, still breakfast time, the Danish of the morning were but a vague memory and it seemed to me that some hot victuals would not be abhorrent. "Next week," she chirped, "the season's really not quite here."

"Well..." I stammered, "would it be O.K. if we tied up here for a while?"

"How long?" she wondered.

"Well... the weather's supposed to break later this morning. Just until it does?"

She pondered the question like an ancient philosopher and then allowed as how that would be all right as long as we did not overstay our welcome.

With visions of bacon and eggs, hash browns, pancakes, English muffins and other restaurant delicacies receding from my mind, I turned to a necessary chore: pacifying the locals. It is one of the odd tasks that since the beginning of time mariners have undertaken and one that can become critical when begging dock space. Traditions of the sea being what they are, it was far from my intention to stray from customary behavior. Thus it was that The Skipper ordered The Crew to prepare to go ashore.

In my experience, aboriginal souls of all sorts can be mollified with a neighborly purchase or two of the local trinkets; usually said natives can be brought around and will tolerate all manner of exploitation without whimper as long as future exchanges remain on the horizon. With that end in mind, we readied ourselves for a bartering expedition.

As we were preparing the ship for our departure, and outfitting ourselves for the intended sortie, a dilapidated 16-18 foot aluminum boat with a nondescript outboard dangling from its transom limped up to the marina and landed, sort of, next to the gas pump. A bedraggled man of 50 or so, doing a fantastic impression of a half-drowned rat, clambered out of the open boat and walked directly into the store. Recalling poet Robert Service's commentary on life in the far north, i.e., "There are strange things done in the midnight sun…", I put my curiosity on hold and continued to dress for dry land. (Comparing our mental notes about that event later, both The Crew and I agreed that if the ragged swab that disappeared inside the store was a representative of the citizenry, it was a hard and benighted lot indeed!)

We made a quick survey of the marina, determining that it was long, narrow and attached to land only by a single, metal ramp. We decided that before we ascended that structure to survey the community, the stop at the store was imperative. As indicated, this would convey a proper regard for the pecuniary interests of the owners and it might net us useful supplies and/or intelligence.

SECRET'S SECRET?

As is common to such establishments, the building we entered was filled with groceries, snack foods, souvenirs, marine necessities, nautically themed home decorating items and a complete line of baseball caps, tee shirts and sweatshirts. The latter items, now apparently mandatory at every North American shop situated within a ten-mile radius of a named crossroad, were festooned with written descriptions of the hidden delights of Secret Cove.

We poked and puttered around, not really needing anything, until the gentleman traveling by aluminum boat began conversing.

"Do you have any idea where one might find a taxi here?" he asked.

Since there were only four of us inside the store at that time, the man, the clerk, The Crew and me, and since none of us were physically close to him, I wondered exactly who he was addressing. In order to begin unraveling that mystery I looked first at the visitor who as standing a good 15 feet away from me, then I looked over his right stranger shoulder at the clerk who was sitting at the cash register another 10 feet or so beyond him, and finally, to complete the survey I looked at Cookie, who was rooting through some culinary delicacies at the rear of the establishment. The facts that the mariner had his back to the attendant and that Cookie was too far away to have been involved, seemed to make me the logical recipient of the inquiry. That notwithstanding, the body position and the direction of the visitor's gaze suggested that he was not really speaking to anyone, per se, but rather was communing with that part of the store that housed both the pay telephone and the ubiquitous cork bulletin board. Still, since I had heard the call and no one else responded, I felt obliged to say something.

Stating what I thought should have been patently clear to any but those socially challenged in the extreme, I worked my way off the proverbial hook by saying, "Geez! I haven't a clue. We just got here by boat; this is our first trip into Secret Cove." That, I hoped, would complete my involvement in the affair. It did not.

For seconds later he responded with a rather taciturn, "Oh!" followed by a, "I was supposed to meet someone around here, but I don't know how to get there…"

I belayed the urge to draw his attention to the obvious, i.e., that I could not help him at all, but that the 'someone' he was supposed to meet in the vicinity probably was much better prepared to find their way to him, than he to them, considering his mode of transportation. Instead, in an unbridled fit of human compassion, I suggested that he might ask the clerk.

He took a shuffling step or two toward the counter and the girl who was clerk, dock boy, fuel attendant, store manager, marina director, and local information center. As he crossed the gap to present himself more directly to her, he raised his coffee cup to his lips and took a draught that appeared to please him so greatly that I was sure the Styrofoam chalice he hefted could contain nothing less than pure ambrosia.

Before posing his basic question again, he supplied the young woman with some background. Although I did not catch its name, I did divine that he lived out on one of the local islands. At a time in the not too distant past, he had arranged to meet 'someone' in Secret Cove this very morning. Usually a half-hour run in his small, open boat, today it had taken him more than two hours to make the trip. In the process he had gotten quite a chill – more like frostbite from my perspective – but despite the cold he managed to keep himself amused during the extended journey by frantically employing a rubber bucket to bail out the seawater that kept washing, uninvited, into his little skiff. Looking as bedraggled as any man ever should, he said that he now only wanted to try to connect with the person he came to see. That he had no land transportation, no viable telephone number and was only a couple of hours late seemed to me to pose some significant hurdles to the accomplishment of that goal, but having pawned him off on the clerk mere moments before, I felt that civility required that I stay out of the discussion now.

In a manner akin to the way that flames draw moths, I had

inched over toward the clerk, the clerk had stopped doing whatever it was that had occupied her just moments before and even The Crew had made her way to the front of the store, all enthralled with this mariner's tale of need and daring do. Being too polite to pelt him with questions about the "someone" who drove him to this extreme, and also not wishing to offend by declaring that he was nuts for being out on the open water in a vessel like his in the conditions of the day, we collectively stared at him in sympathy and hoped that he could get to wherever he was going as soon as he could identify it. With concern, and certainly no malice, the shop girl broke the bad news that there were no taxis within 50 miles of Secret Cove.

When ships pass in the night, at the very least they leave their wakes. Both The Executive Officer and I turned away from this poor creature and found something extraordinarily interesting to look at in another part of the shop. A decent sense of propriety demanded that we give this sad soul some space to wrestle with his anguish while he was drying off. By the time we returned to the cash register area the man was gone. An hour later, unseen and unheard, we confirmed that the battered aluminum boat had disappeared as well. No one knew, precisely, when he had gone or where.

* * * * * * * * * * *

On our first sortie from the boat we followed the planked decking through the marina and toward the shore. We climbed the steel ramp up to the parking lot that led to a paved road that dumped us at the junction of what should have been a main thoroughfare. Along the way we passed in front of a number of summer homes and townhouses perched on the hillside overlooking the cove. Excepting these things, and the trees all around them, we found no sign of community or town center. Even the main highway was more like a country road than a village street. With two narrow lanes split by a faded white line, and with little more than a narrow strip of gravel separating the broken edges of the asphalt from the adjoining forest, and with nothing else in sight, including moving vehicles, it was hard to imagine that we were in the vicinity of a village.

With nothing of particular interest to draw us forward, we instead strolled back to the marina and checked the weather on the VHF. Whoever was compiling the data must have been sitting in a darkened cave. With clouds swirling overhead, the odd shower coming down and the wind still blowing a gale, the comedian behind the broadcast microphone repeated that the skies would be clear, the winds would be calm and the seas flat all through the morning. Only late in the day would atmospheric conditions become worrisome he asserted. Since late in the day was creeping up on us, we decided to pack it in and spend the night at the marina.

We visited the waterfront store again and told the girl of our plans to overnight there. She directed us to the proper slip and added that we could get dinner later at the local ptomaine palace if we wanted. However, because the latter was not within walking distance and was a mom and pop lash-up that was the only game in town, she advised that we needed to tell her well in advance of our intentions. With that information in hand she then would have to call them, convey our wishes and in most instance they would send a car to haul us back and forth to the event. It seemed to us like an awful lot of trouble for just another meal, but we did not want the natives to become restless. Without committing to anything we thanked her profusely for her thoughtfulness.

After moving *Minstrel's Song* her new parking place, we entertained ourselves with a late lunch, some reading, and possibly a quick nap – confirmed by the discovery that the book I had been holding while sprawled on the saloon couch had migrated, surreptitiously, to the floor beside me. Relaxed and refreshed we sought something else to do.

Donning raingear to ward off the occasional shower that moved through – undoubtedly part of the "clearing" process the weatherman kept telling us to expect – we embarked on a close study of our environment. Thus, we made our way up the steel ramp again to the parking lot. The latter was a couple of hundred yards long and about 30 yards wide. It overlooked the marina on one side and was overlooked, in turn, by a steep, tree-covered hill on the other. Its northern end provided no outlet; on the southern side the pavement passed through a chain link gate where it connected immediately to the previously trod public road that came down to the cove. The lot's surface was done up in chip-sealed stone. At the moment we passed through it the expanse contained a handful of cars and a couple of dumpsters. The aforementioned gate was festooned with a small sign that read, 'For Marina Patrons Only.'

Feeling that we had plumbed the depths of the parking area thoroughly, we walked out onto the municipal lane and decided next to make a full survey of the 'government dock' that connected the dry land just there. From the top of its ramp we watched as two 30-something couples bought fresh shrimp from a commercial fishing boat that was tied up there. We commented favorably on the convenience of the location and the enterprise displayed by the sellers. Lacking a more pressing engagement and with nothing else to occupy our attention, we commenced the task of memorizing every word written on all the officious signs that somebody, most probably from "the government," felt were needed to improve the ascetics of the pier. Whoever worked this project spared no expense and left no corner un-placarded. We guessed that the intention of the creator was to educate the public; about halfway through the process of reading them all we realized that we had learned so much already about what could and could not be done in and around that 125 foot quay, that we each qualified for two master's degrees and were well on the way to earning a Ph.D. in Government Docksology! At the same time we realized we had undertaken a fools errand.

Not seeing any particular point in walking back up the steep access road that would dump us at the juncture of the other thoroughfare atop the hill – an exploration we had already completed, completely – we meandered back to the marina for a detailed look at each and every craft that found residence there. While so engaged, we crossed paths with the marina owner, Scott. In the course of exchanging the usual pleasantries, he suggested that we take dinner at the greasy spoon previously named by the shop clerk. He underscored the urgency of making that decision as soon as possible by saying that the marina store closed at 5:00 p.m. and the wheels of progress had to be greased well before then if we wanted to go there.

The Crew and I are independent souls. We march to the beat of our own drummer and dislike, greatly, schedules and expectations established by others. Still, we were all but trapped. Having been invited, twice, to partake of the culinary delights offered by the hometown eatery, civility demanded that we succumb to the gentle pressures of our hosts. Bolstering that position was the fact that Cookie had not been able to decide what she felt like making for dinner onboard. (When she gives voice to that particular dilemma, the prudent listener translates it as, 'I'm sick of cooking. I want to go out!')

Heeding this clarion call of duty, I ask, "Whadda ya think? A restaurant meal in Secret Cove?" With a nod that indicated her ascent, I advised Scott that dinner at 'the inn' sounded like a sterling idea. He then suggested that we immediately give the store clerk that good news so she could set the whole thing in motion.

Having been worn down by the physical exertions of the afternoon and now with a plan developing for the evening, we both felt psychologically prepared to spend the remainder of the day lounging safe and warm inside our little ship. Thus, bidding Scott a good morrow we headed back to the snug saloon of *Minstrel's Song,* our favorite books and the prospect of a second nap.

As her wont is to leave no dangling ends to such affairs, as we approach our craft The X.O. announces that before she goes aboard she intends to run over to the marina store to make the requisite eating arrangements for the evening. When she returns I stirred enough to ask, "Is everything all set?"

"Not exactly," she responded. "The store clerk called over to the place, but couldn't reach anyone. The phone just rang and rang. Unfortunately, the girl said she wasn't sure that she had the right number and even if she did, she advised that the phone often didn't work. As if that wasn't confusion enough, she mentioned that it might still be too early to expect to find anyone on the premises."

"And what does that mean, in English?" I inquired.

"It means that we sit and wait for a while and then I'll run back over there to see what's happening."

"Have I mentioned lately that I hate these group gropes?" I said to no one in particular.

To pass the minutes, I busied myself by trying to obtain the latest weather forecast. Secret Cove apparently serves as the capitol of a great telecommunications wasteland. Already we had learned that the phones sometimes did not work. Now I was finding out that despite having ten discreet weather channels to choose from and a couple of tall antennas to drag them onboard, obtaining the latest prognostication was 'iffy.' Our VHF could pull in a piece of this one and a snippet of that one, but without fail the "meat" of the presentation either was drowned out by static or 'fell' off the air completely. The only clear broadcast I could pull in was the one sent out in French.

Given the fact that this 'foreign language' transmission always arrived loud and clear, I felt obligated to develop a theory to explain the phenomenon. Hypothesizing that no one on this side of the continent ever listened to it, I imagined that the waves in question were not sucked out of the atmosphere the way the others were and as a result, an overabundance of them built up. Thus, they crammed the ether full, but unseen, and were just hanging around out there, unclaimed and free for easy picking.

Unfortunately, while the French version of the prognosis arrived loud and clear, the fly in the ointment was that it came in in French! And, although at one time I read that language pretty well, mastery of the spoken word had never been my forte. I was left, then, to admire the romance of the transmission while wondering whether the word "grand," that I *thought* I might have heard on the radio translated into 'magnificent' or into 'formidable' or into something else altogether, especially when and it applied to the weather over the Strait of Georgia for the coming day. Obviously, then, this speck of information was of little real use.

While I fumbled and fumed over the atmospheric possibilities, The X.O. made her way back to the store. She returned to the boat with a report indicating that the status quo remained. The clerk was still trying to contact the dive, but her workday ended soon and she could not promise that she would be able to connect with them in time. The only truly useful intelligence gathered on this sortie was that the latest weather report was posted on the door of the store. It called for continued abysmal conditions through midnight, abating in the early morning, to be followed later in the day by more abysmal conditions. Those would slowly change to wretched before settling into downright lousy for much of the coming week. That was not what I wanted to hear!

The Shore Party returned from its next outing with real news. The 'people' had been contacted and everyone involved *hoped* that sometime between 6:00 and 6:30 p.m. a car would be able to come over and take us to dinner. I was not getting a lot of warm and fuzzy feelings about this whole meal deal, but it seemed that now we were committed absolutely.

THE SILVER LINING

Dutifully we stood in the vacant parking lot awaiting our chariot. The minutes passed slowly. We took advantage of the opportunity to complete an on-going scientific experiment. Including the three containers immediately available to us here, we agreed that after having gathered a sampling of sufficient quantity to narrow the margin of error to a miniscule level, we could theorize confidently that once you have seen a single trash dumpster, you have pretty much seen them all. Ditto with empty asphalt parking lots. After that, there was nothing for us to do while waiting for our ride but to make small talk and try not to check our watches more than once every 5-10 seconds. Still, 6:30 marched right up to us and then continued on its merry way. Six forty-five did the same.

As the little hand on my watch neared seven, a van roared up and, throwing gravel this way and that, slid to a stop not far from us. A kid hopped out, announced that he was here to take us to the 'inn' and then opened the doors and invited us to enter.

The trip to the 'inn' did not take very long, I think. The passage of time and/or distance is hard to estimate when one is all but drowning under a constant deluge of cheerful, but uninvited banter. For whatever period it took our driver – who later we dubbed affectionately "Skippy" – to get us to our destination, we were treated to a blow-by-blow description of every possible detail of his short, but boring life. It ended, thankfully, as we skidded to a stop to the front of the 'inn' with an apology for his previous tardiness. Beyond getting all of the sordid details just mentioned, we did learn that he and the 'staff' had spent the afternoon working with a wedding party.

My Shipmate and I had assumed from the beginning that the establishment in front of which we now stood was nothing more than one of a couple of million family run, barely- making-a living, greasy spoon, roadside diner, ptomaine palace kind of a place, the type that ordinary folk frequented only when medical assistance was readily available. We had no idea what fare it might offer, beyond the usual assortment of deep fried frozen foods, grilled patties and the catch of the day – a label that too often has nothing to do with fresh fish – and we certainly had built up no particular expectations of it. Reflecting this haughty view, I stepped out of the vehicle barely washed, with feet adorned in semi-wet, open mesh deck shoes, sporting the same jeans and hooded sweatshirt I had had on for the past four days, while carrying a wad of crinkled raingear in one hand, just in case. Adding a touch of flair to this ensemble was the first rate case of "hat hair" I had cultivated over the past, unwashed 24 hours. The Crew landed in similar condition.

Our youthful driver took us into the bowels of the building via shortcut. Instead of entering through the main entrance, if the place had one, we were directed through a narrow portal and down a short hall at the end of which we were greeted by absolute, unanticipated… opulence! Great wooden posts and beams rose elegantly over immaculate granite floors. Warm expanses of carpeting stretched into the distance and overstuffed leather chairs beckoned invitingly. A fieldstone fountain and a large, matching fireplace brought the outside indoors while promising comfort and warmth if needed. A maître d', dressed in black trousers, white shirt, black tie and a short, black waistcoat hurried over to welcome us. "You are the Greene's, from the marina," he instructed. "It's so wonderful you could join us this evening? And can't I take your raincoats and your baseball caps?"

"Eh, well, sure," I think I managed to mumble, dumbfounded by this strange turn of events.

Treating us like long-lost cousins, our newfound friend politely brushed aside our protestations that we were not properly attired for the 'inn,' while leading us to our table. The latter was outfitted with a spotless white tablecloth, fresh-cut flowers, a flickering candle, silverware – not silver-ish flatware – and an abundance of crystal goblets and glasses. As we arrived, our server appeared from out of nowhere; she helped the maître d' seat us and then commenced to drape snow-white linen napkins over our questionably clean, blue-jeaned laps. Can you spell "embarrassed"?

Once ensconced and with the usual greetings and pleasantries behind us, we took a moment to catch our breaths. Our table was situated in front of and toward one end of the glass wall that spanned the entire back of the 'inn.' Through its huge panes we looked out immediately over the pool complex, located one level down. Beyond the pool, the manicured lawn dropped quickly toward to the sea. The towering presence of the few large cedars that were growing there along the rocky coast barely intruded upon the grand view of the Malaspina Strait we were afforded. This body of water stretched its briny wings north, south and west as if set there just to entertain. Miles away, directly across this wind-swept ocean, rose Texada Island. A soggy sun, fighting its way through the thinning clouds, promised a show as it started to dip down toward the island's ridges. Those heights repaid the favor by shooting up out of the depths as if eager to embrace the yellowish orb before it could reach the sea. Close in and to our left, a fir and cedar forest forced its way over a rugged peninsula that extended well out into the water. Conversely, on the lower reaches of the lawn to our right, a colorful tent, like a huge balloon, gathered and protected from the remnants of day's inclement weather the wedding party that "Skippy," *et.al,* had been working.

Our server, insisting that all was perfect, refused to accept any explanation about how two bedraggled seafarers could possibly have gotten a choice window seat in the main dining room of the 'inn.' She declined our gracious offer to e-mail pictures, upon our return home, of us dressed in the clean, decent clothing we claimed to own. Further, she dismissed out of hand my idea that we make a sign and place it is such a way that our fellow diners – attired in jackets, ties and dresses as they were – could read and understand the situation. To that end I proposed the following statement: "Notice: The scurvy, shipwrecked lot seated here washed up on shore this very afternoon. The 'inn' is pleased to extend a hand of human compassion by feeding them. Please do not take offense."

It is tough to worry too much about the sensibilities of those around you when you are wrapped in a cocoon of pleasure. From the scenic view to the décor, from the place settings to the wine list, from the appetizers to the dessert cart, in short, from soup to nuts, everything about this moment in time was pure luxury. And, the food was superb, exquisitely presented and graciously served.

As we relaxed over a final cup of coffee, The Crew said, "This is the best dinner I've had out in years, maybe forever!"

My Shipmate and I have sailed together for quite a while. Between us, we have trod on five of the six (or seven) continents. (How many there are actually depends on who is doing the counting.) We have both been to 49 of the 50 states. (I have missed Alabama and she Arkansas.) Beyond having resided all over the U.S., we have spent almost 20 combined years living abroad, mostly in the best society. Against this backdrop, suffice it to say that we have seen good food, well served, the world over. Thus, when Cookie starts waxing poetic about any particular repast, she is not just whistling Dixie. And I had to agree with her.

Having lingered so long that I was sure that they were going to charge us property taxes on the real estate we were occupying, I finally agreed that it was time to get back to the ship. The maître d', just as cordial and solicitous as ever, retrieved our raingear and called for the driver to take us back to the marina. Before departing, however, he insisted that we take an evening stroll through their forest of suites. Forest of suites? We had been through giant redwood forests, eastern hardwood forests, western softwood forests, European birch forests, the

Black Forest, temperate and tropical rain forests and even an ancient Alerce forest in South America, but between us we could not recall ever having been through a 'suite forest.' How could we not see this one?

With access key in hand, we made our way to the locked gate marking the beginning of an elevated boardwalk that disappeared ahead of us into the dusky dimness of a grove of cedar trees. About six feet wide, with solid wooden paneling up to the rails on both sides, the walkway followed the contour line around a rocky, tree-covered slope and it ultimately guided us out toward the sea. About 200 yards from its start, we came upon our first 'forest suite.' Instantaneously, a mental light bulb switched on!

A small branch of our timbered pathway ran off to the right at this point and it terminated about 30 feet away in front of an unusual structure. For lack of a better description, what we were looking at was a big tent. It was all beige. It was all cloth. A multi-gabbled, fabric roof held up by a number of large tent poles protected its interior. Cloth panels dropped straight down from the tips of the tent's corner posts forming something that looked a lot like an oversized, rectangular 'bumbershoot' with sides. The "walls" of this structure incorporated sliding curtains, door-like frames, and airy screens. Additionally, large isinglass panels guaranteed that massive amounts of exterior light would penetrate their interiors. These "picture windows" opened magnificently onto the surrounding forest as they looked out over the sea. The built-in exterior doors appeared to be a bit more conventional. They seemed to be made of something stout (wood, metal, fiberglass, etc.) and gave the impression of hanging on hinges. From the outside, at least, what made this apparition striking was that it had no hard walls, no shingled roof and no framed or shuttered windows; it had only tightly stretched fabric and an invisible frame.

Gazing in amazement upon this sight, we might have been shocked and baffled or both had not a single factor entered the equation: T.V. At some point in the past my Shipmate and I had dialed up the Travel Channel on that contraption one evening. To the best of our recollection, this was the first and only time we ever did so, but the Lord works in mysterious ways! Anyway, via the wonders of modern HD video cameras and a svelte Asian travel hostess we had been whisked, on screen, to a fascinating place on the coast of British Columbia. On site, we had followed the star of the show through a weekend at an unusual resort spa conceived and built by a couple of European transplants. The twist, beyond being simply luxurious, was that this destination was built around a bevy of beige 'tent suites' nestled in a cool forest that overlooked the sea. As memory served, each suite contained all the modern amenities and conveniences that one could desire, including large, jetted soaking tubs. And, as memory served, the attraction here was that one could live 'outside' while being pampered inside.

When my yelps of, "Oh. Yeah! I remember this now" and "Golly, we're here! This place is famous! It's been on T.V.," did not elicit a sign of recognition from The Crew, I added, "Don't you remember? It was that show where that crazy Asian woman spent the weekend by herself in a tent and then went to watch a bunch of nut rolls knee boarding on the continuous waves that get up on the Sechelt Rapids at Skookumchuck Narrows!"

Slowly, the glow of recognition grew in The XO's eyes and, 'Bingo! Houston I think we have ignition!' "Wow!" she said, "Now it all makes sense!"[11]

Warbling happily about this alignment of the stars, we strolled along the wooden walkway for a time more and then retraced our steps toward the 'inn.' There, "Skippy" and his chariot waited on call to whisk us back to *Minstrel's Song*. Somehow his seamless chatter on the return trip helped to bridge the gap between the two disparate worlds we had visited this day.

While slogging down the Malaspina Strait neither of us would have predicted the pleasures ahead. Had not the weather been bad, we might have sailed right past an exceptional memory. If Secret Cove had been bustling, we might have never left it. The question then arises: How often do unseen hands shower us with unexpected and undeserved

---

[11] *Subject of our attentions and amazement was the Rockwater Secret Cove Resort.*

bounty? How often does a pilot we neglect shape our true courses? As age begins to slow the spinning world, it becomes more and more apparent that the answer is: Much more than ever we thought!

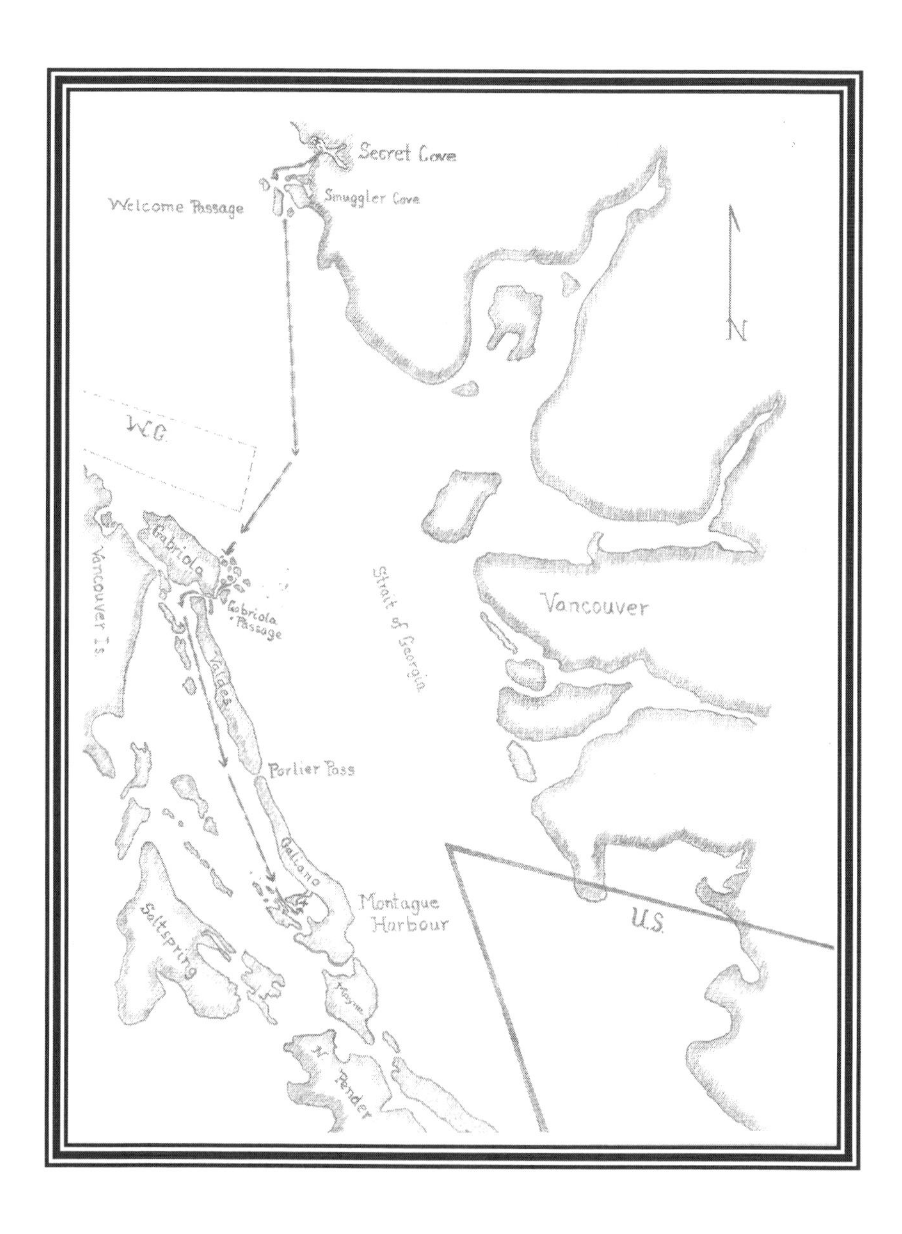
Secret Cove
Smuggler Cove
Welcome Passage
N
W.G.
Gabriola
Vancouver Is.
Gabriola Passage
Strait of Georgia
Vancouver
Valdes
Porlier Pass
Galiano
Montague Harbour
U.S.
Saltspring
Pender

Day Nine

Secret Cove to Montague Harbour
Or
The Moods of the Sea

Not so very long ago, I had a fascinating thought. Now, thoughts are not really all that foreign to me. Despite rumors to the contrary, I seem to have them all of the time. Sometimes I stumble across things erudite, even esoteric, like the continuing effects of the nullification debates on our great republic or the misapplication of the principals of sea power by the Nazi's during the Battle of the Atlantic. Other times, I come up with practical thoughts, like someone should invent a heated ice cream scoop to ease the difficulty of prying a bowl of that rock hard dessert out of a flimsy cardboard box. And then, there are those moments when my mind churns out things that are just plain silly, like I wonder why this flowering plant is a weed when that one over there wins prizes at the fair? But the particular thought I am concerned with now fascinates me because of its fundamental nature. "Why didn't I ever see it before," I wonder?

I was roaming through our home one stormy night when I happened by the refrigerator. It was late – middle of the night late – and the household had been sleeping for quite a while. Not wishing to wake my Shipmate, our trusty watchdogs or possibly even the dead, I refrained from turning on any lights. "Hmmm," thought I, as I neared its magnificence, "Refrigerators are full of all kinds of good things. Maybe there's something inside that will help me go back to sleep." So I threw open the door and that's when it happened!

Bursting forth, literally at the speed of light, came this wonderful brilliance. The whole kitchen lit up. "Interesting," I said as I reached into the cavern for a small slice of pie. I pondered the event as I was stepping away from the box and that caused me to wonder, "What happens to all of that brightness as the door swings shut?" That, in turn, necessitated an experiment. Slowly, I pushed the door closed and at a pace just equal to that movement, the black of night replaced the white light. I contemplated this occurrence for a time, ate my pie and then went back to bed.

Next day when the bustle of the morning had subsided, I made my way to the kitchen for the second half of my investigation. I reached behind the refrigerator and yanked its plug out by its copper roots. That way the pesky 20 watt light bulb inside of it could not skew the results of my work. Then, I pulled the door of the box open as quickly as I could. Incredibly, instead of having the blackness that I knew had to be inside that container stream forth, the opposite happened.

Understanding that the essence of the scientific method turns on observation and repeatability, I worked at this trial day and night until there could be but one conclusion: light trumps darkness every time. Darkness is not truly the opposite of light; it is but the absence of light. Darkness reigns only when light deigns it. The force, the real power, is light and only light.

* * * * * * * * * *

Barely awake, I peered through the pilothouse window in a vain effort to pierce the blackness, the nearly total, seemingly infinite blanket of stifling darkness that enshrouded *Minstrel's Song*. A mere 25 yards away the light from the single bulb that dangled from the pole over the marina's steel ramp was reduced to a faint glow by the time it filtered into the cabin. Although it surely was doing its best, it was incapable of penetrating the drizzle, the fog and the gloom that seemed to be the essence of this new day.

It was early, way early, but based on what little I could discern of the weather forecast from the night before – or of the new one that would have been coming in just then had not the static cut it to shreds – atmospheric conditions were going to be borderline bad for crossing the Strait of Georgia, but if there was going to be a window of opportunity for doing it, it was closing already.

Back in my military days I formulated the First Law of Intelligence. It stipulated, in essence, that regardless of which of that word's definitions one prefers, no one ever has enough of it. Field commanders always want to know more about what the enemy is doing and their thirst for information travels right up the line to the highest levels of leadership. Years later, during my days with that three-letter alphabet group – you know, the one whose central name is "Intelligence" – my advanced training therein led me to add three corollaries to the First Law. The leading one asserts that no matter how much intelligence is gathered, its bulk provides just a tiny slice of life, not a comprehensive picture of the entire shooting match. The second proclaims that ultimately, even the best intelligence can only address human *intentions*. And, the third insists that Homo sapiens are squirrelly as all get out and even having a complete grasp of their intentions 'don't mean nothing at all!'

For those with a deeper interest in this arcane subject, the Second Law of Intelligence clarifies all that precedes it. It cannot be provided here, because it is a closely held secret, but it should be enough to note that the elucidating principle contained therein really just re-states Murphy's First Law and that one is, as the astute reader might recall, totally redefined by its corollary, i.e., that Murphy was an optimist!

So, like every other leader in every other situation, there I stood staring out into the night while pondering what little I thought I knew and wondering what would actually happen. At times like these I find myself wondering why we did not buy one of those cute little boats that one can haul home on a trailer!

The Crew called up from the saloon, "Are we going across?"

Silently, I reviewed my record in struggles against Mother Nature. The score between us stood at 0-14,501,233 in Ma's favor. Nothing I had yet heard on the VHF made me think that today was the day when I would break her streak. Still, I knew it was inglorious enough to have to wrestle pusillanimity privately, but I could expect little good to come out of scaring The Crew to death by waving it around. "I guess we'll give it a try," I chirped. "At the least we may as well go out and see what it looks like."

Beyond my concerns about the weather, we also are fighting time. Our recently amended plan – necessitated by the unscheduled stop we made right where we were sitting – is to cross the Strait of Georgia to a landfall in the Gulf Islands and then head south to an anchorage we would choose later. Successful execution of this entire strategy has the prerequisite of our first getting across the open water and then threading the needle at Gabriola Passage. Accomplishing this latter task safely requires, as the reader well knows, our arrival on site at slack tide. My calculations indicate that we will be where we need to be, when we need to be there if and only if we are underway just before daybreak. And that's fast approaching.

Foregoing the much beloved breakfast that Cookie has been handing up throughout our voyage, to wit, piping hot coffee and a Danish, I start the engine and give the order to take in the lines. With dawn still declining to do anything about illuminating this segment of the globe, we will be feeling our way out of the harbor as much as we will be seeing it. Lacking headlampss, and discounting the green, red and white glows created by our running lights, we depend wholly on the sun to show us the way.

The diesel throbs rhythmically as we begin to move. I touch the bow thruster and spin the wheel to take us off the dock and then twirl it twice more around as we work our way through the narrow opening between two boats that serves as the channel out of the marina. "It's dark…really dark," I think to myself.

We search the blackness ahead for signs of anything, friend or foe. The chartplotter is ranged in as close as possible. It now fills the screen with everything it is privy to only out to a distance of 1/8th of a mile. Overhead, our radar turns relentlessly in its fiberglass dome. From memories of our trip in, I try to pierce the blackness ahead, looking for either of the two orange markers that designate the locally established limits of the anchorage. These devices stick straight up out of the water. They are about three feet high by four inches around and are made of plastic. Hitting them would be no big deal except for the fact that they are attached to the bottom in some undefined manner. Because of that, the primary danger they present lies in the likelihood that as their tether passes under the boat it would find a new home wrapped tightly around our prop shaft. That, in turn, would bring our progress through the water to a screeching halt! The chain reaction thus initiated would have the practical effect of keeping us in Secret Cove for an indeterminate period of time; we definitely would not be getting to Gabriola Passage at slack tide this morning.

After gliding along for a few minutes with no adverse effects, I estimate – a comforting word that really means "guess" – that we are past that first set of obstacles. I guide *Minstrel's Song* to starboard a little, setting her bow more toward the passageway out of the cove that I hope is ahead somewhere in the pitch dark. As I do, I see, rising out of the obscurity, the looming outline of a great landmass that could be only Turnagain Island. We take that event to be a reasonably positive sign since it appears to be about where it should be. Thirty seconds more and the steady white light from the marker perched on top of the barrier island south of the channel pops into view. Beyond that, and almost immediately, the full expanse of the Malaspina Strait clearly takes form before us. It is a beautiful sight.

But how is that possible? Moments before we were steaming south virtually blind, surrounded by a black, gooey nothingness and suddenly, a single, tiny source of brightness seemingly provides enough light to illuminate miles of open sea? It is true that we are moments closer to daybreak than we were and maybe the clouds have lifted a pinch, the drizzle slackened some, and the fog receded, but to this day I am not sure how such a change could have come on so fast and so unexpectedly.

Being now able to see our way quite nicely, The Pilot turned the wheel to starboard and our little ship slipped easily between the last points of land that marked the channel to Secret Cove. Ahead of us loomed...calm seas, great visibility and not much wind. In fact, what we encountered was so pleasing and unexpected that it took a conscious effort to remember that the wide, easy opening we had just cruised through had seemed like the eye of a needle in the wind and waves that buffeted it less than 24 hours before and the ocean ahead of us looked like a duck pond, not a roiling cauldron. "That is what we call perspective," I thought to myself.

Focusing now on the onward journey we picked up the flashing green light on Tattenham Ledge, at the north end of Welcome Passage, and, being well satisfied with our position, The Pilot relinquished the job of steering to Auto. "Take her half mile south of that marker," he silently commanded the machine, "and don't let me catch you wandering about the sea while you're at it!" At the same instant, The Skipper suggested to the Mess Steward that some hot chow (coffee and a Danish) would be nice. She sprang to the task with an alacrity that reflected her sense of comfort, security and happiness. Life was good all around.

By the time we were through Welcome Passage, the sky had brightened about as much as it was going to on this cloudy, rainy day. We picked up some light chop as we passed between South Thormanby Island and Merry Island but pressed on into the Strait of Georgia. The good news was that the wind was down, so the hot coffee and grub that were passed up to the helm offset the foul-ish weather that seemed to lie on the horizon. As we took up our stations on opposite sides of the pilothouse, mugs in hand, we both agreed that if the price of a smooth ride across was overexposure to "greyness," it was one that we would pay happily.

Blizzards always are best endured in front of a cozy fire, locked tightly inside a snug cabin. The same is more or less true of seafaring. For while the day did not hold much promise if sun worshipping was on the schedule, sitting in a warm pilothouse, sipping a hot drink, eating sweets and watching the miles slide by, all to the rhythmic slap of the windshield wipers, created much the same atmosphere.

A tug pulling a barge slowly churned the water five miles or six miles behind us – still in Malaspina Strait – when we veered southward for the trek down toward Halibut Bank. The variegated grey sky hung so low over the steel grey ocean that it was hard to tell where the water stopped and the heavens began. The rain that continued to fall did not make the differentiation any easier.

Slowly we saw Vancouver Island rise dark and surly in the distance. It was not grey, not green nor black nor any other recognizable color. It just sulked up ahead. Two ferries likely out of Nanaimo scurried past, far ahead of our little craft, on their runs to the southeast. They moved quickly, nervously along their separate ways, resembling hunting hounds on a scent they knew was going cold. They paid no attention to us.

Almost imperceptibly the sea began to get up. This is a common occurrence on the west side of the Strait, but one that flies in the face of reason. Everything about the apparent movement of the air suggests that as one gains the lee of Vancouver Island, the wind should fall off and the surface of the water should flatten. For a variety of reasons, just the opposite usually happens. "You'd better go below and stow anything loose," I ordered The Crew. "Oh. And you might as well put the dining table on its side." While she was gone I picked out a cheery CD and put it in the player. I remembered from my childhood days a story that claimed that music calmed the savage beasts.

The waves beset us from the west and southwest, forcing us to take them well aft of the bow, but they never quite became a full beam sea. Thus we were able to slice through them, mostly, as opposed to having to roll incessantly with them. Frothy white caps and the accompanying chop that marched past us in a formation too close for comfortable riding, now defined our watery highway. It was like driving too fast down a bumpy dirt road.

Taking up our binoculars, The X.O. and I try to pick out our route through the confusion ahead. Nearing Gabriola Island, our intention is to cut through Commodore Passage, the same small waterway we used to enter and exit Silva Bay, so as to gain the protected waters just off the eastern end of Gabriola Passage. This tiny, unmarked waterway lies somewhere within a conglomeration made up of seven islands, any number of rocky points and a bunch of semi-exposed reefs. These charming geographical features also include several false channels replete with submerged shelves and assorted other dangers that could suck the life out of a small boat fairly quickly. To navigate this maze successfully we need to come in just off of Gabriola Island's Rowboat Point, which sits almost due east of the tiny Carlos Island. The trick to gaining the right track, thus, is dependent upon correctly identifying these two specs of land.

One of my innate talents has to do with being able to remember a place I have been before and then properly orienting it in my mind. Take me to a specific spot on land, once, and it is likely that ten years later I will be able to tell you that we are coming up on it before we actually get to it, regardless of the approach taken. I cannot say how or why my mind functions this way, but it does and it does so without any effort on my part.

Nearing the islands off Gabriola's coast, we find that the weather that was just grey and wet in the middle of the Strait of Georgia now has turned into a decent little storm. The upshot of this is that any hard object that sits at or near sea level – whether above or below it, rock, reef, shelf or island – is flinging white geysers high into the air. This is the product of the building sea that is now hustling down from the northwest intent, apparently, on committing hari-kari on these local shores. Their actions make it hard to decide where land ends and water begins. Harder still is it to put a name on any particular piece of real estate or, for that matter, on any part of the ocean. Adding additional chaos to this mini-scene is the fact that my aforementioned sixth sense inaccurately insists that we have never been within 10 miles of this location before this instant. (In the abstract it is right, so long as one allows that the changes in the coastline and in the sea's appearance as wrought by wind, wave and tide do create an entirely new setting. Unfortunately, we are not piloting our way in through anything abstract!)

Minstrel's Song now is having a grand old time of it, pitching, wallowing, rolling and trying to turn The Crew a bright green under the gills. The Skipper trains his eyes alternatively on chartplotter, radar screen and the shoreline ahead. The ship is getting pretty close to where it is supposed to be, but being just a little off of spot on – possibly no more than 25 yards – when entering the tiny channel sought after, could be disastrous. To make the game interesting, wind and sea press us ever harder toward the lee shore. And that action diminishes the maneuvering options available to us if we should start down a false path.

Instead of continuing our search for the channel, time enough still remained to swing the boat due east and then loop southward to pick up Gabriola Passage by skirting around the likes of Brant Reef, Gabriola Reefs, Thrasher Rock, and other charming sounding places. The Pilot decided that there was as much out that way to worry about as there was in this little piece of heaven. He stayed the course, figuring that the devil he knew was better than the devil he had not been introduced to yet.

Closing with the coast, The Captain let Auto continue to steer and followed the sage advice of the GPS. Still, he needed visual confirmation. Finicky though it might be, he wanted to know for sure that the sliver of water that was wedged between the two offsetting plumes of spray being thrown sky high by the surf pounding on the opposing rock points was the right one for him to take. Some people are just picky like that!

Studying the scene carefully, the X.O. finally shouted, "That's it. There!"

Decisively, I shouted back, "Are you sure? It looks to me like it's not heading off in the right direction."

"No. That's gotta be it," she responded.

"I'm not terribly comfortable with your 'gotta be.' Tell me again, why you think that that's it?

"Look. Everything is pretty much correct given what the chart says," she points.

"Pretty much right can have us on the rocks pretty much right away if we're not careful," I retort.

Checking everything for the 1,000th time, though, I throttle the boat back to about six knots and let her creep in toward the maw ahead. Ugly thoughts race through my mind. Oddly, such things derive from having lived through too many unpleasant events at sea and not visa-versa. Still, we hold our course.

In what seems to be mere seconds of unabating movement ahead, we flash past the spume and spray of a hostile ocean to enter a calm new realm that instantaneously erases the previous moments of anxiety. This is our channel – Commodore Passage – and we're exactly where we want to be. "Right on time, too," I tell Number One.

Emerging from the south end of our shortcut, we turn to starboard and work our way down between Gabriola Island to the west and Saturina and Breakwater Islands to the east. While we were making our way north though this same neck of water the week before, it had seemed so constricted, so filled with obstacles, so potentially hostile; now, it felt like a little bit of home sweet home.

The Crew and The Pilot laughed and giggled and felt the concerns that had built over the past couple of hours fall away. The Steward heated some more coffee. We watched as the land around us slid by and commented frequently on the hospitable look of the area.

We effortlessly navigated the perils of Gabriola Passage. Having arrived at this bottleneck at top dead center, 100% slack tide, we parted its waters with an ease not unlike that of my old rubber ducky when it slipped gently through the bubbles of my childhood bathtub. Gone was the trepidation. Gone was the uncertainty. Gone was everything except the pleasure. In fact, we so enjoyed the experience that when it was over it would not have taken much talking to get us turned around for another ride through!

Passing what now assumed an air of familiarity, we marveled at all that we had missed on trip the other way through the pass. Nearby homes that overlooked the waterway, many featuring walls of tall windows, exposed wooden beams, prows, stone accents and marvelous landscaping, dotted the shorelines. "Look at that pretty one just there," The X.O. would direct. "Imagine curling up inside that place with a warm drink and a good book and the leisure to watch the parade of ships glide past a couple times a day."

Studying the water all around, we found boats tucked in coves and inlets that had completely escaped our previous notice. And, while we had noted a gaggle of masts in the harbor on the north side of the passage on our trip east, the number of vessels snuggled in there and the expanse of the anchorage itself seemed now double or triple what either of us recalled.

In reality, everywhere we looked we saw what anxiety and a lack of familiarity had hidden from us before. Perhaps this is one of the benefits of cruising the same grounds year after year; perhaps it is just what comes from sailing always with the same dependable shipmate.

Rounding Dibuxante Point, we turned to port to follow Pylades Channel to the southeast. It wasn't even mid-morning yet and we were coming down the home stretch of the day. And even though we did not know for certain where we were going to spend the night we certainly were well on our way to getting there.

WATER, WATER EVERYWHERE...

It undoubtedly is the result of a chemical imbalance in our brains, but The Crew and I like wet, overcast days. For us, a low-hanging sky is as welcome as the bright sun. And, if you throw in a good dose of rain, whether it be a light mist or a healthy downpour, it just makes us that much happier (so long as we don't have to go out and actually slosh around in it).

Regarding this climatic disconsonance, it has been popular for years to try to project our peculiar affliction to an entire segment of the continent's population. Some outsiders, for instance, like to suggest that those who reside in the Pacific Northwet and who don't mind the "gloom" suffer from what amounts to a regionally transmitted form of mass hysteria. Others opine that such unnatural behavior has deep roots in an unidentified environmental cause, traceable, surely, to something in the water.

While mass hysteria may be the base cause of the Northwet's climatological neurosis – for there are, after all, numerous examples of entire nations going off the deep end together – we must reject the notion that alternatively it could be triggered by something in the water. In times past such an assertion might have floated reasonably well, but it can do so no more. The cold, hard facts just do not support that hypothesis. To the contrary, the following proof is offered: So far as anyone can discern, the denizens of this region subsist wholly on three broad categories of liquids. These are, in no particular order: 1.) Energy Drinks, 2.) Bottled Water, and 3.) Coffee.

We should stop here and note that the set, 'coffee,' finely and frequently is subdivided in the Pacific Northwet into a plethora of named consumables that include, but certainly are not limited to, cappuccinos, lattes, Americanos, breves, frappuccinos, double talls, short skinnies, brown cows and a plethora of other esoteric concoctions the names of which are known only to the socially indoctrinated. The general murkiness of this subject is exacerbated by the varied scientific attempts to classify each and assign them their proper taxonomic rank, i.e., their places in The International Code of Zoological Nomenclature according to order, family, genus, etc. Adding considerable fuel to this fire is the raging debate over whether or not chai tea technically falls into the coffee category, as do apparently, hot teas, but not cold ones, the latter tending to be included most often under the 'bottled water' rubric. A few radicals even suggest that chai tea truly constitutes an entirely independent sub-species, if not a complete species in and of itself! (Personally, while not fanatical on the point, the author tends to want to let chai tag along with the 'coffees,' but only so long as the distinctive "tea" is not appended to it. In fairness, it should be pointed out that his view mostly is founded on nothing more than personal preference.)

Thus stipulated, we must search to find the fluid-borne source of this geographic area's so-called madness. With no further fanfare let us dispose of energy drinks and bottled water as the cause. Both, we argue, are the industrial products of other locales. In the first instance, the primary mixes derive from a questionably close association with swamps and alligators – of which the Pacific Northwet has none – or, on a secondary level, from those more cosmopolitan cities where staying up all night and then trying to work one's buns off the next day is considered the norm. As for the bottled water, we have to look no further than to the immensely popular "Evian" brand. It sells precisely because it derives from another continent! Thus either or both of these elixirs must be immune to the charges of causing widespread psychological distress by virtue of their not even being native products!

At first blush, coffee might seem plausibly suspect, especially given its localized, insular production. Regardless of where it is brewed, however, the inescapable truth is that after being thoroughly ground, filtered, heated, vaporized, steamed, pressurized, flavored, deionized and who knows what all else, the likelihood that anything harmful could survive such an onslaught seems to be virtually nil. (And, lest nitpickers attempt to circumvent the obvious by suggesting that it may be the conveyance that is contaminated, we submit that absolutely nothing in the genuine recycled paper cups now in universal use as serving vessels in this region possibly could be deleterious. These, obviously, being subject to the same salutary manufacturing processes as those wrought by the carefully controlled methods of production appertaining to the fluids they ultimately are destined to hold, requires their elimination as the source of trouble as well.)

As a final thought, given the general obsession alluded to above, we suspect, but cannot prove, that nearly all of the leaf and bean drinks prepared daily on every street corner, gas station, free-standing hut and bookstore in at least a three state/two province area is concocted from non-native, bottled water. We rest our case!

Thus, we must leave it to minds greater than ours to find the true source of the apparent craziness that impels, even compels, great sections of this hemisphere's population to not just tolerate, but to exalt in the virtues of cloudy, rainy days!

Since we are on the subject of weather, however, while both The Captain and The Crew are quite happy to own their predilection for grey, wet skies, they remain totally baffled by the unwillingness of the lovers of heat and humidity, i.e., 100 degree (plus) days with a constant 110% dampness factor, to see in themselves any abnormality at all. We would laugh, for instance, at anyone who suggested that they wanted to move to the Sahara Desert for the heat? Yet the same people who would chuckle at that joke flock to the American southwest by the tens of thousands for a similar climate. Likewise, few will admit to wanting to live in the heat and humidity of, say, the Great Dismal Swamp or the Everglades, but the very seat of the U.S. Government is built over a swamp and enjoys similar temperatures and humidity. Odd, isn't it, the way humanity supports its own natural penchants with impeccable logic.

* * * * * * * * * * *

Minstrel's Song has gone from the windy, bouncy, wet and grey of the Strait of Georgia to something very different. Gazing down the slot between Valdes Island to the east and the De Courcy Group to the west, we see raindrops kick up short waterspouts on an ocean surface that is mirror-flat and more blue-black than grey. We see a lowering sky that holds no promise of a brighter future. And, we observe treed hills in the distance that are covered with a dark greenness that is neither flora nor lurking shadow, but rather seems to be a blend of two clashing forces – sea and sky – with neither being able to overpower the other.

The placid seascape that spreads before us is appealing, even soothing. Its embrace conveys a sense of comfort and relaxation that is salve to the soul. Basking in the relief from the trials of the morning, we turn to tamer occupations.

Our stout little ship does not have a dedicated electrical generator, as do many. Instead, everything we need by way of electricity depends on the engine's alternator, our three banks of storage batteries and an inverter that transforms the 12 volts of direct current (DC) held in them to the alternating 110 volt (AC) required for many of today's modern conveniences.

Not having a separate generator is not terribly noticeable most of the time. Between batteries and inverter, our power needs can be met for days without worries. The great exception to this comes when we engage the water heater. Relatively speaking, the amount of electricity that has to pass through a coil immersed in a tank of water in order to make that liquid hot – and thereby produce a product whose temperature is sufficiently high to remove grease from dishes and the bodies of people – is gargantuan!

There are but three reliable sources for that amount of electricity available to *Minstrel's Song*: shore power, our engine's alternator or the batteries. The first requires that we be tied up to a wired dock. When plugged in that way, all of the hot water in the world is at our beck and call thanks to the local utility company and the participating marina. Next, whenever the engine is running, our warm water supply extends right up to the moment when the greedy iron monster below decks sucks the last drop of diesel fuel out of its empty tank. Last, in luxurious silence we can pull hoards of electrons out the batteries alone and use them to push the H20 temperature way up there.

Depending on the batteries for hot water is roughly akin to using your debit card without keeping track of the withdrawals. As long as there is money in the account, the goodies keep flowing. But when there is nothing left, well, there is nothing left! If you opt to do that on *Minstrel's Song* either you had better hope that the American Automobile Association has instituted a seaborne rescue service or that you have one mighty long extension cord for the battery charger you are going to need to start the engine. It is more than an "Ooops" moment when you are anchored out in the middle of nowhere and you 'discover' that the electricity your starter needed to turn your engine over was traded away for a couple of warm showers!

With the certain knowledge that our diesel has produced prodigious amounts of hot water in the run over from Secret Cove, and with the sea's surface being as near dead calm as possible, The Skipper suggested to The Crew that the time for showering had arrived. With the trials of the crossing now behind us, we were anxious for the chance to relax and enjoy the morning's overdue ablutions.

The lovely scenery of the northern Gulf Islands slowly slips by on both sides of our ship. "Islands to the left of us, islands to the right of us, islands in front of us, called out in wonder…" I mumble to myself, paraphrasing, poorly, Lord Tennyson's "Charge of the Light Brigade." Wilderness and untrammelled earth always stoke my poetic fires – even when I know that were it warm and sunny outside the land would come alive with vacation homes and the ocean would fill with recreational boaters. Still, I enjoy these moments of solitude. With the bridge to myself, I think my little thoughts and dream my idle dreams, liberated from the necessity of social interaction. Later, when well mulled, I will share these sentiments with The X.O., but for a time the Lord's grand panorama and the limits of my mind are the boundaries of my entire world. The only "outside" element that presses in is the dim awareness that my "aloneness" is shared with The Crew, just a few steps away. And that is really good to know.

Trading places, Number One assumes the con and I go forward to clean up my act. She always does a nice job of taking over for me, but dislikes the necessity; in the final analysis she doubts her own sea keeping abilities. Alone in the tiny shower enclosure, I take great pleasure in the steamy warmth that cascades down my body, reveling in the pelting I take from the seemingly endless supply of nearly scalding droplets that burst from the shower head. I stand there for long minutes, considering the irony of the fact that such a joy is not available in our spacious bathroom at home because of the "green" setting maintained on the hot water heater there. Although enraptured by the experience, my mind pulls me back to my duty. The Crew will be getting anxious by now and I am needed on the bridge.

Glowing in the pleasures of cleanliness and fresh outfits, we indulge in snacks and another pot of coffee. The cabin heater blows a warm breeze that wards off the dampening chill we know the outside air holds. Rain beats down on the fiberglass pilothouse top and explodes on the surface of the sea all around. Could travel anywhere and under any other conditions ever be better?

Gazing at the charts and the water-world ahead, even though it is not yet noon it is time to decide where we will put in for the night!

Previously, we identified three likely spots. We imagined that all were safe harbors with pleasant surroundings. Two of them were well removed from anything, but entailed anchoring out; the third was a common boating destination, but probably would not necessitate dropping the hook. The choices, really, were between seclusion and getting wet to secure it or enduring a closer brush with human society and staying dryer because of it.

Our boat is a magic carpet. It takes us to wonderful places. Equally important, however, is the fact that it whisks us from the hustle bustle world of thriving civilization to a primeval state – kind of – where barring next door neighbors and buzzing jet skis, we imagine for a moment that the universe outside our doors is devoid of human life. It is a mental construct and a stretch at that, but via this mechanism we find that the farther we get from the press of society, the closer we get to each other. The lure of solitude, then, is the pull of each for the other. Gone are the cares of daily life and the relentless churnings of modern times. Gone are the worries about Aunt Matilda's fungus or the barking dog next door. Gone – if we remember to turn off our cell phones and laptops! – are the unsolicited intrusions, good and bad, that take more and more of our days. Left, only to us, is us.

It was cartoonist Walt Kelly who said, via his beloved 'Pogo,' "We have met the enemy and he is us." It is up to each of us, without exception, to ponder such words and discern their meanings. But contrary to most thoughts on the subject, it seems to me that the target here is an elusive one. In one instance and at one time it might provide a very particular insight and then in another time and place, it may lead us off in some other direction entirely. The job, then, is not to unlock the secrets of the universe in one fell swoop, for that would be a fool's errand; rather, the task always is to interpret and then reinterpret, in light of our new situation, that which seemed incredibly obvious yesterday. The pressures of modern life leave little time for such activities. They are, therefore, too often neglected.

Since the beginning of history a favorite way for people to pass their days has been to build walls. House walls, castle walls, high-rise walls, stonewalls, concrete walls, straw walls and even south-facing, heat-absorbing walls are just a few of the types that mankind turns its attentions toward. Some of these undertakings rank as absolutely essential, while many of them, like the genuine, imitation, full functioning lighthouses people occasionally construct to adorn their seashore homes, are purely for, well...ummmm... reasons they think important or at least interesting.

Visit any city and wander past one of its downtown building sites. Despite its dusty wooden fences, its dirt, its din, its disruptive, even its dangerous character, if you study it for any length of time, you will find that amazing numbers of people stop by to admire the way the walls there are going up. Moreover, if you persist in your efforts it will not be long before you will be able to identify a group of dedicated followers who show up just about everyday, rain or shine, to gauge the advancement and breathe in the heady smell of human progress. People love walls.

Walls keep all manner of bad things out. Wind, rain, heat, cold, murderers, thieves, pillagers, plunderers and perhaps even the odd dragon or two are held at bay by these things.

As a group, human beings are exceptionally good at transforming ideas into reality. Think a marvelous thing, like a pyramid, and putting it together is a piece of cake (especially if you have several hundred thousand skilled slaves standing around with nothing particular to do!) Unfortunately, and for lots of good reasons, we are equally capable at taking this creativity in the other direction. For example, if the average 'Joe' stumbles across an especially fine example of a wall, the first thing he will do is generate a copy of it, even if only in his mind, for further use. Next, however, instead of sitting back and enjoying the creation for its designed purpose, as like as not he will hunker down behind it. When such individual acts are stretched over a lifetime, even plain old, ordinary 'Joe' will wind up with a wondrous collection of walls that are both seen and unseen. Regarding the latter, being ever practical creatures, we disdain allowing useful things to languish; instead we put them to work serving purposes never dreamed of by physical builders. With hardly any effort at all we throw up so many mental barriers that ultimately we cannot turn around in the isle of the grocery store without plowing head-on into two or three of them!

The boat traps us, like a couple of rats, between fiberglass bulkheads. There, protected from sea, wind, sun, rain, cold and heat, it keeps us well removed from the distractions of the day. Sojourning therein we find that we gain the time and space needed to evaluate our internal walls and to determine the utility of each. Usually we learn that we have practiced the art well, but a little too independently, and as we compare our prizes we discover that much superfluous effort has been expended to no worthy end. By sharing this information, we are able to identify those walls that best should be demolished. Thus, in seeking solitude The Captain and The Crew find time to tear down the structures that keep us apart and then we recycle that discarded material to improve those constructs that are good and productive. This makes each of us stronger and safer.

In considering the trade-offs concerning where to put in for the night, the deciding factor is the rain that now is coming down hard. The real question is do we want to grab a buoy and quickly tie off or do we want to spend a lot more time standing around in the rain while setting the anchor and possibly deploying a stern line. In the first instance we will have to go into a busier harbor and suffer from more crowded surroundings; in the second, we get more serenity but also have a better chance of getting thoroughly soaked. Decisions, decisions.

Naturally, I put the question directly to The Crew. As a seasoned commander I know that unilateral decision making in cases like these runs the risk of surliness or even outright mutiny and a happy ship is, well, a happy ship. Concomitantly, by letting The Foredeck Hand cast the deciding vote, the onus for what happens thereafter rests on her.

The common seaman frequently is not the brightest bulb on the tree. It is true that there are exceptions, like Richard Henry Dana, Jr. (*Two Years Before the Mast)* or Herman Melville (*White-Jacket, Moby*

Dick, etc.), but like as not the fo'c's'le hand is referred to as an "ordinary" sailor for good reasons. While I know full well the capabilities of my Crew – after all, I handpicked her – she sometimes does not have the experience necessary to think shipboard situations through to the end. As I gauge the strength of the deluge outside our snug wheelhouse, I bank on that shortcoming to set up the preferred scenario.

In the kind of rain we were enjoying, two developments seemed likely. The first, if we opted to anchor out, was that someone would have to go up on the bow to let the hook go. That same someone would have to stay there while the boat was backed, several times, in order to feed out the anchor, the rode, etc. Then, someone would have to rig the stopper line – a process necessitating groveling on one's knees and handling wet ropes and chains. Thereafter, should a stern line be needed, someone would have to drop the dinghy, affix the outboard, motor in to shore, tie the line to something dripping wet but solid, and then make his or her way back to the boat. Through all of this, despite being in foul weather gear, each of the 'someones' involved would be getting soaking wet. And, given that I am in charge of most of the aforementioned duties, from the point of 'groveling on one's knees' on to the getting the RIB back onboard, one of the 'someones' getting drenched, then, would be The Captain.

Conversely, should we chose to run right up to a buoy, where someone standing on the bow of the boat dressed in foul weather gear and having a boathook in hand would thread a mooring line through the buoy ring and then tie it to the cleats on the vessel, the job could be completed by just one 'someone.' And oh, did I mention, that the 'someone' in charge of performing those machinations would be The Crew? Hmmmmm. Stay inside, nice and dry and warm and do little more than bark the occasional order to The Crew or flail around in a variety of situations that invite streams of cold water to run down your sleeves or to drip relentlessly on the back of your neck, and very well may necessitate jumping into a foot or two of chilly ocean. Let me see. Do I choose what is behind Door #1 or will it be Door #2?

Tangential considerations in the decision we must make about where to go pertain to access and navigation. The mooring buoy grounds are entered easily, the harbor is safe and deep and it includes no worrisome hazards. The others require more maneuvering, are of varying depths – some of which shoal dangerously – and each includes a bunch of submerged rocks that must be avoided.

After explaining all of this to The X.O. – excepting the part about who has to get wet, when – we settle on Montague Harbour as our destination. It has the buoys!

Montague Harbor sits just off the main trunk of Trincomali Channel. Its configuration, relative to the main thoroughfare, is reminiscent of the pit area in a NASCAR race. Ease out of traffic by steering a bit to the left (on approach from the north) and then roll straight down the access ramp to the rest area. After that just sit back and relax while The Crew goes to work!

Our course takes us southeast down the "slot" formed between Valdes and Galliano Islands and the smaller, 'inside' Gulf Islands that parallel the coast of Vancouver Island. No other boats are in sight, so beyond keeping a weather eye out for floating dangers, we are free to enjoy the scenery as it glides past the large windows of the pilothouse.

Soon Porlier Pass opens on the port side. The greyer waters from the Strait of Georgia push their way through the narrow break between Valdes and Galiano, but with the turning tide just beginning to run, we do not see the roiling and churning seas that we witnessed on the way up. Instead we marvel at the subtle changes in the color of the water, from a cold, hard grey to a warmer, softer green, as the ocean washes in through the barrier islands. We wonder whether the pallet of even the most skilled artist could do justice to the transformation.

As happened at Gabriola Passage, we find that this time around we see more of this interesting confluence than we did before. For instance, we note that a full array of fine homes cling to the rocky shores of the opening. In a Walter Mitty way we imagine how grand living in them would be. In our minds eyes we look out over the moving waters, studying the animals that swim by, noting the transiting vessels, fearing the storms that break and enjoying the seasons as they change. Almost at the same time, though, reality sets in and we imagine the difficulties of having any goods or services delivered to these distant ramparts, the cost of transporting the necessities of life out here and the constant, raging battle between Mother Nature and the homeowner over whether the various, flimsy structures erected there will continue to function whole. We conclude that while the views would be gorgeous, we would prefer not to become foot soldiers in the war that takes place there everyday. Well…maybe just for a long, romantic weekend.

Leaving the fun of daydreaming about houses, again, we turn our attentions to the plethora of lights and lighthouse situated in and around this pass. With binocular trained, we scan the shores as well as the distant horizon to try to find all of the dots that we can see on the chart. It's like playing "Where's Waldo." Ultimately we fail, but there is no joy lost on the exercise!

The trip on down Tricomali Channel is splendid. When you are safe and warm inside and everything's working just the way it should, there is just something about a rainy day that is hard to beat. Add to that general statement the slowly unfolding panorama of tree covered islands and distant mountains, of channel markers and sea birds, of raindrops and low-slung clouds and who can say where one goes to find anything better?

Necessitating hardly any change in our ruler-straight wake, I direct Auto to head up to port a point or so. As we leave to starboard the southeast tip of Wallace Island we must begin to bear to the east a tad if we are to steer straight into Montague Harbour. A line of rocks and islets that runs northwest to southeast commences at the Walker Rock Light and includes Ballingall, Wise, Charles, Sphinx and Parker Islands. These landforms create a mile wide funnel between Galiano Island (to the east) and the Trincomali Channel proper (to the west) that leads the seafarer directly to the northern opening into Montague Harbour. Keep the boat between Galiano and the lesser islands and you just about have to wind up at your destination.

On the trip north we had noted the other, southern, entry to Montague Harbour. Based on the few quick glimpses we were afforded of it at that time, we imagined it to be a snug little harbor, although trending toward the crowded end of the scale due to it being positioned about equidistant (+/- 25 straight line nautical miles) from the cities of Victoria and Vancouver. Since it was nearing mid-day on a rainy Sunday early in the boating season, we figured that whatever else it was, it should be pretty empty.

As we motored through the pass separating Gray Peninsula (part of Galiano Island) from Parker Island we observed an expanse of water that was considerably larger than most of the harbors we had encountered on this trip. Liberally extrapolating and rounding up, we were looking at a bay that we guessed might cover a square mile of surface area or more. Much of this water, especially that on the Galiano Island side, was populated by tens if not hundreds of pleasure boats of one sort or the other. It surely was not empty!

Hoping that there might be a mooring buoy available, we made a great loop, counterclockwise, around the south end of Gray Peninsula. This brought us into immediate proximity of the largest public parking lot we had ever seen on the water. Bobbing along in front of us was an expanse of white buoys, all laid out in neat little lines. They seemed to stretch for about as far as the eye could see. And while the field was well populated, there remained a nice selection of empty parking spots off the southern tip of Gray Peninsula. That suited us perfectly especially since that was the part of the lot that was farthest removed from the crowd.

I love approaching mooring buoys. Bringing a vessel up to one of these wonderful spheres allows the pilot to show off all of his boat handling skills without the real fear of hitting anything very substantial! Even though these beach balls are subject to the whimsy of wind and water, their firm anchor chains effectively hold them in nearly static positions. Dock slips share this same motionlessness, but they include lots of very hard, very solid things upon which to wreck a boat. Mooring buoys do not. In fact, if you accidentally hit one – and I don't recommend it – the ball just floats away. No harm, no foul, no dock rash, no gel coat repair and best of all, there are no costly apologies to the owners of neighboring yachts. Sweet!

"Muster The Foredeck Crew for docking," I order dryly. Having donned her foul weather gear and thus having transformed herself into something looking a lot like a great red lobster, The Foredeck Crew squeezes through the port door of the pilothouse and makes her way, boat hook in hand, to the forepeak. "By golly, but it is raining hard, isn't it," I think as I slide her door shut to keep wind and rain on the outside where it belongs.

Easing the boat a few feet forward, I bring *Minstrel's Song* to a dead stop. The buoy bobs gently next to the boat. Its ring stands upright, directly under the station taken up by The Foredeck Crew. I crack my door enough to yell out, "Got it? Yes? Great work. Now double the lines and make her fast." With alacrity I slam my door closed before any more rain can come in to wet my tee shirt. Whew! Docking is a chore.

Through the wall of glass before me, I supervise The Crew's work. I watch intently as she kneels to tie the lines off neatly and make the boat fast. It looks like she has done another good job. This pleases me because although she is fairly new to the arts of the sailor, she is a quick study, a fast worker and given what I had just seen, she does not seem to mind, too much, getting wet.

After stowing her boat hook properly in the stern, The Crew enters the saloon through the cockpit door, aft. Shaking the surface water off her attire, she hangs her stuff up in the wet locker and makes her way forward.

"How'd we do?" she asks.

"Very well," I respond, "but I'll make a closer inspection of your handiwork later, when it's not raining so hard."

Standing hand-in-hand in our cozy cabin, we take a few moments to survey our surroundings. Because of our mooring spot, the northern channel through which we entered is blocked from view by land and trees; in like manner the southern passage out of the harbor cannot be seen. What seems most apparent is that we are in the midst of a fine little bay that is sheltered, in the main, 360 degrees around by rising, tree-covered hillsides. The impression left by the combination of land and sea is akin to the one that anyone might have if floating serenely on a remote crater lake.

The terrain just north of our position, constituting the western end of the low-slung Gray Peninsula, is fairly flat. It is forested with tall evergreen trees. The truncated horizon we can see starts to climb to the northeast as the trees ascend a hill up to the ridgeline of Galiano Island proper. From a height of a hundred feet or more above sea level, this escarpment visually takes off first to the southeast before it begins its loop back to the southwest. From the southwestern extreme of this little bowl, the land comes roaring back to the north along the tree-covered spine of Parker Island. That terminates just a couple of hundred yards across the water from the tip of Gray Peninsula just in front of us.

While not geometrically perfect, the harbor seems to have four basic parts: the buoy area (where we are), in the northeastern corner of the bay; the zone extending southeast from the buoy field, which runs parallel to Galiano's beachfront; the southeastern end of the basin; and that which sits directly off Parker Island's northeast shore.

Montague Harbour Marine Park includes all of Gray Peninsula, the mooring cove where we lingered, as well as a chunk of Galiano Island to the northeast. The peninsula is a low-lying landmass with beaches on both its north and south sides that slope very gently up from the sea. These strands looked to be perfect places for clamming, for taking a quiet stroll along the ocean or for shell collecting. Beyond the tidal reach, evergreen forests rein. Even from our bobbing observation platform we identified a number of the walking paths that circumscribed and crisscrossed this portion of the park. Midway around the arcing shoreline of Gray Peninsula, as it makes its way from the west toward the east and Galiano, a public wharf of about 100 feet or so extends southeastward into the water. A couple of small sheds and buildings huddle near the base of the pier.

A ferry landing, replete with all of the terrors associated with the presence of those monstrous creatures, sits on the southeast extreme of the Marine Park – undoubtedly to help control the local boating population. Where not reserved for park purposes, the land all around the harbor, including that of Parker Island, is dotted with homes tucked into the trees. While the total number of visible structures did not seem excessive or even suggest that a dense population had developed, even a cursory count of the ones that could be seen peeking through the timber, or latter an inventory of the lights twinkling around the cove required a different conclusion. Still, whether by dint of size, terrain or foliage, and despite the apparent truth, the impression left was that of a fairly quiet, even a largely overlooked, backwater haven.

Looks can be deceiving, especially on the water. A quick count of the buoys in the marine park yielded a surprising number: 40 or more. And, although the sense we had from the decks of *Minstrel's* Song was that there were plenty of vacancies and no crowding at all, even after the Sunday afternoon stampede back to home and workplace, no less than ¾ of the total spaces available remained occupied.

This same phenomenon was apparent across the entire face of the harbor. Whereas the buoy area constituted a small fraction of the bay available for hosting waterborne visitors, most of the boats we could see were anchored elsewhere. And while logic dictated that if that were the case, there must have been several hundred vessels cohabitating in the bay, the senses did not support that conclusion at all. Thus, we happily bobbed around on wonderfully protected waters that were unencumbered by the demands of encroaching humanity all the while remaining within arms reach of several hundreds of our fellow creatures. Odd, that!

The great thing about beginning any journey in the wee small hours of the night is that by the time you have passed the sun's zenith you are beset by a virtuous feeling of having done your duty, of having travelled enough, of having put in a full day! It was with just such satisfaction that we ate the grub that Cookie rustled up, played a couple of games of cards, read a bit and then napped, luxuriating all the while in a wonderful, self-congratulatory sense of accomplishment. All of which was made even better, if possible, by the incessant drumbeat of raindrops on fiberglass.

As the afternoon wore on, we found additional entertainment in watching group after group of raincoat-clad hikers make their ways along the shores adjacent to our little sea. Since parts of the various paths were but a few feet above the waterline and since we sat less than 200 feet from several of them, we had grandstand seats. From our little nest, you could see rain dripping from noses and could hear, almost, the squish, squish, squish of wet feet in drenched shoes. It made us feel glad to be alive!

RAIN, RAIN GO AWAY...

The joy of sitting warm and dry inside the cabin while watching others slosh through the afternoon gloom began to wane with the passing hours. One of the quaint customs practiced on both sides of the border is that of charging real money for the use of certain improvements. On the Washington side of the line, a buoy fee is levied whenever one passes a line through the ring of any of the State's tethered, white, public balls. Frequent visitors can cut the fee so charged to next to nothing, however, by pre-purchasing a heavily discounted season's pass. With said item in hand – actually one is supposed to display the authorizing sticker in one of the vessel's windows – the boater is free to pull into any State moorage and tie up without further payment. When properly equipped, the pleasure boater has to do little more than to find a vacant spot, pick up the mooring ring and then sit back and enjoy a pleasant stay!

Canada, too, sees fit to charge for parking. However, to the best of my knowledge, they levy their fees on a pay as you go basis. Pull in, tie up, pay up, it's just that simple. And, while bobbing in Washington State's seawater costs $10. a pop, in 2011 U.S. dollars, Canadian brine is more expensive. (Because they have less of it?) As a rule, a Canadian ring runs $12 per night – as counted out in the local currency, which sometimes is worth more and sometimes less than their southern neighbor's greenbacks. The Canadians sweeten the deal, however, by allowing free parking at some places between certain hours. Moreover, in certain locales they waive their fees completely or charge reduced rates during certain seasons of the year. Also, they extend additional discounts and allowances to some groups and individuals, e.g., Scout troops and the physically incapacitated.

It is probably only of passing interest to the reader to note that the disparate economic advantages offered willy-nilly by our northern neighbors, although frequently significant, tend to be offset by the fact that unless one has satellite communications, on-board computers and a hotline to the Prime Minister, it is nearly impossible to know ahead of time what a boater is going to have to pay for a buoy in any particular shelter on any given day.

As in the U.S., it is my understanding that one is legally obligated to pay whatever the assigned, daily toll is for a Canadian buoy very shortly after attaching to it. Such is certainly the case in U.S. waters, but happily it is truly a trivial matter there since most boaters choose to disregard that requirement in whole or in part. And, whereas such acts of civil disobedience rise almost to the level of patriotism below the 49th parallel, the keepers of the common good on the other side, who safeguard their home waters rather zealously, see no virtue whatsoever in such deeds. Toward that end, they remain ever vigilant for scoffers and rarely fail to cause such ne'er-do-wells serious pecuniary pain. But with the north's long list of rules and exceptions to the rules, even the intentionally law abiding struggle to discern whether they are within or without the regulations at any given time or place. A Philadelphia lawyer or a Congressional committee could obfuscate those points nicely were the issue hauled up to the bar of justice south of the line, but above it, well, above it the ordinary seaman is just on his own.

Suffice it to say that as the hours slipped by, I became increasingly nervous about the legal ramifications of being tied up to Buoy #15 without actually having bought and paid for it. Upon arrival, my intentions were good. In fact, the moment it stopped raining cats and dogs I had ever intention of dropping the dinghy off its rack, firing up the old outboard and whizzing directly to the park's dock to pay monetary homage to the local, political gods. What my scheme lacked was a fallback option in the event that the deluge continued unabated, as it did.

With rain still pounding on the cabin top, dinner in the offing and the big hand on the 12 and the little hand on the six, I was becoming a knotted ball of indecision. Harking back to a prehistoric moment, I recall that the fee in Bedwell Harbour had been waived until this calendar day. "Maybe it has been suspended here too," I hoped. But if it was the same in both places, the pressing question became what was meant by 'this day'? Did the authorities intend to convey, by use of that expression, the idea that on this day the money had to be paid, or did they anticipate that through this day the berth was to be toll free? And if one settled on the latter interpretation – an especially useful argument on account of the rain and all – would anyone really know or even care?

The answer to that question was a very strong, probably yes, for through the discordant cacophony of thoughts that filled my skull, there came an insistent little voice that reminded me that I had heard something, at sometime, that a waterborne portion of the local constabulary actually cruised these mooring areas each night to assure that all have given the government its due. And, if that voice was to be believed, it seemed to be saying that the aforementioned itinerant ticket-writers worked for the money they sucked up. Thus, it stood to reason that entrepreneurs compensated by the fees they could gather were unlikely to skip over potential contributors. Worse, I could only imagine that if all of the above were true, these patrolling cousins of the Sheriff of Nottingham might even earn extra bounty for discovering foreign scofflaws. According to this train of thought, it seemed likely, then, that they would spare no effort to sniff out any who had failed to pony up the mooring fee precisely because they could collect that and a hefty fine to boot. Based on such well-spun whole cloth, I could only imagine the worst possible scenario and that led me to ask the final question: "Well, punk, are ya feelin' lucky?"

When not promulgating rules and regulations with Kafka-like clarity and precision, the various controlling Solons of Western Civilization engage in another interesting activity: hide-and-seek. As pertains to parks and recreation areas of one sort or another, in one country or another, the scenario is always the same. The boater pulls in and, by dint of being a boater, is located on the water. All applicable requirements for a lawful stay in that vicinity clearly are posted, somewhere, on shore. Thus, to determine what one may or may not do – or worse, what one is obliged to undertake immediately and without fail if harsh penalties are to be avoided – when "using" any one of the designated portions of the sea that has been set aside for visitors, one must leave that medium, i.e., get off of the water, and then go and flail about up on shore.

I mention specifically 'hide-and-seek' and 'flailing around' because both are essential ingredients in the game the mariner joins the moment his foot sets down on *terra firma.* Rational human beings might imagine that some sort of "sticker" could be affixed to mooring buoys to convey basic instructions to the casual user. (That officialdom manages to include on the face of parking meters everything the average driver needs to know about leaving his car in a regulated space suggests that such an act is within the technological reach of our modern society.) Those same dreamers might imagine that barring the posting of all essential information at its point of need, the fundamental principles could, at least, be prominently displayed at the designated wharf or landing area. Sadly, neither seems ever to be the case. Instead, the hapless traveller must wander here and there, peering into every conceivable nook and cranny, under rocks and logs, around posts and buildings until, by pure chance, he stumbles upon the pot of gold, replete, always, with officious forms, envelopes, brochures and lock boxes, but never with any kind of writing instrument.

* * * * * * * * * * *

Forearmed as I was with the certainty of what awaited, and compelled by the passage of time and the incessant pounding on the overhead of raindrops that seemed to be growing to the size of baseballs, at least, I grudgingly announced that I was going to the dock to learn what had to be done about paying for our mooring. Donning my foul weather gear, I moved to the rear of the saloon, opened the hatch to the cockpit and was rewarded immediately by a stream of cold water that went straight for my warm, dry neck. With that I knew that the tone for the outing had been set.

I pivoted the dinghy from its upright, stowed position down onto the water. Because the dock was a healthy quarter of a mile away I opted to use the outboard to push the inflatable in that general direction. After turning the screw clamps on the engine to full open so as to release it from the bracket on the ship's rail, I wrestled the beast off its perch, carried it onto *Minstrel's Song's* swim step and then prepared to transfer both me and it into the dink.

It seems that we have explored previously the propensity for floating objects to roam when not attached to anything stationary. What we did not discuss was their natural tendency to see it coming. Much the way a dog that has been restrained inside all day can anticipate his master's intentions and transform himself instantaneously from inert lump to whirling dervish, so too do boats, particularly the small ones. Thus, while a vessel, such as a RIB, might seem to be resting quietly next to a dock or alongside a ship, hard, cold experience teaches that that is just a ruse. Set but a single foot in the bottom of a tender and it will come alive, every time, like an electric bull in a crowded barroom.

Winning half the battle when on the water comes from knowing what is likely to happen next and the other half comes from knowing what any given boat can and cannot do. As pertained to our dinghy, I knew that it was as skittish as a colt away from its momma for the first time and I also knew that prematurely cutting it loose was a recipe for disaster. Against this backdrop, before stepping into it I elected NOT to free it from the two stainless steel davit hooks that held it close to the stern of *Minstrel's Song*. In transferring a 35-pound outboard and myself into the dink, the last thing I wanted it to do was to think that it was about to be set free.

There is a proper, safe way to enter small, open boats. This involves using one's hands to grasp something solid for support and balance, like a pier, and then, setting a single foot gently into the target vessel. This movement is continued by keeping the body as low as possible and then sliding the bulk of oneself in over the gunwale like a snake, while simultaneously latching one's free hand onto some immovable part of the craft being entered. Only when a modicum of stability has been achieved within the confines of the conveyance should one's weight be shifted further and the second foot (and the rest of the body) be directed to move, gingerly, into the craft. As this process progresses one's grip on the external support is transferred to a similar hold on the boarded craft itself.

From this the reader now should have a clear mental picture of what a safe entry looks like. He will compare that with the visage of me standing on *Minstrel's Song* swim step, dripping wet, bolt upright, hefting the 35-pound motor in both hands, while getting ready to move from the relative stability of the big boat down into the relative instability of the rubber inflatable. Keep in mind, too, please, that the RIB resembles a seasoned roping calf that has been trapped in a metal chute an inordinate number of times. It knows the gate is going to open soon and when it does, it plans to run hell bent for leather.

Since safety is the theme here and everything we touch these days comes with a warning label, we need to take this moment to admonish the reader not to try this at home – and especially not on a boat! Additionally, we ask that the student of this event refrain from envisioning a new outboard motor being inadvertently dropped into the depths by an off-balance skipper. There is no need for this latter image especially since both The Captain and The Crew generate enough of them to last a lifetime.

Remaining as low as the load I carry will allow, and moving as gracefully as the rain-drenched swim step and wet tender bottom will tolerate, I transfer my cargo from big to little. The latter bobs and weaves, shivers and shakes, but manages no greater harm than that before I am able to get to a kneeling position on its wet deck. From there I wrestle my load toward the stern. Next I lift the aluminum propulsion system over the transom and then carefully tighten the clamps that attach it to the boat. I begin to breath a sigh of relief as I snap the outboard's heavy safety cable to the dinghy. At this point the motor cannot go anywhere on its own and The Captain now indicates that the passengers are free to move about on the thwart seat of the little rubber terror.

Crews can be wily things and mine more than most, it seems. While my usual duties include those things attendant upon machinery and boat handling – in this instance all subsumed under the rubric 'Getting Ashore' – The Crew always stands by to lend a hand when necessary. That is an activity that we treat as wholly voluntary, but much appreciated. However, at this particular moment, despite the fact that I can barely see anything through the deluge of the century, it is crystal clear that she has opted not to come out to wish me 'bon voyage.' Adding insult to injury, through my raindrop-distorted glasses I catch a glimpse of her visage peering out of the saloon window, warm and dry, blowing the steam off a cup of hot tea…and smiling!

"Cut her loose," I said to the empty sea, realizing immediately that barking verbal commands has become habitual. It is at this point that I realize, too, that the stainless steel davit restraints protruding from the stern of *Minstrel's Song* are still attached to the dink. I move to disconnect them from the rubber monster but instantly realize that my weight has depressed the little boat sufficiently to keep the eyes popping free as usual. With The Crew helping, overcoming this problem is a piece of cake. Alas, The Crew is inside, laughing her eyeballs out while I am outside drowning.

Clambering back out of the canvas fiend and back onto *Minstrel's Song,* I free the reluctant hooks and then, as gingerly as possible, re-enter the dinghy. Except for the handful of painter I hold in clutched claws and the restraint provided by a single foot set gingerly in her waist, she's as free of her shackles as the proverbial bird.

When ensconced on the rear thwart again, I start the engine, turn the handle to "Forward" and rev it a little. The barely-under-control-yet inner tube bumps once against the swim step and on the rebound begins a mushy turn away from the bigger boat. Gaining a modicum of speed, The Coxswain is able to herd it in the general direction of the park dock. Like big beach balls, most RIBS don't steer, really. They wallow through the sea, inclining this way or that in response to the thrust of the engine, but they rarely proceed anywhere on purpose.

Looking for a convenient spot to tie off, one that would make entry and exit from the dink easy, I spy an area at the base of the wharf that is designed just for vessels of this type. There, a row of undersized slips beckons. Consisting of tiny U-shaped slots each of which is wide enough and long enough for a single boat only, I set my course for one of these pens. Built with of the handling characteristics of RIBS in mind, these semi-enclosed niches allow drivers of one of these torments the luxury of not having to try to wring precision out of something inherently imprecise. All one has to do, really, is to get between the fingers and then bump to a stop. As an added bonus, these thoughtful inflatable pens are built low in the water so even when singlehanded, it is no trouble to tie off and quickly and safely get out of them and up on the hard surface.

Sloshing along the wharf in my soaking deck shoes – I left my foul weather boots at home for this cruise – I was able to devote my full attention to ruminations on the topic of the protective limitations of a baseball cap when worn in a driving rain. I had neglected to bring proper waterproof headgear on this voyage as well.

Doing my award-winning impression of a drowning rat, I made my miserable way toward the shore and to the information board that I hoped would be there. About 25 yards beyond the end of the wharf I found it. It offered succinct instructions for payment, some soggy envelopes and a lockbox for deposit. It provided neither cover from the rain nor a pencil to complete the requisite paperwork.

But for once I was prepared. At Bedwell Harbour I had had the foresight to liberate several registration envelopes against an unspecified need for future use. Presuming a modicum of universality at Canadian marine parks, I had even gone so far as to dig out one of these, fill in the requisite blanks, in ink, and stuff it full of Canadian loonies *before* leaving the dry confines of *Minstrel's Song.*

As frequently seems to be the case, theory and practice here diverged. Sadly I discovered that the Montague Harbour Marine Park's soaked envelopes required that a slightly different set of data be entered on its forms. The fee to be paid, though actually less, was different too. With trembling, wet, cold, hands I removed the dry packet I carried within the bowels of my raingear and compared and contrasted it with the one I was supposed to use. I stood there pondering, and dripping, while watching the two slimy pieces of paper held in my hands disintegrate. The 'wrong' one was filled out and set to go, but it was the wrong one. And getting the 'right' one stuffed and properly annotated, under the conditions, was about as likely as finding a pot of gold at the end of a rainbow. I glanced around in a vain effort to resolve the dilemma, hoping against hope to see something that would direct my hand. Finally, I shoved the Bedwell Harbour registration into one of the Montague Marine Park's envelopes and then managed to pour the oozing mess into the metal lockbox. I took consolation in the knowledge that any jail time to be served as a result of my crimes of commission and omission would be spent inside someplace that was warm and dry.

On the short, straight path back to the dinghy I took a moment to get some relief from the poring rain. Sheltered in the lee of a small building adjacent to the pier was a bulletin board affixed to a wall. By standing very close to it one could remove oneself, if only temporarily, from the universe which otherwise seemed to be filled with nothing except liquid air. Taking advantage of that opportunity, I soon became enthralled with the notices neatly tacked up on the cork. And it was there, protected from the weather in that hidden nook, that I discovered incredible wisdom. Who, for instance, did not need to learn a lot more about the neglected art of setting up a proper camp tent? (Was it pure genius to post this at that precise point where the itinerant yachtsman would be off-loading his shelter halves for the night?) Then, too, how could guidance on the oft glossed over fundamentals of starfish collecting (in both word and picture) fail to excite the imagination. Surely, too, the reader will appreciate my despair upon learning that while the public was welcome to attend all of their sessions, the park docents gathered there to discuss the compelling issues of the day just one Saturday each month, May-September.

Facing what had to be faced, I made my way back to the RIB and readied it for the trip home. No less than two inches of rainwater covered its bottom, but that was merely icing on the cake. Reaching the stern of *Minstrel's Song* a short time later I made a command decision. The dink with outboard would stay just where it was until it either filled with rainwater and sank or the rain stopped. Frankly, I didn't care which. After attaching this craft to the swim step with both of the stainless steel davit eyes and with the nylon painter, for insurance, I headed inside.

If The Crew was entertained by my waterlogged sortie into the great out of doors, she had the good sense to keep it to herself. Dripping water everywhere, I dried what I could as I slithered out of the wet and soggy and donned the clean and dry. My mood might have remained grim for the rest of the night, but the scent of food-like delicacies wafting into my nostrils and the promise of a hot meal changed my perspective noticeably. Whether because of the rain or not, Cookie outdid herself with the feast she laid on our table and by the end of dinner all memory of discomfort of inconvenience had evaporated.

We lounged after dinner, whiling away a pleasant hour or two by playing cribbage and then reading. Although I have long suspected that The First Mate once made her living playing cards on a Mississippi riverboat, I humor her by pretending that the competition between us is keen and our matches are close. On any good ship, The Captain has to wear many hats.

As dusk began to descend, the rain abated. In preparation for nightfall, I laid off the course for the following day and engaged Number One in a discussion that centered on the enthralling topic of whether or not we should sail on the tide in seamanlike fashion – despite it arriving at an indecent hour and being wholly unnecessary – or just wait until we felt like getting up and moving. With plans well formulated and our nighttime rituals started, there came a light tapping on the side of the boat. At first I dismissed it as just the bump of the mooring buoy on the hull, but its persistence necessitated at least a look.

Shoving the port pilothouse door open to go out and investigate, I was surprised by the vision of a woman who at first appeared to be floating on air given the fact that her eyes were nearly on the same level as mine. As my mind mulled the likelihood of such a thing, I realized that she not levitating but rather was sitting on the elevated seat of a bobbing RIB. So high up was she, however, that she steadied both the inflatable and herself by holding onto our stainless steel rail, a safety device that stood a good 5 feet above the water. Looking at me from her perch, the seasoned sailor politely said, "I'm here to collect the buoy fee."

"You're what?" I stammered incredulously.

"I'm here to collect the fee. You know, for the buoy. I'm running a little late tonight on account of the rain. We're usually out earlier, but I couldn't see getting drenched just for a few bucks!"

Mulling this startling intelligence while trying to re-gain my composure, I managed to mumble, "But I already paid."

"You did?" she queried.

"Uh-huh. Here's the receipt. See?" I volunteered, as I held up the still gooey strip of paper that had a faint line of running, fading numbers on it. "I put it in the box ashore a couple of hours ago!"

"Oh…so you're the one…Yeah, I saw a ball of something in there, but it was too oozy to identify. I'll rescue it tomorrow. Meanwhile, thanks. Sorry to bother you. Have a great night!" And off she sped into the gathering darkness, making her appointed rounds.

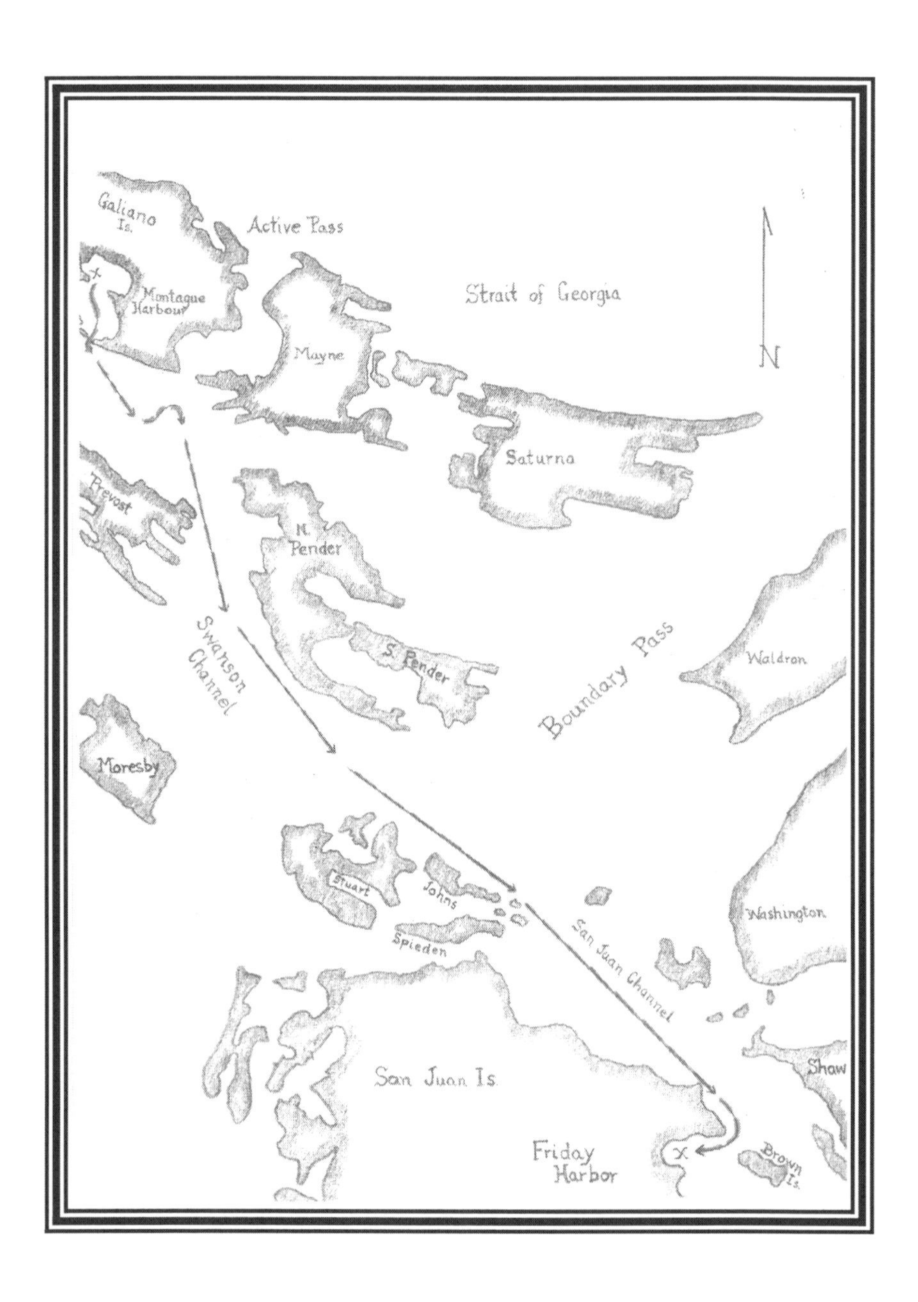
Galiano Is.
Active Pass
Montague Harbour
Strait of Georgia
N
Mayne
Saturna
Prevost
N. Pender
S. Pender
Swanson Channel
Boundary Pass
Waldron
Moresby
Stuart
Johns
Spieden
Washington
San Juan Channel
San Juan Is.
Shaw
Friday Harbor
Brown Is.

Day Ten

Montague Harbour to Friday Harbor
Or
Culture Shock, Revisited

We settled, the night before, on the casual approach to this day. Arising at a comfortable hour we dressed leisurely, sipped a couple of cups of coffee and ate a Danish…or was it two?

Departing Montague Harbour was an equally laidback endeavor. After going through our usual pre-departure checklist I ignited the diesel and we prepared to get under way. The Line Handling Crew stood ready by the cleats on the foredeck to free us from our mooring. On The Skipper's command she slipped the line easily from the buoy and then began to coil it for stowage. Pushing the transmission lever into its one forward gear, The Pilot slowly guided the boat out of the anchorage.

Leaving a place where one has found shelter for a time usually is a pleasure. Whenever we begin a new leg of our journey, we run the engine at an idle for the first 10 minutes or so. During that period the bow of *Minstrel's Song* gently cleaves the water, generating little wake and breaking the silence of the day only with a cheerful gurgling sound that rolls down the hull to the point where it meets the deep, throaty, diesel rumble that resonates through the exhaust system before leaving us forever someplace astern. We work our way toward open water like this in part out of courtesy to nearby boaters, in part to preclude generating a damaging shore wake and in part to give the power plant time to warm to its operating temperature. This latter consideration helps to limit wear and tear on the motor. Even without the impetus of these practical considerations we would continue this ritual indefinitely; it is one of the best parts of any day's travels.

Cruising along at just a few knots, usually over flat water, allows one's senses to awake and the mind to retune to the rhythms of the sea. In this mode, one gains a feel again for the responsiveness of the rudder, the force of the water against the hull and one's own tiny place in the universe.

The gift of flight was a thing denied mankind for millennia. Perhaps because humans were not meant to soar naturally, the ability to float freely above the earth's surface – fear notwithstanding – generates a feeling not soon to be forgotten. Any trip into the heavens involves three parts: slipping "the surly bonds of earth," (in the words of John Magee, Jr.), sailing unfettered through the sky and the process of returning to one's regular, earthly domain. As most any pilot will tell you, all three parts are grand, but each in its own way, differs vastly.

Lazing through the sky, wings extended like some great bird, drifting this way and that, sometimes up and sometimes down, riding, floating, effortlessly conveyed along by invisible currents of air, is a pleasure that titillates the senses. Skydivers, too, enjoy this same perception. They miss, however, the equally exhilarating aspects of leaving the earth on command as well as deigning to return to it, more or less, as one will.

The act of transitioning back to the hard ground from the sky is both challenging and elating. During the process one goes from the grandly three dimensional nature of free flight – with the earth below amounting to little more than an intellectual construct – back to the more constrained and normal situation wherein terra firma is immediately and always 'down under.' In some ways the change can be likened to the difference between the world as viewed from our regular 5'-6' vantage points to that which we experience when standing on the edge of a cliff.

In the first instance everything is normal; in the second, there's NOTHING out in front of us! Beyond having to adjust to this very different vertical perspective, when landing an aircraft of any sort one also must allow for the speed, both horizontal and vertical. Imagine that you are 'flying' a baseball that has been pitched at 100 mph and is closing with the ground at a rate of 10 feet per second. Contemplate having the orb gently connect with the earth at one very specific spot, from a starting point that is, maybe, 2,000 feet up and three miles out. Suffice it to say that doing so is complex, counterintuitive and astounding all at once. Such is the challenge of returning to earth.

Taking off has the opposite effect. From the constraint of the forces ordinarily found on our planet, we lift free and enter a different realm. We float above it all, impervious for a time to the limits suffered by those beneath us. It is incredible, lovely and terrifying, all at once!

Leaving an anchorage has much the same feel as taking to the sky. In sailing away from a place where we have been held tightly to the earth, mechanical though the restraint might have been, we find ourselves suddenly free to float anywhere we wish, riding gloriously on the face of the sea. As the airplane breaks its bonds from the grasping land below it, in a way, the boat heading out from a harbor does the same thing. Probably the greatest difference is in the time it takes for both processes to occur. In the former, the aircraft takes wing quickly; in the latter much more slowly. And, while both sensations can be deeply satisfying, I prefer the second because it provides more time to reflect on and savor the change.

Steering slowly southwest toward the pass out of Montague Harbour, Number One and I occupy ourselves again as usual. Beyond attending to the water ahead, we study the surrounding shorelines – 360 degrees – making mental pictures and comparing notes. Interesting homes, unusual geographic formations, docks, piers, boats, float planes, even landscaping comes under our relentless scrutiny. Fleeting thoughts stirred by something seen or done drives the conversation in unpredictable directions.

Taking in new things and thinking new thoughts is one of the reasons we travel. But the joys we derive from these activities are meager compared to all the rest. The great motive for putting to sea together (or taking a hike or going for a drive or doing anything in company) is to learn about each other. That seems, and even sounds, like an odd thing to say, especially considering the decades we have spent living and oft times earning our keep cheek and jowl. Yet the inescapable truth is that personal and interpersonal discoveries must needs occur as a continuum and not a single ticket punch or check mark on a list. Coming to know someone is a constant, never ending endeavor; people either grow closer to each other or they drift off in separate directions. There is no happy medium.

From this perspective, one might suggest that really getting to know someone else is like dropping a bucket into a deep well. You can bring up water from the top, water from the middle and even water from the bottom of the cistern, but what you can never do is to bring all of it up at once. And, because the well is always replenishing itself, what is lifted into the light of day this instant, will not be the same tomorrow. So no matter how often you dip your pail, what ultimately comes to the surface contains something fresh and new. Plumbing those depths continually yields incredible riches.

Life is a complex business for which there is no recipe or instruction manual. Attentive and desirous souls find hints and clues and ancient signs posted along the way, but the actual, the precise, the 'what do I do this second' directions remain, at best, fleeting shadows moving quickly through the fog of necessity. One can march straight through this boggy wilderness, alone, without pause or even speculation and reach an end to it of sorts; that is fairly easy to do. What is hard to do is to identify the right path to take today, the one that leads us where we most need to go this instant. Because two heads are better than one, wise travelers embark in tandem and search nonstop for the track that best will get them to their destination. And, just as a ship's pilot momentarily spins the wheel this way or that for some perceived advantage, so too, must life's voyagers adapt and amend and give way to each other if they wish to remain on course.

As do many other species, Homo sapiens seem to prefer living in pairs. And while the arguments might rage over whether the reasons for that propensity are the need for security, the division of labor, procreation, or just being tired of one's own cooking, what seems inescapable is that even when left wholly to our own devices, at liberty to choose to do anything we want, to live completely unrestrained and as we will – sooner or later we pick out someone else to help us build a nest...or some walls! Sometimes these unions last forever, but increasingly often today they are of a much shorter duration. Of the brief ones, it seems doubtless that they fall apart because the binding glue is too weak. It is easy to get someone to go for a boat ride on a lovely summer day; it is much harder to get them stay out when the clouds roll in, the wind gets up, and the seas turn tempestuous, as they always do.

If the weak link in the act of conjoining two people is the cement used, then the solution to the problem is to find a way to make it stronger and more resilient. While that search occurs within the context of uniquely personal wants, needs and desires, what is universal is that it does not just happen in an instant, but it comes only with time, patience and a desire to learn and understand. As such, it is always becoming and never, ever is.

As on many other occasions, The Captain and The Crew savor this morning's quiet time together, lazily floating past interesting shorelines, the ship's diesel purring at an idle. Before long they will be pushing the engine's RPMs up to cruise speed and be totally free from the land again. Until that happens, they sip their coffee, share their thoughts and spend a few more minutes getting to know each other once more. Leaving an anchorage is always a pleasure.

THE GREAT SAILBOAT RACE

The southern exit from Montague Harbour lies between little Julia Island and Philimore Point, a part of Galiano Island. It is an agreeable opening, about 300 yards in width, with plenty of water down below. Passing outbound through it puts one immediately back into Trincomali Channel. From this position nothing more is required than a lazy turn to port and a three and a quarter nautical mile run southeast down Trincomali to put one off Portlock Point, the southeastern tip of Prevost Island. About halfway to that landfall, off our port beam, we will cross the southern extreme of Active Pass. Were we to turn to port to follow it, it would take us from the interior of the Channel Islands back out to the Strait of Georgia. But we go to starboard, into Swanson Channel and on toward the U.S. of A.

It's a greyish day, with low, thin clouds that don't quite let the sun through, but hold no real suggestion of rain. The water and even the land that flanks it on all quarters assumes the flat, dull, two-dimensional aspect that photographers hate. A fresh breeze wafts down the channel from the northwest, rippling the protected seas. Although it sets up a chop of a foot or so, its reach is insufficient to incline *Minstrel's Song* to roll or even to notice it much.

Excepting the sailboat that is a mile or so off to the south of her, our fine little ship has the ocean all to herself. With forecasts that vacillate between cloudy and breezy and cloudy and 'watch-out-for-the-blow,' later, we are anxious to cover the 20-25 miles that stands between us and the protected waters of the San Juan Islands (south of the border), our general destination for the day. Our primary goal at this instant is to work our way to the southeast and then east, avoiding as much as possible the predicted winds out of the southwest that will make life uncomfortable for us as we transit the lower part of Swanson Channel and then turn east for the San Juans via Boundary Channel. If the weatherman is right, these areas will be exposed to some nasty seas kicked up by a shrieking wind. Being the good-timing, fair weather sailors that we are, our options are to skedaddle southward before it gets bad or hole up in Bedwell Harbour. Thinking that it was time to get on home, The Pilot pushed the throttle forward and watched the boat's water speed increase to over 9 knots (slightly less than 8 knots over the ground due to an incoming tide). For *Minstrel's Song*, this is flying!

It was with both pleasure and appreciation that we surveyed the sailboat that shared our little slice of the brine this dreary morning. If the experiences we had had on this cruise were accurate guides, this charging beauty was a freak of nature! Unlike virtually all of the rest of the 'wind-driven' craft we had encountered on this voyage, this one was running on a beam reach with every stitch of cruising sail she could fly set and pulling beautifully. Heeling along with her rub rail teasing the surface of the water, it was obvious that this boat's cast iron mains'l (engine) was not in use. The breeze alone drove her on her merry way; the bone in her teeth (bow wave) said she was making really good time. From our perspective she was a vision of loveliness, a wonder to behold.

At about 50' in length, this charmer was sloop-rigged (a single mast forward of amidships that flew one mains'l and one fores'l) with classic, sweet lines. She cut through the water effortlessly. And, although I knew that the rush of the water past her hull and the press of the wind through her rigging and in her sails would be generating a cacophony of noises that only could be those of pure, unbridled power, from where we sat, she created the beautiful sound of silence. Dancing across the waves without any apparent effort, she was the picture of what sailing is all about; I envied her crew.

Much to their credit, and despite the low clouds and the mediocrity of the day, the stalwart mariners manning this ghost-like vision not only made exclusive use of their sails for propulsion, but they mocked the damp chill that hung in the air by balancing themselves artfully on their open gunwales like lords of the sea. Concomitantly, we sipped our coffee in the warmth of the pilothouse and admired their hardiness.

In terms of travel, there was no doubt that they were making all speed to the north, driving for Active Pass and the Georgia Strait. We were bond southeastward toward Swanson Channel and Boundary Pass. Without change, the craft were on crossing courses. *Minstrel's Song* had the stranger's bow well aft of her starboard beam. Our vessels represented the proverbial ships that pass in the night; in almost every way imaginable they were as different as light and darkness.

As the distance between our boats narrowed it became apparent that the rules of the (maritime) road were soon going to require action and that under them we were the stand off or burdened vessel. By virtue of our opposing courses what that meant was that because it appeared likely that both craft would find themselves trying to occupy the same space at the same time in the not too distant future – a violation of the laws of physics that carries a particularly stiff penalty – someone had an obligation to change his ways in order to avoid a big crunching noise that would be followed by massive insurance claims. That obligation, resting heavily on our shoulders, was squared or even cubed by the fact that sails alone were propelling the other boat while we were driving a stinkpot! Under these circumstances our opposite number was entitled – borderline required – to keep doing exactly what she was doing so we could maneuver out of her way. And, under the circumstances, how we chose to accomplish that was not precisely defined.

The observation that our compatriots were skipping along on a bearing that did not change relative to our position, i.e. that her form loomed ever larger in the same quadrant of our starboard window, without moving up or back, warned that we were on a collision course. To remedy this there were three alternatives: 1.) We could stop and let the other vessel pass ahead of us; 2.) We could slow and swing hard to starboard for a time and then cross back behind her; or 3.) We could speed up to move well in front of her before crossing her bow. With the thought of the deteriorating weather dogging The Pilot's mind and the desire to stay politely out of the sailboat's wind – cutting behind her could slow her by blocking for a time the breeze she enjoyed – he chose Option Three. It was the wrong selection.

The plan mentally formulated involved first telegraphing our intentions to the other skipper – not scaring fellow seafarers to death with unanticipated antics is both wise and safe – by turning 20 degrees to port and then speeding up. According to my calculations, doing just that would allow us to open sufficient distance between the converging vessels to let us safely and comfortably make a 90 degree turn, later, across the other's bow. The Pilot liked this strategy well because it was simple and polite. Ultimately it fell short only due to his poor math skills.

The maneuvers concocted had but a single flaw: their success hinged on *Minstrel's Song's* ability to pull ahead of the sailboat. In scientific terms, we could manage the operation safely if, and only if, our powerboat went faster than did the sailboat. When originally devised, my thought was, "Pewfff! Speed is not a concern when it comes to sailboats. Most of them rarely see anything better than about six knots." (Unfortunately, this misguided impression had been reinforced recently by the army of sailing craft we had encountered that were just plodding along – under engine – at about a snail's pace.)

Now, having made the aforementioned turn to port, I watched the sailboat carefully, expecting to see the distance between the two vessels begin to open. It did not. Not one wit! "Dang," I thought, "She's cutting a breeze! Must have a skipper who knows what he's doing." Pushing the throttle forward some, *Minstrel's Song* climbed up her bow wave as her speed jumped from 9 to 11 knots. "That should do it," I opined with smug self-satisfaction.

Convinced that the America's Cup contender we had engaged would be falling behind quickly now, I tuned and took her measure. The space between us had increased, some. Unfortunately, I judged that given the rate at which the gap seemed to be widening, we would be somewhere in upstate New York before we could get far enough in front of this devil to safely cross the T! "Double dang," I said (or words to that effect). "How's she's getting that much speed out of this wind? She's doing 10 knots at least. This isn't natural. Who is that guy?"

As a matter of pure physics, the rapidity with which any boat can move through the water is constrained by a hoard of factors. Without plumbing those dark depths, suffice it to say that the average person can get a fair idea of how fast a craft can go by taking the square root of the length of the hull (where it touches the water) and multiplying it by a factor of 1.34. The resulting number, theoretically speaking, equals the top speed of a boat. For instance, a 36 foot hull should be able to go no faster than 8.04 knots (the square root of 36 being six and then that multiplied by 1.34). In principle no engine or set of sails, regardless of size, could make it scurry any faster. In principle.

The great asterisk appended to this assertion concerns hull shapes. While the aforementioned formula is absolute (to a degree?), clever men have figured out ways to circumvent it! Just as an airplane wing provides lift to raise the attached heavy object called a fuselage up into the sky – apparently defying the law of gravity along the way – so, too can a boat's hull be designed to lift itself out of the water. A hull so lifted is said to be on a plane – think hydroplane – and an entirely different set of scientific parameters begins to rule. It is this arrangement that lets 20' speedboats skitter along at 40, 50, even 60 knots or more.

Since classic sailboats do not have hulls that allow them to plane, the academic question I should have been tackling was, 'How is that sailboat going so fast?' (The reader will forgive me for not diving into that inquiry at that particular moment, interesting though it might have been; I was preoccupied with trying to figure out what we were going to have to do to outrun this flying ghost.) Instead, as testosterone impels the males of the species in any good competition, the idea of turning away, turning back, stopping, backing off, going sideways or trolling for fish never even crossed my mind. 'Faster, faster!' was all I could think!

Dropping the hammer, *Minstrel's Song* leapt forward to her top speed. (Our boat has a semi-planing hull and that allows her to exceed her expected natural velocity of about 7.7 knots. It does not, however, let her break the sound barrier!) Jumping up out of the water as far as a 16,000 pound boat may, within seconds we have achieved a mind-bending 14.5 knots, through the water. Traveling at such an incredible pace caused the engine noise to double. The vibrations shaking the ship from stem to stern doubled as well. Most importantly, the rate of our fuel consumption increased to 'I don't even want to know what the bill's going to be!' Faster, ever faster was the only thing that mattered to The Skipper right now. "We just achieved Warp Speed, Mr. Sulu," I shout toward The Crew. Without even bothering to glance back, I assure myself that we are getting way out ahead of our nemesis now. And that is a really good thing because as I focus on the water ahead of us, I find that I am staring directly at the navigational light that marks Enterprise Reef. It it is moving toward us with great alacrity. And that is a bad, really bad, thing.

Enterprise Reef is nothing more that a tiny bulge in the earth's crust that manages to stick its scruffy head up out of the water about half a nautical mile south of Active Pass. On it sits a lighted tower that serves to warn the wary or to suggest to the stupid that you cannot drive a boat directly over this part of the sea! I will leave it to the reader to determine into which category The Captain fell at this instant. Suffice it to say he had not given this big rock's presence nearly the attention it deserved.

Nervously now, The Skipper split his time between peering ahead and looking back. In his favor was the fact that the gap between the sailboat and his ship had widened markedly. Sadly, the opening between his vessel and the reef looming just ahead had narrowed an equal amount.

It is one of those oddities of life that we often do not really know where we are going, or even why. Worse, too often the direction we have chosen is inconsequential. Enshrouded by such an existential fog, often we plow ahead willy-nilly, frequently getting nowhere in particular and as often as not just spending a lot of time covering mere distance. It eats up a lot of energy and makes us feel like we really have done something, but the truth is that we have just lost another precious chunk of life. Adding insult to injury, in retrospect it's always easy to see how the destination one chooses – as much by chance and default as anything else – soon rules every choice and every action.

The astute reader may recall that we had but a general outline for traveling this day. Where we stopped for the night depended on several variables, but nothing had been carved in stone yet. Despite having plotted a specific course on the chart, a few degrees this way or that or even a grand detour around an island or an entire Continent really would not have changed the course of history nor would it have made much difference to us. That notwithstanding, however, so attached had The Skipper become to following the particular, petty, insignificant, trivial, who gives a darn Option Three, the very one that he pulled out of his own…eh, well…ummm…hat, generated a neat little crisis.

Given the situation, the navigational options left to our High Commander seemed to be threefold. Either he could give it all up, stop dead in the water and let the other boat pass at his leisure. Or, he could loop north, circumnavigating the Reef by leaving it to starboard, and thus avert disaster. Or, finally, he could stay the course and hope that he did not run out of ocean before he arrived at Enterprise Reef. Being human he chose the prize behind Door Number Three once more!

With the intensity of Sherlock Holmes hot on the trail of Professor Moriarty, I study our microcosm. Any change in conditions, even the slightest reduction in engine RPMs, might doom The Plan! The seconds tick by until, finally, judging that we are far enough out front to make the requisite 90 degree turn, I command, "Hard a starboard," mostly to myself, and the bow or our little ship swings sharply southward. Quickly we cross well in front of our trailing archrival. We watch intently as she continues safely on her way.

Relieved and reflective, I put *Minstrel's Song* on a new course toward Swanson Channel. The great race is over. Leisure sets in again. Still, I regret the whole tawdry episode. While it is true that the margin of safety we pursued was not in the least compromised, the series of decisions that I made – and stuck to – had, if nothing else, created anxiety onboard our ship while they caused our vessel to generate a wake that our antagonist had had to climb. From experience I knew that nothing spoils a good sail like the manmade waves of a "stink-pot!" I also knew that the other skipper would never know how good my intentions had been, how faulty my calculations, nor how much we respected what he was all about. If he is reading this, my apologies, sir!

As the racing fiend faded from sight, I was left to wonder why this fine sailing vessel had not passed through our truncated universe in the expected way. And then I grappled, for a moment with the uneasy feeling that such is the norm usually and not the exception. Our lives tend to be nothing but normal, routine, boring, dull, standard, and predictable, except when they are not; and that seems to be most of the time.

* * * * * * * * * * *

Steering into Swanson Channel proper, our surroundings change considerably. Replacing the immediate beauty, tranquility and relative protection that we have enjoyed down the Trincomali Channel, we are now met with a seascape that exposes a watery horizon far, far distant. The ocean ahead appears to be unbroken by land. Islands still abound, for sure, punctuating this microcosm in almost every direction, but they grow recessive, oddly cautious, almost leaving the impression that they are poised to flee something unseen, something awful. Perhaps because of their increasing distance from us they seem to have lost some of their charm. They appear lost, dull, faded, washed out and without any particular interest.

Above us the fight between the cloud layer and the sun goes on unabated, leaving the ocean a sickly grey. A bit of haze hangs in the air, making the dividing line between the heavens and earth a blurry approximation. The continuing breeze has stirred a fair chop on the water's surface, but it is of no great consequence yet.

Movement off the port bow reminds us that we are approaching "Ferry Alley." One of those great, white, hulking creatures we abhor now thrusts its flat, ugly snout out of its island-lair as if to sniff for prey. From a safe distance we watch as it charges across the channel in front of us snarling and snapping vainly for the sustenance it is not to get on this trip over. Another one quickly swings from behind a rock point off to starboard, but blinded, perhaps, by the greyness of the day or more likely by blood lust, it dashes past us going northward without ever picking up our scent. A smaller and possibly a younger one scoots from right to left across our bow. It seems more intent on cutting through the building chop than on hunting. Nonetheless it is a dangerous field we play on, but at least this time we come forewarned.

The weather people had the wind making up from the south-southwest and building through the day. There was talk of gusts well into the 30s. If accurate, our trek down Swanson Channel and into Boundary Pass – a route that changes our course from south to southeast – will be the most exposed of the day and, if we dawdle, the roughest. Although we anticipate gaining protection from fresh breezes and building seas as we enter the lee of the western San Juan Islands (Stuart, Johns, Spieden and others too numerous to mention), the fact remains that we must make a longish dash across exposed waters that could be fairly unsettled.

We begin to pick up slop and chop off the west coast of North

Pender Island, but whether due to our recent bouts with the Georgia and Malaspina Straits or our direction of travel, we encountered nothing that caused us even marginal concern. True, the wind and the seas got up some – maybe 15-20 knots with four foot waves that had short intervals between crests – but with them both coming in just a few points off the bow, *Minstrel's Song* frolicked through them happily.

Sometimes everything falls right into place. And nothing can change it when it does. Too often, however, it becomes lost in the events of the day and we do not recognize it for what it is: a great gift! That was not to be the case this time around.

Cavorting along our chosen route, the sun suddenly broke through the clouds and immediately transformed everything in sight. The sky turned blue, the sea went from grey to green and the islands came into sharp, beautiful focus. And for once, instead of adding misery, the white caps that topped the waves around us conveyed a holiday air inside our ship that was half carnival and half 'school's out!' Sadly, even though The Captain and The Crew reveled in this unexpected turn, they noted that others did not.

While carving a path through the sea along the southern end of North Pender Island, we met another trawler headed in the opposite direction. She was a few feet larger than we, but a product of the same factory. Starting her run northward up Swanson Channel, she seemed to be spending as much energy rolling and wallowing as she was in pushing ahead. The Crew and I exchanged glances and wondered if we gave the same impression. The greenish visages staring out at us from the other pilothouse made us giggle shamefully. "Did we look like that the other day?" we asked each other? Better yet, "Have we ever looked that way?" And, "Why would you ever be out "having fun in a boat" if that is what it really looked like?" We had no real answers for those questions.

Ten or 15 minutes later we sped past a commercial trawler that was churning her way northward into the Gulf Islands. She was quite involved with hauling her nets, and had no time for those of us who were skylarking, but her skipper watched us as we went our way and the look he gave us seemed to be one of, "Gosh. I wish I was sailing with you today." Again, sometimes everything just seems to fall into place.

Reaching the lee of Stuart Island put us back across the international border, at least mentally. It is a bizarre set of Never-Never Land rules that apply to international travel by air and sea. When on land, set one little foot beyond the imaginary line that constitutes the border and you are across – and in lots of trouble if it was without permission! Sail in or fly in and it is a whole new ballgame. Whether by air or sea, one has not legally entered either country unless and until one actually touches ground. Airplanes can fly all over Canada as long as they don't land; boats can float wherever they wish as long as they do not anchor or otherwise attach themselves to the earth's surface. Thus, while we passed over the international border mid-way across Boundary Pass, we would not be back in the U.S. legally until we came to rest (or until we hit something).

"Asteriskize" that last statement heavily with the proviso that while one cannot be said to have entered either country until secured to terra firma, all of the laws and regulations appertaining to each are operative immediately when the line is broken.

HELLO? IS THIS THE PARTY TO WHOM I'M SPEAKING?

"O.K. It's time we got in touch with the constabulary and let them know we're back," The Skipper advised The Crew. "See if you can raise them on the cell."

Immersed in thoughts about the realities of being home, of leaving behind the idyllic realm of limitless adventures and soaring dreams, The Skipper pays little attention to The Crew or what she is doing. After all, she is dependable, capable and does not need supervision every minute of every day. However, in the midst of watching Satellite Island glide by the starboard door, and while anticipating the vision of John's Pass coming abreast soon, it occurs to our erstwhile leader that The Crew is no longer available for duty. Oh, she is at her station in the pilothouse all right, but apparently she is immersed deeply in a rather complex telephone conversation. While idly contemplating the way in which time may pass by completely unmarked when one becomes engrossed in one thing or another, The Captain begins to emerge from his mental happy place and now starts to wonder: "How long has this been going on?" While searching for a reasonable answer to that question, our man at the helm simultaneously takes the precaution of devoting no less than half of his brain to the task of actively monitoring The Administrative Officer's activities for quality control purposes.

"No, as I said, I don't have a BR number to give you," The Admin Officer offered somewhat testily to someone, somewhere out there in telephone land.

"Yes. I know I need one, but I don't have one. You see the problem, don't you?"

"...Because when I called the local U.S. Customs and Border Patrol office to inquire about getting one before we left the country they assured me that they only issued those to people actually returning to the U.S...Hello. Hello! Helloooo..!"

"Can you believe it?" The Crew snapped. "No one knows what they're doing anymore including the cell phone people!"

The receipt of this intelligence requires that I respond with my most sympathetic smile while turning to find something terribly important to do on the starboard side of the house, near the ship's wheel. Doing anything else runs the risk of having The Crew transfer her wrath from the person on the other end of the line directly to me. Being a veteran of foreign wars, I have no desire to fight that battle again. So, while she re-dials the number I listen, very quietly.

"Hello. Yes you may. I called just a moment ago and...Oh, great. I was afraid I would have to start all over...Oh, terrific...Now, about that BR number, I do understand the requirement for it, but I hope you can appreciate the fact that I tried to get one before we left but your office wouldn't give it to me then…Which office? I don't know. I called this number and spoke to the officer who answered…His name? I don't know…Well, you're right, I should have gotten that. I just didn't think it would be necessary…Certainly, but the point remains that someone there assured me that all of this could be taken care of over the phone when we were coming back. (Longish pause…)

"Absolutely. Yes. Uh-huh. Yes. I can see where it does create a major dilemma for you…Sure, I know, and I know how easily things get way out of hand when someone hands out bad advice." (Another pause…)

"So, what do we do now? Uh-huh…O.K…but if we have to go through all of that again, of what use is the NEXUS pass?" (Very pregnant pause…)

"…Oh, no. You're absolutely right and we definitely do want to get this thing straightened out today…"I see, uh-huh…Hello…Hello!..Helloooo..!" The X.O. eyes me suspiciously and spits, "I lost them again."

I do my best impression of dead silence!

"…Hello. Hi. I was just on the phone with… Uh-huh…O.K., well at least I'm glad it's you again…This is getting to be a regular habit!...Excuse me?...O.K…Right. It's *Minstrel's Song*...Hello. Can you still hear me? You're breaking up. Hello…Hello!...Helloooo!...Darn! They're gone again," she splutters at no one in particular.

This latter fact is very good because while she has been talking, I have busied myself in a concerted effort to become invisible! Apparently I have achieved a modicum of success!

"Hello…Oh, hi. Yeah. It's me again. Did you get the name of the boat? Great! My husband's date of birth and Social Security Number? Sure it's…And mine is…Hello… Hello!...Helloooo! Can you believe this stuff?"

I watch as she slams her finger into the touch screen of her phone, commanding the machine to re-connect her immediately with her lost party.

"...Right. Sure. His mother's maiden name and the color of her third grade Easter dress? No. No! Just, kidding...Hello...Hello!...Helloooo!"

"...Well, I guess I am glad to hear that it happens all of the time, but it's still a little frustrating...Really? I can only imagine...Everyday? Wow! Sure. He has brown hair and brown eyes; mine are brown and blue, my eyes, that is. Our address is...And before that? We lived at...What? Oh. Fourteen years...And before that? I don't have that address in front of me but can't you pull that out of your records? (Long pause) Well, yes, I do know all about that. Ours crashes all of the time too! Absolutely...Yes...It's been well over five years...Our drivers' license numbers? Hold on...Hello...Hello!...Helloooo!" (Look of total disgust.) "Gone, but not forgotten."

"...Yeah. I know. That's O.K. It's not your fault. Everyone said it would be really easy with the NEXUS pass...Yeah, I'm sure it usually is. Oh, yes. You seem to be coming in better now too. No. He's retired...U.S. Government...Central Intelligence...Absolutely. Oh, yes, very exciting...Um-humm, very interesting...Yes, me too...Uh-huh...Right, all over the world...Yeah. For years...Yes, well I'm sure you'll get the chance someday...Of course, I know how these things go...Me? Now? No, I work in our community...What? Well the best way is to contact the main office and request an information packet. No, I don't have that number here on the boat, but if you give me your name and number I could probably find it and get back to you in a few days...No, I wish I could,_but for that you pretty much have to do it all on your own...Oh, sure, I can only imagine how much training you've had already...Uh, huh...Well it's clear that all of that responsibility is a weight on your shoulders...O.K...Great. That would be...Hello...Hello!...Helloooo? Good grief Charlie Brown!

"Yes, back again! No. I didn't get that last bit. Yes, it is highly irregular, but we do appreciate the way you've been able to slash through the red tape and work with us on this...Yes. I do have a pencil...Uh-huh, that's B.R...Oh, thank you...and does that mean we're cleared? Hello...Hello!...Helloooo!"

Sitting back on her duty perch, The Crew very uncharacteristically spits out the word, "Shit!" and nothing more. Turning slowly toward me and with complete malice and forethought she said, "I'm done!"

Inclined though the circumstances made me, I resisted the temptation to respond to her with, 'Aye. Aye. Ma'am,' or with anything else that might have been interpreted as provocative. She had been through enough for the boat already and there was nothing to be gained by baiting the bear.

* * * * * * * * * * *

We began the day's trip with no firm notion of where we would spend the night. We were agreed that while we could get all the way home in one jump, we were not inclined to do that just yet. Besides, the weather for the crossing did not look good. Thus, entry into the San Juan Channel was occasion enough to force a decision regarding our stopping point. As so often happens, we picked the course of least resistance. We agreed to run down the channel another seven or eight miles and then put into Friday Harbor, i.e., "harbour" without the "u" for our Canadian readers!

With the possible exception of Key West, Florida during the high season, I do not believe that there exists anywhere in the Western Hemisphere a "zoo-ier" place in the summertime than the confines of Friday Harbor and its public marina! (Although I would allow that the prize might justly be split with Roche Harbor, another San Juan Island destination that sits a few short nautical miles to the northwest of Friday.) This alluring place is tucked into an arcing indentation punched into the lower end of San Juan's southeast coast. It fronts directly onto San Juan Channel. This neat little paradise would be open to the northeast and the wind and the seas that might come out of that quarter were it not for the protection provided it by hulking Brown Island. Said chunk of land shields the entire anchorage so well that due to the number of boats that press to enter it via the narrow channels at either of its ends, the casual mariner may find the chore of making his way safely through the throng more trouble than it is worth during tourist season.

The main event in Friday Harbor is the public dock. Nestled in the northwest corner of the bay, it's the first thing most seaborne visitors encounter. Extending almost 400 yards out from land and paralleling it for an equal distance, not only is this facility large, but also its masters pack boats into it like sardines into a tin! We have observed vessels squeezed in so closely that they rub fenders simultaneously with their finger docks on the outsides and with their stable mates in the middle. In fact, we have studied a couple of parking jobs that were so tight that we were forced to go away scratching our heads and saying, "How'd they do that?"

Probably because the 'islands' are almost exclusively a summertime destination – and in the Great Northwet that translates pretty much into just July and August – the city fathers definitely work to make hay while the sun shines. Every possible inch of dock space is used and double and even triple rafting in the transient areas is not unusual. The boat traffic in the fairways can rival that of a Los Angeles freeway on Friday afternoon and the jostle and jockeying thereby created can try the nerves of the most seasoned skipper.

Even the wharfs are filled with crowds of people who are constantly coming and going. Not limited to actual tenants, boat watchers of all descriptions wander up and down the concrete floats and by their presence create an atmosphere not unlike that of a Middle Eastern bazaar. From the newly arrived seaman hustling off for a cooler full of ice, to frantic revelers worried that by being away from the action they might miss something, to the crusty old sea dogs struggling to get to the main office building for their five minute, 50 cent showers, these quays are alive with humankind all pursuing, together, their differing passions and agendas.

Veterans of the scene swear annually that it just is not worth the hassle to put into Friday Harbor. But most of them show up there like clockwork, year in and year out, ready once again to pronounce it an abomination that should be avoided at all costs. Such is its charm and its allure!

The marina backs up to a lovely, tree-shaded public park. In the summer months, live music emanates from the bandstand there. Steer a southeast course from the top of the ramp – through the park – and one can enjoy a smooth, flat walk to the ferry terminal and the city's downtown shopping area. Take the stairs up, instead, and the visitor will top one of the hills upon which the town itself sits. The panorama of the anchorage, the San Juan Channel and some of the San Juan Islands, spreading out in front of the viewer is a pleasure to behold.

Being the largest village on San Juan Island, this compact burg caters simultaneously to the wants and needs of the flood of sojourners who come by private vessel, airplane and ferry to see its dim lights, as well as to the 7,000 people who call this speck of land home. Thus, the hardware store stands cheek and jowl with the ship's chandlery, the whale museum, a host of art shops, souvenir stores, super markets, book sellers, the Courthouse, antique emporia, restaurants too numerous to mention and the plumbing supply house, at the very least!

Day visitors, summer residents, vacationers, true islanders and boaters of all descriptions converge on the town of Friday Harbor to do whatever it is that these folks set about to accomplish. While a full description of all of its semi-Victorian charms – I say semi-Victorian because it has the feel of a Victorian village, but not having been founded until 1897, it all but missed that era – might fill a volume or two, suffice it to say that people roll in by the boatload to enjoy the enchanting atmosphere and to shed their worldly concerns for a time at least.

During the high season, it would be difficult, if not totally impossible, to get a slip at Friday Harbor without reservations. This early in the season, however, we know that the place will be less than half full, accommodating only its year round tenants and a few vagabonds like us. All we have to do to claim a choice slip is to give the Harbor Master a shout on the VHF when we are within a mile or two of the port.

We favored the west side the San Juan Channel as we headed down the slot toward our destination. This allowed us to stay in the lee of San Juan Island. A surprisingly fresh breeze had sprung up and was ripping along out of the west at a steady 25 knots, gusting to 35. Even though the seas had little room to make up any real trouble, the surface of the water got bumpier and bumpier the further out toward the middle of the channel one strayed. Thus, holding closer to the protection of the island made life better for us.

Like all other things, storms arrive in all different shapes and sizes. Some crash in, wreaking havoc everywhere they go and others sneak in, going almost unnoticed. Depending on where you are and what you are doing, they can be damaging or, oddly, pleasing. This particular one – ultimately building to between Force 6 and 7 on the Beauford scale and rightly described therein either as a "strong breeze" or a "near gale" – arrived with little fanfare. The weatherman earlier indicated that the afternoon might see some breezes, but those he claimed were to be of the common garden variety. And, perhaps because the building winds were not preceded by the onset of dark, roiling clouds, the change from nice to not so nice remained undetected by us until we watched a sailboat of about 25' in length struggling against the forces of Nature to remain topside up. She was flying little more than a couple of handkerchiefs for sails but still her rail was buried under foaming water. Her two-man crew was feverishly trying to counterbalance her heel while still maintaining a course toward shelter. Her narrow keel, frequently visible, was fighting valiantly, but vainly to counteract the power of her sails. From experience I knew that the sailors aboard her would be getting home both wet and exhausted; depending on their skill levels, one might throw in 'terrified' as well!

Watching the small boat do battle with the elements added new perspective to our day. Tucked safe, dry and warm inside our pilothouse we could laugh and chatter and enjoy our surroundings despite the howling wind. The poor souls struggling out to keep out of the 50-degree water could not.

Having reached the relative security of the San Juans, the howling wind was as nothing to us, a mere zephyr and no more. Had we been on the outside of the islands – just a few miles distant – contending with air and wave and a lee shore as well, everything would have looked different. Same day. Same wind. Same ocean. Just a different point of view. "Hmmmmm," I thought, "maybe everything depends on where you are in the voyage."

Rounding Point Caution, we turn to starboard and make for Friday Harbor's northern channel. As we do so, we see, looming gigantic before us, was a U.S. Coast Guard cutter. "All hands to battle stations! Man the deck guns! Stand by the torpedoes! Prepare to repel boarders!" I want to shout. For although the bright orange stripes and sleek lines of this relative leviathan bespeak her civil mission, the black snout of her forward gun and the way she bestrides the channel leading into the harbor equally suggest warfare and trouble.

"What's this?" I ask The First Mate. "She looks ready for action. But why?"

My follow-up question of, "Are you sure we got clearance back into the States?" was greeted with a cold stare and dead silence. "O.K., yeah. Dumb question. They're definitely not sending all that boat out here just to capture a couple of criminals like us!"

Ever notice how it is the good guys and not the bad guys who immediately conclude that they are doing something wrong when confronted by the forces of truth, justice and the American way? Why is that? Even when I task the four memory cells I still own to dredge up whatever information I have left about that time in my life when I dealt with bad guys for a living, kind of, it seems that their reactions were always just to the contrary.

"Rob a bank? With a gun? Shoot somebody? Oh, yeah, that. Well, you see, I…I…I was really strapped for cash and I wasn't planning on hurting anyone, but then the cashier made that quick move and, well, you know, accidents do happen. Why did he have to tie his shoelace just then anyway? I mean, you know, I wasn't really doing anything wrong." And that was the usual song sung! Again, hmmmmm, why does it look so different from the other side of the fence?

Deep breath. Calm down. Get a grip. "Oh. There. See it?" I point to a flashing dot on the surface of the water. As it grows larger we identify a Coast Guard RIB flying toward the bigger ship a breakneck speed. It slows alongside, exchanges a few lines, etc., and within what seems like seconds it has been hoisted into its place on deck. All the while the cutter, apparently anxious to find some real bad guys, is springing forward so as to make its way down the channel. Relieved, I call the Harbor Master on the VHF.

As expected, the marina's pretty empty. We are assigned to a berth on H dock.

Of all the things that *Minstrel's Song* does exceedingly well, maneuvering in tight spaces is not one of them. Like most trawlers, her lack of a deep keel and her relatively round hull means that she turns on a dollar, a large, paper one, rather than on a dime. Instead, of squaring corners the way some sailboats can, she carves graceful arcs that have diameters that approach triple digits! Thus, the dimensions of most marinas do not conform to her preferences.

The trick to docking our little vessel is to gauge, right down to the foot, precisely when one must change course from straight down the fairway to hard a-something in order to glide into the assigned slot. Spin the wheel too late and our craft will slop around until she is in position to plant her beam squarely on the stern quarter of the neighboring boat, an adjoining piling or an extended finger dock, whichever lies off in that direction. Turn too early and you begin to get a diagonal thing going that puts her more or less athwart the actual opening. This latter development features the added benefit of being able to plow into two things at once: whatever is dead ahead – most frequently another vessel or a finger pier

– and whatever chances to be passing by the stern quarter of the hull at that moment (usually a piling or a sharp corner of some type). In either instance there ensues a lot of running and shouting and fending off with anything that comes easily to hand. However these things play out, rest assured that in sum it is not a pretty sight to behold. And, while everyone tries to walk away from such performances as if they were sterling, slinking wharf rats, comparatively speaking, move with greater dignity. The ignominy of such an event might be likened to that endured by the local deacon when word leaks out that he is the father of an illegitimate son.

Knowing what could await us, it is with great relief that I identify our slip. It is a starboard tie, e.g. the finger wharf will be on the starboard side of the boat, and the space to port is empty. We like tying off to starboard because it is easier to get on and off of our boat. (*Minstrel's Song* has a storage locker on the port side of the cockpit and that makes boarding over, around or under it awkward.) Better still, the slip itself is located on the starboard side of the fairway and, mirroring the one at her home port, that's the side The Helmsman is most comfortable hitting (oops, I mean sliding into!). Thus, all he has to do is go straight down the fairway, spin the wheel at the right instant and even if everything is not just so, he can still nestle in snuggly with a blast or two of the bow thruster. Piece of cake!

As we near our assigned position, I study it for anything that might cause problems. I double-check the number on the piling against the number we received from the Harbor Master. "Yup. That's it," I mutter to myself. The Crew is already standing by, mooring lines in hand, at her post in the cockpit. I look at the finger pier jutting from the main wharf around which we must turn. "Looks short," I think, "but I gave the lady our size and there's no shortage of space around. Must be right."

With just enough speed to maintain steerage, I put the helm down and we start the slow circle that I hope will bring us up parallel to the dock. Grinning with pleasure, I watch as *Minstrel's Song* carves a path precisely to the desired spot; I do not even have to touch the bow thruster. Having by now lost almost all way, I let her drift forward to her final resting place, her bow about a yard short of the main part of the pier. "O.K. Tie her down," I shout back to The Crew. I do not even bother to look back because I know that the boat's hull is exactly where it should be, picture perfect, not touching anything but no more than six inches from the hard walkway all up and down the line.

Then, in the distance I hear: "I can't."

Leaving for a moment the electronic gadgetry I was preparing to shut down, I glance toward the stern through the pilothouse window and say, "What do you mean you can't?"

"Look!" she replies.

So I look and what I see surprises me. We are nestled into the slip as snug as a bug in a rug except for the part about having most of the stern still hanging way out in the fairway! Indeed, so much of it is sticking out that The Crew cannot step out of the cockpit and get to the wharf without first walking on a yard or two of water!

I engage the engine for a split second to ease our craft forward a foot or so. This needs to be finely done because the bow can go ahead no more than about a yard or so before it will start cutting its teeth on the concrete decking there. Discontent with this mode of adjustment, I grab a line and jump out of the starboard door and down onto the dock. If this procedure is to be accomplished without damage, making the final amendments will have to be done by hand. Pulling our ship ahead with the line, I yell back, "Are we there yet?"

"Almost!" came The Crew's response.

Hustling around to the head of the dock, I find that the bow of the boat is so close to the pier that I am able to grasp the anchor that protrudes from the bow roller without having to lean out over the water at all. Pulling gently on it, I coax our craft ahead another six inches. Her stem is but six inches from the concrete. That is as close as I dare bring her.

"How about that?" I bellow.

"O.K., but just," comes the reply.

"Then tie her off."

I busy myself with tethering *Minstrel's Song* front end and then stroll toward the stern. Our craft fits in the space available to her like a kid in last year's shoes. She is in the slip, no doubt, but with no room to spare. And any movement at all is likely to raise up blisters.

The Crew and I examine our work, paying special attention to the overhang in the front, where the anchor juts across part of the walkway, and in the back to where the RIB that rests on the swim step partially obstructs the fairway. Without saying a word we climb back onboard and silently break out another set of lines. If our boat moves more than a few inches in any direction there is going to be trouble. "With all of these open slips, I wonder why they put us here?" she asks.

"Summertime habits are hard to break, I guess."

With The X.O. still on the dock, I climb back onboard, shut the engine and the peripherals down, and then close and lock the doors. Only after we have scrutinized our vessel, fore and aft once more, do we turn our attention toward the marina office and the village lying beyond it.

The water in the basin that lies in the crook of the elbow formed by the two intersecting, sheltering ridgelines above Friday Harbor is calm despite the winds that buffet the summits. Nothing more than gay, laughing ripples disturb its surface, driven casually by the light breeze that meanders down the hills to touch it gently. The late spring sun beats down on the bowl and all things in it, soaking everything it hits with a warm, yellow glow that has been absent in these parts for many months. Situated in the lee of San Juan Island, free from the scourge of fast moving air, the temperature seems to rise to that pleasant level that causes people to just sit and contemplate life.

The serenity of the marina belies the gale that is sweeping the heights behind it. Surveying the southwest hill, above and beyond the Harbor Master's office that sits at the top of the dock ramp, our eyes are drawn up the steep slope painted in forest green by the conifers and shrubs that cover it, to the old, brick buildings at its summit and then, especially, to the flag that surmounts it all. This poor shred of cloth is standing out straight, rent unmercifully by gargantuan, invisible hands. Wriggling and twisting as if to dodge a cruel lashing, the force of its struggles slightly bends the huge pole to which it is tied tightly.

"Guess we'll have a little wind," The Skipper advises The Crew. But uncaring now about what wracks this part of the world, he takes his messmate's hand and they march happily up the dock together.

After paying the slip fee and climbing the stairs to the top of one of the hills that overlooks the marina, we partake of a feast at our favorite deli. Sitting in front of one of its large windows, we happily munch as we look out over the harbor, San Juan Channel and a slew of distant islands. The sky and the water are blue and beautiful; from this perspective it looks like a perfect day to be out there!

Strolling a block or two down the street, we drop in on the good people at the Whale Museum. We are there for a couple of replacement coffee cups. A few summers back we purchased a pair of them there for our son. Later, he asked that we ship them to him at college, questioning at the same time whether such prizes possibly could survive the trip through the mail. I assured him that they could, no sweat, and confidently wrapped them and sent them off. Days later he received a box of colorful, ceramic shards. Guilt-laden this way, The X.O. and I spent many months tromping through every gift store in a four state area vainly trying to find two more cups like the ones I had been destroyed. With the Whale Museum being our last best hope, the stop here is obligatory.

The remainder of the afternoon is spent at the fine little used bookstore we know from experience to be in Friday Harbor. With joy we devote several hours to pawing through dog-eared volumes of books that neither of us really needs. Stuffed to overflowing, the rickety shelves that fill the innards of this dilapidated house of pleasure plays host to thousands of well worn tomes that are bought and sold through all times of the year. With just enough organization to get one going in the desired direction, whether serious or casual, the unsuspecting book addict is well advised to cancel all other activities for the day before entering its depths.

Laboring out of the emporium with bags of new treasures sufficient in bulk to give a string of pack mules pause, we saunter nonetheless back toward the water, stopping to peer into every shop window we encounter. The tourist crowds have not yet arrived, so leisure is still permissible. A final feast at a Chinese restaurant caps our afternoon. From there on everything is gravy. The trip back to *Minstrel's Song* is all downhill, literally. And the remaining hours of the day are spent delighting, carefree, in our new discoveries, and in the jolly company we find in each other through the last night of our epic voyage.

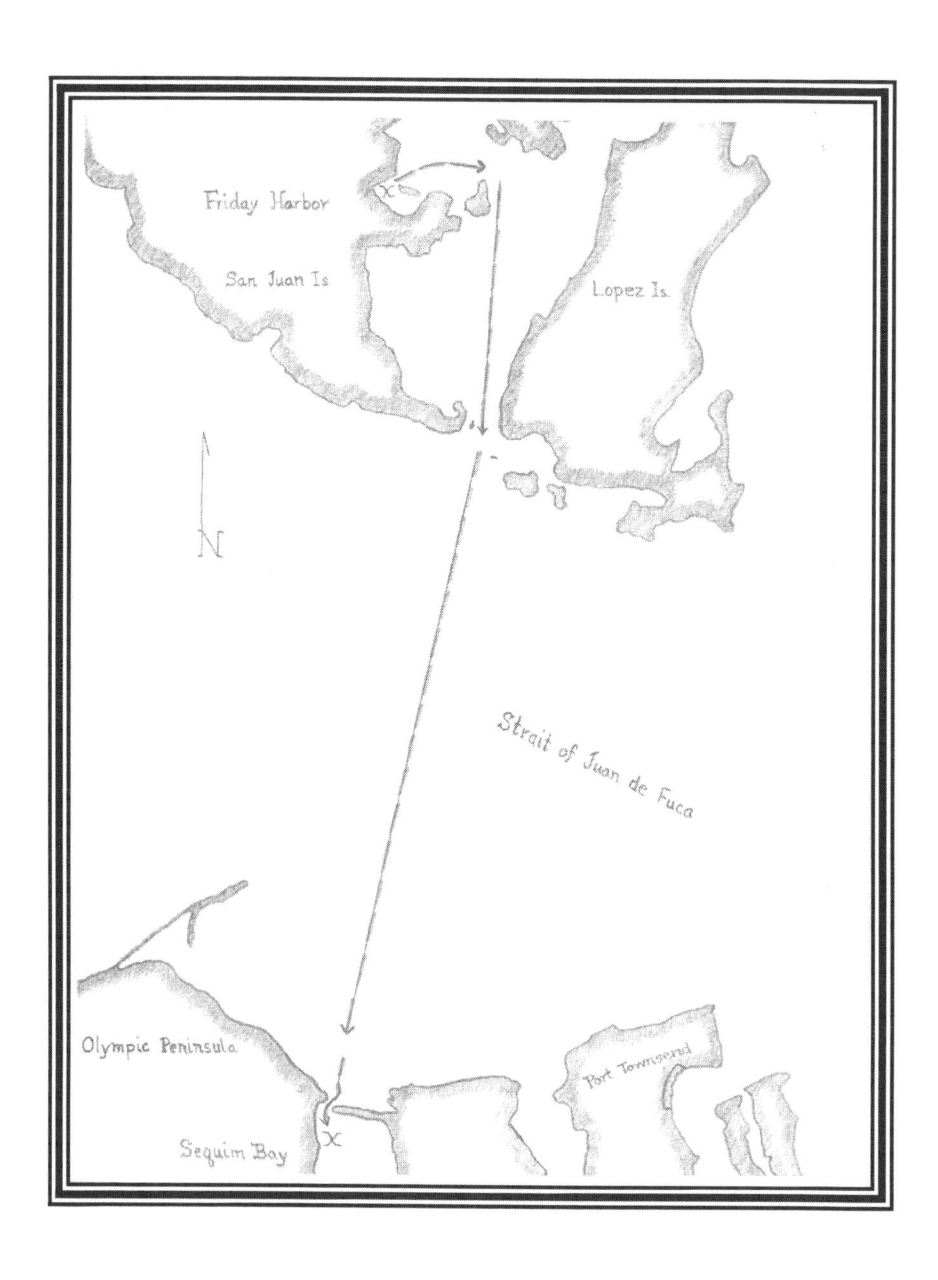
Friday Harbor
X
San Juan Is.
Lopez Is.
N
Strait of Juan de Fuca
Olympic Peninsula
Port Townsend
Sequim Bay
X

Day Eleven

Friday Harbor To Sequim Bay
Or
You Can (And Must!) Go Home Again

As always, the dawn unapologetically broke in on a perfectly lovely period of darkness. In this particular instance, it did not matter too much to us since we were up and moving anyway! The good news was that with daylight brightening the confines of the galley Cookie was able to dish up coffee and the usual Danish with greater ease than she could when we are running in the dark. Come to think of it, consuming them was more pleasant under those circumstances as well.

The weather forecaster predicted another clear day, but just like the previous one he said we would see building wind and high seas through the afternoon. According to him though, if there was going to be a good time in the next 96 hours to skitter across the Strait of Juan de Fuca, it was going to arrive this morning. So we decided not to dawdle.

Life is full of little ironies, but one of the most universally shared – at least in the western world – is the one that pertains to the weatherman. Day in and day out we listen intently as he tells us how he thinks the gods of the heavens plan to entertain themselves in the hours that will follow. Day in and day out we gird ourselves according to his instructions for the weather wars we will have to join. And day in and day out his prognostications hardly come up to the accuracy standards routinely expected from the "Magic 8 Ball." In recognition of his unerring fallibility, we berate, belittle and besmirch the character, if not the entire life's work, of this cultural miscreant. Yet back we go, day in and day out, imploring this demi-god for mercy while seeking anxiously his divinations – often via The Weather Channel – and hoping against hope that this time he will get it right.

As we quietly slipped our lines the stillness of the morning was so complete that even when totally unattached to dry land the usually exuberant *Minstrel's Song* showed no inclination to move at all. In fact, it seemed likely that she would have remained in her berth, unperturbed by any force or even by any particular desire to leave, for hours to come. Nary a ripple graced the surface of the sea; the sky overhead that was transforming itself from a bright golden umbrella to a cloudless blue bowl seemed intent on doing so without calling attention to the massive makeover. The Ship's Photographer recorded the tranquil scene for posterity's sake and then, having no other rational options, The Skipper backed his little ship slowly away from the dock and turned her bow toward San Juan Channel and home. The diesel engine and the circling gulls overhead produced the only sounds heard in Friday Harbor at that instant.

In company with our frequent companion, "Sammy the Seal," we shaped a course southeast down San Juan Channel. I remained at the helm until we were ready to swing to starboard around the shoals off Turn Island. Thereafter I directed Auto to take us south toward the pass that separates San Juan and Lopez Islands and leads out to the strait.

As usual, our engine hummed to the beat of a steady 1,650 rpms; it pushed us easily along at our cruise speed of about 8.5 knots. Oddly, however, instead of that number, the GPS insisted that we were moving along, over the bottom of the ocean, at about 10.5 knots. The ebbing tide, for once, was with us.

Even the most inattentive reader should have discerned by now that I tend to be a planner. Almost without exception surprises are the things you do not want at sea and the best way to avoid them is to prepare for every conceivable situation. Doing that does not really forestall problems, but it does give you something to do while waiting for them to occur.

For the better part of half of the preceding winter, I plumbed the depths of all of the tide and current tables available to mankind appertaining to this region. Thereby, I had gleaned every possible morsel of the wisdom available to the prudent mariner. Not content with just that, however, we carried the gold standard reference work on the subject of the in and out flows of the oceans that sweep the Salish Sea, *Washburn's Tables,* and we supplemented that monumental tome with a notebook full of localized graphs that I had picked carefully and individually off the internet. So thorough were my preparations that there should not have been a ripple made in the entire Northwet that could not have been immediately and completely predicted and explained by one or another of the studies we had at our fingertips. Forewarned is forearmed, after all.

How then to explain the fact that our entire journey, right up to that moment, had been made uphill, into the teeth of a counter-flowing sea? As might have been noted already, each evening The Pilot dedicated a significant amount of energy to the business of planning the next day's voyage. During that time he carefully scribes lines onto charts, marks off distances from point to point, calculates travel times, determines optimum departure and arrival hours and makes notes to himself about everything possible – right down to what he hoped Cookie might prepare for lunch!

Naturally, the bane of that work was compromise. To get here you have to go there and to go there you have to pass that place, only that place cannot be transited during the particular period in question so you have to start the process all over again. The art of the endeavor is to find the happy medium that sort of, kind of, almost meets all of the requirements of the day. Sadly and almost without exception, the compromises The Pilot made on paper transformed themselves into abysmal failures at sea.

So, what was this? Instead of moving through the water at 8.5 knots, but only really covering the 6.5 nautical miles of real distance per hour we had come to expect, the opposite was happening. (The progress of any vessel is calculated by the rate of speed it makes through the water plus or minus the force of the current, depending on its direction.) Despite expectations, this morning, even though we were lazing along at 8.5 knots, we were actually flying toward our destination at 10.5!

Reflecting, later, on this unanticipated turn of events, it occurred to me that this inversion should have been expected. For, in making all of my careful calculations I had failed to factor in the two unwritten, but inviolable Laws of Nature appertaining to travel. These are: First, 'No one ever gets to their desired destination as fast as they hope'; and second, 'Everyone always arrives at those places they do not really wish to reach – like back to their home port following an idyllic voyage – faster than they want.' Both were at work during our adventure, but I had neglected them throughout.

In keeping with these natural mandates, the closer we came to Cattle Pass the faster we sped along. The funnel created by the adjoining islands caused the water to speed up as it tried to force its way, north to south, into the Strait of Juan de Fuca. Beneficiaries of that surge, the GPS on *Minstrel's Song* inched up from 10.5 knots to 11, then 11.5, to 12, to 13 and finally topped out at 13.5. Wow! We were cooking! And the amazing part was that we were making that time and only burning fuel at the normal cruising rate.

Looking southward, beyond the strait, the Olympic Mountains sprawled, east to west, across our horizon. Neither The Ship's Photographer nor The Skipper could resist capturing forever, in miniscule pixels and digits, the intervening lighthouse that perches on the extreme end of Cattle Point, along the south coast of San Juan Island. Set up to warn mariners of the dangers lurking off that particular head and to guide seafarers safely out of the strait and into San Juan Channel, on a morning like this one, one easily might imagine instead that the structure was situated there solely for the delight of itinerant shutterbugs. With blue water between us and it, with its bright, white, sun-drenched walls rising boldly from the rocky extreme it dominated, and with the snow-capped peaks of the Olympic Range forming, in the distance, an incongruous backdrop, few scenes could have been more worthy of the effort. We split our attentions between this grand view and the more mundane, but potentially dangerous water just in front of us.

As the sun rose higher in the sky, we passed out into the strait, jauntily sailing across a placid sea that so often is whipped to a frenzy by the prevailing winds. Golden yellow rays pierce the pilothouse windows, warming us to a sleepy turn. Slowly the mountains ahead grow and the identifiable features of home begin to come into view. The Captain and The Crew chat, but it is that slightly nervous kind of 'I don't want this to end' conversation that is intended to saturate the air with mindless sounds in hopes that the noise will fend off the flood of memories, hopes and dreams that might overpower our emotions were we to remain silent.

"How do you think the dogs are doing?" I ask.

And she, "We might need to stop at the store for some stuff for dinner."

With every mile the mundane looms larger. And somehow the press of tides and currents, dinghies and anchors, charts and ferries, sailboats and fjords, tight passes and narrow entries grow weaker and weaker. What had just defined our physical universe begins to take on an ephemeral, ghost-like aspect. Reality fades to memory and then begins the shift back to the new, but really just the old.

We sail past Dungeness Light, a deep-voiced beacon we hear from our home when fog blankets the ocean. We thread our way carefully into Sequim Bay, scene of many a delightful sailboat race, cruising day and the manmade shelter that houses *Minstrel's Song* when she is forced to live alone.

We stop at the fuel dock to top off our tanks and to pump out our waste. The attendant falls into the easy dialog of a familiar face, not understanding that we are not really from around there, yet. We have, after all, just returned from a different galaxy.

Gracefully, perfectly, we ease *Minstrel's Song* back into her slip. She is home. Independently The Crew and I stow, log, check, secure, open and close all manner of things in preparation for disembarkation.

Not much is said until all is done.

Drawing a wistful breath I casually remark, “Well, I guess it’s time to start hauling gear to the car.”

“Whaddaya want to do for lunch?” Cookie asks. “We could stop somewhere on the way home or I could whip up something here. We’re not really pressed for time.”

Cautiously I respond, “Let’s eat here if it’s not too much trouble.”

Knowing that it is over, but not wanting to leave, we sit once more at our little saloon table – the one that so likes to take a dive in a heavy sea. We munch our sandwiches quietly while mentally ordering the thoughts we each have about the exotic places we have just explored. We know we will want them again and again in the future; we fear losing even just one. For a moment or more we hold hands and say nothing. We listen intently to the gentle lap of the zephyr driven wavelets as they play on the hull. Then slowly we climb the three-step ladder up to the cockpit. Another life awaits our return.

Epilogue

The Days Thereafter
Or
The Journey Continues

In the beginning, The Lord made the dark, formless, empty earth as well as the deep waters. Then, He separated light from dark, naming them day and night and He set the sky in its place overhead. Next he gathered the water so that the dry land would appear and he named these things Earth and the Seas. So begins the ancient story of creation. One of its striking features is the separation of the parts of our natural home into wet and dry.

It is with delight that mankind takes to the sea. Perhaps it is because we get away from 'it all' there. Perhaps it is because of the different places we can visit and the different things we can do while moving upon it. Perhaps it is the distinctive perspective we gain while bobbing upon it. Perhaps it is because our Maker's presence lingers there strongly. Whatever it is, it is a special place.

One cannot help but feel a certain sense of sadness then, when we return to our rightful domain on the high and the dry. The natural rhythms, the comings and goings, the things we have known forever, take on all consuming aspects when we linger there. As always, we move, we do, we hope and we dream while our existence continues on unabated. Still, we savor that ancient slice of time when, in all practicality, all things revolved around the water.

Every night when we were at sea I worked in the pilothouse, laying out the course for the following day and making and amending our plans. Up on the hard we do the same things, although certainly with much less formality. Everyday we follow a general strategy with the hope of reaching the desired end. Just like on a boat, everyday a hundred things come up to surprise us, to enchant us and force us to change and to grow. But unlike when afloat, the contempt of familiarity ashore frequently keeps us from seeing clearly how all of the pieces of the puzzle lock together to form an incredible picture. We need to stop and smell the coffee, the Danish and the seaweed more often!

As the days and weeks passed after our return to *terra firm*, life took for The Captain and The Crew an unexpected turn. The earth rotated, the seasons came and went, and nothing could (or should) stay the same. When we purchased *Minstrel's Song,* it was with the ultimate intention of letting her take us to the far off reaches of Alaska, stopping at all of the remote backwaters along the way just to see what could be seen there. At times we even dreamed of building a delightful new life for ourselves in our little craft's spaces, wandering forever, like true vagabonds, upon the bounding Main. While these idyllic thoughts still wafted warmly over our lives a different breeze came up quickly. To meet the unexpected shift, we had to alter course.

Minstrel's Song went up on the auction block and she now is someone else's pride and joy. Having been called without much introduction to investigate a different realm, one too far from the ocean to allow us to enjoy as we had our boat's charms, we were faced with a difficult decision. Ultimately, our love for her gifts convinced us that it would be neither just nor right to keep her tethered and tied against her nature, month after month, expectantly awaiting our return in hope that such an event might mean that she would get a short romp on the great sea. Better, we thought, to send her on to someone else, someone who was waiting patiently for his chance to take her for a magic carpet ride, than to hold her tight.

If, when, and under what circumstances we return to the briny ocean we cannot predict. We can confide, however, that we still spend luxurious hours at boat shows and more than a few moments, from time to time, perusing many a fine little craft offered for sale on-line. Whether dream or reality it is hard to say, but both The Skipper and The Crew still share a vision of their next little ship!

The unexpected tack we have taken does not mean that the adventure has stopped or even slowed. It cannot and it will not. All we have done is to put the helm hard over so as to come up on a different course. As always, we guide by a single star…wherever it might lead us.

Since greetings and goodbyes are just the obverse aspects of the same process, we wish to say to the reader, to all well-found vessels at sea, and to our fellow mariners wherever they may be, *bon voyage.* We are all off, together, on a fantastic, new journey. May you enjoy smooth seas and calm winds all along the way!

Drop us a note at MinstrelAuthor@Ronan.net.

Made in the USA
San Bernardino, CA
08 January 2014